The Stories Behind Country Music's All-Time Greatest 100 Songs

THE STORIES BEHIND
COUNTRY MUSIC'S
All-Time Greatest
100 Songs

ACE COLLINS

BOULEVARD BOOKS
New York

The Stories Behind Country Music's All-Time Greatest 100 Songs

A Boulevard Book / published by arrangement with
the author

PRINTING HISTORY
Boulevard trade paperback edition / March 1996

The Putnam Berkley World Wide Web site address is
http://www.berkley.com

ISBN: 1-57297-072-3

BOULEVARD
Boulevard Books are published by The Berkley Publishing Group,
200 Madison Avenue, New York, New York 10016.
BOULEVARD and its logo are trademarks
belonging to Berkley Publishing Corporation.

PRINTED IN THE UNITED STATES OF AMERICA

10 9 8 7 6 5 4 3 2 1

TO LOUISE

Whose talents always draw the spotlight,
but whose generosity shares so much of it with others.

Thanks for casting the spotlight's warm glow my way.

A special thanks to those who have made this book possible:
Sue Redlauer and Terry Choate, John Hillman, Ronnie Pugh, Mike Holman,
Dave Stricklin, Steve Tucker, Evan and Linda.

To all the songwriters, managers, and performers who shared their time,
talents, and stories.

To Clint and Rance for giving up some of their time with me.

Most of all, to Kathy.

Contents

Introduction

My formal introduction to country music began when my father let me have some old 78 rpm discs when I was just five years old. In that collection were Spade Cooley, Gene Autry, and the Sons of the Pioneers. When I wasn't listening to my small turntable, I joined Dad and caught his long-playing recordings of folks like Hank Williams and Jimmie Rodgers. On clear Saturday nights the two of us would often tune in the *Opry* and listen to Ernest Tubb and Marty Robbins. I guess that country music was a part of my life since the day I was born.

My aunts and cousins got me into Elvis and the rest of the rockabilly acts before I entered grade school in the late fifties. From there my love of country music spread beyond listening to the old songs, and began to include finding out where they came from and who wrote them. This was the beginning of an interest that would lead not only to my learning guitar and playing with a band, but eventually to writing country music biographies and scripting country music stage shows in Branson, Missouri.

To write this book I have drawn upon twenty years of country music writing and forty years of country music memories. Over the course of a year I visited with hundreds of songwriters, music historians, performers, producers, disc jockeys, and even fans. Thanks to the folks at the Country Music Foundation I was able to search through scores of magazines,

books, interview transcriptions, and record albums. Using the *Billboard* playlists as a foundation, I was also able to survey not only the country charts, but pop charts going back to the last century. Assembling this massive amount of information, I then called upon a host of experts and we began to take a list that once contained over five hundred songs and whittle it down to the one hundred you will find within these pages.

The songs in this book are not necessarily the best one hundred or the one hundred records with the highest sales, though many from both groups can be found here. What we have tried to do is look at the history of country music and choose the songs which were the most important. Some of these numbers, such as "Wildwood Flower," made this list because they started the career of a performer or songwriter who had a massive effect on country music. Others, like "The Night Life," are here simply because they stand out as monumental efforts in writing or performance. Many, including "Statue of a Fool," are included because they are timeless: they have continued to be recorded over and over again even decades after they were written. Some, such as "Tennessee River," started trends that dramatically changed the course of country music. Finally, tunes like "Smoke on the Water" were chosen because they defined an era or a time.

Within in these pages you will find train songs like "Wabash Cannonball," truck songs like "Six Days on the Road," cowboy songs like "Tumbling Tumble-weeds," songs with social significance like "Detroit City," sports songs like "Are You Ready for Some Football?," and pain songs like "Your Cheating Heart." Yet even more fascinating than the songs that we highlight are the stories behind them. In these pages we have pieced together bits of lost history and sewn them into a quilt that reveals the rich fabric and influences of country music.

Casey Jones

Written by Wallace Saunders

Before Michael Jordan there was Babe Ruth. But before Babe Ruth there was Casey Jones. And before there was Garth Brooks, there was the American Quartet.

There was once a period of time when boys everywhere dreamed not of dunking basketballs or hitting home runs, but of piloting a surging machine along long expanses of woodlands or through high mountain passes that seemed to reach to the sky. For decades millions went to sleep each night with visions of guiding a great black locomotive, with its steam, bells, whistles, and unlimited power, down twin ribbons of steel as the world clicked by at a mile a minute. Belching smoke and fire, the iron horse drove a generation's collective imagination and made the captains of these mighty land ships some of the most revered men on the planet.

With the sounds, the sights, and the smell of trains so much a part of a growing and expanding American society, with every engineer a hero and each engine given a special life of its own, it is little wonder that during this period most boys would have rather driven a train for the MKT than been President of the United States. The fact was that most grown men would have also given almost anything to put on a pair of bib overalls and climb up into the cab.

Because of the railroad's importance in redefining American history, there were countless train engineers who drove machines whose nicknames conjured up images of monsters and gods. Most of these men went to work, piloted their huge hunks of steel safely down long stretches of track, and when their work was done went home. While local youngsters may have run after them, few people outside the engineers' hometowns or regular stops knew their names. In almost all cases these faceless men eventually retired and drifted off into obscurity with only a pocket watch and a whistle to remind them of the exotic life they once lived. But circumstances often dictate that a few men stand apart from the others with whom they share a profession, and in an era when the train was at the heart of the American story, one special engineer became famous not just along his line, but around the world. And it was all thanks to a song.

Casey Jones would have been just another anonymous man at the throttle if not for the events that surrounded an April 30, 1900, Vaughan, Tennessee, train wreck. Jones, a longtime railroader who by the turn of the century had earned a justified reputation as one of the Illinois Central's best pilots, was also one of the line's most beloved employees, friendly, outgoing, quick with a smile and a handout. Jones's "Old No. 3" was a welcome sight in and around his Jackson, Tennessee, home. His record for on-time runs was so well known that some rural folks set their watches by his wave and whistle. Solid, good-looking, blessed with clear vision and a commanding presence, he was the American ideal, a clean-living husband who loved fast trains almost as much as he loved his family, a responsible grown man who still laughed like a child when he felt his engine roar along the tracks at more than sixty miles an hour.

On a fateful early spring night Casey was attempting to make up time on a mail run through rural east Tennessee. For hours he had pushed "Old No. 3" to the limit, cutting precious seconds off with each mile. Jones had almost gotten even when tragedy cut both his run and his life short. Rounding a curve, he spotted a passenger train that had been pulled off onto a siding. Unfortunately, the passenger train's engineer had failed to notice that several of his cars and a caboose were still resting on the main line right in the path of any oncoming train. There was barely time to pray as Jones's No. 3 screamed towards the exposed cars. Grabbing his brakeman, Casey pushed him out of the cab; then the engineer put all of his weight on the brake rather than leaping off the platform to save himself. His heroic efforts slowed his train enough to preserve scores of lives, but it cost Casey dearly. He died with his hand still riding the brake.

Up until the Vaughan wreck, Wallace Saunders was probably destined to be remembered as just another railroad worker. For years he had made his living as an engine wiper at the Canton railroad shop. He and Jones had been friends, and when Saunders heard the events of the Vaughan wreck, he was deeply saddened. As a tribute to the dead engineer, Wallace wrote the story of Casey in verse. He then added music to his lyrics, and began to sing the ballad of a "great engineer" to his railroading friends.

Saunders's song quickly spread up and down the Illinois Central line, and eventually fell into the hands of two vaudeville performers, Frank and Bert Leighton. For the next two years they sang "Casey Jones" as a part of their act. In late 1902, T. Lawrence Seibert and Eddie Newton heard the Leightons' version of "Casey." Upon delving into the composition's history, they discovered that composer Saunders had never registered his song. In a move that was a common business practice during this time, the two men copyrighted and published "Casey Jones" listing themselves as the song's authors. Thus Seibert and Newton gained all rights to the sheet music.

Eight years later the ballad, which had by this time become fairly well known on the theater circuit, fell into the hands of Billy Murray. Murray, known as "The Denver Nightingale," was then America's most successful recording star. A veteran of vaudeville and honky-tonks, he was best known for his interpretation of George M. Cohan's works. Murray had just put together the soon-to-be-famous American Quartet, and needed a composition to help him establish the group. As he guided his new group into the Victor studio, Billy considered several different numbers before settling on the tune about the train engineer.

Murray himself could not have predicted America's rush to purchase this tale of a man who had died a decade before the song about his life had been recorded. The fact was, like Murray, most people had not previously heard of either Jones or the train wreck at Vaughan. Yet the record quickly changed that. From coast to coast and border to border customers actually lined up when shipments of the American Quartet's version of "Casey Jones" arrived. Over the course of just a few weeks the song steamed up the national charts to the #1 position, and held it for eleven straight weeks. No pre–World War I song was as popular.

Murray, sensing that sharing royalties with the three others in the American Quartet made little sense, cut his own version of "Casey Jones" and rode it solo to #3. Arthur Collins and Byron Harlan, two of the nation's other top voices, also cut a single, which topped out at #5. It quickly became apparent to the music industry that "Casey Jones" was more than a simple hit, it was a phenomenon. City folks were buying this "country" ballad even faster than rural customers. By the beginning of 1911 sales of the American Quartet's single had topped one million. Eventually the record would go over the two million mark. "Casey" was a country standard which had ridden to town in a big way.

The success of "Casey Jones" should have stoked the fires for a number of other rural-hero songs. Yet it was fifteen years before "The Death of Floyd Collins" would follow "Casey" up the charts. For a while some of the major labels did experiment with other country-type releases and acts, but with little success. After a short time Victor, Edison, and the other labels went back to the Broadway show numbers and Tin Pan Alley themes which had always been popular with the buying public. Novelty songs replaced songs about true-life heroes, and the American Quartet began to record tunes about college boys.

Still, this song about an unknown engineer had opened the door a crack and proven not only that America had a deep romance with locomotives, but that the sounds and stories of rural America could be brought to the city and folks would pay good money to hear them. It would take another fifteen years and an opera-singing Texan to really put country music on the rails to success, but thanks to the tribute that Wallace Saunders paid to a friend, a country music songwriter earned his first gold record. Sadly, neither Saunders nor the Jones family ever received a penny for "Casey Jones."

1925

The Prisoner Song

Written by Guy Massey

Marion Try Slaughter was born in 1883 on the Texas plains. While in his teens he and his mother moved to Dallas, but before he left the ranch he learned to rope, ride, and sing the songs of the local cowboys. Young Marion studied classical music at the Dallas Conservatory of Music, and was a popular soloist at some of the city's finest churches. Encouraged by his teachers and local critics, he left Texas in 1910 to pursue an operatic career in New York.

Though blessed with some natural talent, Slaughter was out of his league in the Big Apple. Time and time again he found himself competing for parts in plays and operas against seasoned musical veterans. Though he landed a few small roles in productions such as *H.M.S. Pinafore* by Gilbert and Sullivan, he sustained himself and his growing family by working as a piano salesman and a paid funeral singer. In 1914 he noted a very small advertisement located on the back pages of one of the city's many newspapers. With some enthusiasm he informed his wife that a New Jersey recording company was auditioning new talent. Taking what little savings they had, he purchased train fare and arrived at the audition, only to find himself surrounded by many of the same men who had beaten him out for scores of opera jobs. Discouraged, he stayed for the audition only because he had nothing else to do. Surprising everyone, including himself, he was the only person signed to a record deal.

Over the course of the next decade Slaughter released a host of songs under scores of different aliases. Though there was no known reason why he recorded under so many different names, it was probably done in order to keep his own name pure for the stage. Classical singers who had been employed to record "lesser" music were usually shunned by major producers. Slaughter still desired a shot on the New York stage, so as a practical matter, when recording he rarely used his own name. His most commonly used recording monicker, Vernon Dalhart, was taken from two of his favorite Texas towns.

Up until 1925, Slaughter, using aliases, was best known for singing songs in a Negro dialect. Most were humorous, and a few sold fairly well. It was during a "Dalhart" recording session for the Edison label that Slaughter and the producer opted to have the song sung in a style the singer had heard on the Texas range. In the midst of recording these songs of the country, Slaughter and his cousin, Guy Massey, took a break to grab a bite to eat and get some rest. During this break Massey took an old envelope and jotted down a poem about a lonely man who was doomed to die in prison. Slaughter read the words and then helped Massey come up with a tune to fit. Within three hours Slaughter as Dalhart had cut the song and the two were on their way home unaware that they had just made history.

"The Prisoner Song" was released in March of 1925. Within weeks the mournful tune had climbed to #1. It would own this position for five weeks. Slaughter, now growing famous as Dalhart, raced back into the studio to cut some more folk-type numbers. This time he was working with the Victor label. He again cut "The Prisoner Song," and backed it with a song written by and recorded in 1921 with minor success by Henry Whitter. Once again the record took off, reclaiming the #1 spot and staying at the top for another seven weeks. The former opera singer had now found his niche—doing storytelling songs as Vernon Dalhart.

Johnny Cash would later explain that prison songs work because all people put themselves in some kind of jail. Maybe Cash was right, but what fueled "The Prisoner Song" was probably the simple, easy-to-remember melody and the haunting words. Seemingly falsely accused, deserted by everyone who knew him, the prisoner was destined to die alone and unloved. No country song would seem so sad and hopeless until Hank Williams penned "I'm So Lonesome I Could Cry."

"The Prisoner Song," coupled with the almost equally popular "B" side, "Wreck of the Old 97," would assure that Slaughter would always be remembered as Dalhart. "The Prisoner Song" alone sold over seven million copies. Outside of three Christmas favorites, it was the largest-selling record between 1900 and 1950. No "rural" song had ever generated this kind of popularity, and the record companies took note. They began to wonder if there was a place for real country music at the local music stores.

Within months of the reformed opera singer's huge hit, talent scouts were hitting the back roads looking for authentic country acts. In makeshift recording studios set up in stores and barns, hundreds of backwoods musicians were asked to sing their own compositions for the hungry scouts. A few of these "finds" were brought to the city for more professional auditions. Some were even signed, but over the next three years none could come close to duplicating the success of Slaughter's Vernon Dalhart.

During his career Slaughter would sell more than fifty million records. Most of his songs would be forgotten almost as quickly as they were released, but not "The Prisoner Song." On sales alone this song is one of the most momentous in American music, but more importantly, it put wheels to the search for rural music. Its success began the process that would see Ralph Peer journey to Bristol, Tennessee, to become the midwife for the real birth of country music.

An added note concerning the authorship of "The Prisoner Song." Guy Massey claimed to be the sole writer on the song's copyright. He had even tried to sell the song to a record company before he miraculously jotted down the words from out of thin air in early 1925. Yet for years his brother, Robert, claimed to be the song's acutual composer. It was said to be a combination of several songs Robert had heard while traveling around the country. Robert claimed that he had taught it to his brother. Upon his death, Guy seemed to acknowledge this fact by willing all future royalties from sales of "The Prisoner Song" to Robert. Yet while it is Robert's heirs who receive the royalty checks, to this day Guy's name remains as the hit's sole author.

1928

Wildwood Flower

Written by A.P. Carter

As has been revealed in these pages, there was country music before August 1927, but before this time country music's real impact on the national markets was only marginal and very inconsistent. By and large those like Vernon Dalhart who had made their name recording "country music songs" were not from the hills and hollows or plains and valleys. These recording stars sang both rural music and city music, and most knew more about Broadway than they did about hillbillies. Their rural image was often manufactured for the moment and the dollar. And none were solely devoted to a country style. Thus it was really only when recording executive Ralph Peer came to Bristol, Tennessee, in August 1927, looking for new recording acts, that he uncovered the genuine article. In a yodeling drifter and a religious family trio, Peer finally found the first real voices of what we now know as country music.

The Carter family consisted of three individuals, A.P. or Doc, his wife Sara, and A.P.'s sister-in-law Maybelle. With A.P. singing bass, Sara singing lead, and Maybelle adding harmonies, the family group had entertained around Maces Springs, Virginia, since Maybelle had married into the family in the spring of 1926. Unlike other rural bands who played just for their own amusement, the Carters saw their music as both expression and a paycheck. Ambitious, they were one of the few rural acts in search of bookings that paid real money. A.P. even dreamed of cutting records.

Legend has it that the family read a want ad in a newspaper and learned about Ralph Peer looking for new acts. Recent research has turned up no such advertisement. More than likely A.P. heard the news of Peer's arrival through the rural grapevine or caught a brief mention of the event in a newspaper story. In any case, the group's leader was determined that he was not going to miss the opportunity to audition for a major label. Thus, on the appointed day, dressed in poor people's best, the family made the twenty-five-mile drive across the state line to Bristol, Tennessee, to the audition.

Those who witnessed this group's arrival were probably more amused than inspired. Dust-covered after a hot ride over unpaved roads, the small Carter band hardly appeared to be the focal point of country music's "big bang." Sara and A.P. had brought their seven-month-old son Joe and eight-year-old daughter Gladys. Maybelle was seven months pregnant with her first child. For all the world they simply resembled hill folks on a monthly trek to civilization for supplies. Rather than producing a supply list, the Carters pulled their musical instruments from the mud-spattered vehicle. As they wandered into the makeshift storefront studio to meet the Victor Talking Machine executive, it must have seemed that this was just another rural, hayseed string band that had made a fruitless pilgrimage to town. But looks can often be deceiving, and under this plain veneer were three unique talents that would blend together to bring Ralph Peer much more than he had ever dared hope.

Sara Carter was a strong vocalist. Although she was raw and untrained, her phrasing and emotion set her apart. Much more than a singer, she was an interpreter of lyrics. She had a quality that made her distinctive in a world where most rural female singers sounded the same. Even as she was pregnant, Maybelle was a woman in a man's world. When most girls had been content to sing, she had learned to play. She was a talented instrumentalist who brought a whole new style of playing to both the autoharp and guitar. Her unique method of picking the chords on the low strings with her thumb while playing the lead on the high strings with her fingers created a sound that Peer had never heard. It fascinated him. Even though the record producer didn't realize it then, Maybelle's was the rhythm on which country music was to be built. Joining the two attractive but unadorned women was A.P.

While the two women may have had more visible talent, it was A.P.'s insight and drive that fueled the team. A.P. Carter was a promoter, a booker, a public-relations man, and a salesman. It was his ambition that drove the trio past family get-togethers and into schoolhouse programs and local fair platforms. It was his desire for material that sent him into the backwoods. He listened to and transcribed folk songs, old hymns, poems, and country jigs. He then took the best of these often primitive lyrics and melodies and refined them, shaping them into something that seemed to have the Carter Family identity written all over it.

With Maybelle's guitar featured equally with Sara's vocals on A.P.'s arrangements, the group was the most

original thing Ralph Peer had ever heard. He was so excited that he devoted much of his day to getting six of their cuts on sides. He also obtained publishing rights to their material. Yet while this day in August put the family on the way to a recording deal, it was a few months later before they would cut the song which would assure them a place in country music history.

In the spring of 1928 the Carters again emerged from the Virginia hills, journeying this time to Camden, New Jersey. Here the group cut "Little Darling Pal of Mine," and their theme song, ""Keep on the Sunny Side." While both of these numbers would become standards and country music hits, it was another A.P. Carter song that would fully mesh his song-gathering genius with Sara's rich voice and Maybelle's revolutionary guitar style.

"Wildwood Flower" is in itself a very curious song. The lyrics are confusing and far too poetic to have come exclusively from a unpretentious rural environment. Part ode, part folktale, the song contains phrases which are filled with unexplained symbolism. It is anything but a simple love song. How much of it A.P. actually wrote remains unknown. Sara would later admit that her mother had sung it more than two decades before. Yet no matter its origin, the song is a testament to A.P.'s research, his knowledge of folk music, his own sense of style, and his ability to blend the rural music of the times with Sara's voice and Maybelle's picking.

"Wildwood Flower" was a huge hit. Released in late summer, it would race up the pop music charts, peaking at #3 (country charts would not exist at a national level until 1944). It would be fifteen years before another country act climbed this high on the more sophisticated ratings system. This kind of success was unheard of for a hillbilly group. While "Wildwood Flower" was a big hit in the city, in rural areas it quickly became an anthem. No one could have predicted the sales it generated in both sheet music and records.

Throughout the first few decades of country music, whenever a country act had a strong hit vehicle, a host of pop acts would cut their own versions of the song. For years these cover versions would outperform and outsell the originals. It is therefore a lasting testament to the Carter Family's cut of "Wildwood Flower" that in spite of the song's huge success, no pop versions followed. As a matter of record, no country acts even dared challenge the original until two future Country Music Hall of Famers, Merle Travis and Hank Thompson, rode their tribute to the Carters up the charts some twenty-seven years later. Yet despite the fact that few have dared to record it, probably no single song has been played as much or as often as A.P.'s "Wildwood Flower." Upon release it set a new standard; now, some sixty plus years later, it is still the standard!

Yet it wasn't the chart numbers and million-unit sales success that made this song one of the most important in the history of American music. The fact is that this was more than a simple hit. "Wildwood Flower" was the cornerstone on which country music finally built its own identity. The Carter song didn't just expand the audience for country music; with Maybelle's unique guitar style, it also expanded the role of the guitar. It might be hard to appreciate today, but the licks that were captured on this and other later Carter Family recordings radically changed music. Up until this point, a country vocal number had little or no room for instrumental leads. Now guitar players were learning from and expanding on what Maybelle had created. There would be no turning back; from this flower a new kind of expression would grow.

1928
Blue Yodel #1/T for Texas

Written by Jimmie Rodgers

Jimmie Rodgers's plaque in the Country Music Hall of Fame states that this "Singing Brakeman" was "the man who started it all." Should this sickly, uneducated, Mississippi-born, guitar-playing minstrel showman really be called "The Father of Country Music"? In a word, "Yes!"

There was country music before Ralph Peer recorded Rodgers and his soon-to-be friends the Carter Family in August 1927. It didn't just suddenly begin that day in Bristol, Tennessee, but country music did start to really come together then. And it was there in the backwoods South, not in New York or New Jersey, where the voices that would inspire a generation of country pickers and singers were first captured and identified.

In retrospect it was the Carter Family that was Ralph Peer's tie to the hills and hollows, to lost loves and found faith, but it took Jimmie Rodgers to connect the publisher with some of country music's other most beloved symbols—trains and saloons, jails and the blues. The Carters identified with the white South, but Rodgers drew from much broader sources.

Born in the last few years of the nineteenth century, Rodgers lost his mother to tuberculosis when he was four. What compounded the boy's tragedy was that she had probably passed the disease on to Jimmie before she died. Often sick, pushed from relative to relative, Rodgers grew up feeling unwanted and

alone. By the age of fourteen he had given up on family life and hopped a freight train. He was hoping to find both adventure and peace. What really followed him were more pain and hard times.

The teenager didn't hesitate telling friends that he longed to live the life of a railroader. He yearned to be an engineer or line foreman, but with his small frame and hacking cough, it was a dream he could never realize. Because of his health, Rodgers was relegated to being a menial water carrier, a position usually given only to inexperienced black workers. Yet this obvious slight probably paved the way for Jimmie's later fame. Here, with the men and boys most saw as having little worth, Rodgers learned to play guitar and banjo as well as sing the workingman's blues.

Over the course of time young Rodgers found he could make a bit of extra money by using his guitar and voice to entertain the railroad workers during breaks. He sang a few folk standards, but mainly he "invented" songs of his own that combined several different musical styles. It is doubtful that at the time Jimmie envisioned that he was creating a whole new sound by combining the white rural music he had heard as a child with the Negro odes he was now playing. At that moment the boy just knew that people seemed to like it, so he continued to improvise.

By the mid-twenties Rodgers had given up railroad work even on a part-time basis. With his guitar in hand he turned to roving tent shows as a way to make a living for his wife and new baby. Nomadic life was hard on the sickly Jimmie and his family. In 1927 he landed a steady job on WWNC in Asheville, North Carolina, and vowed to settle down. His dreams of stability were dashed when his show was canceled less than six weeks after it premiered and he was forced to once again hit the road.

As with the Carters, it was probably a newspaper article that led to his seeking an audition in Bristol with Ralph Peer. At age thirty, for the first time in his life it looked as if he had finally caught a real break. After playing only two traditional folk ballads Rodgers was given a Victor contract. Just before Christmas "The Soldier's Sweetheart" landed on the pop charts, earning the singer almost $400 in royalties. For Jimmie's wife Carrie it was a dream come true. The singer saw it as just the beginning.

Impatient for more success, Rodgers journeyed uninvited to New York and informed Ralph Peer that he was in town and ready to cut more records. The producer quickly arranged for a session in Camden, New Jersey. Four songs were cut, one an original Rodgers composition.

Carrie had wanted her husband to play "T for Texas" at his Bristol audition. At that time Jimmie hadn't felt confident enough to share his own "amateur" work with a professional music man such as Peer. But now, with two royalty checks in his pocket, a self-assured Rodgers cut loose and displayed his version of white rural blues. Peer loved it more than anything he had heard Rodgers sing. He deemed that it would be "The Singing Brakeman's" next release.

There was nothing complicated about "T for Texas." It was a tale about a man who was very mad at the woman who had done him wrong. It was obvious from the phrasing that the writer had combined both rural black and white influences in a somewhat haphazard manner to make up the song's five verses. And there were only two lines per verse! Yet none of that mattered in the least. The words were simply in the song in order to have something to sing. It was what Jimmie did when he wasn't singing that made this recording special.

The yodel at the end of each verse, Jimmie's "hey, hey, hey," combined with the black blues feel, created a song that was completely unique. With "T for Texas" Rodgers had captured an informal sound that New Yorkers, or most of white America for that matter, had never heard. The label knew that this style would easily set the singer apart from not only Vernon Dalhart and the Carters, but from every other recording act, both black and white. It was an incomparable sound, but some still questioned if it could be marketed. It didn't take long to find out.

Victor released "T for Texas" as "Blue Yodel" in March 1928. Across the nation radio stations immediately began to play Rodgers's rural voice accompanied by his simple guitar runs. After each verse came Jimmie's mournful yodel, and the listeners couldn't get enough. In a matter of weeks Rodgers's success was the talk of the nation. To capitalize on their find, Peer and Victor began to call the singer the "The Blue Yodeler."

Within weeks fan mail had literally poured into the Victor's New York office. A hastily booked tour sent Rodgers to theaters throughout the Midwest. This wildly successful tour proved that the Mississippi product was as hot in Chicago as he was in the Deep South. Within two months Jimmie's royalty checks jumped to more than $2,000 a month and his "Blue Yodel" made it to #1.

Rodgers was so successful that a host of other labels used their own artists to cover "T for Texas." The public would have none of it. They wanted real country music from the man who wrote it. In a fairy tale come true, the once sickly and unwanted orphan had become a national sensation and no one could find a worthy challenger.

It took Jimmie Rodgers scarcely a year to go from being completely unknown to selling millions of records, working on stages with the likes of Will Rogers, and appearing in a talking film. The singer was also making more money in a month than most Southerners would see in a lifetime. By 1929 Rodgers had earned enough in royalties to spend $50,000 for a custom home in Kerrville, Texas. He was on top of the world, but as he would later sing, "My time ain't long."

By themselves the Carters would have had a major impact on beginning the form of music that came to be known as country. But without Jimmie's "Blue Yodel," and the more than one hundred Rodgers recordings which followed (eleven more labeled "Blue Yodel"), it is doubtful that this hillbilly music would have expanded as rapidly or included the black blues sounds that have so shaped country music.

Jimmie Rodgers earned the spotlight and acclaim as he forged black and white influences into a new sound that stood apart from folk and blues. Because of this marriage, his influence would be felt in all forms and styles of country music for years to come, including the formation of rock 'n' roll. A simple man who was always running from a lifelong death sentence, Jimmie Rodgers and his "Blue Yodel" laid a foundation on which Ernest Tubb, Gene Autry, Roy Acuff, and a host of others would soon construct a viable industry.

1928

In the Jailhouse Now

Written by Jimmie Rodgers

In early 1955 Webb Pierce released what was to become the best-selling single of the year. This record would go on to become the second most successful song of the decade and country music's third-highest-charting release of all time. For the former *Louisiana Hayride* star it was the biggest in a long list of hits that would ultimately make him the sixth most successful recording artist in the history of the country music charts. As important as these numbers may have been in establishing Webb's place in Nashville, all this chart and sales success on the eve of the rockabilly revoluaiton may have been an even more important reminder of the powerful influence of country music's first real star.

Jimmie Rodgers cut "In the Jailhouse Now" in 1928. It was "The Blue Yodeler's" follow-up to "T for Texas." Though it did not make as much noise on the chart as its predecessor, its impact was felt all around the nation.

When he put together the original version of "Jailhouse," Jimmie took an old American ballad and groomed it to fit his mesh of white hillbilly and black blues. With his casual treatment of the melody and lyrics coupled to his unique yodel, the simple moralistic song went far beyond what any other singer had ever done with it. Though much of the standard's heritage may have been in folk music, the singer expanded the number's potential. Much as he was later

able to do with another familiar standard, "Frankie and Johnny," Rodgers transformed "In the Jailhouse Now" into one of his own works. For decades he would be the only person music fans identified with the song.

Over the course of the next two years after the release of "T for Texas" and "In the Jailhouse Now," "The Singing Brakeman" became so hot that at some concert stops frenzied patrons tried to tear his clothing off his body in order to secure souvenirs. In the rural South families would patch old dresses, shirts, and pants in order to save their money for Rodgers's latest 78. Conservative and sensible farmers went into hock to purchase radios or Victrolas just so that they could hear Jimmie's songs. His singing style and guitar licks were learned by every rural boy (and many a city slicker) who had any kind of love of music. If you could yodel like Jimmie, you were almost guaranteed an opportunity to earn some spare change playing at local dances. With this kind of devotion, it is little wonder that Rodgers continued to sell records by the millions even in the midst of the Great Depression's worst years.

From the very beginning Ralph Peer and Victor Records had encouraged their star to write a series of "Blue Yodels" in order to satisfy the public's passion for this unique song style. With each release in what was to become a twelve-song string, the fans would rush to buy the records. It was the success of this line of releases that caused the producer and the label to suggest that Jimmie write his own version of "In the Jailhouse Now." With their request in mind, the singer retired from the studio for about twenty minutes before returning with the new original set of lyrics. "In the Jailhouse Now No. 2" was released in 1930, and as was expected, the single quickly became a successful follow-up to the first hit. As Peer and Victor had surmised, the song and Rodgers's style were a perfect marriage. If Jimmie hadn't died in his prime, there would have probably been an "In the Jailhouse Now No 3."

In his brief recording career Jimmie Rodgers wrote and performed several songs, such as the upbeat "Peach Pickin' Time in Georgia" or the mournful "Waiting for a Train," that were probably better examples of writing and performance than either version of "In the Jailhouse Now." When measured simply on pop chart success, "The Brakeman's Blues" and "Blue Yodel No. 3" climbed higher and lasted longer than the "Jailhouse" releases. Yet it was "In the Jailhouse Now" that was most often included in the shows of Rodgers imitators Ernest Tubb and Gene Autry, and until his death in 1933, it was to be one of Jimmie's most requested live numbers. For some reason this was a song that touched a chord when Rodgers was alive and continued to win fans after his death. Still, few expected or would have predicted that it would become such a monster hit again more than twenty-five years later.

Just a few months after Webb Pierce released his version of Rodgers's "Jailhouse," RCA brought Chet Atkins and Hank Snow into the studio, combined them with a number of session players, and over-dubbed Jimmie's original 1930 version of "In the Jailhouse Now No. 2." Released as a single at about the same time Webb's version hit #1, the version by Jim-mie Rodgers and the Rainbow Ranch Boys cruised up the country sales list and settled in at the seventh spot. Because country charts were not introduced until 1944, it would mark the first and only time that the "Father of Country Music" ever had a hit record in the genre he helped create. But the success of the song didn't stop there.

In 1962 Johnny Cash released his "In the Jailhouse Now" and used it to get into the top ten for the first time in almost three years. In the early seventies Merle Haggard included "Jailhouse" on a widely acclaimed tribute album to Jimmie. Sonny James spent eleven weeks on the 1978 charts and peaked at #15 with the Rodgers classic. Like Cash, the Southern Gentleman used the 1928 lyrics for his version. Webb Pierce teamed with Willie Nelson in 1982 and spent five more weeks in the top one hundred with a duet version of the song. When his two releases are combined, Pierce spent forty-two weeks on the charts with this classic. More than any other song recorded by Hall-of-Famer Rodgers, "In the Jailhouse Now" seems to have influenced the most country acts.

Yet maybe country music in general is too quick to claim Rodgers as strictly its own founding father. By combining blues and folk, white and black, and by even experimenting with jazz and Broadway standards, Jimmie didn't adhere to one musical influence. In some of his recordings he relied on black sidemen for special licks, and in others he called in Maybelle Carter. Until tuberculosis claimed his life, Rodgers continued to grow by constantly seeking out ways to expand his audience and his music. Maybe this was why the Rock and Roll Hall of Fame inducted "The Singing Brakeman" in 1986.

Rodgers once told a group of pickers, "I'm trying to pick up a couple of musicians. Boys who will work schoolhouses, barn dances, roadhouses, and beer joints—anything and anywhere. Folks everywhere are gettin' tired of all this Black Bottom–Charleston music junk. I want to give them something different."

What the singer gave them was a mix of music that we now call country. Even though he never named it, Rodgers "invented" it by taking the best not only from his musical heritage, but from all types of music. He then played this mix as he felt it. He thus drew from everyone he met, but imitated no one. He set the standard for Hank Williams, Elvis Presley, and even Garth Brooks and Reba McEntire.

Without the contributions and influence of this star of the common people, country and rock music would probably be far different today. Jimmie Rodgers, the first of country music's tragic heroes, was a man ahead of his time, and thousands of songwriters and performers owe him a debt that can never be repaid.

1929
I'm Thinking Tonight of My Blue Eyes

1938
The Great Speckled Bird

1952
The Wild Side of Life

1952
It Wasn't God Who Made Honky Tonk Angels

Traditional

The tie between American country music and traditional English folk songs is a deep one that goes back centuries. During the New World's first three hundred years the American upper class may have continued to listen to the classical music of Europe, but the real pioneers were adapting and revising folk music to fit their situations and tell their stories. Many of the tunes that gave birth to what we now call country music were brought to the New World by men and women fleeing England's oppression. Music was one of their most powerful links to a faraway homeland. It was the fabric of what they had been, as well as being an oral history of their lives. After several generations of evolution, the instruments and words had dramatically changed. In many cases there was only a faint hint of the original melodies left intact. Yet by and large, there was a bit of the feel of the British peasant class in this "original" American music.

Country music legend A.P. Carter collected many of these ancient tunes and their new lyrics when he was looking for performance material for the Carter Family. "I'm Thinking Tonight of My Blue Eyes" was one of the hillbilly folk songs he uncovered. In 1929 it became a huge hit for the family. While this hauntingly sad story of a love that had been lost far across the sea was new to most of the listening public, the melody must have seemed familiar to many who had been raised around the English folk music tradition.

The fact was that the musical riffs and strains had come across the Atlantic a couple of hundred years before Mr. Carter had collected the tune's Americanized verses. While "I'm Thinking Tonight of My Blue Eyes" might have been the first popular use of the tune at that time, it was certainly not the only one. Sara Carter, A.P.'s wife, remembered hearing other versions of it when she was a child. Still, for the purposes of the recording world and country music history, this early version, which climbed to #10 on the pop charts, was the initial popular use of the tune. As time would prove, it wouldn't be the last.

In early 1937 Roy Acuff was a former baseball player turned struggling medicine-show singer when he heard The Black Shirts use much different lyrics with the same English folk tune as "I'm Thinking Tonight of My Blue Eyes." Acuff was captured by both this new song's message and symbolism. He paid singer Charlie Swain a very hard-earned fifty cents to transcribe the song's words. It was probably the best half-dollar Roy ever spent.

Within weeks this new song, "The Great Speckled Bird," would become Acuff and His Crazy Tennesseans' most requested number. He even sang it on his first *Grand Ole Opry* guest shot. Knowing very little about "The Great Speckled Bird's" origin, Acuff began to dig into its history. Tracing "The Bird's" roots revealed that the religiously framed story had been composed by a minister, Guy Smith. Acuff also discovered that the song's unusual words had been inspired by the twelfth chapter, ninth verse of the Book of Jeremiah.

Mine heritage is unto me as a speckled bird, the birds round about are against her; come ye, assemble all the beasts of the field, come to devour.

By October 1937, the American Record Company's William R. Calaway had also heard several different versions of "The Great Speckled Bird." It was both his and ARC's belief that this would be a great song in the hands of the right recording artist. Upon listening to Acuff's version, he knew he had found that perfect match. Acuff would later remember that he wasn't signed because of either his outstanding voice or great fiddle talent; instead the record label used him because they believed that he could deliver "The Bird."

Around the same time that Acuff recorded his first session, ARC was purchased by Columbia. During this period the merged labels were unsure what to do with their hillbilly acts. Thus Acuff's recording of "The Bird" was held in limbo. Finally the company decided to record Acuff in early 1938 on its Vocalion banner. By this time Roy had written four additional verses to go with the song's original six. In order to include all ten, the producer put the first five on side one and the other five on what was usually called the "B" side of the record. In retrospect it would seem to have been a very wise move. By the end of the year Roy's first release had climbed to the #10 pop chart and Acuff had been invited to become a regular part of the *Grand Ole Opry*. Acuff's place in country music was thus assured, and his next release would make him "The King of Country Music."

Two major national hits with the same tune was a phenomenal accomplishment, but the best days for the old English folk tune were still ahead. Over a decade after "The Bird" hit the charts, William Warren's wife of eight months left him. As she packed up, she issued this ominous warning; "Don't write me. If you do, I'll just tear up your letters. If you call me, I'll just hang up." A few weeks later Warren saw his now-ex-wife dancing and drinking at a Texas honky-tonk. Devastated, he went home and immediately wrote lyrics that he matched to the same tune used in "Blue

Eyes" and "The Bird." He then gave those words to Jimmy Heath and the Melody Masters, a local group that played in the honky-tonk his wife now regularly visited. As soon as she heard the song, she knew who and what had inspired the lyrics.

The Melody Masters cut "The Wild Side of Life" on a local label and put it in area jukeboxes. Hank Thompson and his wife Dorothy heard it on one of Thompson's east Texas swings.

"My wife immediately liked the song," Hank recalled, "but I told her that the tune was worn out. It had simply been used too many times before." Nevertheless Dorothy did convince Hank to copy down the lyrics. In doing so, he combined verses two and three, thus simplifying Warren's original story.

Hank Thompson was not a typical country music performer of the day. The Waco, Texas, native had studied electrical engineering at Princeton University, and was using this background to create the industry's first portable lighting and sound systems. He was also rewiring guitars and amplifiers to come up with far better concert sound quality. To say that he was innovative and constantly pushing the envelope was an understatement. Yet his developments in the technical area would eventually pale in comparison to his on-stage showmanship. Hank first hit national prominence in 1946 with "Humpty Dumpty Heart." A series of top-ten hits had followed, including 1949's "Whoa Sailor," but by 1950 Hank Williams and Hank Snow's surge had left little room in the spotlight for the Texas Hank. In 1952 he needed a hit just to relaunch his career.

In the early part of the year Hank and his band traveled west to cut a new series of records for Capitol. Ken Nelson, a producer assigned to work Thompson's Los Angeles recording session, asked Thompson if he had anything for the "B" side of Hank's self-penned "Crying in the Deep Blue Sea." The singer

mentioned "Wild Side of Life." He pulled the scribbled lyrics out of his bag and, without a rehearsal, Hank and His Brazos Valley Boys cut it in one take. Then they packed up and went home.

Thompson's "Crying in the Deep Blue Sea" could only manage to chart in the Southwest. Nationally it went nowhere. But after two frustrating months, a few disc jockeys began to flip the single and play "Wild Side of Life." In one of the more bizarre events in recording history, without any public-relations push, this "B" side moved like a tidal wave across the nation and became a huge hit. It stayed #1 for fifteen straight weeks. It would not only resurrect Thompson's career, but would become 1952's biggest country release. Hank and Burl Ives would also score near the top of the pop charts with this third version of the old English standard. Could it get any better?

J.D. Miller saw no reason to stop the tune's chart success with Thompson's latest hit, nor did he waste any time pushing his idea to Decca Records. Miller heard Hank's "Wild Side of Life" while driving in a car near Rayne, Louisiana. He pulled off to the side of the road and wrote a woman's response. While Hank was still holding country music's top spot, Decca took Miller's lyrics and called Kitty Wells.

"Kitty was in semi-retirement," Hank Thompson remembered, "and she wasn't that interested in recording again [her first efforts with RCA had failed to chart]. Her husband, Johnny Wright, convinced her to cut the song for the session money."

Decca liked the demo that Kitty cut so much they not only wanted to release it, but also to sign her to a contract. Some would have questioned the label's actions. No female soloist had ever posted a major country music hit single. Except for Patsy Montana's pop hit of "I Want to Be a Cowboy Sweetheart," few female country-oriented songs had even bumped the charts. Country music was a man's world, so why waste time and money on a girl singer?

There was also another problem. When Wells heard Miller's new words it had to have shocked her. She was a devoted mother, a pillar of the church, and a happily married woman who didn't drink or smoke. This song spoke of a woman being condemned to the sinful world of taverns and liquor by the actions of an unfaithful man. It was just the opposite of the image she had always tried to project. "It Wasn't God Who Made Honky-Tonk Angels" thus would have seemed totally inappropriate for Wells to promote. Still, in the face of opposition, Kitty and Decca forged ahead. In doing so, they changed the world.

Decca would have been satisfied to have simply charted on their initial time out with Wells. A top-ten song would have been cause for a huge celebration. What they got must have caught them in a dead faint. With Wells's mournful voice pleading "not to blame us women," "It Wasn't God Who Made Honky-Tonk Angels" became the first #1 single for a country music female artist. It would remain at that position for six weeks, and hit #27 on the pop charts. Suddenly Kitty was a major star. With an old tune and new revolutionary words, country music's female liberation movement had begun, Kitty Wells was the "Honky-Tonk Angel," and she was on the threshold of a career that would span hundreds of recordings and more than five decades of performances. And country record labels were having to take a second look at their female acts.

When taken by themselves, each one of these four vocal versions of this old English folk tune was a remarkable piece of country music history. Each was a major hit, has been recorded and performed on numerous occasions by scores of artists, and has struck a special chord with fans. Yet the most remarkable record set by these four different lyrical renditions of the same tune is that all of the original recording artists have found their way to a special place on the hallowed walls of the Country Music Hall of Fame. The Carter Family probably would have made it even without "I'm Thinking Tonight of My Blue Eyes," but Roy Acuff himself admitted that he was signed to record "The Great Speckled Bird." Without the fifty cents he invested in the words to that song, he might have never become the "King of Country Music." Hank Thompson hadn't had a hit in three years when he cut "The Wild Side of Life." Would he have ever had the opportunity to record the long string of special chart-busting records without this song? And what about Kitty Wells? She didn't even have a recording career before "It Wasn't God Who Made Honky-Tonk Angels." Without that song, how long would it have been before country music recognized the power of female performers?

Four recordings, four sets of lyrics, four members of the Country Music Hall of Fame, and all with the same tune. That is a bit of history that will probably never be repeated—unless, of course, another songwriter comes up with another set of unforgettable words to this ancient British folk standard.

1934
Tumbling Tumbleweeds

Written by Bob Nolan

The man most responsible for the inspired lyrics and melodies which would define America's premier western group was born not in the arid Southwest but in the province of New Brunswick, Canada, in 1908. From a fun-filled freedom that included endless hours in the woods tracking wildcats and shooting the rapids, a twelve-year-old Bob Nolan moved to very civilized and proper Boston. In the city the bright boy was educated and refined, but the urban life couldn't completely tame or satisfy him. He longed for places where the trails were long and the people were outnumbered by the animals. So it was with great joy that in 1922, at the age of fourteen, Bob and his father left the East Coast and settled in the desert around Tucson, Arizona. It was here that Nolan was to get his first unforgettable glimpse of the Western vistas which would so shape his life and career.

Four years after moving across the nation, the young well-traveled high school graduate earned an athletic scholarship to the University of Arizona. Surprisingly, the hearty pole-vaulter would choose to major in music and spend his spare time writing a poetry column called *Tumbleweed Trails* for the student newspaper. The inspiration for his poems was centered around Bob's own wanderlust. He loved nothing so much as drifting around the barren desert or through the unsettled mountains. He often sat for hours watching eagles fly, listening to wolves howl, or just waiting for the setting sun to paint the skies with a myriad of beautiful hues. While the rest of his generation seemed to yearn for fast times and faster cars, alone and on foot Nolan found peace and comfort in the quiet harsh beauty of the arid wastelands or the moist lushness of the dense mountain woods.

It was probably his unsettled gypsy nature that caused Bob to drop out of college and begin a wandering trek that would last for several years. He often lived off the land for weeks at a time, and his instincts kept him alive and his pioneer spirit kept him moving. Finally, in 1929, Nolan found his way to California. He took a job with a traveling Chautauqua troupe reciting tales and singing songs that revolved around his adventures in the wild. With his unlimited stories he was a cast favorite. He was also a good draw for the show. Yet the profitable times didn't last long, as the Depression not only closed the tent show, but seemed to obstruct almost all other avenues of work open for young men. A job as a lifeguard fed Nolan for a while, but then it too played out. If he had not noticed a talent ad placed in a Los Angeles newspaper, Bob probably would have given up on city life and returned to the desert to live off the land.

In 1931 Leonard Slye, an Ohio-born singer and guitar player, decided to form a new western-style singing group. He began his search for prospective band members through the newspaper. Several out-of-work musicians answered his ad, but only Bob Nolan came with a yodel and a bag full of original compositions. Slye immediately hired the young man to play and sing with his Rocky Mountaineers.

For several months the Mountaineers eked out a living singing on a local radio show and playing for small dances. Sleeping in cheap, dirty rooms and living off thrown-away fruits and vegetables, they found the life of musicians harder than any of them had dreamed. Frustrated by the lack of opportunities, Nolan left the group in 1932. Slye replaced Bob with a Missourian, Tim Spencer. While Nolan went back to lifeguarding, Spencer and Slye worked with three different unsuccessful groups over the next year.

In the fall of 1933 Len and Tim convinced Nolan to join them in forming another western group. This time they called themselves the Pioneer Trio. Working hard at developing a unique sound, the group began to sing in three-part harmonies. It was this close-knit sound that was to become their trademark and earn them their first job. With Slye singing lead and playing guitar, Bob adding baritone and playing bass, and Spencer chiming in with tenor and seconding on guitar, less than a month after pooling their limited resources the group won a radio job that paid thirty dollars a week. For the hungry men, this was like a gold strike.

Within months the Pioneer Trio began to achieve a bit of local fame and success. In early 1934, with the audiences and paychecks expanding, the three boys felt rich enough to add another member. They chose a Texas fiddle player named Hugh Farr. At that point the trio changed their names to the Sons of the Pioneers.

While all the Pioneers' members were involved in songwriting, it was Nolan whose writing and style seemed most in touch with the group's western theme and drew the greatest audience response. Of Bob's

songs, the one which captured the most interest had been inspired by the blowing leaves Bob had observed during his long autumn treks in the Arizona wilds. Yet for some reason the radio listeners who called in requests couldn't seem to remember the song's title. Instead of asking for "Tumbling Leaves," they would beg the group to do their song about the "tumbleweeds."

At first Nolan tried to explain that the song was about leaves, not weeds, but eventually he gave up. To satisfy the fans he reworked the lyrics and melody in time for the group's first recording session. Instead of "drifting along with the tumbling leaves," the catch line became "drifting along with the tumbling tumbleweeds." Hence, rather than "Tumbling Leaves," Decca released the Sons of the Pioneers singing their new radio theme song, "Tumbling Tumbleweeds." Thanks to the promotion and identification created by the group's show, as well as the special sound that came from their smooth western harmonies, sales response was immediate. The single shot to #13 on the pop charts in late December.

A few months after the Pioneers struck gold with the Nolan composition, Gene Autry was tested and hired by Republic Studios as their first true singing cowboy. In an attempt to spin interest from both his and the Pioneers' radio audiences over to Gene's new film, the studio entitled the picture "Tumbling Tumbleweeds." Gene even cut the song for the Melotone label. The highly successful movie assured Autry's stardom, and Gene's version of the record hit the top ten.

"Tumbling Tumbleweeds" made the Sons of the Pioneers the nation's foremost western group and Autry the nation's best-loved cowboy. Gene would follow up his initial picture with scores of other singing range movies. The group followed "Tumbleweeds" with another Nolan classic, "Cool Water." With national radio coverage, appearances in several Hollywood westerns, and demand for a heavy tour schedule, the Pioneers had gone from outcasts to stars in less than a year. This exposure paved the way for Len Slye to get a movie offer of his own and leave the group to become "The King of the Cowboys," Roy Rogers. It created a new popular musical genre that was soon filled with a host of other talented western groups such as Foy Willing and his Riders of the Purple Sage. "Tumbleweeds" also helped make western music the vogue, with Bing Crosby, the Andrews Sisters, and a long list of other pop singers covering the Pioneers standards. Composers like Cole Porter tried their hand at writing western ballads. It can even be argued that the success of the Sons of the Pioneers marked the beginning of America's two-generation-long love affair with anything cowboy.

In 1948 the Pioneers again recorded "Tumbling Tumbleweeds," this time releasing it to the country market. It charted at #11. Over a decade after its original debut, the song was back as a hit. Even now, more than sixty years after it was first recorded, most Americans know at least some of "Tumbleweeds's" words and most of its tune.

The Sons of the Pioneers went on to earn a well-justified spot in the Country Music Hall of Fame. Their harmonies and showmanship had a great deal to do with establishing them as the greatest western group in country music history. Yet it was probably the wanderlust and vision that inspired Bob Nolan's songwriting which most defined and immortalized the Pioneers. Just as the West was being tamed, he drew the word pictures that brought it to life again and gave a voice to the cowboy's lonesome song.

1935

That Silver-Haired Daddy of Mine

Written by Gene Autry and Jimmy Long

Gene Autry was born in Tioga, Texas, in 1907. The son of a rancher and livestock trader, Gene grew up in an authentic cowboy setting, learning how to rope, ride, and drive cattle at an early age. It was this impression of the real West, coupled with his love of music, that was to shape both his life and career, as well as dramatically alter the way that Hollywood marketed movies, music, and products to children.

Autry's grandfather was a preacher and it was in services at the Indian Creek Baptist Church where young Gene first lifted his voice in song. Impressed with her son's musical talent and enthusiasm, Autry's mother bought him a guitar for his eleventh birthday. By the time the family moved to Oklahoma, where Gene would eventually be "discovered," he was a high school student who made his pocket change singing in medicine shows.

It was during this time when Gene began to refine his musical talents. By the time he graduated and took a job as a telegraph operator in Sapulpa, Oklahoma, he was accomplished on several instruments and knew hundreds of folk standards. By chance, when Will Rogers was passing through the small town, he noted Autry's guitar sitting against the telegraph office wall. "Why don't you play something for us," the noted entertainer suggested to young Autry. Within minutes Gene and Will were entertaining a handful of onlookers with a rousing rendition of "Casey Jones."

Rogers liked what he saw in Autry. Will suggested that the young man take his talents to a larger venue. For a young Oklahoman this was like receiving a directive from God Himself. Within weeks Gene took a train to New York and gave show business a shot. Not unlike most unseasoned rural dreamers, he found reality and the city a hard pill to swallow. Within weeks he was back home working for the railroad.

Autry might have continued living in Oklahoma and singing for his own pleasure if the Depression hadn't hit. Like millions of others who had never heard of Wall Street, Gene was hit hard by the stock market's collapse. By late 1929 he was unemployed. Hard times dictated radical moves, so while thousands of Okies were preparing to hit Highway 66 and go west, the twenty-two-year-old native of Texas picked up his guitar and headed back to the East Coast. His timing couldn't have been better.

Record labels were eagerly looking for the next Jimmie Rodgers and signing almost anyone who could sound like him. Autry knew every one of the "Blue Yodeler's" releases. First at Victor, then at Columbia, Okeh, Gennett, and Grey Gull, Gene cut several different sides under a host of different names. None charted nationally, but the records did receive enough play in his home state to get him a good job on KVOO in Tulsa. Coming back home and singing on the 50,000-watt station gave the young cowboy his big break.

Arthur Satherley had somehow missed Gene in New York, but when the ARC talent scout heard him on KVOO, he knew that he'd uncovered a property who could sell product for his record label. He signed Autry, and soon Gene found himself in Chicago on one of the nation's most-loved weekly radio shows, the *WLS Barn Dance*. WLS was owned by the Sears corporation, and Gene's signing with the *Dance* meant that all of his Melotone (ARC) releases would be sold in all the chain's stores and catalogs. Thanks to these combined forces, within a year of his arrival in the Windy City the Oklahoman had become one of the nation's biggest hillbilly radio personalities.

In a world where once-wealthy men were selling apples and pencils on street corners, Gene was now making enough money to be considered rich in Sapulpa. Singing songs like "The Death of Jimmie Rodgers," "Moonlight and Skies," and "The Last Round-Up," Autry had hit his stride. He was also beginning to develop a style of his own—a sound that set him apart from his idol, Rodgers. Working with his old railroad boss, Jimmy Long, Gene was also now writing much of his own material. It was from this collaboration that sprang Autry's most successful non-holiday record.

"That Silver-Haired Daddy of Mine" was far from an original concept. Scores of times composers had embraced sentimental songs of parental love and sacrifice. This had been one of the constant themes in the rural music on which both Long and Autry had been raised. Later quizzed, the two men couldn't even remember being "inspired" by any one idea when they put the song together. It was simply a solid commercial concept that they thought would sell. Yet their composition's unencumbered story about a man

living out his golden years in a vine-covered mountain shack after having given his life for his son immediately struck a chord with the WLS audience. The listeners rushed to Sears and Kress stores to buy the ballad. If there had ever been any doubt that Gene was the station's rising star, it disappeared entirely with this release. Ironically, this popularity would also cost WLS dearly.

Hollywood took note of both "Silver-Haired Daddy" and Autry's radio ratings. Republic Pictures had been having success with cowboy epics, so they brought Gene to the West Coast and gave him a part in a Ken Maynard movie. The test proved so successful that the studio spun Autry off into what was to be a long line of singing cowboy pictures. The first, *Tumbling Tumbleweeds*, capitalized on a new hit by the Sons of the Pioneers.

Gene may have been the standard-bearer for hillbilly music in the Midwest in the early thirties, but the movies made him a truly national voice for the genre. In film after film Autry sang songs that were as much country as western, and by doing so introduced the musical form to millions of city folks, especially kids, who had never ridden a horse or strummed a guitar. Ultimately Gene's stardom and success would open Hollywood's doors to Roy Rogers, Rex Allen, Spade Cooley, Tex Ritter, and a host of others who would help to popularize country music.

While Autry would find his way to country music's Hall of Fame, "That Silver-Haired Daddy of Mine" did not become a country music standard. Few of today's entertainers and fans can even hum the old tune. In 1980 Slim Whitman did take the song for a short ride on the country music charts, but it could climb no higher than #69. Yet, while never enjoying huge country chart success, the song which made a star out of a future baseball team owner and gave him a chance to transform into a trailblazing "B" western star was very important. For it was in those pictures that Autry groomed America's future country music fans, America's youth.

Gene once said, "I was the first of the singing cowboys. Maybe not the best, but that doesn't matter if you're first." Somewhere his silver-haired daddy must have been proud that in being first, Gene changed music history for millions.

1935

Can the Circle Be Unbroken

Written by A.P. Carter, based on a hymn by Ada Habersoln and Charles Gabriel

The Carter Family's final appearance on the popular music charts was on August 24, 1935. The landmark group would not make their next entry into the hit list for twenty-eight years. Yet the clan never completely disappeared, and their influence remained strong in country music for decades to come. In a very real sense the Carters cherished their roles as the standard-bearers for the hillbilly songs that traced their heritage back to the first British folk melodies. They had popularized the "folk" sounds which were at the heart of the music genre, and while a host of other influences would shape and reshape country music, the Carters continued to remind folks of the real roots from which it all sprang.

Few fans realized that by the mid-thirties the family was no longer a real family. A.P. and Sara had divorced, and while they still worked together, their lives were focused in different directions. Maybe this lack of unity was why A.P. was especially drawn to an Ada Habersoln and Charles Gabriel hymn, "Will the Circle Be Unbroken." Working with the 1907 song's chorus, Carter rewrote the verses and asked the haunting question "Can the circle be unbroken?"

As A.P. composed it, the song was now set at a funeral. The mourners were questioning if they would ever be reunited again with their mother. Would there be a time, by and by, when their family circle would once again be unbroken? (For A.P. the an-

swer was no. Sara married one of his cousins in 1938.)

"Can the Circle Be Unbroken" was a big seller in rural areas. While the city folks may have passed it over as just another hymn, those suffering through the Depression in the hills and valleys clung to it as if it were a personal statement of faith. It quickly became one of the most popular funeral hymns. In a world where few folks had any individual wealth, family relationships were cherished deeply. This song spoke to these heartfelt emotions as few songs ever had.

Beyond the song's emotional content, "Can the Circle" brought to the forefront the gospel and religious elements which had so helped to shape early country music (this combination of gospel and secular was continued in such classics as "Wreck on the Highway"). By and large those who sang and would continue to sing country music could trace their singing roots to the church. It was there that they were first exposed to organized music. It was there where the joy of singing really entered their being. This was the foundation that led to them seeking out other forms of musical expression. And from time to time, on stage shows and in recordings, it was gospel music to which almost all of them returned.

In its original release "Can the Circle Be Unbroken" made it to #17 on the pop charts. It remained there for just one week. Then, just like the family, the song quietly disappeared from national view. Yet like the Carters, "Can the Circle" lingered in the public rural consciousness, where it would remain for decades.

Carl Perkins was traveling with Johnny Cash in 1968. An accomplished songwriter, rockabilly artist Perkins had composed such classics as "Blue Suede Shoes" and "So Wrong" and had grown up listening to the Carters and "Can the Circle Be Unbroken." In the guise of Maybelle and her daughters, the Carter Family was now backing Cash on stage, and the family's music was again all around Perkins. One night while waiting in his dressing room for a show call, the noted guitarist began to play around with a new song built on the Carter gospel classic. As soon as he had roughed it out he took it to Cash. The man in black was impressed and urged Carl to finish it. When the song was complete, Johnny earmarked it for his next recording session.

"Daddy Sang Bass" borrowed from the Carter classic by asking the question "Will the circle be unbroken?" On his way to his best year in the business, Cash recorded Perkins's composition with both the Carter Family and the Statler Brothers adding harmonies. Sandwiched between the release of "Folsom Prison Blues" and "A Boy Named Sue," "Daddy Sang Bass" hit #1 five weeks after its chart debut and remained on top for six weeks. While this was an important step in revitalizing the original song and continuing Cash's Hall of Fame climb, "Can the Circle's" complete rebirth happened in 1972 with a rock group acting as the midwife.

In the midst of the acid-music era, Jeff Hanna and

John McEuen had formed one of rock music's most successful folk groups. With its soft sounds, the Nitty Gritty Dirt Band was to produce one of the era's most unforgettable hits, "Mr. Bojangles." Their chart and album success presented the band with the freedom to stray from normal marketing parameters from time to time. Thus they hatched an idea that would lead to one of the most important albums in music history.

Journeying to Nashville, Hanna and McEuen teamed the likes of Roy Acuff, Doc Watson, Earl Scruggs, Merle Travis, and Maybelle Carter with Music City's best acoustical pickers. What resulted from this marriage of young and old and folk and country was a Grammy-winning effort that celebrated some of country music's most treasured songs. These cuts would reawaken both the public and the industry to the genre's rich living history and some of its most important older contributors.

For the Carter Family this reunion was really special because the thirty-six-song three-record album took its name from the Carters' old gospel classic. This time the cut was retitled "Will the Circle Be Unbroken." With Mother Maybelle playing autoharp and singing lead, this unique cross-generational recording session cemented the song as the binding tie between country music past, present, and future. Almost twelve years after A.P.'s death, it also enthusiastically and affirmatively answered the song's haunting question. Yes, as far as country music is concerned, the circle will be unbroken. As a matter of record, Carlene Carter, Maybelle's granddaughter and one of Music City's most imaginative songwriters and performers, is carrying on the family tradition to another hungry generation of fans.

1936

Orange Blossom Special

Written by Ervin T. Rouse

The Rouse Brothers were a Florida hillbilly band who made their living playing fiddle-based country music. While Ervin, Gordon, and Earl never placed a single record on the national charts, didn't become members of the *Grand Ole Opry,* and have all but been forgotten by those who both play and love country music, one of their songs stands as an instantly recognizable country music icon. It would be hard to imagine country music without it.

In 1936 Ervin Rouse was constantly fooling around on stage with a fiddle piece that he had never really named but occasionally referred to it as "a little bit crazy." No matter that it didn't have a handle, the crowds at dances and fairs ate it up. The way the brothers played their instruments the audience swore that they could hear a train coming right through the middle of the song. Observing the reaction to the rapidly paced instrumental, the group's manager, Lloyd Smith, had a brainstorm. Why not make it a real train song?

Smith convinced the manager of the Seaboard Railroad station in Miami that the Rouse Brothers had a number that would be perfect to play at the christening of the company's new Miami-to-New York passenger service. He even promised the folks at Seaboard that the fiddle tune would be named after their new train, The Orange Blossom Special. The railroaders were quickly drawn in by Smith's smooth

salesmanship, and even helped the promoter create a carnival-like atmosphere for the debut of the train and this "new" song.

When they learned about being booked at the Miami station "gig," the Rouse Brothers were probably overjoyed. During the Great Depression any kind of paying date was to be treasured, but one that included a large number of government officials, some of the city's and state's most prominent citizens, and several members of the press was a real stroke of luck. And to beat it all, their song was going to launch the newest train on the line! It didn't seem that things could get any better. At that time the Rouses had no idea that their manager had copyrighted Ervin's song in his own name and that any profits would be forwarded to Smith, not the song's writer. It was to be some months before Ervin noted that Lloyd Smith had been given credit for composing "Orange Blossom Special." When he discovered that his song had been taken away from him, he and his brothers geared up for a fight.

It took Ervin Rouse over a year, but he finally won the right to have Smith's name removed from the song's copyright, as well as winning the rights to all future publishing royalties. With the "Orange Blossom" again all his, Ervin sat down and wrote words to his crazy little fiddle tune. Keeping the railroad theme, he came up with a lyric centered on the fastest train on the line. In 1939 the Rouse Brothers journeyed to New York and recorded their song for RCA. While it enjoyed some regional play, the Rouses' "Orange Blossom Special" never hit the national pop charts.

While the Rouses may have largely been forgotten by country music fans, their song wasn't. Bill Monroe used it in his bluegrass shows. Bob Wills and his country jazz band, the Texas Playboys, played it at their dances. By the late forties it was hard to find a hillbilly band, famous or unknown, that didn't do some version of "Orange Blossom Special" in their live shows. Yet while the song was recorded scores of times on albums and had become a concert and dance favorite, it didn't gain any single-release success until almost four decades after its debut.

In 1962 Johnny Cash had ridden Jimmie Rodgers's classic "In the Jailhouse Now" to hit status. In looking for another old classic, he turned to a number which had worked well in his concert sets, "Orange Blossom Special." Cash's version was far different from any which had preceded it. Rather than using a fiddle as the lead instrument, Johnny played a pair of harmonicas. The entertainer's showmanship and flair came out even in the studio. The recording wasn't anything like what Ervin Rouse had intended when he wrote the crazy little fiddle tune, but that didn't stop it from

being a hit. Johnny's rendition of the old standard climbed up the charts, not stopping until it peaked at #3.

After Cash scored with "Orange Blossom," Charlie McCoy came out with his own classic harmonica interpretation of the tune in 1973. His instrumental made it into the top thirty. A year later Johnny Darrell hit the top one hundred for the eighteenth and last time with another version of the classic Rouse composition.

When Ricky Skaggs brought bluegrass back onto the national scene in the late seventies, the standard fiddle versions of "Orange Blossom Special" came back strong too. It now seems that every American, young or old, knows the tune that launched the passenger train. It would be hard to imagine showmen like Bill Monroe, Charlie Daniels, or Louise Mandrell leaving a stage without bringing out a hot fiddle arrangement of the song.

The Rouse Brothers began "Orange Blossom Special's" long ride into immortality with a short concert at a Miami train station. Ironically, they never bought a ticket and took a ride on the real Special, yet thanks to Ervin Rouse, millions of country music listeners have had a chance to ride this special train and will for many years to come!

1938
San Antonio Rose

Written by Bob Wills

In 1915 Jim Rob Wills was a nervous ten-year-old guitar player waiting to appear in his father's dance band. Already an accomplished musician, he didn't have butterflies jumping in his stomach at the thought of playing before his family's friends and neighbors; instead, young Wills was concerned about his father. John, the group's leader and fiddle player, was late. As the time dragged by and the crowd grew impatient, Jim Rob took it upon himself to save the family pride. Stepping up to the front, he picked up his father's fiddle and began to play. As the incredulous crowd watched the small child, he expertly performed one of the audience's favorite fiddle standards. He led the band for the rest of the evening, and from that night on, John Wills lost his place as the family's most famous fiddler.

Born in Kosse, Texas, Jim Rob Wills was a product of a family that had played the fiddle for generations. Like most white boys from rural Texas, Jim Rob learned country and folk music at his father's feet, but it was in the cotton fields where the child absorbed a sound which would help him create a new American musical style. Young Wills worked side by side with blacks who sang blues and gospel as they toiled in the hot sun. It was this influence that reshaped a Southern boy's musical outlook. At night, when he sat on the porch and took up his bow, Jim Rob played old country standards, but he also added something new.

He tried to combine the white and black sounds into a singular strain. Something that was uniquely Bob Wills. It would be years in the making, but it was during these long Panhandle nights that the boy initially began working on the music the world would someday call Texas swing.

Running away from home at fourteen, Jim Rob took any job he could find. During his travels he also stopped and listened to every band, both black and white, country and blues, rural and city, he came across. In Fort Worth he donned blackface and became a minstrel singer. At other times he fronted for medicine shows as a comic. As months grew into years, Wills would do almost anything to make a dime and entertain the crowd. By the early thirties Jim Rob had dropped his given names for Bob and replaced the comedy and stage makeup with his fiddle. On radio, first with the Wills Fiddle Band and later with the Light Crust Doughboys, Wills continued to evolve and build on the sounds that he had heard as a child.

As the Light Crust Doughboys' fame grew and they expanded their markets to include large, clear-channel radio stations, so their sound grew too. As a probable outgrowth of his days in the cotton fields, Bob took a strong interest in black jazz. Bob was trying to combine this urban musical style with the western sounds of rural Texas, and folks were responding.

The group even cut a few sides for Victor Records in 1932. Then, in a move which paralleled his father's own reasons for missing the dance date that made Bob a local star, the fiddle player got drunk and missed a radio broadcast. Just when it looked as if Wills was on his way to success, he was fired and forced to start all over.

Migrating to Waco, Bob formed a new band, the Texas Playboys, and continued to tinker with what he was calling "western jazz." It was during this time he put together the solid group of musicians who would help the creative Wills invent this new sound. With the vocals of Tommy Duncan, the jazz piano of Al Stricklin, Johnnie Lee Wills's banjo, Kermit Whalen's steel, and June Whalen's bass, Bob's sound was beginning to really cook. Beginning in 1934 the band was the star attraction on KVOO in Tulsa. From this base the Playboys grew to include more than twenty members and become the Southwest's definite swing band.

Wills's composing and band-leading success could be traced to his free-wheeling style. He added instruments that no one considered hillbilly in order to enlarge the country/jazz sound. He was using drums when no country bands would even consider them. At a time when electrical instruments were deemed unfit for the Opry stage, Wills was featuring them in long solos. He even used brass. Surrounding himself with some of the era's most talented and creative musicians, he was generating and refining a country big-band sound that quickly became the mainstay of Texas dance halls during the pre-war years.

Beginning in 1935, Bob and the Playboys recorded sides that caught and preserved the dawn of this special sound. One of the first numbers they cut was a Wills original, "Spanish Two Step." This Tex-Mex dance number combined the western and Spanish musical influences which were so much a part of the

Southwest sound with a black jazz flavor. In Texas and Oklahoma the release sold well, but just like the Wills records that followed "Two Step," it went nowhere on the national charts. It was evident that like so many other bands, Bob Wills and the Texas Playboys were just a regional phenomenon. Wills was satisfied with this status. Both he and the group were making a nice living in the midst of some very hard times and they couldn't have asked for much more. None of them could have guessed that lightning was about to strike in the form of a reworked old melody and a flower.

During a 1938 recording session the Playboys needed one additional tune to fill out a side. Sitting down, Bob worked out a new instrumental by rearranging "Spanish Two Step's" melody. As the band finished rehearsing the number, Art Satherly of Brunswick Records inquired as to the tune's name. Shrugging his shoulders, Wills told the executive to name it himself. Satherly wrote "San Antonio Rose" on the master.

Released on the Vocalion label, "San Antonio Rose" became Wills's biggest hit up until that time. In 1939 the single climbed onto the national pop charts, peaking at fifteen. The record's national play caught the attention of the Irving Berlin Music Company. Noting that the song was unpublished, they tracked Wills down in Tulsa and inquired about purchasing the sheet-music rights. Over the phone Wills agreed to write out the charts if Berlin would give him a $300 advance against royalties.

Berlin sent an agent with the check to Oklahoma to pick up the charts and get Bob's signature on the contract. "Where are the lyrics?" the music representative asked when Wills handed him the scores.

"Ain't none," Bob replied.

"You can't have the advance without the words," the agent shot back. "Mr. Berlin doesn't publish songs without lyrics."

Over the course of the next few hours Bob, Tommy Duncan, and Everett Stone sat down and tried to come up with a story for a song which they hadn't even titled. With a $300 check hanging in the balance, Bob finally came back to Berlin's emissary with a set of scribbled lyrics. He would later say the words were "two years in the making." The deal done, the parties went their separate ways, and Wills soon began receive regular royalty checks from the music and the recording.

In late 1940, the Playboys went back to Dallas to record the old song with the new lyrics. In order to differentiate it from the instrumental, Okeh Records released the single as "New San Antonio Rose." This version of the "Rose" would become Bob's biggest pop hit ever. The single would hover on the charts for five weeks and top out at #11.

A few months later Decca would record "New San Antonio Rose" with Bing Crosby supplying the vocal. Der Bingle's release stayed on the charts for eleven weeks, pegging out at #7. Crosby's version did more than make Wills money. It helped to legitimatize his form of country music in the pop world.

During World War II, probably because so many Southwestern soldiers took country music with them as they were shipped around the world, "New San Antonio Rose" reentered the pop charts for a week. It also leapt up the new hillbilly charts, stopping at #3.

Over the course of time Wills would become known as "The King of Western Swing," and his versions of "San Antonio Rose" would be eclipsed by other singles with more impressive chart showings. These included "New Spanish Two Step," a vocal version of the song which Wills rewrote into "San Anto-nio Rose." Yet even though six of his songs would find their way to #1, none would come to mean as much to audiences as "Rose."

There is no doubt that the song's instrumentation, beat, and jazz-like feel shaped the way songwriters and musicians thought for years. Long after big-band music had faded, the Wills influence could be heard in scores of performers, especially Ray Price and Mel Tillis. Today, Asleep at the Wheel is little more than a nineties Texas Playboys, and they are proud of it too. It would be hard to imagine a country band performing a salute to swing and not playing "San Antonio Rose."

Hundreds of groups and individuals have recorded "San Antonio Rose" since Wills's Playboys first laid down their tracks. In 1961 Floyd Cramer took his piano treatment of the tune higher than he did his own famous composition, "Last Date." Yet of all the wonderful renditions of the song, including the half dozen that Wills himself put on tape, perhaps none can match the original for enthusiasm, energy, and joy. There is a passion in that 1938 record that expresses the essence of what Bob Wills wanted to create. Here is a sound that combines black blues and jazz with white western and hillbilly music and makes it danceable. Here is where western swing found its most wonderful vehicle. Here is the wonder of creation at its finest. This was music that was played by men who were having fun, and almost six decades later it is just as fresh as it was then. From Al's piano to Bob's kidding asides, it is hard to listen to that first session and not smile. No wonder "San Antonio Rose" has left such an impression anchored so deep in country music's heart.

1938
Wabash Cannonball

Written by A.P. Carter

Roy Acuff scored only a dozen times on the country music charts, never hitting any higher than #3. His recording career after the 1944 debut of what was then the hillbilly record tracking system is so insignificant that few except hardcore fans can even name one of those releases. His pop chart appearances numbered only four, with a total of just seven weeks spent in the top one hundred. Yet Acuff is widely known and revered as "The King of Country Music," and was the first living artist ever inducted into the Country Music Association's Hall of Fame. In spite of not having the "numbers" to make him any more than a minor bit player, Roy Acuff remains a true star.

A one-time baseball player, young Roy was a Baptist minister's son who dreamed of playing in the majors until a heat stroke confined him to bed for most of one year. It was the illness and the boredom that resulted from his long recovery that caused the young man to rethink his career aspirations. Too weak to work heavy labor, left too frail to continue in sports, he wondered if he wasn't being led to preach. Then, while listening to his father's collection of fiddle records, Roy began to scratch around on one of the family violins. In no time he had taught himself to play almost all the fiddle jigs he had heard as a child.

Always blessed with a strong voice, when he regained his health Roy listened to the advice of a local doctor and hit the road playing in medicine shows. By 1933 he had formed his own band, the Tennessee Crackerjacks, and worked dances all around the Knoxville area. His first real break came in 1932, when he and his band landed a regular spot on the locally popular *Mid-Day Merry-Go-Round*. After being heard daily on WNOX for almost a year, Roy then negotiated a deal that gave him his own show on WROL. A slip of an announcer's tongue may have changed the band's name to the Crazy Tennesseans, but it did nothing for their financial status. Blessed with just minor local fame, no recording contracts, and small-time dates, the group was starving and was probably crazy in continuing to push its musical career. Still, for three years they forged on.

In 1936 (as covered in an earlier part of this book), Acuff bought the words to "The Great Speckled Bird" for fifty cents. This buy landed Roy a recording contract with ARC. After his rendition of "The Bird" hit the national charts in 1938, Acuff was invited to join the *Opry*, where his showmanship and antics soon made him one of the show's favorite performers. After seven long years, he was an overnight success.

During his first recording session Acuff's band not only cut "The Bird," but also another old standard, "Wabash Cannonball." Far more than any song that had preceded or would follow it, "The Cannonball" would become America's most beloved and remembered train epic.

Roy had probably heard versions of the tune for all of his life. He would later say that he remembered singing the song as a child. As with many country music standards sung during this century's first three decades, at least part of the song's text was based on fact. There was a Wabash line passenger train that carried the name Cannon Ball as early as 1885. While its total run was far short of "the great Atlantic" and "the wide Pacific," starting in Chicago and stopping in Kansas City, the unique name created a far more romantic picture than the "New York Limited" or "San Antonio Express." There was something distinctively poetic and American about the Wabash Cannon Ball. Here was an image made to order for a songwriter's imagination!

Combining fiction with a patriotic theme, William Kindt used the very fabric of the American heartland to set up a version of the song he wrote and published in 1905. Kindt's "Wabash Cannonball" was probably not the first, but it was the initial "Cannonball" to be both copyrighted and noticed by the public.

The initial recorded versions of Kindt's composition didn't appear until the late twenties. Record companies eager to cash in on the success of Jimmie Rodgers and the Carter Family were releasing scores of new versions of old songs. By this time Kindt's copyright had fallen into public domain, and a shrewd A.P. Carter "rewrote" the song and claimed ownership of a new published version of the Kindt number. The Carters themselves sang the epic on many occasions. Yet even with A.P.'s strong backing, "Wabash Cannonball" remained uncharted and, outside of the rural reaches of hillbilly music, fairly obscure.

It took Acuff's 1938 release to put the song and the by-then-defunct passenger line on the map. In December Roy and his band rode the "Cannonball" to #12, one spot further up the pop chart line than his version of "The Great Speckled Bird." From that mo-

ment on, he owned the song. Any Acuff performance was incomplete without hearing his band take the audience for a ride on America's finest passenger train.

As was noted earlier, Acuff became a country music legend without ever having a #1 record (his highest charting song, "I'll Forgive You But I Can't Forget," reached #3 in 1944), or without ever establishing a sound or style which was embraced by a long line of imitators. In one of country music's strangest quirks, Roy didn't even sing the vocal on the 1938 hit version of "Wabash Cannonball." One of his band members, Dynamite Hatcher, earned the right to supply the lead. All Roy did was provide the song's unique whistle beginning. It is important to note that many scholars and historians do believe that this whistle was what made the number a real showstopper.

Almost a decade after Acuff and the Crazy Tennesseans hit the pop charts with "Wabash Cannonball," the star went back to the studio with his band, now known as the Smoky Mountain Boys. In his customary one take, Acuff laid down a new version of the song using his own voice on the lead vocal. This version was never a hit and did not land on any national charts, but is the one most frequently heard today. So why was it that Roy became such an American icon that during World War II Japanese soldiers were often heard to cry out, "To hell with Roosevelt! To hell with Babe Ruth! To hell with Roy Acuff!"?

Radio and clear-channel WSM were a large part of the reason. The rise of the *Grand Ole Opry* coincided with Acuff's arrival at the Ryman. To those who listened each Saturday night, he was the *Opry*. Also, the two songs with which he was so associated were both uniquely rural and uniquely American. His edges were rough, his voice was pure country, and he was one of the first to carry the title "hillbilly" proudly. Millions of poor rural Americans lionized him for these qualities. This same group also responded to his adherence to old values, his gentle demeanor with fans and industry insiders, and his love of performing. Visiting after all of his shows, signing autographs for hours, and answering his mail, Roy was the fans' star. The country music faithful of the day may have loved Pee Wee King's music and Bob Wills's style, but they just plain and simple loved Roy Acuff.

Overlooked in the image of Acuff the man and performer was his business savvy. He "sold" his weekly concerts on the *Opry,* and therefore grossed bigger gates than most of his other contemporaries. He also created, with Fred Rose, a publishing company that became the most dominant in the industry. While never changing his own style, he foresaw music trends and invested in them before they happened. This seemed to prove that, in Acuff's case, he hung around for so long because he was not only a good man, but a smart good man. Still, how did he become "The King of Country Music"? It seems that the title should have gone to Eddy Arnold, Ernest Tubb, Hank Williams, or at least a half dozen others. In the long run these men's musical contributions were far more significant, so why Roy?

For the answer you must come back full circle to Acuff's first love, baseball, and to maybe the game's most colorful Hall of Famer, Dizzy Dean. As a baseball television announcer on CBS, Dean sang "Wabash Cannonball" live on the air countless times. This, and not the Acuff record, was the place where millions of Americans first heard the classic train song. Diz's version become so popular that thousands of fans wrote in each week begging him to sing the song during every broadcast. And he did. The former St. Louis Cardinals pitcher was even invited to the Opry to perform "Wabash Cannonball" with Roy himself. At the Opry, and then hundreds of times thereafter, Dean referred to Acuff as "The King of Country Music." Just as few would ever successfully challenge a Dizzy Dean fastball, few ever argued with his coronation of Acuff.

On the wings of a bird and in the cab of a train Roy had ridden to the Opry, but it was through his own personality that he became the man who most signified country music. Roy Acuff may be dead, but his presence is still felt on the stage where his reign began.

1940

You Are My Sunshine

Written by Jimmie Davis and Charles Mitchell, based on a song by Paul Rice

James Houston Davis was born in a shotgun cabin in Jackson Parish, Louisiana, on September 11, 1902. The son of a sharecropper, one of eleven children, he rose from street singer and dishwasher to movie actor and governor. Through hard work and brains he moved from poverty to national acclaim to the Country Music Hall of Fame. Certainly Jimmie Davis's story is the stuff of American legend. This tale is made even more remarkable in that he used country music every step of the way from his humble beginnings at the bottom to his lofty status at the top.

Desperately poor, Davis grew up singing both folk and gospel songs. His family preached to him that the only route of escape from poverty was grounded in education, something his father and mother lacked. Walking two miles each way, Davis was one of the few local boys who made it through high school. He then hopped a freight train and continued his schooling at Soule Business College in New Orleans and Louisiana College in Pineville. It was in college where the country boy saw his first indoor shower and visited his first library. At first Jimmie was overwhelmed, but eventually he settled down and earned not only a B.A., but a Master's at LSU. At his every stop along the way he found a singing group to join.

Davis was a criminal court clerk in Shreveport in 1929 when he landed a moonlighting position as a singer on radio station KWKH. Like Gene Autry and Ernest Tubb, he cashed in on the success of Jimmie Rodgers as he sang in the "Blue Yodeler's" style. An RCA record scout heard Davis and took him to Memphis. Over the next five years Jimmie cut more than eighty sides for the label. During this formative period Jimmie began to both write his own songs and purchase the original compositions of other local musicians. In the latter case, Davis would do what A.P. Carter and a host of other artists of the era did; he would rework the originals and then register them in his own name, thus claiming all royalties as his own. Far from being frowned on, this was the accepted practice at the time. There was nothing underhanded about it. In retrospect Davis should probably be applauded for paying the composers a fair-market value for their work. Many other recording artists and publishers simply stole them.

Davis landed a deal at Decca Records in 1935, and had a hit in "Nobody's Darlin' but Mine." It was one of two songs which Jimmie would place on the national pop charts. "Nobody's Darlin'" struck nineteen, spending one week in the top one hundred in 1937. A year later "Meet Me Tonight in Dreamland," a rehash of a 1910 Henry Burr hit, peaked at #13, lasting only a single week at that position. Because of his strong local following, moderate regional record success, and his radio show, Davis not only drew large crowds on the regional fair circuit, but also climbed up the political ladder to a position as Shreveport's Commissioner of Public Safety.

In 1940 Davis happened on the title which would pave his way into the Hall of Fame. Paul Rice, a member of a fairly well-known Louisiana band, the Rice Brothers Gang, had written a song entitled "You Are My Sunshine." The number soon became a Rice Brothers fan favorite, and the Gang recorded and released it in November 1939. After the Rices, Bob Atcher, Bonnie Blue Eyes, and the Pine Ridge Boys all cut versions of "Sunshine."

Early in 1940, steel guitar player Charles Mitchell heard the tune and played it for Davis. The story goes that the two men then contacted Paul Rice. Because of a love of alcohol, Rice was in constant need of cash, so he sold all rights to the song to Davis and Mitchell. The rumored sale price was as low as $17.50 and as high as $500. The actual price was most likely somewhere in between those figures. Reggie Ward, a bass player and local disc jockey, witnessed the sale and confirmed that all parties were happy with the deal.

Reworking the tune to fit his style of singing and the words to meet his own needs, David cut "Sunshine" in March. His version had considerable success in the South, but failed to stir up many sales in other regions. When a national audience paid little attention to any of the first four versions of "You Are My Sunshine" and it failed to hit the charts, Rice's deal looked pretty good. Yet one of those who had noted the song and loved its message was Gene Autry. The cowboy star's image and popularity guaranteed the composition's hit status. Gene rode it all the way to #23. Autry's "Sunshine" might have even gone higher except that Bing Crosby had also realized the song's growing following and cut his own version. Bing's baritone carried "Sunshine" all the way to #19.

With its easy-to-follow melody and sweet inspirational message, "You Are My Sunshine" became not only a hillbilly classic, but a children's favorite. Recorded by more than three hundred different artists, it would generate sheet sales and albums cuts for years. It would also become Davis's 1944 campaign theme song. Jimmie would sing "Sunshine" all the way into the governor's mansion, and later use it in Hollywood when Monogram Pictures filmed a motion picture loosely based on his life.

When the hillbilly charts were posted beginning in 1944, Davis hit them six times. His biggest single was "There's a New Moon over My Shoulder," which topped the charts in 1945 and lingered on them for eighteen weeks. "Sunshine's" lone appearance on the country charts was as a Duane Eddy guitar instrumental in 1977, but this lack of country chart success didn't keep the song from generating a breakthrough chart-topper for one of the industry's most important groups.

By 1978 the Statler Brothers had made thirty appearances on the country charts without a #1. At a concert, Harold Reid, the group's bass singer, was asked by a young woman, "Do you know 'You Are My Sunshine'?" The more he thought about the question, the more he was convinced there was an idea for a song there. Later, when the group was between dates and snowed in in Nashville, he teamed with brother Don and the two quickly wrote "Do You Know You Are My Sunshine." Released in March, the song hit the top spot in May and stayed there for two weeks. It is the only #1 single for the original group members (when Jimmy Fortune replaced Lew DeWitt in 1982, the Brothers added three more #1's to their total), and "Do You Know" remains the Statlers' most successful release.

Today "You Are My Sunshine" is still one of the most known and most loved country music songs.

Like "Can the Circle Be Unbroken," "Wabash Cannonball," and "I Saw the Light," "Sunshine" has joined a handful of other classics to become a country music anthem. And because of this unique status, at one time or another every country artist is probably going to be asked, "Do you know 'You Are My Sunshine' and can you play it just one more time for me?"

1941
Walking the Floor over You
Written by Ernest Tubb

As a child growing up in the small central Texas town of Crisp, Ernest Tubb would spend hours playing cowboy. Until he heard Jimmie Rodgers on the radio, his life's goal was to be a western movie star. But the Brakeman's plaintive yodeling changed all of that. Dreams of riding a horse through a Hollywood set gave way to music. Throughout his teens Tubb diligently saved every one of his hard-earned pennies and nickels in order to purchase each new Rodgers record on the day it was delivered to the store. Such was his devotion that when Jimmie's body finally gave in to TB in 1933, it seemed like a part of Ernest died too.

Until Rodgers's death, imitating the "Blue Yodeler" had been strictly a Tubb hobby. A common laborer, Ernest was working construction when a friend suggested that he purchase a guitar and make some money in music. The twenty-one-year-old man followed that advice, taught himself guitar, and within two years had wrangled a singing spot on KONO, a San Antonio radio station. A few weeks later he boldly walked up to the late Jimmie Rodgers's home and talked his way inside.

Unlike so many of his friends, Jimmie's widow Carrie didn't think Tubb sounded that much like her late husband, but she did respond positively to the stranger's frank nature and country charm. Sensing that a young musician who had a wife and new son

needed every break he could get, Carrie called RCA and convinced the label to offer her uninvited "discovery" a contract. In an attempt to give the man a dose of good luck, Rodgers even lent the singer her husband's favorite guitar. In Tubb's mind this was like receiving a divine blessing. How could he fail with all of this working for him? Ernest had to believe that success was just around the corner.

RCA cut eight sides with Ernest. These songs were largely Tubb-penned efforts paying tribute to his idol Rodgers. The four singles that RCA released went nowhere. Soon the label lost all interest in the Texan and dropped his contract.

Over the course of the next three years Tubb worked one-night stands around Texas for as little as two dollars a show. Frustrated by his lack of success and just one step ahead of the bill collectors, he again contacted Carrie Rodgers. Ernest knew that this was a last desperate act. As was her nature, Carrie again came to Tubb's rescue.

In the spring of 1940 Mrs. Rodgers recommended Ernest to Decca Records. Tubb sang four songs for Dave Kapp. By this time Ernest was no longer just another Rodgers clone. He had developed his own easily paced style. Kapp liked what he heard, thought with the right material he could sell this voice in the rural markets, and signed the singer to a royalty-based contract. Using the Decca deal as leverage, Tubb then landed a spot on KGKO in Fort Worth. Finding a flower company to sponsor his show, he suddenly found himself pulling down the unheard-of sum of $75 a week. The Tubb family felt rich. Still, a year later, after his first six Decca releases went nowhere, Ernest was again having doubts.

While preparing for what was to be a monumental recording session, the singer was presented with a batch of bills. It seemed that his wife Lois had gone on a shopping spree and had run up charges Tubb couldn't pay. An argument ensued, and Mrs. Tubb left with their son to visit her mother. Ernest, now known on radio as the Troubadour, was left at home to fret. The next day when he came back from work, Lois was still gone, and the usually upbeat Tubb sank into a deep depression.

Alone, angry, and worried both about the finances and the upcoming Decca session, Ernest began to pace back and forth in the small upstairs apartment that the family called home. The more he walked, the madder he became. After several hours of mindless steps, he stopped to consider what his all-night anguish was accomplishing. It was then that inspiration struck. Sitting down with a pen and paper, he quickly wrote out his emotions in song.

When Dave Kapp put together Tubb's next cowtown session, Ernest suggested they record the song the singer had written on that long night. As the session concluded, Kapp admitted that while he liked "Walking the Floor Over You," he favored putting "I Wonder Why You Said Goodbye" out as the single. The lanky singer had a gut feeling that "Walking the Floor" was a song with which the public could identify, so he argued to have it released first. After some discussion, Dave and Decca finally gave in, and in August 1941 shipped *Walking* to radio stations. By doing so they insured that Tubb's career would soon be off and running.

"Walking the Floor over You" hit #23 on the national pop charts and became one of the South and Southwest region's biggest sellers. The song was a jukebox favorite, and quickly became a honky-tonk anthem. It also bought Tubb's ticket to Nashville and the Grand Ole Opry, as well as assuring his long association with Decca Records. Over the course of the next dozen years the Texas Troubadour would chart another ten times on the pop side. Over his long career he would hit the top one hundred ninety-one times in country.

"Walking the Floor" would find its own way onto the country charts two more times too. Once in 1965 when George Hamilton IV took it into the top twenty, and again in 1979 when Ernest himself placed it there as his last chart song.

Maybe more important than his own recording success was Tubb's eye for recognizing talent. Never forgetting what Carrie Rodgers had done for him, Tubb was constantly bringing new acts to the attention of the record labels. He would also put unproven entertainers on a bill just to give them a chance to win audience recognition and gain valuable experience. Country music stars Cal Smith and Jack Greene were among many future acts who got started in his band. Ernest gave superstars Tanya Tucker, Loretta Lynn, and a host of others some of their initial breaks.

In 1947 Tubb was the first country performer to appear in New York's famed Carnegie Hall. When country was still a regional music form, he became a worldwide traveler who entertained the troops in several different countries. Not blessed with immense talent, he nevertheless shared a generous spirit that millions of fans could see in every one of his shows. While others may have had a better voice, none seemed to have a heart that wanted to give as much as Tubb's did.

On the back of Ernest's guitar he painted the word "Thanks." After every show he flashed a large smile and spun his guitar around to spell out just how much he appreciated the fans turning out for him. Even today, over a decade after he passed away, that image remains fresh, as well as the image of Ernest Tubb walking the Opry floor over, or rather in front of, thousands of worshipping fans.

1943
Born to Lose

Written by Ted Daffan

Ted Daffan did not grow up listening to Jimmie Rodgers or the Carter Family. He was not a young man who constantly dreamed of putting together a hillbilly band and touring the South in a woody station wagon. Though he was born in Louisiana and raised in Texas, in 1932, two years after his high school graduation, Daffan fell in love with the sounds of the Hawaiian guitar and first contemplated a career in music. This led to his forming a band that concentrated on playing songs with a Pacific island flavor. Ted's reputation for being a master of the Hawaiian guitar quickly grew to the point where he was able to successfully open his own studio and teach both island and classical music. With a solid income coming in, country music was a long way from any of Daffan's plans.

In 1937 a Houston-based country band, the Blue Ridge Boys, needed a steel (Hawaiian) player. They begged, and finally convinced, Ted to join them until they could find someone else.

"I had never listened to country music," Daffan remembered, "and I had problems learning how to play it."

A year later the Hawaiian player had figured it out, and was now good enough to leave the Blue Ridge Boys and move on to a band which played better, higher-paying dates. It was his days spent with the Bar X Cowboys that convinced Daffan to not only stick with country music, but to also consider putting together his own band and composing his own hillbilly songs. Within a few months he had done both, and sunk his money in a small recording setup.

"I had my own little group that we used to cut demo records on my songs," Daffan explained. "I then pestered all the A&R people who came down our way to listen to them. The first of my songs that was accepted by a major label was 'Truck Driver Blues.' "

When Decca had tremendous regional success with "Truck Driver Blues," other label representatives began to stop by and visit Ted's studio. One of them was Art Satherley of Columbia. After listening to Daffan in person, he signed the steel player and his band to a record deal. By 1940, just three years after backing into country music, Ted Daffan and His Texans were releasing singles on the Okeh label. One of their first, a Daffan original, was "Worried Mind." It didn't hit the national pop charts, but it gained a strong enough regional sales push to insure the Texans a long list of good-paying dates. The only problem was that they had to travel all over the big state of Texas.

"One night we were coming back from Corpus Christi in an old station we used for travel," Ted remembered. "The wagon's back two seats were facing each other with a table placed between them so that we could play poker as we rode to and from our dates. As we were headed back to Houston that night, our accordion player thought he had a winning hand and raised our drummer's bet. Freddie laid down his three kings and two tens and reached for the pot, but then he saw the other boy's four threes laying on the table. He couldn't believe that he had been beaten again.

"I was laughing because this old boy just couldn't ever seem to win a hand of poker. I remember telling him as he watched the money being swept off the table, 'You were just born to lose.' "

As soon as the words had left his mouth, Ted realized that he had come up with a great phrase. Getting the band's attention, Daffan announced, " 'Born to Lose,' now that is a hell of a song title!"

Upon getting home, Daffan sat down at the kitchen table and fleshed out his concept. It took just five minutes. He would later remark that it seemed like he was taking dictation as he jotted the lyrics down. As he ran over his work he knew he had a good song, but he didn't have any idea if it was hit material.

In early 1942 the Texans traveled to California to cut twenty-four sides for Columbia. Most of the songs were Daffan originals. In the middle of the session the A&R man pulled Ted to one side and informed him that Irving Berlin Music wouldn't publish that many songs from one songwriter. If he wanted Berlin to take them all, Daffan would have to use an alias on half of them. "Born to Lose" and several others were thus registered under the name of Frankie Brown.

"No Letter Today" was the single Columbia released before "Born to Lose." With Chuck Keeshan and Leon Seago providing the vocal work, the record lingered on the pop charts for seventeen long weeks. In August of 1943 Okeh released "Born to Lose." It jumped to nineteen on the pop side, and was such a strong seller that it was still grabbing interest when the hillbilly charts made their debut at the beginning of 1944. Daffan's ode to a poor card player stayed on the new country charts until summer, topping out at #3.

Sensing that he needed to get full credit for this hot new single, Daffan contacted Berlin and Columbia and requested that they put his real name on the songwriter credits. They fulfilled his request, and by 1944 the song was linked forever to Ted.

"Not long after 'Born to Lose' hit the charts," Daffan laughingly recalled, "*Billboard* had a headline that said, 'There Is Gold in Them There Hillbillies.' You know, in the case of 'Born to Lose' they were right!"

Ted Daffan's classic song of a man who just couldn't win would be released forty more times as a single in every genre from soul to pop music. In Daffan's favorite moment, Ray Charles would use it to prove to the world that a black man could sing a white man's blues. The song has also been a part of more than three hundred albums. Daffan's composition has gone beyond classic and has become a music standard.

"Born to Lose" was an innovative song that seems to fit in every era and time, and maybe that is because the writer was so far ahead of his own time. His style of play would help to revolutionize the country music sound for the next three decades. Daffan was one of the first to use the electric guitar in a country band. He helped to pioneer the use of lead instrumental work behind vocals. He embraced drums and jazz-type influences. Yet as complicated as his musical concepts appeared, it was his ability to write a very simple song that made Daffan's career.

"You know," Ted admitted, "that song has supported me all my life."

Here's to the losers who made the winners. Here's to Freddie!

1944
Smoke on the Water

Written by Zeke Clements

Zeke Clements came to the Opry in the 1930s as one of the first western singers to be welcomed to the Ryman. Decked out in flashy cowboy outfits, he was a crowd favorite, but in spite of this he never placed a single of his own recordings on the national pop or country charts. Still, of all of the country music old-timers, he is the performer whose voice has probably been heard by more children than any other. In the Disney classic *Snow White*, Zeke Clements supplied the voice for Bashful.

The songwriter Zeke Clements wrote several hits for a host of different performers. Eddy Arnold scored big in 1948 with Zeke's "Just a Little Lovin' (Will Go a Long Way)." That release camped out at the top of the charts for eight weeks. Yet Zeke's most inspired strike occurred five years before. This 1943 Clements composition would not only launch the career of one of country, gospel, and pop music's most beloved stars, it would also become one of World War II's most important songs.

The war years were a unique time in American music. With so many boys stationed all over the world, and with so many people from vastly different cultures thrown together in a random fashion, our nation was in the midst of a massive and very direct information exchange. Men from the Deep South were swapping stories and songs with guys from New York City. Chicago boys were trading guitar licks with Texans. In the thirties the Okies had migrated to California and taken their music with them, thus spreading a sound that would evolve into the Bakersfield version of country. Now, with the war, hillbilly music was being taken around the world, and for that reason its influence was spreading faster than ever before.

It is quickly obvious when listening to the records of the era that country music writers felt the war deeply and personally. They had relatives and friends who were wading ashore on Pacific islands or battling Hitler's forces in Europe. Many of them knew well soldiers who had been injured or died. This emotion flooded out in "A Soldier's Last Letter," "Mail Call Today," "Stars and Stripes on Iwo Jima," "The White Cross on Okinawa," and a host of other war releases. These songs served double duty, and the writers and performers knew that. They were used to build morale not only on the home front, but overseas as well. In many cases country music songs became the themes for units. Hillbilly song titles were often chosen as the names for bombers. While country music was certainly not the only musical form to embrace the subject of war, the genre's writers seemed to relate to it in a very meaningful manner.

Like so many others, Zeke Clements was deeply concerned by the death and dying which were part of the worldwide conflict. It was a time that tested faith.

As millions did, Zeke often turned to the Bible and prayer for a source of comfort. On a dark night in 1943 when the horrors of war seemed so very close, a haunting vision hit the songwriter and would not let him go.

"I had a dream," he later recalled. "It was from a Bible passage. It said that God put a rainbow in the sky and the world would not again be destroyed by water. The next time it would be destroyed by fire. I felt that it was possible that this war would consume the world with fire as the Bible had predicted."

With the image of World War II setting the world on fire smoldering in his mind, Clements asked Earl Nunn to help him write a song. The two men then composed words that were only meant for this one moment in time. And for a war-weary public, the images they created worked ever so well.

Just as soon as Zeke premiered the song, a host of other performers lined up to cut their versions of "Smoke on the Water." The first single to make the charts was by a thirty-three-year-old Kentucky native, Red Foley.

Foley had been in the entertainment business since college. A veteran of both the *WLS Barn Dance* and *National Barn Dance* in Chicago, he had spent a decade doing comedy, as well as singing with a number of different groups. During these times the spotlight had rarely fallen on his great talent as a solo vocalist. Thirteen years after leaving home and arriving in Chicago, Foley was doing a show with Red Skelton. It was from this pairing that he finally caught Decca's interest.

For his first record the label matched Red with Clements's new composition. They shipped the Foley single in the summer of 1944. By August it had climbed on the hillbilly charts, and in September it made the hit list on the pop side. Foley's initial Decca release would ride the national pop charts for eleven weeks, peaking at #7. On the country side "Smoke" would hang on for an incredible twenty-seven weeks, thirteen of them at the top position.

Decca used Foley's "Smoke" success to groom him into one of the nation's biggest recording stars. Red cut a version of Spade Cooley's "Shame on You" that hit the top spot, following it with more than a dozen other huge hits. Within five years of his first record he was so popular that Red's "Chattanoogie Shoe Shine Boy" topped the country and pop charts at the same time for eight straight weeks (it stayed #1 for a total of thirteen weeks in country). Yet in spite of the huge success of "Chattanoogie," notwithstanding the fact that eight of his other songs reached the top spot and he recorded sixty-five chart singles, the future Hall of Famer's biggest hit remained his first effort. Such was the power of this wartime epic.

Bob Wills and the Texas Playboys also recorded "Smoke on the Water." Released in early 1945, their record topped the charts too. This time "Smoke" was #1 for two weeks, and remained on the hit list for fifteen. A relative unknown, Boyd Heath, cut a version of the song and landed it at #7.

Overseas "Smoke on the Water" became a password for certain Marine groups, as well as the inspiration for many men caught in the midst of kamikaze raids and close fighting. For years Clements received fan mail from war vets telling him how his song had inspired them to continue fighting when they were convinced they could take no more.

World War II was a special time for America. It was an occasion when a nation banded together to contribute to paying freedom's high price. Zeke Clements's contribution was born in a vision and reached its zenith in a song. The war is long over, but the song remains as a testament to how much so many gave to make "Smoke on the Water's" message ring true.

1946
Shame on You

Written by Spade Cooley

The postwar period was a magical time, an era that saw country music grow from a mainly regional product to one considered national in scope. The world was exploding with both technology and growth. Television was in its infancy, everyone was back from the war, for the first time in four years we were at peace, and there could be no doubt that America was the most powerful nation on earth. Maybe it was because so many hadn't gotten to dance in so very long, or maybe it was just because we were just so happy, but this was also the golden era of the country dance hall.

By now Nashville had rightfully begun to claim its place as the center of country music, but middle Tennessee didn't have the monopoly on the genre. The West Coast was also producing its own special brand of hillbilly music. It was music with a swing and a beat. It was music to dance to. It was a combination of cowboy and hillbilly with a dash of jazz all played by large bands. One of those at the heart of this "western" influence was a former Okie named Donnell Clyde Cooley.

Like so many from his state, Cooley had migrated to California with his family in the midst of the Depression. A fiddle player, by the time he reached his mid-twenties he had worked with various western bands including the famous Riders of the Purple Sage. A bit player in a host of different movies, Donnell was performing with the Jimmy Wakely Trio in the early forties when he was hired to form the house band for the Venice Pier Club. Spade, as he was called by his friends, recruited some of the best talent in Los Angeles, including vocalist Tex Williams, for his group. Playing their own version of the western swing sounds made popular by Bob Wills, the Spade Cooley Orchestra quickly became one of the most popular dance bands west of the Lone Star State.

In 1943 the fiddler moved his band to the even bigger Riverside Rancho Ballroom, and played to overflow crowds for the next three years. Everyone knew that if you wanted to see Spade, you had to get there early. In 1944, Columbia, in the form of Okeh Records, noted the excitement created each night on the dance floor and took an interest in the Orchestra. To capture Spade's unique big-band country music sound, they plowed through the band leader's own compositions. The producers settled on a simple song with a catchy title, "Shame on You."

"Shame on You" had enough instrumental breaks to spotlight most of the band's great musicians. It also gave the nation a chance to hear the smooth sounds of Tex Williams. An instant hit on the West Coast, by the late spring of 1945 it had climbed the country charts to the #1 spot. It would remain there for nine weeks, and hover in the top one hundred for almost eight months. The song put Cooley on the national map, and Bob Wills's "Spanish Two Step" was the only true western swing single that would stay on top longer than "Shame on You."

In a great irony, "Shame on You" also opened country music's door for the nation's polka king, Lawrence Welk. With Red Foley supplying the vocal work, the Welk Orchestra took the song back up the charts in 1946, hitting the top spot in early fall. Foley and Welk's version also did well on the pop side. Against a host of great postwar competition, "Shame on You" ended its run at #13. For several years the popular Cooley tune was covered by a number of other country and dance bands. Over the course of the dance and swing craze, "Shame on You" was to be one of the era's most requested songs. It stayed on jukeboxes throughout the forties.

Cooley's ride on the hit parade that began with "Shame on You" continued for almost four years with songs like "A Pair of Broken Hearts," "Detour," and "Crazy 'cause I Love You." The demise of the big-band sound, the passing of swing music, and the departure of lead vocalist Tex Williams led to Spade's break with national fame, but it did not end his career. A television pioneer, the band leader kept his unique orchestra intact and continued to draw big crowds in Los Angeles country dance halls for years to come.

Tex Williams and His Western Caravan also carried on the sound for more than two decades. Williams's chart impact in the late forties was almost as great as

that of Bob Wills. Overall Tex scored more than twenty times on the *Billboard* roll of hit songs, with the silly "Smoke! Smoke! Smoke!" becoming his biggest hit. Yet for many fans of the day, Tex would always be associated with the Spade Cooley Orchestra.

Cooley's "Shame on You" represented the best in the California swing influence and signaled just how much the demand for country dance songs had grown during the war years. With the return of millions of G.I.'s, country music was now a national commercial force. The dispersion of Southern troops had spread its popularity to the extent that no longer would the musical genre be limited to just barn dances, local radio shows, and the *Grand Ole Opry*.

While Tex Williams continued to happily perform into the eighties, and the Original Texas Playboys even longer, Spade Cooley, the self-proclaimed "King of Western Swing," fell on hard times just a decade after his biggest hit. During the rise of rock 'n' roll, the demand for swing music waned and the band leader's disposition soured. Taking up the bottle, he often drank heavily. In a tragedy that some would consider more typical of a Hollywood movie or country song lyric than real life, Spade got drunk, then beat and stomped his wife to death. Cooley's remaining eight years were to be spent entertaining prisoners from the inside of a cell. As he was sentenced to prison newspaper headlines read, "Shame on You."

1948
Bouquet of Roses

Written by Steve Nelson and Bob Hilliard

He was born less than 150 miles from Nashville in 1918. Fatherless from a young age, he grew up so far back in the sticks that it was said he had to work his way through a long educational process just to be considered a hick. Dirt poor, this baby of four kids learned to chord on a cousin's borrowed Sears guitar. By the time he grew into his teens his favorite singers were Gene Autry and Bing Crosby. This hardworking lad, Eddy Arnold, made the money to buy his idols' latest records by plowing fields with a mule team.

Fearing being permanently trapped in the life of a sharecropper, Arnold left home at seventeen and put together a country band in Jackson, Tennessee. Over the course of the next few years he drifted first to Memphis and later St. Louis with his guitar and his songs. Though he continued to play clubs, he rarely made much more than a dollar a night. The poor kid from the country had become a poorer kid in the city, and there were few signs that Eddy's luck would ever change.

Almost as if by magic, fortune smiled on Arnold in 1940 when Pee Wee King heard the young man sing. The band leader loved his smooth country style and offered the boy a spot in King's Golden West Cowboys. Arnold couldn't wait to pack his bag and hit the road. For the first time in his life he had a regular music job that paid solid money.

Pee Wee King's Golden West Cowboys per-

formed at some of the South and West's best clubs and night spots. These big-time venues offered a tremendous opportunity for Eddy to hone his talents. But what was more important to Eddy than the regular club dates was the fact that King owned a regular spot on the *Grand Ole Opry*. It was here that young Eddy would make the most of his "golden" opportunity.

For three years Eddy provided vocals for the Cowboys on the road and at the *Opry*. In 1943, feeling he was sufficiently seasoned, he walked away from the band and talked WSM into giving him a show of his own. Within weeks Eddy was so popular on radio that he was given a solo spot on the *Opry*.

Then what looked to be a huge break fell in Eddy's lap. Impressed with his voice on radio as well as his *Opry* following, RCA offered the singer a record deal. This big break turned out to be a false start. A union strike shut down the recording business for over a year. Because of this, it was 1945 before the record label was able to introduce its newest act. By then, thanks to Arnold's *Opry* work, the "Tennessee Plowboy" really needed no introduction.

Eddy's first records failed to hit the national charts. It took Arnold almost a year to produce a smash country release in "That's How Much I Love You." Eddy, who was now being managed by a former carnival circuit promoter, Colonel Tom Parker, followed up that

1946 hit with "What Is Life without Love" and "It's a Sin."

Arnold's success with these smooth ballads seemed out of place at the *Opry*. He was sharing a stage with fan favorites such as Ernest Tubb, Bill Monroe, and Roy Acuff. Dressed in his tailored country-style outfits, Eddy looked as if he could be Tubb's cousin, but when he opened his mouth he sounded as if he should have been on Broadway.

While many in hillbilly music saw this crooner style as an affront to "real" country music, RCA and Colonel Parker saw potential beyond the rather confined borders of Nashville-based music. Very quietly they began to market Eddy to both country and pop markets. They also began to look for material away from the usual country songwriting circles.

The table was set for this orchestrated country/pop move in March 1948. Arnold placed his "Anytime" atop the country charts for nine weeks while also sliding it over to #17 on the pop side. With this release Eddy *had* broken over to the big chart, but only in a very small way. "Anytime" spent one scant week in the pop numbers.

For the next single, RCA turned to a songwriting team, Steve Nelson and Bob Hilliard. The composers had just come up with a romantic ballad that seemed perfect for some of the nation's top pop crooners. RCA had something far different in mind.

"It was a sweet tune," Nelson would always say, "so we wanted sweet words to go with it." When the royalties began to roll in they realized just how "sweet" this song really was.

In a sense, "Bouquet of Roses" was a manufactured piece. It was written not to exorcise a bad life experience, but in order to marry words to an already written score. Such was often the case with pop material, and this was almost always how it worked on Broadway. But in Nashville songs were supposed to be

"lived." Songwriting was not a nine-to-five job. It was a gift from the heavens, and songs were always supposed to be "inspired."

While "Roses" might have gone against the Music City grain, having been simply "produced" rather than "lived," the song's lyrics did have a country feel. This was the story of a jilted lover whose heart had been broken over and over again by one uncaring person. Still, even with its theme of lost love, "Roses" was far different from the era's other big country songs such as "One Has My Name, the Other Has My Heart," "Sugar Moon," "Smoke! Smoke! Smoke!," and "So Round, So Firm, So Fully Packed." It would have been hard to imagine Ernest Tubb or Bob Wills playing "Bouquet of Roses" at a country dance hall.

Inspired or not, Arnold's "Roses" would quickly shoot up to #1 on the country charts. It would hold the top position for nineteen weeks. It would remain in the top one hundred for more than a year—fifty-four long and profitable weeks. It was the biggest country release of 1948 and one of the biggest of all time. Yet it was on the pop side where it made the most important waves for the Tennessee Plowboy. "Bouquet of Roses" climbed up the pop charts to hit #13. It stayed on those charts as a best-seller for twenty-seven weeks. While pop covers of "Roses" did appear, none came close to the original in sound or sales. In Arnold, country music had finally produced an artist who didn't need to have his songs covered by a popular artist to be accepted. Eddy was welcomed anywhere.

With startling speed Eddy Arnold changed the very fabric of country music. With his effortless style, his sophisticated touch, his country charm, he opened up the industry for a new type of star. No longer did you have to work your way up via the beer halls and honky-tonks. Now, to sell records you didn't have to sing with a twang or yodel. And a country music fan could now have a college degree and be from southern New York City. Jim Reeves, George Morgan, and Tennessee Ernie Ford among others followed in Eddy's footsteps, and with their smooth style and country values they won fans in both rural and urban areas.

Over the course of a Hall of Fame career that continues even today, Eddy Arnold has hosted scores of network television specials, has regularly dressed in a tuxedo, has become the first major country act to appear on numerous mainstream television shows, and was also the first to appear on the major stages of the nation's biggest cities. During this period he has also become the most successful act in country music chart history. All told, Arnold has dropped 145 songs

on the *Billboard* singles charts and seen twenty-eight of those go to the top spot. Over his remarkable recording career he has spent 145 weeks, or almost three years, at #1.

When considering what made Eddy Arnold a worldwide star, one has to only look at the boy's earliest musical influences. On an old record player, listening to records bought with money he made plowing neighbors' fields, Eddy memorized the words to all the Bing Crosby and Gene Autry standards. Years later, with huge crossover hits like "Bouquet of Roses," Arnold successfully meshed those two vastly separate styles into one, thus bringing millions of new fans into country music, expanding the scope of his musical genre, and bringing the country hick and the city slicker a bit closer together.

One Has My Name, the Other Has My Heart

Written by Hal Blair, Eddie Dean, and Dearest Dean

During the decades after World War II Hal Blair was one of the nation's most successful songwriters. Blair's best known composition, "Frosty the Snowman," would come while he was on staff at Hill and Range Songs in 1950, but just after World War II his special genius had already been recognized. Strangely, when one stops to consider just how profound his effect on the music industry would be, Blair had very little concept of how to marry a set of lyrics to an original melody. He couldn't compose music at all, nor did he write as a poet would. When creating a song's lyrics he always wrote those new lyrics to fit the tune of another familiar song. Once he was satisfied with his work, he opened his desk drawer, dropped the new copy in among his other lyric sheets, and waited for the right moment to show them to someone who could write original music. In this particular case that person was Eddie Dean.

Dean was a Texas native who had migrated to Chicago in the early thirties and worked on the *WLS Barn Dance* before joining his friend Gene Autry in Hollywood. For a decade he sang western songs on the radio and grabbed bit parts in "B" movies. He worked his way up to starring roles during the war years. By the time Hal Blair dopped the lyrics to "One Has My Name, the Other Has My Heart" in his hands, Eddie was starring in his own western series

and was one of America's ten best-drawing cowboy stars at the box office.

On screen Dean was playing typical all-American-type roles. He was a hero for American youth. Thus Hal's risque lyrics must have surprised him. Radio stations simply didn't play records that romanticized illicit behavior. Beside that, Blair's story all but endorsed cheating in marriage. Going back to Hal, Eddie demanded and got the story behind the song's haunting lyrics.

It seemed that when Blair had come home from military service a young woman to whom he was engaged had dumped him. On the rebound he had quickly married someone else, and been caught in an unhappy situation. The lyrics he wrote were therefore not merely formula words, but were straight from his heart. Blair also genuinely believed that his life story was one with which a large number of other people could relate.

Even though Dean was happily married, he could now see how a song of this type might be commercial. So he took it home to work up a tune. With the help of his own wife Dearest, he easily came up with a melody that fit Hal's words. As he sang it for the first time he must have wondered if any radio stations would have the guts to ever play it.

California-based western singer Jimmy Wakely was the first to test the waters with "One Has My Name, the Other Has My Heart." He released the song on Capitol three weeks before Dean released his single on the Crystal label. While both records met some initial radio play resistance, this only seemed to fuel their chart performance. The more people talked about the song's scandalous message, the more they wanted to hear it.

W_____ version _____ _____ fact that it was on a mo_____ powerful label and had come out of the _____ fir_____ won _____ battle to get on the _____ playlist. While D_____'s _____ _____ _____ _____ faded away entirely by October, Jimmy's moved steadily up the charts, u_____ it reached the top, and by November, held that p_____ _____ _____ _____ _____ _____ the _____ ra_____ So popular for a total of thirty-_____ _____ Wakely was well known in all music circles for his Hollywood movie work. So he was able to put his song over to the _____ cherished fans _____ _____ _____ _____ _____

_____ 1949 record Jimmy Wakely could not record the song for Dean, he hired Hersh, who was probably best known as Belew (_____ Connelly _____ _____ and termed a band). But this Rockabilly Sextet was. Eberly released his "One Has My Name" in January, and_____ al in its seven days on the country chart it rose to _____ The _____ _____ _____ Eddie D _____ _____ _____ ew remade _____ a company Make it for him, he _____ ew still hit. _____ _____ It was the tune number _____ _____ _____ _____ and for the _____ _____ _____ _____ the story's Eberly w_____ _____ _____ _____ _____ _____ _____ _____

Even after it had finally reached its long, slow run, "One Has My Name, the Other Has My Heart" remained a jukebox favorite for years. It also became a

popular album cut and one of the favorite local band covers in the country. This popularity caused it to reach classic status in a manner of years, not decades. And though Eddie Dean didn't sell a lot of his own records, he did profit handsomely from the royalties he earned from Wakely's version.

Twenty years after the Blair/Dean song first hit the charts, a former rocker returned to his musical roots. Jerry Lee Lewis had been raised on country and gospel. A one-time big rockabilly star, he had fallen from grace in the face of both personal scandal and the invasion of British rock groups. Grabbing a contract with the Smash label, he had remade himself as a country music singer in the mid-sixties, and after getting close three times, hit the top of the charts with "To Make Love Sweeter." For his follow-up Lewis elected to sit down at his piano and pound out a new verison of "One Has My Name." Released in May, the song climbed to #3 and solidly anchored Jerry Lee as a country music star. The next three years would be the best hit-making period of his career.

In today's "anything goes" era it might seem strange that "One Has My Name, the Other Has My Heart's" message was once considered racy. Yet it was one of the first cheating songs to make a huge splash on radio stations and the charts. While people have long forgotten the taboo that was broken by the Blair/Dean effort, fans are still being caught up in the song's haunting lyrics. These wonderfully crafted words, once stored in a crowded desk drawer, will insure that "One Has My Name, the Other Has My Heart" will be performed and recorded for years to come.

[Handwritten note on attached paper: APRIL 8, 1966 — IS GOD DEAD?]

1948
Tennessee Waltz

Written by Pee Wee King and Redd Stewart

The co-writer of one of country music's most popular songs was not from the South nor was he raised in the country. Julius Frank Anthony Kuczynski, the son of a violinist, was a city lad born in Milwaukee, Wisconsin, in 1914. He was a mechanical draftsman by trade, but from his youth his passion was music. By fourteen he had already formed his own group and was playing fiddle and accordion at polka dances. He soon began appearing on radio as well. Bitten hard by the entertainment bug, Julius gave up on a career as a draftsman and left home while still in his teens. Moving to Louisville, he landed a job with the Gene Autry Show.

By 1934 Kuczynski had become completely immersed in country music. Sensing that Julius Frank Anthony Kuczynski was not a great name for a hillbilly act, he started going by Frankie King. While performing on the *Crazy Water Barn Dance,* King would meet another young man who would become one of his best friends and his closest and most trusted musical advisor.

Redd Stewart was a talented Kentucky native who sang as well as he played guitar, piano, and fiddle. Stewart had performed with a number of local Louisville groups for several years when King, now going by the name of Pee Wee instead of Frankie, was forming his Golden West Cowboys band. In 1935 the talented Redd became one of the first men King hired for the Cowboys. Over the course of the next two decades Stewart would play every instrument in his friend's band as well as sing the lead on many of the group's greatest hits.

Less than a year after they first played together, the Golden West Cowboys had developed such a strong following that they were invited to leave Kentucky and move their show to the *Opry*. The group would remain WSM regulars for over a decade.

Sensing that this was a prime opportunity, Pee Wee branched out. He traveled to Hollywood and worked in cowboy movies. He also took his band to both coasts and appeared on several national radio shows. With their polish and shine, as well as their solid dance numbers, the Cowboys were favorites wherever they worked. Despite some personnel changes, the group remained popular throughout the war years too. When World War II ended, Pee Wee was ready to really take them to the top. He was determined to get the Cowboys the one thing they lacked, a nationally charted record.

In the late forties King collaborated with Stewart to write "Bonaparte's Retreat." Using their special relationship, the two then began to write together more often. They found that some of their most productive hours were when they were riding on the road. It was on a long trip from Texas back to Nashville that Pee Wee and Redd caught magic and fleshed it out into song.

"It was a Friday night in 1946," King would later recall, "and we were coming back from Texarkana. We did a lot of writing together, and Redd and I would get off by ourselves in the luggage truck so that we could concentrate."

On this night the two men were listening to the radio as they drove across the Texas/Arkansas border. In the silence a Bill Monroe cut came over the speaker. Listening to the familiar "Kentucky Waltz," Redd noted an irony.

"Why is it, Pee Wee," Stewart observed, "that no one has ever written a waltz about Tennessee?"

King thought about that fact for a few moments and suggested that it was probably just an oversight. He also figured that if the two of them had any brains, they would take advantage of that oversight before someone else did. Turning the radio down, Redd grabbed the matchbox he had used to light his last cigar. Pulling a pen out of the glove box, he waited for King to share his thoughts.

"We could put words to the 'No Name Waltz,' " Pee Wee suggested. Stewart quickly agreed.

The "No Name Waltz" had been Pee Wee's theme for years, but the two men had never considered putting lyrics to its melody. Now as the Arkansas countryside flew by, they both wondered why they had waited so long to work out words for the old tune. With the dome light lighting up the cab, the two men wrote a sad song about a dance and a lost love. When they got back to Nashville they turned it over to Fred Rose of Acuff-Rose Music.

Pee Wee couldn't wait to record "Tennessee Waltz." In 1948 King used the "Waltz," already a concert favorite, to propel the beginnings of his RCA career. With Redd singing the lead, the Golden Cowboys cut the "Waltz." On April 3, King's "Tennessee Waltz" danced on the charts, staying there for thirty weeks and topping out at the third

position. The song also moved up the pop charts to #30.

Meanwhile, others took note of the "Waltz's" natural appeal and headed to the recording studios. The first to record an alternate cut of the "Waltz" was former King band member Lloyd "Cowboy" Copas. Cowboy issued his single on King Records in May. It also climbed to the #3 position, and managed a seventeen-week chart ride. Then Roy Acuff released his "Tennessee Waltz" in November. "The King of Country Music" pushed his version to the twelfth spot on the hit parade. Yet all of these successful releases paled in comparison to what would transpire just two years later.

Patti Page had been recording for Mercury since 1948. She had scored with several minor hits, while earning just a single #1 with her "All My Love." In 1950 she entered the studio hoping to make a follow-up to that song. What she actually made was history.

Mercury was just beginning to use multi-track recording when Patti arrived on the scene, and "Tennessee Waltz" seemed like the perfect song for Page to sing a duet with herself. Recording her first in the lead, they next taped Patti singing a harmony line. After sandwiching the tracks together, the producers felt that the new record had a pleasant feel. They also figured it would become a hit simply because of the voice-over harmony gimmick. The Mercury public relations people knew that Patti singing a duet with Patti would make for some good press.

Released in November, Page's "Waltz" jumped to #1 almost immediately. Patti hit the top pop spot nine days before Christmas, and didn't give it up until March. The single would remain on the hit list for half a year. Pee Wee King had once observed that former Golden West Cowboy Eddy Arnold had bridged the gap between country and pop. Ironically Patti Page used Eddy's bridge to bring her pop sound back to the other side. On the country charts Page's new version of the "Tennessee Waltz" also scored well, staying #1 for three weeks.

Sensing the power of the "Waltz," others raced to record it. In popular music Guy Lombardo, Les Paul and Mary Ford, Jo Stafford, Spike Jones, the Fontane Sisters, and Anita Day all released singles in 1951. Three of those cuts made the top ten. In country, RCA rereleased Pee Wee's version. This time it climbed to #6.

The "Tennessee Waltz" had quickly become one of the most powerful moneymakers in music history. By now it has been recorded by hundreds of performers. The song that was written in a luggage truck made not only Pee Wee King's career, but also Patti Page's stardom.

With sales in excess of six million copies, Page's "Waltz" is the best-selling single ever recorded by a female artist. It is also the sixth best-selling pop single released before 1954, and three of the songs ahead of it have an unfair advantage because they are perennial Christmas classics.

In 1965 Pee Wee King's and Redd Stewart's answer to Bill Monroe's "Kentucky Waltz" was named the official song of the state of Tennessee. Three decades later it is still being recorded in all musical genres and remains one of the nation's all-time favorites. Not bad work for a Polish guy from Milwaukee and a musician named Redd content with riding in a luggage truck.

1949
Lovesick Blues

Written by Irving Mills and Cliff Friend

Of all the thousands of country music performers who have made their marks on the charts and in record sales, Hank Williams stands apart. In his brief six-year recording career he touched more hearts and won more fans than any musician of the era. At a time when larger-than-life stars such as Ernest Tubb, Eddy Arnold, Hank Thompson, and Hank Snow dominated airwaves and playlists, Hank dramatically dwarfed them all. He was like nothing that had come before, and probably nothing like his genius will ever be seen again. He was one of the common people elevated with a special talent that enabled him to take all of the gut-wrenching emotions of a tragically sad life and spin them into songs that were haunting in beauty and meaning. He was in touch with a people's collective soul even while never being able to find his own. He played under the brightest spotlights while roaming the darkest streets. He was country music's Babe Ruth, but he was also a lost little boy.

Hank was an often directionless and hopeless alcoholic, but his genius was obvious even in the midst of his deepest depressions. Self-destructive and moody, he was and probably remains country music's most creative and endearing writer of timeless words and melodies. His music would not only transcend his own life, but transcend the genre of country music. He would not just inspire a new group of honky-tonkin' country stars, but through his mesh of gospel,

blues, and country, as well as his embracing of the sounds and soul of black rural music, he would shape the Southern boys who would shake the world in the mid-fifties with the brand new sounds of rock 'n' roll. Though the term wouldn't be used until after his death, and is even today rarely used to describe his work, Hank was the first wildly popular prophet of rockabilly. By simply spewing out all of his great pain and small joys into his music, setting it to a unique, heartfelt rhythm, he touched the world and reshaped music as no one had ever done before.

There is little need to document the fact that Hank Williams is to country music songwriting what Mark Twain is to American literature. No one could turn a phrase like he could. No one could paint the pictures. No one could compose such simple but awe-inspiring melodies. And no one could do it as often or as quickly as he did. So, with those facts established, one of country music's most interesting ironies remains the origin of Hank Williams's first huge hit record.

Hank recorded "Lovesick Blues" largely because it was a favorite of the *Louisiana Hayride* crowd. (Hank's excessive drinking had relegated him to this venue by causing his exclusion from the more prestigious *Opry*.) Every time the skinny young man jumped on stage and hunkered over the microphone to perform this number, the crowd yelled its approval. Much more than any other song, "Lovesick Blues" brought his fans to their feet. Yet even as he stepped into the recording studio and duplicated the sound that had made the song a concert favorite, not everyone sensed the potential sales and power of this release.

It may be hard to appreciate now, but in early 1949, Hank Williams was not a huge star. He really wasn't much of a star at all. At this point in his career there was good reason for many to wonder if the young self-abusive Alabaman would ever really score big. By March of that year Hank had released just three singles for MGM. The first, "Move It On Over," had been the biggest hit, charting at #4 in the summer of '47. The other two, "Honky-Tonkin'" and "I'm a Long Gone Daddy," hadn't even made it into the top five. By the time he recorded "Lovesick Blues," the singer's total weeks on the chart at any position numbered just seven. During this same period of time Eddy Arnold had spent over fifty weeks just at #1.

Hank's publishing company, Acuff-Rose, headed by Fred Rose, had little reason to want to push "Lovesick Blues" either. Even though he claimed he had purchased all rights, Hank hadn't actually written it. He really didn't know who had. If Acuff-Rose was going to publish this number, they needed more proof. Legally, they would have felt much better dropping "Lovesick Blues" in favor of one of Hank's own compositions. The publisher had signed him because of his songwriting abilities, and they wanted to use them. Still, Hank convinced them it was his, so they gave the go-ahead and filed the rights to the song. It was only after it was released and hit the playlists that they discovered the song's rights were actually owned by Mills Music.

The words had been written by Cliff Friend, a vaudeville pianist from Cincinnati. Friend had found inspiration for the song as a flyer stationed at Wright Field during World War I. He watched as lovesick fly-boys hovered over every phrase in every letter they received from their sweethearts. The words and Friend's music were then "massaged" by a Russian-born Jewish band leader, Irving Mills. Mills would later write such classic big band songs as "It Don't Mean a Thing (If It Ain't Got That Swing)." "Lovesick Blues's" first commercially released recording was done by Elsie Clark in 1922. Ukelele Ike also cut it about the same time. Jazz singer Emmet Miller tried the number three years later with the same results as Clark—absolutely no chart action and few sales. During the Depression a few others attempted to score with "Lovesick Blues," but none of the records took off.

In 1939 Rex Griffin of Alabama cut his version of "Lovesick Blues." It was Griffin's country yodeling style that had helped the song make its final transition from a bluesy Broadway number to a country and western piece. Yet it would be another decade before the genius of this change would be fully realized. Like the earlier releases, the Griffin recording failed in every possible way but one—local bands around the South began to play it. One of these local bands' singers even convinced Hank Williams that it was an original. Hank then "purchased" all rights for the song for $100. A few weeks after he released "Lovesick Blues," he realized he had been conned.

When MGM released "Lovesick Blues" in March 1949 it became an instant hit. On April 7 it climbed to #1, a position it wouldn't relinquish until the bloom was well off the summer roses. Sixteen weeks on top and forty-two weeks on the charts turned the struggling singer into a national sensation. "Lovesick Blues" even raced up to #24 on the pop charts. Suddenly Hank Williams had to be recognized.

The Opry finally did so on June 11, 1949. Even as a sober and smiling Hank dragged his tall, thin frame on stage that evening, he scared them. His erratic behavior, his thirst for booze, his failure to show up at bookings—these were among the reasons they had closed the door to him in the past. Now, with "Lovesick Blues" the nation's hottest song, they had been forced to hold their collective noses and invite him to join them. Still, they were afraid that he would embarrass them. It was no secret that many were hoping he would fail. Yet at his debut the Opry audience called him back more than a dozen times just to sing another verse of his first #1. Whenever anyone else appeared on stage, the crowd howled for more Hank. It was an evening never to be forgotten.

Hank Williams now had what he had craved all his adult life—stardom. He forgot about the bad times, went on overseas tours with Bob Hope, sold millions of records, performed before huge crowds all over the nation, built a massive home, and bought Cadillacs. Yet as time would soon prove, commercial success did little for his personal life. The pain that had so dominated him since childhood continued. Fed by newfound wealth and fame, his addictions grew, and what the Opry management had most feared eventually drove him off their stage. Yet even these demons couldn't drive Hank out of country music fans' hearts. They forgave him time and time again because they saw his weakness as their own. When he tragically and needlessly died, a wasted, used-up man at the age of twenty-nine, the fans still loved him. And they forgave him.

It is his own compositions that would prove just how deeply the blues had ensnared Hank Williams's life. It is these songs which have immortalized him and have made him a timeless music icon. Which makes it all the more ironic that his biggest single, "Lovesick Blues," the record that launched country music's still-growing love affair with Hank Williams, had been co-written by a Russian Jew. Only in America could a redneck and an immigrant swing composer from two different eras somehow find common ground and touch immortality together.

1949
I'm So Lonesome I Could Cry

Written by Hank Williams

There are times when men create art without ever realizing what they have done. In the case of songwriters, this art is the result of the fragile marriage of words and music. Out of that crystal-like union comes a message that transcends all musical genres and springs directly into a listener's soul. The song that results is timeless, its meaning just as strong in each successive generation. Using no gimmicks, no play on words, no sophisticated breakthroughs, the piece becomes a simple but profound testament for every man or woman who hears it. As years pass it remains fresh and haunting. Because it transcends time itself, it is as if the song is suspended in time just waiting to be rediscovered by each new generation.

Inspired by waves of emotion that no one seemed to fully understand, Hank Williams created art on several occasions. Using the tragic flavor of his own life, he wove simple words and unadorned music into songs that seemed to have endless layers of substance. He seemed to sense that he had a great deal to say, but very little time in which to say it.

Mitch Miller, the noted band leader, once observed, "No matter who you were, a country person or a sophisticate, the language [Williams's writing] hits home. Nobody I know could use basic English so effectively."

Much like Edgar Allan Poe, Hank Williams was seemingly possessed by forces which kept pulling him down into the depths of darkness and shadows. It was there, in the hopeless mire of booze and pills, where he sought refuge from demons only he saw and understood. Yet like Poe, there were moments in Williams's life when he pulled himself up to the sunshine. During these brilliant times he shared the anguish of his other world in songs. His creations not only proved his genius, but often confirmed his fears.

In 1949 Hank penned a hopeless epic that was to become not just a country classic, but one of the most powerful and emotional songs ever written. No one knew what drove Williams to so eloquently describe the very essence of loneliness, but in simple language he nailed this void like no one ever had or probably ever will.

"I'm So Lonesome I Could Cry" was not one of the thirty-nine Hank Williams singles that MGM released between 1947 and 1955. While rumor has it that it was one of the last songs he ever sang, to the fans of Hank's day it was an almost forgotten tune. "Lonesome's" magic, its autobiographic symbolism and beauty were all but lost, hidden behind the long list of Hank's hits that dominated the charts at the time.

Though picked up and performed by many country acts in the decade after Williams's death, "Lonesome" did not really gain a great deal of national notice until the song resurfaced as a vital part of the 1964 movie

Your Cheatin' Heart. Still, even then, no one released the song as a single.

In 1966, an unknown Oklahoma-born rock singer recorded "I'm So Lonesome I Could Cry" in the same haunting manner as Hank had. This revived country classic would become the first rock chart hit for B.J. Thomas. Thomas's version was beautifully pure. His voice revealed the lyric's ultimate sadness. Listeners must have related to the standard's loneliness in a special way because sales pushed it up the rock charts. By late spring B.J. would take "Lonesome" into the top ten, launching a career that produced major hits in three different musical genres, rock, country, and gospel.

"I'm So Lonesome I Could Cry's" ride in pop music drew a reaction in Nashville. Going back into their vaults, MGM added backup vocals to Williams's original recording and reissued it. The song rode the charts for four weeks in 1966, peaking at #43.

Hank's "Lonesome" was now being recognized as one of his greatest works. In pop, rock, country, and even soul, artists were using it in their stage shows. Numerous album cuts also began to appear. Beginning in 1971, several country performers even tried to produce a hit single with this ode to sadness.

Linda Plowman charted with "Lonesome" in 1971. Charlie McCoy created a wonderful harmonica hit with the song a year later. McCoy carried his release to the twenty-third spot. In 1982 Jerry Lee Lewis also cut the song. Yet the country version of "I'm So Lonesome I Could Cry" which remains the most successful belongs not to a performer, but to an athlete.

Terry Bradshaw loved country music almost as much as he did football. By 1976 the Pittsburgh Steelers All-Star had not only become a household name, but had used his gridiron fame to reveal his singing skills. Sensing an opportunity to capitalize, Mercury Records rushed him into the studio so that he could cut "Lonesome" as a single. Bradshaw, whose happy-go-lucky lifestyle didn't at all reflect the pain and misery of Williams's life, nevertheless did a solid job on Hank's classic. Country fans bought it and Terry pushed his way up the charts to #17. Today, over four decades after it was written, "Lonesome" has grown into one of Hank's most beloved compositions.

One of the first men who reviewed "I'm So Lonesome I Could Cry's" lyrics was Jimmy Rule. After Rule had read the words, Hank asked, "Do you think people will understand what I'm trying to say when I say this?" Jimmy assured him that they would.

Those who worked at Acuff-Rose Publishing during Williams's time would later say that the song's original title was to have been "I'm So Lonesome I Could Die," but that it was changed because Fred Rose felt that this message was simply too hopeless. Maybe he was right, but the song's lyrics seem to fit that first sentiment and Hank's life so very well. Either way, with "Lonesome" Williams had stepped beyond simple songwriting and created timeless art.

1949
Slipping Around

Written by Floyd Tillman

Floyd Tillman was a native Oklahoman who as a child moved to Texas. He was in his early teens when he grew to idolize Jimmie Rodgers, and the "Blue Yodeler's" influence helped to create a strong musical drive in the young man. By his sixteenth birthday Floyd had mastered guitar, mandolin, and banjo and was playing at local dances and parties. Before he was out of his teens Tillman was already entertaining in local honky-tonks.

Migrating to Houston in the mid-thirties, Tillman worked with a number of different local groups. At one point he and Ted Daffan both played together as a part of the Blue Ridge Playboys. Like Daffan, Floyd was drawn to the world of writing as well as performing. One of his early compositions, "It Makes No Difference Now," earned him an introduction at Decca Records. Through this connection a string of other Tillman-penned songs found their way into the hands of various artists in both pop and hillbilly circles. So while his own recording career would never create big waves, his songwriting kept Tillman going.

Floyd may have been a country boy, but his voice and style seemed a bit closer to Bing Crosby than Ernest Tubb. A rural crooner, he often had more success selling his songs in popular, rather than country music, circles. Yet even though ninety percent of his writing royalties were coming from outside country music, he still worked the honky-tonks, pioneering a single lead style of guitar playing that would be taken up by almost everyone in the industry.

Living in Houston during the late forties, Tillman was driving back home from a late-night gig when he stopped at an all-night diner to drink a cup of coffee. Still hours from home, he wasn't anxious to get back in the car, so he lingered and observed the local night owls. He couldn't help but note a pretty young woman as she passed by his stool and headed toward a nearby phone. Floyd wondered who it was she would be calling at three in the morning. His curiosity getting the best of him, he leaned close enough to catch most of her conversation.

"Now, honey," the woman explained, "you call me. But if a man answers, you hang up. Do you understand?"

Tillman couldn't help but feel a little sorry for the lady. Here she was getting out of the house in the middle of the night just to sneak around on her husband. He felt that she must have been pretty unhappy to take those kind of chances in a small town. As he watched her slip out the door, an idea that was to grow into his biggest song was born. Not long after that experience he sat down and scribbled out the words to "Slipping Around."

Just a year before, "Slipping Around" might have had problems being cut and released. Just twelve months before, radio stations had had a rule not to play cheating songs. But Jimmy Wakely had broken that taboo with "One Has My Name, the Other Has My Heart," so Floyd felt sure that his song would get by the record "censors." Still, he wondered how it would play to the audience.

Tillman released "Slipping Around" on July 2, 1949. The song immediately drew radio play, and soon landed on the country jukeboxes. Columbia sensed that they might have finally produced the song that would make Floyd a real force in the recording world and one of the industry's big stars. Yet other labels also noted the immediate positive response to the song. They were not going to give Floyd the charts without a fight.

Decca brought Ernest Tubb into the studio and cut their own version of the Tillman hit. "The Texas Troubadour" followed Floyd onto the charts in late July. Tubb, who at that time probably had the greatest fan base in country music, killed all of Floyd's momentum. Tillman's version of his own song stayed on the charts for three months and would peg out at #5. Tubb's cut would hit the top for a week and remain on playlists for twenty more. Ernest would also roll up the pop charts to the seventh spot.

Jimmy Wakely, who had enriched his bankroll greatly with "One Has My Name," thought that he could add a unique touch to "Slipping Around" by recording it as a duet. He contacted a successful pop singer, Margaret Whiting, and she joined Wakely in the Capitol studios. Their version of Tillman's composition exploded onto the country charts in September. It reached #1 less than a month after its release, and stayed there for more than four months. It also crossed over on the pop charts, holding #1 for three weeks and staying in the top one hundred for six months.

"Slipping Around" would ultimately chart in country music on seven different occasions. It was 1949's biggest song and one of the most successful crossover hits ever. Over four decades after its release, the Wakely/Whiting cut remains country music's most successful duet.

Floyd Tillman went on to write more than two hundred other songs, but none ever had the success of "Slipping Around." Given a chance, he certainly would have liked to thank a certain young woman in a little Texas town for giving him the idea for his greatest hit. Floyd always wondered if the visitor to that all-night diner ever guessed that the songwriter had shared her affair with the world.

1949
Candy Kisses

Written by George Morgan

George Morgan was born in 1925 in Waverly, Tennessee. Like a host of other Southern families, the Morgans were caught in hard times during the Depression. In order for his father to find work in a factory, George's family left the South for Ohio in the mid-thirties. As a teen, young Morgan killed many hours playing guitar and listening to music. Though many of his friends seemed to think that George was doing little more than wasting his time, the boy made money with his hobby long before any of his friends had even figured out what they were going to do after high school. While he was still in his mid-teens his reputation as a singer had grown to such a point that WAKR, an Akron radio station, gave young Morgan his own show. After a successful run at WAKR, George left for a better-paying gig up the road in Wooster.

What was to become one of the most important moments in George's life grew out of a broken romance. On one particular day during the early 1940s, he felt like a heartsick teenager as he drove from his home in Barberton to his job in Wooster. A girlfriend had treated George badly for the umpteenth time. Angry, upset, and filled with all the wounds that were created by high school love, the young singer began to wonder just how much he really meant to the girl. George finally decided that she prized the candy kisses her mother gave her more than those that came

from his lips. This realization did more than just frustrate him. It inspired him.

Arriving at the radio studio early, Morgan sat down at a table and allowed a song to write itself. Within ten minutes he had not only finished the lyrics, but fully polished the music. With his guitar in hand, he premiered "Candy Kisses" live on the radio just moments after he had completed it. At that time the only real satisfaction he felt as he sang the song was that he had finally informed the selfish young lady just how he really felt about their relationship.

Even at an early age, George's smooth sound was far more pop than country. If not for the success of Eddy Arnold, Morgan probably would have had to pursue a musical style outside country music. Yet because of the success that Eddy was having in both country and pop, a door would open up for Morgan not long after he graduated from high school. The *WWVA Jamboree*, a very popular radio show out of Wheeling, West Virginia, called George and offered him a spot on their program. He accepted, packed his bags, and moved to Wheeling. Once on the air, he introduced "Candy Kisses" to an audience that included listeners from most of the eastern portion of the nation.

In short order successful road dates and large bags of fan mail quickly made George one of the show's biggest attractions. So big that, even without a single hit record, he received an invitation to join the *Opry* in late 1948. Just as he had done in Wheeling, Morgan rapidly charmed both the show's fans and its management. He also caught the eye of Columbia's talent scouts. Within a few months the label had Morgan under contract and in the studio. Their foremost goal was getting George's theme song on the market.

Late in February "Candy Kisses" was shipped to radio stations and sales outlets from coast to coast. Columbia's leadership felt the record would do well, but in their wildest dreams they just couldn't have guessed how well. By the first of April Morgan had placed his initial single at #1. He would register three weeks at the top, and keep "Candy Kisses" on the charts for twenty-three weeks. It would be his all-time biggest hit, and would quickly become one of country music's most covered records.

Five other country music acts cut "Kisses" in just 1949. These artists—Elton Britt, Red Foley, Cowboy Copas, Eddie Kirk, and Bud Hobbs—all planted their records in the top twenty. The first four acts even went to top-ten status. Altogether, the six country cuts of "Candy Kisses" spent sixty-five weeks on the charts.

On the pop side, Eddy Howard and His Orchestra quickly noted Morgan's country cut. They hurried to the studio to engineer a big-band version of the song. By late spring Howard had jumped "Candy Kisses" into the top twenty.

In country music's long and proud history there have been a host of novelty or gimmick songs which have done well on the charts. A few rose above their own catchy titles and novel lyrics to become some-thing special. Hank Thompson's "Humpty Dumpty Heart" was one of these. Another was "So Round, So Firm, So Fully Packed," by Merle Travis. Many, such as Tex Williams's "Smoke! Smoke! Smoke!" or the Bellamy Brothers' "If I Said You Had a Beautiful Body Would You Hold It against Me," were chart-busting smashes, but still had little going for them other than their gimmicks. Most other novelty numbers were forgotten almost as quickly as they had been written and produced. Yet of all of the songs which fit into this category, George Morgan's story of high school romance stands apart.

"Candy Kisses" became more than a gimmick because you didn't even have to know what candy kisses were to fall in love with the song. Simple, direct, and filled with a message which almost anyone at any time could relate to, more than forty-six years after it first hit the charts and two decades after the star's death Morgan's classic is still one of country music's most familiar songs. It has such great staying power it might even outlast the candy which inspired its title and theme.

If he had lived long enough, George Morgan would have seen his record success surpassed by a member of his own family. His daughter Lorrie became a major recording star in her own right in the mid-eighties. When she was just four years into her RCA career she already had racked up more chart-toppers than her father. Yet even though most of Lorrie's fans had never heard George sing, they rarely let her leave the stage without crying out for "Candy Kisses." It seems that the sweet taste of great songs lingers for a long time.

1950
Faded Love

Written by Bob Wills and John Wills

One of the first songs which Bob Wills heard as a child in Kosse, Texas, was a fiddle tune that had been written by his father. John Wills often played this old tune at night, long after everyone else had gone to bed. Some thought that the elder Wills's song had such a mournful sound that as it drifted across the dark countryside it must have even caused the stars to weep. Yet John's son could only hear a peaceful beauty in the fiddler's strokes, and that was why this unnamed Wills family original became one of the first tunes the young child learned when he picked up his father's bow.

By the time Bob Wills began forming his own fiddle bands and striking out in station wagons to play dances across the Southwest, John Wills's piece had a name, "Faded Love." Year after year Bob taught it to his bands, and rarely a day went by that he didn't play the number himself. When Wills formed the Texas Playboys, the song became one of their standards. But just like Bob's other great song, "San Antonio Rose," it lived without lyrics. For decades "Faded Love" remained what it been when John had first composed it, a simple little fiddle tune.

In late 1950 MGM was seeking music for the Playboys' next single. The label, like Columbia before it, was beginning to lose faith in Wills's brand of music. With his large band and dance music, Bob seemed old and outdated. Solo acts were now ruling the charts, and most of that year's hot artists were a good deal younger than Wills. The days of swing seemed numbered, and MGM doubted that Bob could or would change the Playboy sound to conform with country music's new direction.

Wills too could see that his place in country music was shaky. Other swing acts were either fading from the national spotlight or trying to change their sound. The kids who had once come to dance to his Playboys were now sending their own children out to see Hank Williams and Eddy Arnold. The band leader knew that changing times often meant the changing of the guard, and yet he felt that there was still a bit of magic left in his swing music.

Sitting down with his brother Billy Jack, Bob began to jot down words to fit his father's old tune. In short order the two siblings had given a new look to the family anthem. With Rusty McDonald supplying the lead vocal and the Playboy trio hitting background harmonies, Wills returned to the MGM studios. He had a much smaller band than when he had cut "San Antonio Rose," but the sound that had earned Bob the title "King of Western Swing" was still there. So maybe, he thought, they did have a chance at scoring another winner.

In retrospect it is hard to realize that "Faded

Love" would not immediately become the nation's best-loved fiddle ballad. In late 1950 Bob helplessly watched as his father's old tune struggled up the country charts, peaking at the eighth spot. In an era when Hank Snow's "I'm Moving On" stayed on the top playlists for over a year, the Playboys' "Faded Love" only managed five weeks. Almost before radio stations quit playing the song, MGM dropped the act. It would be ten years before Bob Wills again hit the charts.

For all practical purposes "Faded Love" should have been forgotten, yet it wasn't. The combination of the song's beautiful old melody and new heart-breaking words wouldn't let it die. It began to gain fresh life almost as soon as it fell from the playlists. Within months "Faded Love" was appearing not only in country albums, but in big-band and solo pop releases too. "Faded Love" remained alive via LPs and concert sets for over a decade. Then the song really began to bloom.

Patsy Cline had just come off her best year, and was expecting even more great things in 1963. Cline was about to go back into the studio to try to follow up her biggest hit, "She's Got You," when she heard folk/rocker Jackie DeShannon singing "Faded Love" on a car radio. As she listened, the country star got caught up in the old song's potential. She was determined to convince her producer, Owen Bradley, to let her cut it. In what was to be her last recording session, Patsy laid down a dozen songs. The first thing she completed was the Wills swing standard, only she did it in her own torchy style.

A month and a day after she cut "Faded Love," Patsy Cline died in a plane crash. Six months later Decca would release her version of Bob's classic. In country the song climbed to the seventh position, and then crossed over to make some noise on the pop charts. Bob himself would call Cline's cut of

"Faded Love" his own favorite. It would certainly be one of the most remembered.

That same year, Leon McAuliffe, one of Bob's original Playboys, cut a swing version of "Faded Love." Leon rode the charts for eleven weeks. As good as McAuliffe's rendition was, the next "Faded Love" single was probably the best.

Tompall Glaser and his brothers had grown up listening to Bob Wills. As a part of the country outlaw movement, they often toured with Willie Nelson and Waylon Jennings. Yet far from separating themselves from country music's old sounds, the Glasers often embraced them. With their easy harmonies and smooth instrumentation, they re-created old classics as well as anyone in Music City. More than most, the brothers seem to realize that the power of a good song never died.

In 1971 the Glasers cut "Faded Love" in a fashion that seemed to really capture the sound of John Wills's lonesome fiddle singing out across the Panhandle night. Then, adding just one instrument at a time, the Glasers built the song into a performance masterpiece. Perhaps not even John Wills himself could have done it as well. The Glaser Brothers' Wills tribute became a huge favorite in Texas, and moved up nationally to a respectable #22.

As the years have gone by, "Faded Love's" hit power has actually gotten stronger. In 1980 Willie Nelson and Ray Price teamed and took the Wills fiddle number to #3. For more than three months this single stayed firmly entrenched in the charts. These two Texans could thus lay claim to having the biggest hit of John and Bob's old song.

There are some standards whose classic status can never be fully explained. These songs are so great and their sound so peerless that they give off a special aura. Such is the case with "Faded Love." Bob Wills had a host of songs which were "bigger" hits than his father's fiddle tune, but he never produced another which so captured the beauty of Texas swing music. Yet time has proven that "Faded Love" is more than just a swing tune. It is more than a fiddle standard. "Faded Love" is a song which can reach out and touch listeners in any style and in any era. Maybe it *can* even cause the stars to cry.

1950

I'm Movin' On

Written by Hank Snow

He was given the name Clarence when he was born in a small Nova Scotia town in 1914. By the age eight the Liverpool, Canada, boy had witnessed his parents' divorce and watched as two of his sisters were shipped off to an orphanage. Meanwhile, Clarence was sent to live with his grandparents. There he would endure three long years of physical and emotional abuse. What kept him going was a mail-order guitar and some old Vernon Dalhart records his mother had given him before she left. When things were at their worst, the boy escaped into his music.

When he was eleven, Clarence's mother remarried and brought the boy back into her home. Rather than rescuing the child, the woman almost signed his death warrant. Her new husband beat the boy daily. If young Clarence Snow had stayed in this nightmarish existence, he might have been killed. At the age of twelve he picked up his guitar, said good-bye to his mother, and left to become a cabin boy at sea. Four years later, bigger, stronger, and more able to defend himself, he returned home. His mother, overjoyed to have her son back, couldn't wait to share something special with the boy. Grabbing a new Victor disc, she put it on her record player. The boy was entranced as he heard Jimmie Rodgers for the first time. At that very moment he decided to escape the pain of his miserable life by becoming an entertainer.

He worked a long series of hard jobs before landing his first radio gig. Just twenty-one years old, he starred on a Halifax station with a show called *Clarence Snow and His Guitar.* The seemingly insignificant local program led to an audition with RCA Canada. He cut two records for the label under the name of "Hank, the Yodeling Ranger." The sides definitely showed just how much the young Canadian idolized Jimmie Rodgers. He sang in the "Blue Yodeler's" style. The releases also spelled an end to Clarence. Snow was now to be known as Hank.

Over the course of the next decade Snow cut a few more songs and crisscrossed his native land time and time again. He also made some U.S. appearances, and twice tried to break into the movie business in Hollywood. Discouraged and broke, he called on friends in Dallas, Texas. In the middle of the Lone Star State Hank Snow was about to get his first real break.

Fred Edwards was a DJ on KRLD, one of the Southwest's most influential country music radio stations. Edwards was impressed with Snow, and with the jock's pushing, Hank got a spot on a local radio show and began to sell some records. By the end of 1949 the Canadian had a strong Texas following and a local #1 song. Then Snow met Ernest Tubb. Ernest gave the powerful baritone his next break, a regular slot on the *Grand Ole Opry.* Unfortunately, Hank bombed. The only reason he was invited back was because the powerful Tubb put pressure on management to do so.

What Snow really needed to mesh with the *Opry* crowd was a hit record. To the crowd this "foreigner" was simply an unknown commodity. Based on his Texas success, RCA's U.S. division decided to put their weight behind the "Singing Ranger." They set up a session that could provide some quality material for Snow. Then, going into the studio, Hank suggested that they cut and release one of his own compositions, "I'm Movin' On."

The singer figured that his chances of recording the song he had written five years before were slim. Hank had earlier tried to get the label interested in "I'm Movin' On," and they had turned him down flat. Now, with Hank's *Opry* status hanging in the balance, he had offered it to them again. He figured that again they would reject it, but if they did, he was going to point out the strong response he had gotten to it in his shows. Ultimately he didn't have to put up a fight. RCA bowed to Snow's wishes and let him record his composition.

Probably no one understood "I'm Movin' On's" message any more than Hank. For almost three decades he had been on the move, running from a past that was too painful to think about and trying to find a future where he would be loved and accepted on his own merit. This train song thus spoke volumes about Snow's gypsy-like lifestyle. After all, it seemed that Hank had spent his entire life moving on. Yet the song reflected a bit more too.

"I'm Movin' On's" message and music were an updated tribute to the styles of both Vernon Dalhart and Jimmie Rodgers. Snow had used the two music pioneers' themes and concepts, then built a story that

was so energetic and catchy that people seemed to immediately respond to it. In spite of the fact that the song's message was all about an unfaithful love, it somehow made people feel good. Finally, and maybe most importantly, not only did it show off Hank's mellow voice, but "I'm Movin' On" was also easy to sing. After only hearing it once, crowds left shows humming it.

"I'm Movin' On" was Snow's second American release. His first, "Marriage Vow," had lasted but a single week on the *Billboard* chart. RCA hoped for a lot more than a week when they shipped "I'm Movin' On" to stations in late June. The label got more too! By July 1, 1950, the single had made the charts. On August 19 Snow's first national hit became #1. It would stay at the top for an amazing twenty-one weeks, and hold a place on the charts for forty-four weeks. It still ranks as the most popular country music chart song of all time. "I'm Movin' On" also crossed over onto the pop charts. The song would ring out at #27 in mid-summer.

Hank Snow used a self-penned train song to cement a solid place with both the *Opry* and his fans. Using this as a base he would go on to score more than eighty chart singles and reach the Hall of Fame. More than fifty artists, including Don Gibson and Emmylou Harris, who would both reach the country charts, and Elvis Presley, would eventually record "I'm Movin' On." It stands as not only one of the best traveling songs ever written, but as the all-time king of the country charts. Ironically, to Snow the success of "I'm Movin' On" meant that he finally got the chance to settle down and quit running. In Nashville he had found acceptance, love, and a place to call home.

If You've Got the Money, I've Got the Time

Written by Lefty Frizzell and Jim Beck

William Orville Frizzell was born to a family that chased rainbows. Frizzell's father was an oil well driller and his pot at the rainbow's end didn't contain coins or nuggets. It was filled with black gold. So while William may have been born in Corsicana, Texas, as a child he saw a lot of both his native Texas and neighboring Oklahoma. By the time he hit his teens he was both an amateur fighter and a seasoned singer. His quick left hook earned him the nickname of "Lefty," and his nasal tenor voice earned him a strong reputation as a local radio star.

Before his twentieth birthday Lefty had formed a band and worked most of the central Texas honky-tonks. From Waco to Dallas his fiddle-and-steel-driven music served as background for barroom fights and late-night two-stepping. A fan of old-timers like Jimmie Rodgers as well as new folks like Hank Thompson, Frizzell was tough, confident, and a bit of a loner. And even though he liked the music of a number of different country music acts, he was so intent on being himself he copied no one.

Through the smoke and noise, Dallas radio personality Jim Beck saw something in the young club singer. Jim thought that Lefty was so well seasoned that even at twenty he was ready to make a move to the big time. He encouraged the young man to write songs and set his sights on a career in the business. He didn't have to push Frizzell too much.

Lefty also thought he was ready to make the trip to Nashville.

In 1950 the singer brought Beck a song on which he had been working. The radio man was impressed. With a little bit of Jim's help that composition would earn Lefty a contract with Columbia Records. At the young age of twenty-two, Frizzell was about to step out of the local dives and onto the nation's brightest stages. He was going to perform with the likes of Hank Williams. And the Corsicana native was going to make all of this happen by recording one of his biggest records the first time out of the chute.

The inspiration that would take Lefty to the big time was the song he had taken to Jim Beck. The idea behind that composition had come when the singer and his band were working a West Texas nightclub. On that night, an old friend had driven down from Oklahoma to catch Frizzell work. After the show the Okie had tried to convince the performer that it was too early to call it a night. After some gentle prodding, the man had inquired, "Lefty, do you want to go or not?"

Smiling, Frizzell had answered, "Well, if you've got the money, I got the time!" Before the words had fully cleared his mouth, Lefty had realized that he had just created the perfect hook line for a honky-tonk song. The idea was so good that it wouldn't leave him alone. Over the course of the next few weeks the singer crafted a story around that hook. Jim Beck finished what little polishing there was left to be done on "If You've Got the Money, I've Got the Time," and then took it and Lefty to Columbia.

Lefty's style went well with his new song. His voice naturally blended or slurred words together, and he loved to extend single syllables for an extra beat or two. When he sang the word "time," it seemed to joyfully drag on forever. The same was true of almost any word that possessed a long vowel sound. Everyone who knew Lefty well realized that he was a real character—a one-of-a-kind original—and his voice seemed to reflect his wit, his style, and his confident stance. No wonder Jim Beck had been so impressed and Columbia had signed him so quickly.

"If You've Got the Money, I've Got the Time" jumped on to the country charts just before Halloween. The release's early success must have made a lot of Music City veterans think that this young man was going to *trick* them out of a piece of their action, but from the first time they heard him, the fans knew that Lefty was a *treat*. "If You've Got the Money" climbed into the big money just before Christmas, and held the #1 position for three weeks. Hank Snow's "Golden Rocket" knocked Frizzell out of the top spot for a couple of weeks, only to have the Texan again hit #1 in January with the flip side of "Money," "I Love You a Thousand Ways." All told, the double-sided hit stayed on the charts for thirty-two weeks.

Of all of the stars who have been overlooked by the Hall of Fame, Lefty is one who raises the most questions. Few new performers produced a style which influenced so many up-and-coming singers as Frizzell. His chart reign probably could have won him baskets full of awards and accolades, but the independent streak that gave him such a unique sound and style also placed him on the outside of Nashville's in-crowd. He refused to play political games to fit in, and

seemed to resent the Music City powers who had the greatest ability to do things for him. In fact he often seemed to take real pleasure in making the establishment mad.

For a while Frizzell went against the grain and didn't join the *Opry*. He bluntly stated that he didn't need the old radio show, saying his records were selling just fine without it. Finally, when he did give in and join, the marriage was short. Lefty quickly found differences with management and quit. He eventually became so at odds with the Nashville establishment, he took his show to the West Coast and worked on television. This move seemed to kill both his chart success and his ability to find play on national radio. By 1955, just five short years after his career had jump-started with such a rush, the singer was dead in the water. After recording some of the era's biggest songs, he had lost his following. Lefty would have just one more #1, "Saginaw, Michigan," in 1964. After a string of chart-topping records, and after having achieved superstar status alongside Hank Williams, Hank Snow, and Hank Thompson, he was a has-been.

Twenty years later Lefty had made peace with old enemies and was again living in Nashville. He was starting to write strong material and people were talking about a comeback. The timing seemed perfect. The outlaw movement was just around the corner, and many of the men who would start that Texas-based music style owed a great deal to Frizzell's influence. As if anticipating this sound, ABC had signed Lefty to a new recording contract. It pleased the singer a great deal to realize that for the first time in over a decade a record label was genuinely excited to be working with him. Yet it all came too late. Lefty Frizzell ran out of time on July 19, 1975. At the age of forty-seven, a massive stroke killed him.

A year later Willie Nelson released a new version of

Lefty's first single. Willie's "If You've Got the Money, I've Got the Time" earned him his second number-one record, and stayed on the charts for fifteen weeks in the late summer and early fall of 1976. Nelson would then cut an entire tribute album called "To Lefty from Willie." It started a movement where almost every major entertainer began to talk about just how much Lefty's music had meant to them. It was a shame that Frizzell wasn't around to hear all the praise.

In the fifties honky-tonk music exploded out of Texas and took the nation by storm. This music was the product of singers who had been raised on country's first generation of stars. Yet these new performers were much different from their idols. Many of them had a rebellious streak. They had come to Nashville after working their way up through the dance halls and barrooms and they were tough and proud. They gave no quarter and asked for no special treatment. The best of these first honky-tonk pioneers was Lefty Frizzell. Without his blazing of the trail, Waylon, Willie, and the boys might have never had the money or the time.

1951
Cold Cold Heart

Written by Hank Williams

The inspiration for the song which would really open Hank Williams's music to the whole world was born in a hospital. Hank's wife Audrey had been fighting illness for some time when she took a turn for the worse. Ultimately Mrs. Williams was confined to a hospital bed for several days. Lonely, as well as remorseful for some of the harsh words he and his wife had exchanged, the singer decided to make a peace offering. Without first consulting Audrey, Hank went shopping and bought her a mink coat. Williams then gathered up the children and happily headed down to the hospital. He felt sure that his expensive gift would tear down the wall that had come between the couple. After all, logic told him, what woman could refuse a mink?

It was immediately obvious that Audrey was happy to see the kids, but she didn't even acknowledge Hank as he walked into the room. Even after he had presented her with her first mink coat, she continued to ignore him. During the entire visit, Mrs. Williams never spoke to Mr. Williams, nor did she act as if she'd heard his apologies. She treated him as if he were not even there, and his expensive gift seemed to go completely unappreciated. He soon left the room defeated and dejected.

As Hank rode home that day, he was filled with both anger and pain. He simply couldn't find a way to get the woman he loved to trust him. He knew that a lot of what was wrong had been his fault. He realized that his drinking was driving a deep wedge between them, but he thought he had made it clear that he loved her even more than he loved his vices. In his mind he was willing to give up whatever it was that was keeping them apart, but to the singer it didn't seem that his wife was willing to give an inch. She didn't seem to have any faith in him, nor did she seem to want to do anything which would end their feud.

The family housekeeper, Audrey Ragland, had come with Hank and the children to visit Mrs. Williams. The singer rarely drove, and on this trip Miss Ragland acted not only as the children's nanny but as the driver too. While she was driving through Nashville, she silently observed the brooding man to her right. After several minutes Miss Ragland finally asked Williams how he thought Mrs. Williams was doing.

Looking over to her, his eyes sad and mournful, Hank replied, "She's got the coldest heart I've ever seen." Then he turned his head back to watch the road, and seemed completely lost in thought. He said little more for the remainder of the trip.

That night, long after everyone else had gone to bed, Williams took a piece of paper and pen and jotted down some of his random thoughts. As was often the case, his words quickly fell together into a song.

Each of the new song's lines was drawn from the most important relationship Hank had ever known. He must have realized as he wrote "Cold Cold Heart" that he had no chance of ever melting Audrey's anger or healing her heartache. Nevertheless, this expression of his desire to do so would become his personal favorite of the more than one hundred songs he wrote.

Williams cut and released "Cold Cold Heart" in 1951. The song entered the charts in March and made a slow climb up to the top spot. It reached #1 on May 12. While he had a host of other singles which stayed on top longer, he never had a release which endured so long on the charts. "Cold Cold Heart" lingered on radio station playlists for forty-six weeks. It also caught the eye of an up-and-coming pop singer.

Tony Bennett had noted with great interest Hank's latest appearance on the pop charts. The smooth singer fell in love with the country star's new song. Bennett felt that "Cold Cold Heart" could easily be transformed into a classic piece for his own style. Tony quickly cut "Cold Cold Heart," and watched as the Williams-penned tune not only hit #1 on the pop charts, but held steady there for six weeks. Many critics credit this single with fully establishing Bennett as a star. "Cold Cold Heart" certainly had a huge impact on the man's career, and today it remains one of Tony's biggest all-time hits. Joining the parade, a host of other pop acts cut their own versions of the country song in 1951. Four of these artists landed their cuts on the pop charts.

For years country performers left Williams's original material alone. While many of the day's best-selling songs were recorded by several different acts in direct response to chart movement by another act using the same song (see "Slipping Around"), most artists felt that Hank nailed his songs so well that no one else could cut another version that would be accepted. Jerry Lee Lewis was one of the first to not be intimidated by the Williams mystique. Jerry Lee had already scored a big hit with a wonderful rockabilly version of "You Win Again" in 1957, so it was with great joy and anticipation that the singer cut "Cold Cold Heart." Lewis saw this 1961 Sun release jump to #22. It would be his last hit for the famous Memphis record label.

Since his death, Hank's "Cold Cold Heart" has remained one of country music's most beloved songs. A multitude of people have learned its words and felt its message. Countless fans have come to know Hank Williams because of this classic. Other of Hank's songs might have sold better upon initial release, but "Cold Cold Heart" remains one of just a handful of true Williams classics. This is the song which reveals not only what Hank most wanted, but how helpless he was in trying to obtain it. In "Cold Cold Heart" one finds the essence of Hank Williams displayed for all the world to see. Here is where he cries out for a love he just couldn't seem to have.

1952
High Noon
(Do Not Forsake Me, Oh, My Darlin')

Written by Ned Washington and Dimitri Tiomkin

Dimitri Tiomkin was born in the country just outside St. Petersburg, Russia, in 1899. A natural music talent, he graduated from the prestigious St. Petersburg Conservatory of Music, then earned a degree from St. Petersburg University. He continued his education by obtaining a law degree from St. Mary's. Gifted in several different fields, Dimitri was conducting some of the finest orchestras in Europe before his twentieth birthday. More than just talented, the young composer was innovative too. On one of his earliest concert tours of the continent, Tiomkin departed from classical offerings and introduced the music of George Gershwin to sophisticates who normally turned up their noses at anything American. Caught up in the excitement of this new music, Dimitri became fascinated with the creative flair he saw in the work of U.S. jazz composers. The Russian left his home for the United States in 1925 to experience jazz firsthand. By the early thirties he had found his way to Hollywood. The film community quickly noted Tiomkin's talents, and by 1931 he had established himself as one of the industry's greatest composers.

While working on such epics as *Alice in Wonderland, Lost Horizon, The Great Waltz, Mr. Smith Goes to Washington,* and *It's a Wonderful Life,* Tiomkin became fascinated with American folk songs. He partic-

ularly loved the music of the West. Over time Dimitri found that he enjoyed few things as much as scoring westerns. His passion showed in his work, as few composers captured the genre's atmosphere as well.

Just six years after Tiomkin was born in Russia, Woodward Ritter was delivered to a poor farm family in Murvaul, Texas. An outstanding student, Woodward would also advance quickly through the academic ranks. He first earned a degree from the University of Texas, and then began law school. Before he could finish his studies, he was bitten by the acting bug.

By 1928 Woodward was singing in the chorus of an Austin production of *Maryland, My Maryland.* He followed the show to New York and acted in various roles there, before drifting to Chicago in 1930. It was in the Windy City where Ritter would get his first big break. Woodward won a secondary lead in *Green Grow the Lilacs.* During the course of the play he sang "Git Along, Little Dogies"; "The Old Chisholm Trail"; "Good-Bye, Old Paint"; and "Bury Me Not on the Lone Prairie." With his deep voice and Texas accent he seemed made to order for the part.

His outstanding reviews won him a return ticket to New York, where Ritter worked both Broadway and radio. Art Satherley of Decca Records caught one of his western radio shows and signed the young star to a recording contract. Ritter's initial release, "Rye Whiskey," became a hit in many areas of the South and West. A series of singles followed, and by 1936 Woodward, now known as Tex, had been brought to Hollywood to appear in "oaters" for Grand National Pictures. Over the course of the next ten years Ritter would star in more than sixty "B" westerns, and a number of his movie songs would become minor hits for Capitol Records.

Country songs and "B" pictures went together hand in hand for almost twenty years, yet for the most part, first-run releases stayed away from rural songs and singers. If a "folk" tune was inserted into a major motion picture, a pop star was generally employed to perform it. Country acts were good box office at matinees, but the motion-picture moguls knew that the hicks simply couldn't cut it for the nighttime shows.

Dimitri Tiomkin thought this bias against country songs and singers in top pictures was blasphemy. If a classically trained Russian composer could like hillbilly strains, he thought that the American public would too. So when Dimitri was contacted in 1952 about supplying the score for Gary Cooper's newest picture, he hatched a plan. First Tiomkin used the film's script—the story of a man who must take on a slew of bad guys on his wedding day—as the basis for the movie's theme. He then turned the song on end by making this big tough hero seem to actually beg for his girl not to leave him. The melody he had composed was lonely, drifting, and filled with an ominous sadness not usually found in pop music. There was a hint of jazz influence in this work, but by and large it was country and western in both sound and style.

Dimitri felt that there was only one man who could do justice to his "Do Not Forsake Me, Oh, My Darlin'." The composer called Tex and set up a face-to-face meeting just so Ritter could hear the theme from *High Noon*. Tex listened and was intrigued. Still, he couldn't imagine someone wanting him to sing in an "A" picture, especially a movie starring the likes of Gary Cooper and Grace Kelly. When Tiomkin explained that Ritter's sincere deep voice was the only one the composer felt could do the song justice, the singer agreed to join the project.

High Noon broke box office records, and would become the most honored western movie of the period. The picture would elevate Cooper to superstar status, make a movie queen of Kelly, and win an Oscar for Ritter and Tiomkin. Tex would even get to perform "High Noon (Do Not Forsake Me, Oh, My Darlin')" on the first Academy Awards show ever shown live on television.

In retrospect it seems strange that "High Noon" didn't make an appearance on the country charts. Nevertheless the movie theme did stir up interest on the pop side. Ritter's version went to #12, and camped on the playlist for eight weeks. Frankie Laine then covered the song and took "Do Not Forsake Me" to #8. Laine kept his version on the charts for nineteen weeks. While Frankie had the bigger hit, it was Tex's version which really captured the story and made history. It was his voice which remained deeply etched into the minds of the millions who bought tickets for the movie.

Over the course of the next few years country music began to be used not only for the themes to movies, but to a host of television dramas too. *High Noon* seemed to begin a Hollywood trend of employing the likes of Marty Robbins, Johnny Cash, and a number of other hillbilly stars to sing western movie themes. Several of the television oaters' theme songs developed into hits on the music charts.

Four decades after the fact, it is hard to imagine Hollywood not always using the talents and resources found in Nashville and other rural music centers. Since *High Noon,* scores of top films have relied on country music not only for their themes, but also for the complete background score. Some of these, like *Bonnie and Clyde* and *Urban Cowboy,* began national country music movements. There is now a bridge between Music City and Hollywood, and the flow of talent goes both ways. Yet without the teaming of a Russian-born composer who came to love American country music and a former Broadway actor who just couldn't get away from his Texas drawl, who knows how long it would have taken to build that bridge. Dimitri and Tex brought country off the movie "B" list and into the spotlight.

1953
Your Cheatin' Heart

Written by Hank Williams

During the summer of 1952, less than six months before his death, Hank Williams was traveling by car with his fiancée Billie Jean Eshlimar to Louisiana to visit her family and inform them of the couple's engagement. As he drove through the wilted countryside and felt the rush of hot air blow through the convertible, he switched off the radio and began to talk about his ex-wife, Audrey. For some time country music's master songwriter rambled, telling the new woman in his life all about the "wicked" ways of his last woman. It became quickly obvious that Audrey had hurt him more than even this master phrase-turner could express. The more he spoke, the more painful episodes he remembered, the more bitter and somber he became. In an effort to sum up all of his frustrations he finally sighed and said, "Her cheatin' heart will pay!"

That last phrase seemed to hang in the air for a few moments until Hank repeated it. "That would make a good song!" He then asked Billie Jean to find a piece of paper and a pen. When she had secured both, he began to feed her the words to the song which would become most associated with his monumental career. Billie Jean later recalled that "Your Cheatin' Heart" was completed in less than ten minutes. By the time she had put her tablet away, she and Hank both knew that it was going to be a hit.

At this point in his life Hank Williams was begin-

ning to find a great deal of recognition beyond the often-confining borders of country music. His songs were being recorded by everyone from orchestras to the top pop singers of the day. He was being hailed as the "Stephen Foster of the twentieth century." He was no longer just a country bumpkin. He was a certified genius. Perhaps this is the reason why his manic mood swings, his alcohol and drug abuse, and his erratic stage performances were so easily overlooked and often dismissed. He was Hank Williams, he was one of a kind, his talent was as rare as gold, and he was to be forgiven every sin. Most assumed that his behavior was just the price that had to be paid for his unique and explosive talent.

In the fall of 1952, Hank and his band got together with Fred Rose in the studio for what they thought would be just another recording session. None of them realized that it would be the last time the legend's voice would be captured in a professionally produced manner. To everyone in attendance this was just another opportunity to put on tape some of Hank's newest creations. It was another chance for all of them to make some money. Yet if those gathered had taken a deeper look into the singer's face, surely they would have seen the signs of a young man dying of old age. Even if they failed to notice, others had. At twenty-nine Hank was used up, worn out, and despondent. His skin tone was pale, his face wrinkled, his manner slow, his gait a bit unsteady. He had dark foreboding circles that lined his eyes and seemed to reflect a world full of black nights and dark days.

It was during this period that he would always finish a show singing his own gospel classic, "I Saw the Light." Smiling, he would wave to the crowd and rush to a car to take another hit from a bottle of booze. One evening, as he repeated this routine for the countless time, he turned to another star, Minnie Pearl, and sadly shook his head. As the city lights created strange shadows on the tired man's face, he moaned, "That's the problem, Minnie, there just ain't no light."

The little light that was left in Hank Williams's life was now documented through his recordings. Here was where the barely literate farm boy became the eloquent scribe. Here was where he stepped out of the gutter and walked soberly with the giants of music and poetry. Here was the one place where he momentarily seized immortality. And it was with a mournful wail that he gave his tortured words flight. Here was where he so eloquently shared with the world his pain and anguish. And just maybe it was because those simple words were so masterfully crafted that no one seemed to see a frightened and horribly lonely man reaching out for help.

"Your Cheatin' Heart" would be released six weeks after Hank's abused body gave up. It would stay on the country music charts for twenty-three weeks and rest at #1 for six. On the pop side Hank would top out at #25. Joni James would cover "Your Cheatin' Heart" and ride it up the popular charts to #2, while Frankie Laine, a man who constantly covered country classics, would jump his version to #18. Since that time hundreds of artists from all genres of music have scored

with the song. Ray Charles nailed it on the pop and black charts in 1962, while Elvis, Jerry Lee Lewis, and scores of other rockabilly acts cut their own versions. Today it has even become the fodder for symphonies and "elevator" music. Yet while hundreds have rerecorded "Your Cheatin' Heart," maybe the biggest testament to just how well Hank sang on that 1952 fall day is that no one has ever again charted with the song on the country side. In country music "Your Cheatin' Heart" belongs only to him.

"Your Cheatin' Heart" became so associated with Hank Williams after his death that even the largely fictionalized George Hamilton movie biography about the singer/songwriter's career was given the song's title. And while this act of Hollywood may have helped immortalize "Your Cheatin' Heart," it also probably cheapened it. The movie failed to even scratch the surface of the entertainer's talent and pain, failed to really note what drove the singer to his early grave. Without a knowledge of Hank's anguish, the full impact of "Your Cheatin' Heart's" lyrics can never be appreciated.

More than forty years after it was written, "Your Cheatin' Heart" is a standard for every up-and-coming male and female country singer. It would be hard to find an American of any race or background who didn't at least know a few of the song's words. Millions can sing every line. In its simple lyrics and tune is the essence of what every songwriter wants to create, but the price of this genius was simply too high. In his creative darkness, Hank Williams could see and poetically describe the most mystical of human emotions, but he could never push away that deepest of nights and find the light. As it turned out, it was Hank's heart, not Audrey's, that really paid.

1953

There Stands the Glass

Written by Audrey Grisham, Mary Jean Schurz, and Russ Hall

A song about drinking to forget a love affair gone wrong may not sound scandalous today. As a matter of fact, it seems like country music has always had a host of drinking songs blaring off barroom jukeboxes and radio stations. In the late fifties and early sixties booze seemed to be one of the primary subjects of many honky-tonk performers. Yet it wasn't always that way. Up until 1953 few songs even mentioned an alcoholic beverage. Hank Williams in "Hey, Good Lookin' " took his "two-dollar bill and hot-rod Ford," and drank free "soda pop." In the days between World War II and the end of the Korean conflict, most radio stations didn't even allow "drinking" songs on a playlist. Just as cheating in marriage had been a decade earlier, booze was a subject a writer didn't touch if that writer wanted to make any royalties from a single release.

So when Mary Jean Schurz began writing a song about drinking soothing the pain of lost love, it wasn't surprising that she didn't complete it. No matter how good the idea behind the tune was, Mary Jean knew that there wasn't much of a market for the final product. Schurz's concept might have remained hidden away forever if not for a Louisiana singer who had first made his mark on the national charts in 1952.

Webb Pierce was a former salesman for Sears Roebuck who moonlighted from time to time singing country music. While he had a great ear for picking

out good music, many of those who listened to his whining tenor voice wondered if he really had any business continuing to dabble in his hobby. It seemed that he often hit just below a note and then slowly eased his way up to it. For music purists this technique was painful, yet the honky-tonk crowds who turned out at the places Webb played couldn't care less. They like the dancing songs Pierce chose, and they liked the man who sang those songs. They even liked the way he almost hit notes.

With that in mind, it was probably more Webb's personality than his talent which caught the eyes of the *Louisiana Hayride* talent scouts. In view of Pierce's quick smile and firm handshake, the radio concert show scouts thought they had found a man who represented their region well. Little did they guess that this salesman would quickly become one of their favorite showmen.

Decca, like all the major record labels, regularly sent their producers to the *Hayride* to check out the regulars and guests. One Saturday night, on a bill that included Faron Young and Floyd Cramer, the record company spotted Webb. In Pierce the label felt that it had found a man who was just right for the evolving country market.

Thanks to the success of Lefty Frizzell, the honky-tonk movement had grown into a craze. Smoky barroom music was now the hottest thing on the radio, and labels needed men who could sing those songs. Pierce seemed to have Frizzell's sliding vocal style, with an outgoing personality that Lefty couldn't claim. On those qualities alone, Decca took a chance that Webb was their lead man for the new honky-tonk sound.

Right out of the box as a recording artist, Pierce scored with "Wondering," "That Heart Belongs to Me," and "Back Street Affair." All three cuts went to the top of the charts and made Webb the top new talent in Nashville. In his first eighteen months as a recording star, the former Sears salesman hit the top ten nine straight times and claimed four #1 singles. The thirty-year-old singer felt he could continue to score as long as he found top-notch material. At a meeting with Mary Jean Schurz he discovered what he believed was the best subject a honky-tonk singer could ever want to embrace.

Webb had immediately like Schurz's unfinished ode to pain and booze. Taking it home, he and his wife worked over the lyrics. Then they turned the song over to Russ Hall for a finishing touch. Between Mary Jane and the trio of contributors who followed, "There Stands the Glass" was finally completed. Pierce knew it was a winner, but he didn't know what to do with it. If he recorded it, it might be banned and create enough bad publicity to kill his career. But the song was too good to simply file away.

Over the course of the next few weeks, Webb studied his fans. With his background in sales he knew that in order to ring up the numbers, you had to know your audience and give them a product with which they could identify. What the singer quickly discovered was that at least seventy-five percent of the folks who bought his music drank. He figured that most of these people wouldn't be put off in the least by a song that talked about getting drunk.

In spite of Webb's assurances to the contrary, many

at Decca were still uneasy about the potential of "There Stands the Glass." They argued that country radio simply wouldn't play the song. The moral restrictions that many of the disc jockeys followed when putting together a playlist would knock "There Stands the Glass" out before it even had a chance to be judged on its musical merits. While Webb admitted that several stations might ban the release, he felt that the fans would loudly demand that the record be played. After a while, the singer argued, enough radio stations would give in to the people's requests that it would carve out a niche on the airwaves. Pierce also knew that a song of this type would receive endless play on country music jukeboxes.

Still not completely convinced that they were doing the right thing, Decca released "There Stands the Glass" on October 24, 1953. Just as the label had warned, a number of radio stations immediately banned the single from their playlist. Yet just as the singer had assured his label, Pierce's fans began to flood radio stations with requests for it. The fans won the battle, and by Thanksgiving the single was riding atop almost every radio playlist in the country. "There Stands the Glass" hit #1 in late November, and held onto the top spot for twelve weeks. It also remained on the charts for a half a year, making it Webb's biggest hit up until that time.

Throughout the remainder of his colorful career Pierce's most requested song was his ode to drinking. Whenever he cut loose with his twanging tenor and belted out, "There stands the glass," crowds went wild. As he was to discover, not only had Webb broken down a country music taboo by recording "There Stands the Glass," he had also created the national anthem of barrooms. And just like "One Has My Name, the Other Has My Heart," "There Stands the Glass" opened the door for a long list of great songs which would embrace its theme.

1954
I Don't Hurt Anymore

Written by Don Robertson and Jack Rollins

Don Robertson was born half a world away from Music City. His father was a medical doctor and a university professor heading up the Department of Medicine at Peking Union Medical College. In 1927, when Don was five, the family left China for the States, settling first in Boston, then a year later in Chicago.

Don's early exposure to music consisted of listening to his father's classical record collection. When he was four his mother enrolled the boy in piano classes, and by the age of seven he was already composing his own original pieces. Young Robertson might have kept his focus on a classical bent if it had not been for a vacation that expanded both his vision and his interest. When Don was nine his family decided to summer in Birchwood Beach, Michigan. After settling in, the boy found that a neighboring girl, Helga, was about his age. Within days the two became inseparable.

After a short while Don began to watch and listen to Helga's father. The girl's dad was a gentle man who told fabulous stories and sang wonderful folk songs. Sitting at his feet, the boy began to gain an interest in the simple but fascinating music that seemed to be so important to the older man. As he observed this friendly neighbor, Don also began to realize that his friend's father was not only an extremely interesting person, but a very talented one too.

The Robertsons enjoyed that first vacation so much

that they would continue to summer in Birchwood Beach throughout their son's youth. And as those years quickly passed, Don began to spend more hours with Helga's father than he did with the young girl. The boy even began to understand that their neighbor was one of America's most renowned creative forces. By the time Don had left home for college, Helga's dad, Carl Sandburg, had left a deep impression on him.

Even though his piano talents had progressed to the point where he was making good money playing for dance bands, Don turned his back on music long enough to enter the University of Chicago pre-med program. He had his mind set on becoming a doctor. Yet after four years of study and hard work, he dropped out of college. There was music in the boy's soul, so he followed his heart rather than his mind and talked his way into a job as the musical arranger for radio station WGN. From there he toured the country with a live production show, before finally settling down in Los Angeles in 1945.

Initially he took a job as a demo pianist at Capitol Records. There he had a chance not only to show off his piano skills, but to also play some of his own classical and jazz compositions. When no one seemed interested in buying his pieces, he tried writing the kind of music he had heard at Carl Sandburg's feet. For eight years he made his living at the piano while continuing, with very little success, to try to interest someone in his folk songs. Stubbornly he refused to give up, and kept showing his songs to every publishing employee who came to the sessions in which he played. Finally, in 1953, Hill and Range Songs gave him a songwriting contract.

Within weeks Don had met some of the industry's most talented writers. He first worked with Hal Blair. Then he was handed over to Jack Rollins. Jack casually tossed Don some lyrics and asked him to go home and pen a tune to go with them.

The lyrics Don had taken home told a very personal story. Rollins had been badly hurt by a former lover and try as he could, he could not get over her. The song's words were the story of his own heartbreak, how he felt when he was living in daily pain, and the freedom he finally realized when he quit hurting. Coupling the words to a country folk score, Don took it back to Rollins. They both agreed that it had potential, so they turned a demo over to Hill and Range. While the writers went back to work developing a new product, the publisher shipped their song to Music City.

In Nashville, Hill and Range's song pluggers handed the demo over to Hank Snow. The "Singing Ranger" liked the way the song's melody fit his strong baritone voice. He also thought that Rollins's story line was perfect for the country music market. In a manner of weeks Snow was in the RCA studios cutting "I Don't Hurt Anymore."

Snow's single hit the charts in late May. By June 19, 1954, thanks to Hank's recording, Don Robertson had earned his first #1 melody. The song stayed on top for five months, and remained on the charts for forty-one weeks. Hank's hit was the year's biggest song, and would go on to become one of the biggest hits in country music history. Over the course of the next forty years "I Don't Hurt Anymore" would be recorded more than fifty times, charting in several different years and several different genres.

Hit songs were nothing new for Snow. They just gave him something else to feature on his show. In fact much of "I Don't Hurt Anymore's" success may have been lost on him altogether. Hank was trying to put together a partnership with Eddy Arnold's old manager in order to buy the contract of a new kid who had been opening for Snow on the road. The Canadian native wanted to help put the young talent's career on line. Thinking he had all the loose ends tied up, Snow headed back to Nashville to close the deal. Upon arriving home, he discovered that Colonel Tom Parker had beaten him to the punch by already securing the boy's signature on a contract. It's doubtful that Hank Snow ever quit hurting over the loss of Elvis Presley's management rights.

Meanwhile, Don Robertson would benefit greatly from Elvis's career move. Over the course of the next two decades, the future king of rock 'n' roll would choose to record a long list of the songwriter's compositions. Presley wasn't alone. Eddy Arnold, Connie Francis, Ray Price, and several hundred others made Don one of the industry's most recorded writers. Carl Sandburg would have been proud! After years of being rejected, Don Robertson certainly didn't hurt anymore.

1955
Making Believe

Written by Jimmy Work

When Jimmy Work was still in the small rural Kentucky Pilot High School he had already honed his songwriting skills to a point where he had a contract with Cole Publishing. Young Work was also sure that he wanted to make his living in the music business. No matter the obstacles, Jimmy was determined to end up in Nashville.

Usually dreams take a very long time to be realized, and Work's were no exception. In the forties there simply wasn't enough money in hillbilly music to make a solid living, so Jimmy had to move north and take a factory job in Detroit. He didn't leave the South without his guitar, and almost before he unpacked Jimmy began playing. Late into the night the young Tennessean sang at many of the night clubs where displaced Southerners came to drink away their homesickness and listen to *their* kind of music. Along with serving up entertainment at bars, Work worked a factory job and landed a gig singing on WCAR radio in Pontiac. His plate was full!

For a decade Work slaved night and day trying to pay the bills and get his music career off the ground. With each passing year it seemed that his chances grew slimmer and slimmer. Jimmy finally managed to be in the right place at the right time to be noticed by Dot Records. The company gave the young man a recording contract in hopes that he could turn some of his own compositions into hits. One of the first numbers they decided to try was a song that had taken Work less than a half hour to write.

"I had had a title running through my mind for some time," the songwriter recalled. "One day when I sat down and started playing with some words, it just fell together. In no time I had all the lyrics and the music to a song that I believed could be a hit."

Publisher Fred Rose took it to Dot producer Randy Wood, and Jimmy's confidence was buoyed as the label agreed that his latest creation might just earn the singer a spot on the national charts. As he continued to work the assembly line, Work couldn't help but wonder if this song might just be the ticket that could take him back home to Tennessee. He also considered the irony that he might just be fooling himself, setting himself up for a hard fall into a pit called reality.

With the cold north wind blowing and snow falling on Detroit's gray streets, Dot shipped "Making Believe" to radio stations and record outlets in January 1954. Within weeks it had made the charts, with Jimmy's voice eventually moving it up to the #5 position. With the song registering on all the major playlists for over three months, Work had realized a dream. But his shining moment was short-lived. "Making Believe" would be one of only two songs that Jimmy would ever place on the national charts as a singer.

Work's version of his own composition might have gone even higher and helped Jimmy establish a performing career had it not been for Kitty Wells. "The Honky-Tonk Angel" noted "Making Believe's" success and cut her own version. Decca rushed the Wells rendering of the song out a month after Work's. Country music's reigning queen put "Making Believe" at #2 on the charts for an incredible fifteen weeks. Only Webb Pierce's "In the Jailhouse Now," the year's biggest hit, blocked Wells's attempt to land her second #1 record.

That Work's composition had become a hit twice in the same year was not that surprising. During this period many songs were cut by both guy and gal singers with both versions charting. But what made this song stand apart was Work's special marriage of great lyrics to a perfect melody. "Making Believe" was a hauntingly beautiful song filled with great heartache and pain. Here was a common story of someone not quite ever realizing true love, and then having to exist in frustration in a fantasy world where hollow desires only seemed to play with the emotions. This song's passions were not wrapped in puppy love. The love revealed here was cold, hard, unrequited passion. The scars this love created would last a lifetime.

"Making Believe" was probably too grown up for the teenage market, and far too direct and honest to find a home in the sophisticated city circles of the pop world. But even though it wasn't geared for the pop market of the day, Work's masterpiece was a truly great country song.

Two decades after Kitty Wells and Jimmy Work first charted with "Making Believe," a country music newcomer made the song her fifth straight top ten hit. Emmylou Harris is now sometimes referred to as the "Keeper of the Flame." She has earned the title because she has used her clear rural-edged voice to celebrate the genre's real country sounds. Harris was doing hard country even when middle-of-the-road stars were controlling the charts. In spite of what seemed to be her adoration for the sounds of traditional hillbilly music, when Emmylou first hit country music, many feared and mistrusted her.

Before arriving on the country charts, Harris was known primarily as a folk singer. She often performed on the same bills with some of the better-known rock bands. In a period when country girl singers were wearing "big" hair and elaborate costumes, Emmylou had long straight hair and sang in either old blue jeans or peasant dresses. Even though she sounded like she should have been a member of the *Opry*, folks didn't quite know what to make of Harris.

Over time, with her soft, strong style, Emmylou won converts. She was modest, but always ready with a quick smile, and her angelic voice and a tremendous devotion to old-fashioned country music began to make a deep impression on the Music City establishment. Using primarily beloved standards, Emmylou built a foundation for her career on the Reprise label in 1975. She then appeared on Warner in early 1977, and hit the top ten with an old Chuck Berry rocker, "(You Never Can Tell) C'est La Vie." On her next trip to the recording studio she cut what was to become the definitive version of "Making Believe."

Harris made the standard into one of the era's most beautiful and haunting ballads. As she passionately threw herself into the song, it seemed as if Emmylou had really lived the story. In her unadulterated voice the listener could hear both pleading and hope, as well as sense the realization that this baring of the soul was all for naught. Using Herb Pedersen for harmonies, Emmylou's very simple but heartfelt approach to "Making Believe" revealed the composition as a country music classic and made this remake a top ten song.

"Making Believe" continues to be a favorite concert and album-cut choice for country music artists. At some point it will probably also be discovered in the pop field. With its ability to showcase a dynamic emotional voice, the song cries out for a song stylist like Whitney Houston. With that in mind it appears that the days of "Making Believe" are far from over. As a matter of fact, this classic's best days may be in the future.

1955
Satisfied Mind

Written by Red Hayes and Jack Rhodes

No one ever promised Porter Wagoner that life was going to be a walk in the park, and if he had been the type to be easily discouraged he would have given up long before he had reached adulthood. When Porter was just six, his father was crippled by arthritis and forced to quit working the family farm. A few years later, just as the boy turned ten, his older brother was diagnosed with a heart ailment and Porter was forced to go to work full time doing a man's job on the farm. He would never again spend a day in school.

Those around Porter marveled at him. In spite of the heavy responsibility laid on his shoulders, in the face of backbreaking work, and staring at the realization that his life offered little promise, the boy was outwardly happy and content. His easy smile seemed to proclaim, "I'm fine. Don't worry about me."

An eight-dollar guitar bought with money made selling rabbits started Porter's love affair with music and served as a substitute for the school he no longer attended. Trying to mimic radio singers, the young teenager began to develop the sincere rural style that would one day endear him to millions of fans. Surprisingly, at this time Porter was a painfully shy boy who wouldn't sing or play in front of strangers. More often than not his audience consisted of tall trees, lonesome valleys, and the critters of the Ozark backwoods.

In the midst of World War II a teenage Wagoner found himself working for Sid Vaughan. Vaughan owned a West Plains, Missouri, butcher shop, and had pledged to teach Porter a marketable trade. (In a way Sid would do just that, only the trade wouldn't be the vocation Vaughan had intended.) It was only by accident that Sid first heard the boy singing in the back of the shop. Impressed with the young man's voice, the butcher began to consider how he could use the Wagoner boy to build his meat trade. The answer seemed to be radio.

Within a few weeks of Wagoner's backroom concert, the West Plains radio station began to broadcast a live show from Sid's each day. By offering the poor boy a raise, Sid convinced Porter to overcome his shyness and sing the commercials. The young singer's "ads" soon became the show's most popular segments over time, and caught the attention of KWTO in Springfield. Wagoner's timing couldn't have been scripted any better. Within in a few months of Wagoner's move to his new $70-a-week singing job at KWTO, Red Foley began his weekly television series, *The Ozark Jubilee*, in Springfield. After catching Porter on the radio, Foley invited the young man to join the *Jubilee*.

Through the comments he received on the streets and at live shows, Porter immediately saw the power of TV. Saving $300, he contacted an up-and-coming costume designer and gave him all the cash for a custom-made colorful spangled western outfit. That was the first of the Nudie suits which became Wagoner's trademark. Those often ridiculous costumes focused so much attention on Porter that they helped to carve out an identity which set him apart from the *Ozark Jubilee's* other unknown singers, thereby allowing him to fully showcase his real talents.

In 1953 RCA noted Wagoner's potential and great stage presence and offered him a recording deal. Taking it, Porter soon found his way to Nashville. There he recorded *Company's Coming*. That song would begin a long successful career on the country music charts.

At about the same time Porter was climbing out of dire poverty into the rich life of a country music star, a well-traveled east Texas fiddle player was writing a song inspired by something his wife's father had once told him and by the life his mother had lived.

Red Hayes had spent most of his adult existence trying to make his mark in the music business. He had played in bands and written scores of songs, but none of the playing and writing had brought him fame and fortune.

It was during this period of struggling that Red's father-in-law asked the musician who he thought was the world's richest man. Hayes had considered the question for a short while, then beginning with Rockefeller, listed all the wealthy people he had heard of or read about. The elder man laughed at each answer before finally informing Red that he was going in the wrong direction. He then added, "The richest man in the world is the man with a satisfied mind."

Considering his father-in-law's observation, Hayes began to think back on the many things his Bible-reading mother had told him. She had spun her wisdom in common language and small doses, but what she had said had taken. The woman's moral character was deeply woven into Red's fiber. Early on he had re-alized—just as his mother had preached—that money didn't buy much happiness and that some of the happiest people had spent their lives giving what little they had to others. As Hayes looked back to the days of his youth, he began to understand that his mother's whole life had been a lesson in how to find happiness and joy in each hour of each day. Sitting down, Red began to jot down his mother's thoughts. Scraps from his memory of lessons long ago thus formed the formula for "Satisfied Mind." With a little help from Jack Rhodes, Hayes completed what could be called a testimony in song, then sold the piece to Starrite Publishing Company.

Porter Wagoner was one of the first to recognize the potential of Hayes's demo. Having grown up in the midst of the Great Depression around some of the country's poorest people, the singer appreciated the song's full scope. Though his mother and others he knew had been paupers, they had embraced life in a full and joyful manner. Even if they didn't have a dime in the bank, these people seemed to have a grip on the most important elements of living. As much as Wagoner enjoyed the money his newfound success was bringing to him, he also realized that the good paychecks were only letting him live better, not happier. In "Satisfied Mind" Wagoner had found a way to prove to the folks back home that his values hadn't changed when he moved up success's ladder.

On May 28, 1955, Porter's "Satisfied Mind" made its chart debut. This, Wagoner's second RCA release, would spend more than eight months on the hit list, eventually knocking Faron Young's "Live Fast, Love Hard, Die Young" out of the top spot. The thin man from Missouri would go on to control the #1 position for most of July and August. "Satisfied Mind" would become both Wagoner's breakthrough song and his all-time biggest seller. It would also establish the flashy dresser as a major force in Music City. Over time Porter would gain so much power that he would be able to dictate RCA record deals for others. The best-known star whose career he started and supervised was Dolly Parton.

Jean Shepard noted Porter's success with the Hayes composition and cut her own single for Capitol. A winner in its own right, Jean's version rode the charts for twenty-two weeks and climbed as high as #4. The man who had made Wagoner a star in the Ozarks, Red Foley, next cut the song, now as a duet with his wife Betty. At the very same time that Shepard's and Wagoner's songs were sitting in the elite best-seller ranks, Red landed at #3. Foley's single remained on the hit parade for over seven months.

Over the course of the next four decades "Satisfied Mind" made the country charts six times. It also crossed over and was recorded by a host of different pop stars. Mahalia Jackson, the world's greatest black gospel voice, cut the Hayes song and used it in her concerts. In 1969 "Satisfied Mind" even climbed into rock music's top forty.

The song's writer knew that the Sunday School lessons he had put into verse were doing well by the royalty checks that were delivered each year. Over time Red Hayes even came to realize that his song of praise for a mother's wisdom had done more than simply assure Porter Wagoner's recording career and make Red some money. Yet for years Hayes himself didn't feel the *real* power in his own song's message.

One night Hayes was walking by a Nashville church on his way to play the Opry. Through the sanctuary's open windows the writer heard the strains of a congregation singing "Satisfied Mind" as a hymn. Listening to the voices, he heard the song much differently than he had ever heard it before. Falling to his knees in the street, Hayes bowed his head and said a prayer of thanksgiving. He didn't thank the Lord for the royalty checks or the recognition. Rather he thanked Him for the woman who'd lived its lesson and inspired both the song and the song's writer. As Red got up and continued his walk, he felt great. If anyone at that moment had approached and asked Red Hayes to name the world's richest man, he would have eagerly answered, "I am. I am the man with the satisfied mind!"

1955
Sixteen Tons
Written by Merle Travis

One of the most creative forces in country music history was born in Rosewood, Kentucky, in 1917. Merle Robert Travis, the son of a poor banjo-playing mine worker, grew up in the middle of coal country. He lived most of his youth in a rent-house that had no running water or electricity. The Travises' landlords and best friends had been slaves until after the Civil War. Life was hard, times were tough, and the only joy the Travises could afford was the music they made on hand-me-down instruments.

By the time he had reached the age of eight, Merle was plucking a five-string banjo and a homemade guitar. After local Pentecostal meetings the boy would stay late just so Ike Everly (Don and Phil's father), one of the church's finest guitar pickers, could teach Merle new chords. Young Travis soon mastered the Everly style of thumb and finger picking and began to add to it. Long before he left school in the eighth grade, Merle was known as one of the area's best string men.

In a peculiar irony, the Depression actually improved Merle's life. By enlisting and working in the Civilian Conservation Corps, Travis made enough money to purchase a Gretsch guitar. Teaming with other members of his CCC troop, Travis formed a band and worked streets for nickels and dimes. This eventually led to a radio job in Evansville, Indiana. By World War II the guitar player had moved up to WLW in Cincinnati. In less than a decade he had es-caped the mines and was making good money playing music. The boy who had once been lucky to get patched-up hand-me-downs was now purchasing suits off the rack and driving his own car. Then the Marines called him.

Merle continued to play music during his service stint, and after the war secured a West Coast music job with Tex Ritter. By the middle of 1946 Travis was recording for Capitol and on his way to producing a long string of hit records. The biggest, "Divorce Me C.O.D.," held #1 on the country charts for fourteen weeks.

Cliffie Stone, an A&R man, thought that Merle had pop potential. Stone suggested to Travis and Capitol that the best way to break through to a larger audience might be to emulate Burl Ives. There was a catch. Stone didn't want Merle to sing modern versions of old folk songs. He wanted the singer to write new original folk ballads. Even though this idea failed to stir Travis's imagination, he went along with it. If the label wanted him to write folk songs, then Merle was going to give it a try.

After listening to a number of folk recordings, Travis sat down and began to write. Drawing from the experiences of his youth, Merle came up with several new working-type songs, but he didn't personally like any of them. He felt that none of the compositions were really inspired, nor did he think they had any commercial possibilities. As he told Stone, "These songs are nothing more than a lot of junk." When none of the new tunes charted, his point seemed to be proven. Soon the record label let Merle get back to writing in a country style and all talk about folk music was dropped. It was probably a wise move, as over the next few years Travis turned out a number of country classics including "So Round, So Firm, So Fully Packed" and "Steel Guitar Rag."

At about the time that Merle Travis was trying to write folk music, a Tennessee-born disc jockey and World War II vet was becoming a well-known radio voice in San Bernardino, California. Not only could the man tell great stories between record spins, but he had a powerful deep singing voice. Cliffie Stone noted Ernest Ford's baritone, and soon learned that the young man had been trained at the Cincinnati Conservatory of Music. At the time when Eddy Arnold and George Morgan were crossing over onto pop charts, Ford's combination of country manners and smooth disciplined voice seemed perfectly suited for the marketplace.

In 1949 Stone signed Ford to a record deal and brought him into the Capitol studio. Over the course of the next six years "Tennessee" Ernie Ford would score seventeen times on the country charts, with several of his songs crossing over to pop. One of his records, "Mule Train," stayed #1 for a month in country and moved up the pop side to #9. Ironically, "Mule Train" had been one of Merle Travis's compositions from the writer's folk or "junk" efforts.

Unlike Merle, Ernie loved the feel of Travis's folk songs. As he listened to the old recordings, one of the numbers really stood out. Back in the studio Ford concentrated on putting together a dynamic but simple arrangement to Merle's "Sixteen Tons." Beginning with Tennessee's snapping fingers, the story of a miner who couldn't get ahead was slowly built. In Ford's strong voice the tale came to life. Millions who had never been close to a coal mine, or who didn't have the slightest idea what a company store was, would be quickly drawn in. Even in the studio as they listened to the playback, the musicians felt a miner's pain and frustrations. Everyone agreed that this was a powerful record.

"Sixteen Tons" hit the charts in November 1955. A month later it would be at the top spot and would hold that position for ten weeks. Ernie's record would also cross over to pop playlists and hit #1 there too. In the world of popular music, Ford's single would mine gold at the mountaintop for eight weeks. As late as 1990 it was still one of the top twenty songs of the modern pop era.

Thanks to the coal mining record, Tennessee Ernie Ford was no longer just a "pea-picker." He was a major star. NBC gave him a morning television show, and soon spun that off to a prime-time variety series. He became a spokesperson for the Ford Motor Company, and was used by a long line of other advertisers. From that moment on Ernie was big time, and would stay an important entertainer for the rest of his life.

As the years passed, Merle Travis would also come to be appreciated. Travis would be honored time and time again for his songwriting, acting, singing, and guitar playing. The Country Music Association would even place Travis in its Hall of Fame. His style of singing and picking would be emulated by a long line of country music performers. Again and again the once-dirt-poor boy was called a genius. Deep down Merle must have realized that the accolades which had come his way were due in large part to the "junk" song Ford had made into a smash hit.

"There is not that much in the song that was written seriously," Travis would explain scores of times. " 'Sixteen Tons' is not realistic at all. No man could load a ton of coal in a day. Who could pick up a shovel the day they were born? I did get the key line from the way folks talked around the mines during the Depression. When you'd ask them how they were doing, they would tell you, 'I can't afford to die, I owe my soul to the company store.' But the song wasn't really written to be serious. It was just a fun song."

Fun song or not, "Sixteen Tons" led to news reporters investigating and revealing the terrible conditions many miners faced daily and how major coal companies had long taken advantage of their workers.

Through the new medium of television the plight of millions of forgotten miners was shown in graphic detail. These reports covered everything from black lung disease, to abject poverty, to the plight of those who died in unsafe conditions. So "Sixteen Tons" did more than just make two men stars. It helped generate a nation's awareness and lead a move for major mining reforms. Through these actions "Sixteen Tons" also began to reveal the power of country music to effect social change.

1955

I Forgot to Remember to Forget

Written by Stan Kester

In the early fifties, Memphis, Tennessee, was probably the best home in the world for a young musician. Stan Kester, a steel guitar player, didn't know it then, but he would be present for the explosive birth of one of the entertainment's most exciting and powerful performers. In this historic riverport city, which freely embraced blues, country, and gospel, Kester would soon witness a charismatic young man mix these three different musical styles into a dramatically new kind of sound. What happened at a small recording studio where the steel player worked would change the world forever. Stan would not only be there, he would participate.

In 1954 Kester was freelancing at so many of Sam Phillips's Sun Studio recording sessions that he often jokingly told people he lived there. During this period there didn't seem to be a country session that Stan didn't work. But things began to slow down for the steel player. While traditional country music still paid a lot of Sun's bills, Kester could see that the owner was slowly turning the studio in a new direction. Sam kept saying that he was looking for a white man who could sing black music. If he could find that man, Phillips actually thought he could make a million dollars. When a shy and unpolished Elvis Presley walked through Sun's front door, the record producer found the man he wanted, and Sam almost set himself up to make the million dollars too.

At about the same time that Elvis was cutting his first Sun record, Kester realized that being a steel player might soon make him a dinosaur at this studio. Phillips was now rapidly going to a new kind of style. The guys the producer was auditioning were singing a different kind of music. And it was very apparent that fiddles and steels were not a part of this new sound. This was one paycheck that Kester couldn't afford to lose. Overnight Stan "evolved" into a stand-up bass player, thus insuring that he would get to work the sessions with Sun's new artists.

"Besides switching to bass," Stan remembered, "I started writing songs. I thought that if I could write the kind of things Sam was looking for, I could really cash in on this new music he was recording."

For a late 1954 Presley session, Kester offered Phillips a snappy country/blues-style tune that he had written with another local musician. Sam listened to it first, and then played it for Elvis. They both agreed that it would make a solid "B" side. They assured the writer that it would be used at one of the next sessions.

Phillips had decided to release all of Presley's Sun singles with a hard-driving "A" side and a softer cut on the back. On the upbeat cuts the producer wanted a decidedly black feel, something that he felt kids would love. On the "B" side Sam let Elvis, who was a huge country music fan, record a country song in the

Presley style. This rhythm/country release formula would be the one that Sun would continue to employ until Phillips sold Elvis's contract to RCA.

By the middle of 1955, the "Hillbilly Cat," as Presley was now being called, was pulling down eighteen dollars a week doing a couple of songs each Saturday night on the *Louisiana Hayride*. He was also working small clubs and fairs three to five nights a week. At that time Elvis had released four singles, but none of these records made either the national country or pop charts. While Presley was a strong record seller in the areas around Memphis, Tennessee, and Jackson, Mississippi, as well as in most of Louisiana and East Texas, he hadn't found the right record or gained the right exposure to generate a national hit.

In early summer, Sam Phillips crossed his fingers and shipped Presley's latest double-play single, "Baby, Let's Play House"/"I'm Left, You're Right, She's Gone"—the latter written by Kester. These sides not only hit the country charts, the record actually climbed into the top ten. The single stayed in the numbers for almost four months. Sam and Elvis breathed a bit easier knowing that they finally had a record that introduced the singer to national radio.

Back in Memphis, Stan was thrilled to have one of his own compositions on the hit parade. He knew that this "hit" record would give him an opportunity to sell Sam and Elvis some more of his songs. Yet at that time, Kester didn't have anything that fit Presley's style. With Elvis due to record again in mid-summer, Kester needed to write something very quickly. As time was clicking down and he was hitting dry well after dry well, the songwriter overheard a conversation. One man was complaining to the other about the other man failing to make an appointment. The second man apologized by saying, "I just forget to remember."

"At that time I was on the kick of catchy titles,"

Stan recalled. "When I began to think about that phrase it just expanded into 'I forgot to remember to forget her.' From there I just started working on it and it all fell together."

Once he had finished the song, Kester needed a tape in order to present it to Sam and Elvis. He sought out a local singer who often recorded at Sun to help him turn his idea into a polished demo.

"I didn't know it then, but I made a mistake," the Sun session player remembered. "I gave Charlie Feathers half the rights to my composition for doing the demo work. Once we settled getting his name listed as a songwriter on the song [Stan bought back all rights from Feathers a few years later], I taught it to him and we put it on tape. A few days later when Sam heard it, he approved it. Elvis liked it too and decided that he wanted to cut it."

One of the reasons the producer and artist probably initially jumped on "I Forgot to Remember to Forget" was that it had a similar feel to "I'm Left, You're Right, She's Gone." It was probably only after listening to the playback that Sam and Elvis realized that "I Forgot's" catchy lead line would be so easy for folks to remember that it would make radio requests a breeze. It was also a song that almost anyone could sing, so the two men knew folks would be singing along with the record after hearing it just once or twice. It seemed that all the key elements were in place.

Elvis cut Stan's song in July, and it was shipped on the "B" side of Elvis's sixth Sun single toward the end of the summer. The supposed "A" pick was a blues standard that had been recorded in February. Today everyone remembers that "A" side, "Mystery Train," as the hit side for this release. In fact, it wasn't.

"I Forgot to Remember to Forget" landed on the country charts three months before its flip side. Steadily climbing throughout the fall and winter, it finally hit #1 in February ("Mystery Train" rose no higher than eleven and only stayed on playlists for a month). By the time "I Forgot" made the top in late winter, things had changed a great deal for Elvis, Sam Phillips, and Sun Studios.

With the country chart success generated by "I Forgot to Remember to Forget," and the overwhelming response to a live appearance Presley had made before the Country and Western Disc Jockey's Association Convention in Nashville in the fall, Elvis was a hot property. First Atlantic Records and then RCA visited Sam Phillips's office and offered to purchase the singer's contract. Steve Sholes and RCA won the bidding with an offer of $35,000. The deal was closed just months before Elvis took Stan Kester's song and knocked Webb Pierce and Red Sovine's "Why, Baby, Why" off the top of the country music charts. "I Forgot" would hold the top for five weeks before being knocked out of #1 by Presley's first RCA release, "Heartbreak Hotel." "Heartbreak" would rule the country playlist for seventeen more weeks.

"I Forgot to Remember to Forget" assured the world that no one would ever forget Elvis. From those first five weeks at #1, Presley would go on to become the most successful artist of all time. What is largely forgotten is that not only did he score his first #1 record on the country charts, but that all of his early rock 'n' roll releases made the country playlists. In 1956 alone Elvis ruled the top of the country charts for thirty-four weeks.

When Presley left Sun, he didn't forget Memphis or Stan Kester. Over the course of his career the King would cut "Playing for Keeps," "Thrill of Your Love," and "If I'm a Fool for Loving You," all penned by the old Sun Studio steel and bass player. Over the next few years a host of other artists, including Jerry Lee Lewis, would cut Kester tunes too.

"I think the thing which surprises me most," Stan explained when considering Elvis's unfathomable career, "of all the hit songs he had and of all the records he cut, 'I Forgot to Remember to Forget' stayed on the charts longer than any other. That still amazes me."

Elvis's cut of Stan's song rode on the *Billboard* country playlist for an incredible thirty-nine weeks. The Presley tune with the next longest ride was "Don't Be Cruel"/"Hound Dog" at twenty-eight weeks. While those latter singles may have gone on to immortalize Elvis as the "King of Rock 'n' Roll," it was "I Forgot to Remember to Forget" that made him a country music star.

1956
Singing the Blues

Written by Melvin Endsley

Marty Robbins was born in Glendale, Arizona, in 1925. Unlike most men who would become country stars, Marty showed little interest in any type of music until he entered the service after high school graduation. And unlike so many from this era who grew up idolizing and emulating a Jimmie Rodgers or Gene Autry, as a boy Marty seemed only mildly interested in country music at all. This lack of musical indoctrination probably had a great deal to do with the tremendous style diversity of Robbins's later recordings. It would also help to make Marty one of country music's most unique stars.

During the three-year Navy hitch in the late forties, Robbins would often find himself with time on his hands and nothing to do. While sitting on a ship in the Pacific, he first picked up a guitar and seriously worked at teaching himself how to play. After learning a few chords, he filled his spare hours composing songs.

When the twenty-two-year-old vet was discharged, he returned to where he'd attended high school in Phoenix, Arizona. There Robbins looked up an old friend who owned a country night club. That first night it took a little arm-twisting to get Marty to sit in with the house band and finally sing a solo. No one ever had to beg him to go on stage again. After a few months the audience's reaction was so warm and positive that Robbins was made the club's regular head-

liner. Using that spotlight as a springboard, the young Navy vet began working bills throughout Arizona and New Mexico. As a result of his live shows Robbins put together a large enough fan base to convince a local Phoenix television station to give him an hour each week for a country and western music show. Marty's *Western Caravan* provided the young singer with another opportunity to expand his audience. Soon Robbins was performing throughout the western United States, where he caught the eye of scouts from Columbia Records. It was a union that would last over twenty years.

Beginning in late 1952, Robbins's records began to make appearances on the national charts. "I'll Go Alone" was his first #1. Three years later his cover of Elvis Presley's "That's All Right" stayed on the charts for eleven weeks. Marty's time on the national playlists with "That's All Right" thus beat Elvis's cut by exactly eleven weeks. While Marty enjoyed his hit, the future King of Rock 'n' Roll failed to land the Sun single on any national chart.

Marty's easy style and fabulous sense of humor had quickly made him an *Opry* favorite. His road show also drew well. But with only six chart songs in almost four years of recording, his record career was far from solid. Sensing that the rockabilly artists were appealing to a new generation of potential country fans—a generation which had never heard of Jimmie

Rodgers—and realizing that his "That's All Right" had managed to bring some of those teenagers out to his shows, Marty cut another rock 'n' roll vehicle, Chuck Berry's "Maybellene." This cover single made the top ten, but it didn't win many new fans and turned off some of the country music hardliners. Many of the old-timers thought that Marty was selling out country for that radical new kind of music. Others simply wondered if the singer had any direction at all.

In a sense, Robbins's main problem was one of identity. Even he didn't know who he wanted to be. All Porter Wagoner craved was to be a straight country singer. Webb Pierce was going to stick to his forte, honky-tonk music. Bill Monroe was just an honest bluegrass man. Yet Marty wanted to do country, honky-tonk, western swing, straight western, rockabilly, blues, and even pop ballads. And with his tremendous voice and boundless energy he had the ability to do all of those styles and a few more too. Yet his record label and the critics argued that by scatter-shooting his records in all directions and using so many different styles, Marty was failing to put together a fan base that would buy each of his releases. The experts felt the singer needed to sharply define his sound and concentrate on finding records to fit that one musical area. Robbins was informed that if he didn't follow that advice, his recording career was probably doomed to failure.

About the time that Marty Robbins was moving to Nashville and establishing his career, a young Arkansan had beaten polio and was putting the finishing touches on a song called "Knee Deep in the Blues." Just before Melvin Endsley could send the composition to Acuff-Rose Publishing, the man he had written the song for died. With Hank Williams's death, Endsley's dream of going to Nashville and taking part in country music died too.

"Back in the early fifties," Melvin recently recalled,

"I was trying to write songs that would be hits for Hank Williams. In all honesty, I still was writing songs for him after he died. That is how much I loved that man's music. In the summer of 1954 I thought I would write something that sounded like a Hank song and maybe then get myself a recording contract with it. At that time I had never even been to Nashville.

"I eventually wrote a song that I thought had just the right feel. In the summer of 1955 my friend and fellow musician Jimmy Doug Grimes and I drove to Nashville for the weekend to try to sell my stuff. On Friday night we went to *Friday Night Frolics* at the WSM studios and visited with some of the stars backstage before the show. I got some good advice from some mighty good people on how to go about getting my stuff published, but I didn't get any takers."

By this time Melvin realized that a country boy just didn't drive into town, sell a big song, and become a star. That only happened in the movies. So Endsley and Grimes determined that they might as well just have a good time and enjoy the show. Then they ran into Marty Robbins.

"Marty and I started to talk." A bright smile covered Endsley's face as he remembered the moment. "I explained to him that I had written some songs I thought he might like. He told me that I could visit with him the following week, but I explained that was impossible as we had to go home on Sunday."

Rather than simply rejecting the young songwriter outright, Marty led him back to a corner of the studio and handed Melvin a guitar. After the singer listened to four songs, he stopped the Arkansan.

"My publisher Acuff-Rose wants me to record songs that I write," Robbins explained, "but I like a couple of these songs a lot. I want you to go with me tomorrow to Acuff-Rose's studio and we'll get these on tape."

After Endsley had cut the tunes on Saturday morning, Marty asked Melvin to hold one song, "Singing the Blues," for six months. Marty thought that he might like to record it. The songwriter immediately agreed not to offer the cut to anyone else for that time period.

"He was interested and I was desperate," Melvin said, laughing about why he gave in so easily to Marty's request.

Columbia released Marty's "Singing the Blues" in September 1956, one year after the songwriter had first played it backstage at the *Friday Night Frolics*. Within two months the single had dethroned Elvis's double-sided hit, "Hound Dog"/"Don't Be Cruel." Robbins's record would hold the top country position through November, December, and January before Sonny James claimed the top spot with "Young Love." Marty also took the song up the pop charts, topping at #17. It would be the first of thirteen crossover hits for the *Opry* star.

Two months after Robbins hit the country charts with Melvin Endsley's composition, Guy Mitchell, a Detroit-born singer, copied Marty's arrangement and style and took his version up the pop charts to the #1 position. The record held onto the top spot for ten weeks.

Over the years other country acts have tried to take "Singing the Blues" and make it their own. Because of its deep association with Robbins's career, recording this classic has proven to be a tough chore. Gail Davies's 1983 version has been the most successful remake, landing solidly in the top twenty.

Marty Robbins would use "Singing the Blues" as a foundation on which to build a career that would see him chart ninety-four times in three decades. During this span the singer defied marketing logic and refused to be pigeonholed in any one style. Marty scored a huge rock hit with "A White Sports Coat," hit the top of the country charts with the western classic "El Paso," landed at the pinnacle with the pop standard "It's a Sin," and sang the blues when he took Melvin Endsley's "Knee Deep in the Blues" high on the radio playlist. No one ever knew what to expect next from this recording artist.

Marty was recently ranked as the twelfth all-time most successful country recording artist, and even fifteen years after his last recording session, his records are still selling and much of his catalog remains active. Yet unlike so many other legends, there are no Marty Robbins clones in today's market. Scores of country music stars loved his music and idolized the man, but few have tried to follow in his tracks or recapture his sound. That fact is, there were so many different Marty Robbins'es that no person could sing all of his styles and do it so very well. Marty Robbins became an established star with "Singing the Blues," but rather than classify who he was, it just gave him the power to force Nashville to let him be whoever he wanted to be.

1956

Sweet Dreams

Written by Don Gibson

Don Gibson was born in Shelby, North Carolina, in 1928. A child of the Depression, he spent his youth listening to music and playing an old guitar. By the age of fourteen Don was winning local grade school talent shows. Soon thereafter he landed a job on local radio and was singing professionally. When Gibson was still a teenager he moved to Knoxville and became a featured performer on WNOX's *Tennessee Barn Dance*. Over the course of the next five years he earned a spot as one of East Tennessee's favorite talents.

Many performers would have been satisfied with the local acclaim Gibson had already earned. In Knoxville everyone knew him, and he had even been honored on several occasions by the mayor. Yet Don possessed a drive that caused him to push forward. While it was this drive that would eventually make him a star, it would also bring some lean years along the way.

Organizing his own band in the early fifties, Gibson hit the honky-tonk circuit. He played his music before drunken crowds in smoky old bars. More often than not no one seemed to notice. Though he thought he was ready for a shot at the big time, the right people weren't calling and this frustrated the young man. Even when a label did give him a chance to record, they didn't push him or his product.

One long afternoon at the Knoxville radio station where he worked, Don decided to lock himself in an upstairs office and write his way to fame. Believing that he could shape ideas into songs, he worked on the beginnings of something he would soon call "Sweet Dreams." At first he used nothing more than a guitar and the C, D7, and G7 chords. The words came later. After several weeks he had completed a set of lyrics for his original tune and believed he had something that might get him a ticket to the big time. So he carefully polished his composition and his performance, all the while praying that someone would notice.

Wesley Rose, the son of Fred Rose, heard Don's new song on the radio and drove to Knoxville to meet him. In an old mobile home the two talked about the pieces Gibson had written, as well as the young man's longtime desire to become a recording star. Rose offered to buy the rights to a few of Don's originals, but the songwriter wouldn't sell unless Wesley could get Gibson a better recording contract with a label that would fully back him (his current contract with MCA had shown little promise). Feeling much like his father must have felt when Fred first discovered Hank Williams, the younger Rose headed back to Nashville to work out the necessary steps to bring this supertalent to town.

When Rose started shopping Don's songs, MCA finally realized that Gibson had potential. Too late the company sensed that to keep him the label needed to produce a big hit. They were hoping that "Sweet

Dreams" would put Gibson on the charts and keep him in their stable. What MCA wanted was for the song to produce enough solid chart action to keep him at the studio. What they got would not hold Don at MCA, but it would finally unveil a talent whose skills would enrich all of country music for years to come.

Before Don's "Sweet Dreams" hit the charts in August 1956, Faron Young released a version of the song in June. Faron's record took off fast and stayed solid, hitting the second spot on the charts while taking a thirty-three-week ride on playlists. MCA, which released Don's version way too late, still saw the songwriter's version rise to the eighth spot. While Gibson had hoped for more, the song's publishers were pleased. Acuff-Rose noted with great capitalistic glee that with "Sweet Dreams" Don's writing had been recognized by some of country music biggest stars. As Wesley Rose had anticipated, the publisher was soon answering scores of calls inquiring if this Gibson boy had written anything else.

Seeing a potential star in Gibson, RCA signed Don just as soon as he had fulfilled his obligation to MCA. Gibson, thrilled to be a label which really wanted him as a singer, followed up "Sweet Dreams" with another self-penned number, "Oh, Lonesome Me." This single would go #1 and hold that chart position for eight weeks in 1958. Over the course of the next three years Don would score a dozen hits for his new record label.

While RCA urged Don to keep writing fresh material, the label still saw great potential in Gibson's first chart song. In 1961 they brought Don back into the studio and had him cut a new version of "Sweet Dreams." This time the Gibson single climbed to the sixth spot.

By this time Don believed that his first hit would be put to rest for good. He certainly didn't expect it to be-

come a major hit again anytime soon. So it must have both pleased and surprised him when he found out that Patsy Cline had cut it during her last recording session. Released just a month after her death, Cline's "Sweet Dreams" worked its way to #5. Moreover, the song became so associated with her career that a 1985 movie made about her life was given the song's title too. Thirteen years after Patsy's "Sweet Dreams," another country music woman cut the song.

Emmylou Harris was at the end of her first Hot Band tour when she grouped some talented musicians into a studio and cut her last album for Reprise. Besides three of Elvis's best pickers, former Eagle Bernie Leadon and future superstar Rodney Crowell joined Emmylou for the session. "Sweet Dreams" had long been one of Harris's favorite songs, and she loved singing it live. She wanted this record to reflect both her feelings for Don's piece and the energy which drove her in concerts. The singer evidently accomplished everything she desired and more. Emmylou's "Sweet Dreams" was released in October, and two months later became the singer's second #1 single. Over twenty years after Gibson had written this classic, the song finally felt the rare air at the top of the charts.

Even after four stellar runs up the charts, Nashville was far from finished with "Sweet Dreams." Troy Seals pushed it on the playlists in 1976, and Reba McEntire first tasted the top twenty with the classic in 1979. As a tribute to Patsy Cline, Reba always used "Sweet Dreams" to conclude each of her concerts. This practice stopped only when McEntire's band died in the same tragic fashion as Cline. After the plane crash Reba vowed never to perform "Sweet Dreams" again. Still, scores of others continue to sing and record the song that brought Don Gibson to Nashville, and it looks like Music City will continue to embrace "Sweet Dreams" for years to come.

1956
Folsom Prison Blues

Written by Johnny Cash

Growing up dirt poor in Arkansas, J.R. Cash was a sharecropper's son who almost died of starvation as a child. Living in an old shack, the family wore hand-me-down clothes and ate lots of beans and corn bread. For recreation they sang old hymns they learned at church and country songs that they heard on a neighbor's radio. For the Cash family life in Dyess County was not just hard, it was all but impossible. It was a struggle just to get by each day, and no one seemed to want to give these hardworking people a helping hand to lift them out of their sad world. And always it seemed that things never got better, only a little worse each day.

A neighbor once observed that she could see real pain in those children's eyes. With the heartache caused by losing two brothers, his family's abject state of poverty, and the hard work in hot cotton fields, there was little in young J.R.'s or his brothers' and sister's lives they could look forward to. Christmas toys were out of the question, and so was new clothing or eating at a nice restaurant. Santa didn't have an address for the Cash family either. It seemed that J.R.'s only way out was to make it to his late teens and enlist in the military. So in 1950, J.R. Cash walked away from the family farm and joined the Air Force.

While stationed in Germany, Johnny (the military gave him a name to go with the initial his parents had given him at birth) taught himself how to play guitar.

He also began to jam a little with some of his buddies. Cash mainly sang gospel and old country standards. Then, as he grew more confident, he began to write and sing a little of his own material. Before long he was fielding requests from the boys in his outfit.

Johnny was discharged from the service at twenty-two, and quickly found his way to Memphis. In 1954 alone, Cash went to school, tried to sell appliances, worked odd jobs, and played music with a couple of men Johnny had met through his brother Ray. Those two new friends, Luther Perkins and Marshall Grant, would eventually become Cash's band, the Tennessee Two.

After working with Perkins and Grant for several months, Cash wrangled an audition at Sun Records in March 1955. Sam Phillips was not very impressed with the boys. They were too raw and unpolished. Very matter-of-factly Phillips sent them home to hone their skills. Sensing that he needed some very special material to turn the producer's head, Cash set to work writing a series of new songs. When he found two that seemed to fit the group's style, Johnny called and set up a second meeting at the Sun Studios.

This time Phillips liked what he heard and signed Cash and his band. Those two new songs were also put out on a record, and for a week in late 1955 Johnny could turn on the radio and hear his own voice belting out "Cry, Cry, Cry" and "Hey, Porter." Those seven short days on the country charts didn't mean much in the grand world of music, but to a boy who had suffered through hunger and poverty just to grow into manhood, this #14 ranking was the top of the world.

Sun put Cash and the Tennessee Two on the road, usually hooking them onto Elvis's show. The exposure was a great help in allowing the boys to develop an identity and stage presence. It also opened up their eyes to how Presley was using the fans to build a career that was more than just hit records and high school gigs. He was going to go after big money. The three country boys began to sense that if they could put together a really good record, then there would be some very good money out there for them too.

The song that would put the group and especially Cash over the top got its inspiration from a movie. To kill a few extra hours one afternoon, Johnny ducked into a theater. The feature that day was a documentary entitled *Inside the Walls of Folsom Prison*. Cash was immediately fascinated by the fact that these men were literally caught in a trap of their own making. As he watched, Johnny began to realize that everyone, even those on the outside, was locked in some type of prison. It might be loneliness, poverty, booze, or a hundred other things, but there was something holding just about everyone back. With that thought in mind he reasoned that country music fans should be able to identify with a prison song even more than they could a drinking song or a train song. Within a few hours after the film's final credits had rolled, the singer had composed an ode to Folsom Prison and taught it to Luther and Marshall.

Phillips like "Folsom Prison Blues" better than anything Cash had ever brought him. Putting the number with its very stark arrangement on one side, and "So Doggone Lonesome" on the other, Sun shipped

the single right after the first of the year. Both sides charted, both sides topped out at the fourth position, and both stayed on the playlist for more than twenty weeks. At that time, "So Doggone Lonesome" was considered the bigger hit, but it was "Folsom" that really got the fans going at live shows and set up the market for another Cash record. Riding the wave put in motion by his doubled-sided hit, Johnny's next release, "I Walk the Line," would hit the top spot on the country charts and slip into the top twenty on the pop side. Johnny Cash was now a star.

Over the course of the next decade "Folsom Prison Blues" remained a concert favorite. Long after "So Doggone Lonesome" had become just a memory, "Folsom" was still drawing loud cheers. Yet even as the Cash-penned song's popularity remained steady, the singer/songwriter wavered. Hooked on pills, Johnny was walking a very dangerous line. Several times he came close to dying, and on many other occasions his concert appearances revealed a man so high on speed even he didn't know what he was doing. Cash's own inspiration for writing "Folsom Prison Blues"—the fact that each person places himself in some kind of prison—now had come true in his own life. His addictions had the singer trapped. Without help, these addictions would probably also serve as his executioner.

Fortunately for Johnny, June Carter stepped in and helped him beat his dependencies. When she got him completely free of pills, Cash felt the magic come back into his life and work. He once again felt the desire to go forward. And just like in 1956, Johnny knew that if he could just find that one song, he could again be as hot as he had been during his early days at Sun. As it turned out, the song that would give Johnny his first #1 in five years was an old friend.

Recording a live album for Columbia Records in 1968, Cash took his show to Folsom Prison. The inmates went crazy when Johnny walked out, leaned over the microphone, and announced, "Hello, I'm Johnny Cash." From there the performer went into a fast-paced version of his classic "Folsom Prison Blues." The concert's live energy and enthusiasm was captured so well that when Cash and the producer played the tape back, "Folsom" literally jumped out of the speakers. It was as if the song was "happy" to be home. In the recording you could feel the place and you could sense just how much the number meant to those convicts.

Sensing the song's new market potential and needing something to help plug the live album, Columbia opted to release "Folsom Prison Blues" as a single. This "live" record hit the charts in June, and in just five weeks ruled the country playlists. Cash's prison song would remain at the top spot for six weeks and would help the "Man in Black" claim the CMA's Entertainer of the Year in 1969. In one of country music's most interesting stories, "Folsom Prison Blues" thus became the song which not only first launched Johnny Cash's career in 1956, but which then relaunched the second phase of his career twelve years later. Cash's Hall of Fame journey probably couldn't have happened without a side trip through Folsom Prison.

1956
Crazy Arms

Written by Ralph Mooney and Charles Seals

By the middle of 1956 many were predicting the end of the "real" country sound. The rockabilly movement that had sprung forth and taken root in the early fifties had now found a charismatic leader in Elvis Presley. The music that was propelling the "Hillbilly Cat's" rise, as well as the scores of imitators across the nation, was a mixture of country, blues, and pop, and this bass-driven sound was beginning to dominate not only the pop charts, but the country music charts too. With Presley now being backed by RCA, his music was not only starting a cultural revolution in the nation, but was also dramatically reshaping the country music charts.

Hank Williams had barely been dead three years, and already fiddles and steel guitars were disappearing from country bands. Drums and hot lead guitar licks blasting out a louder, more frantic beat were now replacing the honky-tonk-user-friendly dance rhythm. Record executives were so convinced that yesterday's music was dead that one of them even asked Porter Wagoner to record rock-sounding songs. In a brief instant it seemed that Music City had been turned upside down.

During the first five months of 1956 the *Billboard* country playlist presented five #1 singles. Three of these chart-topping hits, "I Forgot to Remember to Forget," "Heartbreak Hotel," and "Blue Suede Shoes," may have been sung by Southern boys, but

they had very little in common with the music of Webb Pierce or Faron Young. The two legitimate country hits during the first part of the year, "Why, Baby, Why" and "I Don't Believe You've Met My Baby," couldn't hold their top chart position nearly as long as their rocking rivals. With Elvis's "Hound Dog"/"Don't Be Cruel" single just beginning to make its run, things looked bleak for folks who worked the *Opry*.

During the holy war for the radio audience one man would step forward to proudly carry the country banner. He had been born in 1925 in a tiny Texas Panhandle town. This Cherokee County product didn't get into music until he had competed a hitch in the service and was enrolled in college. Far from seeing himself as the man who would become a country music savior, for most of his life Ray Price didn't even foresee a career in entertainment. He really thought he'd end up a rancher.

Price made extra money for his college education by singing at small local events. This seemingly innocent moonlighting experience won him an invitation to join KRBC's *Hillbilly Circus*. Once he was on radio, his audience grew so rapidly through this Abilene-based program that he was asked in 1950 to come to Dallas as a part of KRLD's *Big D Jamboree*. The *Jamboree* was one of the most important country music offerings west of the Mississippi, and segments of the show were actually broadcast on the CBS net-work. Price scored big numbers here too. Letters and calls demanded that the *Jamboree* feature him again and again. In 1952 the *Opry* called, as did Columbia Records. Ray quickly packed his bags and moved east. Texas may have lost a future rancher, but it wouldn't take America very long to find that they had gained a new country music star.

In 1953 Price formed a band out of the remnants of Hank Williams's old Drifting Cowboys. The fiddle-and-steel-driven sound that the Cherokee Cowboys were to provide for the singer would become his trademark for almost two decades. During a time when Nashville was turning to the frantic rockabilly sound, Ray was keeping his shuffle-beat hillbilly music pure and easy.

Price's early recording career was marked with solid entries, but few songs that stood out. "Release Me," which many years later would become a pop standard, was probably the best of these singles, even though "I'll Be There" scored a little better on the playlists. In early 1956 this moderate chart success would give way to something special. One song would make Price the era's most important traditional voice.

While Ray was thrilling traditional fans at the Opry, on the West Coast Charlie Seals was working to a much smaller audience. A musician from a family that had been picking for generations (Brady Seals of Little Texas and singer Dan Seals are from this same family tree), Seals was playing in clubs by night and writing songs by day. His potential for producing hit compositions had been acknowledged when he penned "Two Times Two" and "Let's Make Love Tonight," but he had yet to really score big with any-thing on the national country charts. With this thought in mind he was always looking for new song ideas.

One of his best concepts came on a day when he ran into a friend and old playing partner, Ralph Mooney. Mooney was a talented steel guitar picker who had influenced countless steel players. He was also a pretty good man with a song and a joke. On this day he was anything but upbeat. His wife had caught Mooney with a younger woman, and this wasn't the first time it had happened. Angered beyond words, Mrs. Mooney had taken the next bus out of town.

"Oh, these crazy arms of mine," Ralph had moaned as he told Charlie about his problems. "If only I could control my arms."

Seals immediately realized that Ralph's story would make a great song, and the line about having crazy arms was a good place to start. With that in mind the two men pooled their talents and wrote the story of a man who just couldn't be true no matter how good he had it at home. Once it was completed, Seals took it to Jimmy Wakely.

"I'll publish it," the singer told him, then added, "but Chuck, it will never sell." Wakely continued to repeat this claim even after Charlie and Ralph won over their live crowds with the composition. Rather than getting the song placed where recording artists could hear it, Wakely simply filed it away. Whenever Seals or Mooney would ask about "Crazy Arms," Jimmy would answer, "There is no way that song will ever be cut."

"I kept on doing it in my shows," Charlie recalled, "and I really thought this might drum up some inter-est in the song. And it did. Another publisher asked me about the song. When I told him that Wakely wasn't doing anything with it, he asked me if I could get the rights back. When I asked Jimmy if I could have them back, Jimmy couldn't even find his copy of 'Crazy Arms' in the office. He verbally gave me back all rights, still warning me that it wasn't going to sell."

Seals quickly signed on with the new publisher and cut his own version of "Crazy Arms." A few months later Ray Price heard the Seals recording and liked it a lot. Using an almost identical arrangement, the Texan went into the studio and put "Crazy Arms" on tape. By late spring Columbia had it ready to ship.

The song that Jimmy Wakely said would never be recorded hit the charts in May. On June 23, it knocked Carl Perkins's "Blue Suede Shoes" out of the top spot. "Crazy Arms" would remain # 1 song for twenty more weeks, would stay on the *Billboard* playlist for almost a year, and even cross over to score on the pop charts. With one recording Price had not only become a country music sensation, but had also knocked a large hole in the theory that there was no place for the old country sound in the rockabilly era.

1956
Young Love

Written by Carole Joyner and Rick Cartey

By the early fifties Bill Lowery had been a well-known disc jockey for several years in Atlanta. Blessed with a wonderful voice, he was a solid promoter who had built a station from the ground up, taking it to the very top of the market. In the mid-fifties things couldn't have been going any better for him. He was well known, well respected, and very well connected. With nothing standing in the way of a bright future, tragedy struck. He was told he had cancer.

A friend in the music business suggested to Bill that he use his radio and music contacts to start a publishing company. "That way you can build an annuity for your family," the DJ was told. What his friend was really saying was, "Cancer is probably going to kill you. If you have some songs making solid royalties, at least your kids won't starve to death." Lowery didn't plan on dying anytime soon. He planned on being around to play with his grandkids. But starting a publishing company did sound like a good idea. After all, Bill knew a lot of good writers who could supply him with solid material. He also knew both artists and A&R men who could then take those songs and get them on radio.

As he fought his disease, Bill built Lowery Music and cruised into the rockabilly movement by picking out songs and acts which would sell well in the teen market. Soon Steve Sholes from RCA and Ken Nelson from Capitol were regularly phoning him to see what

hot acts or potential hit songs Lowery had signed that week. In the midst of the craziness of trying to keep up with a brand-new musical genre and fight a killer disease, Bill also left his door open to almost anyone who thought that they could write or sing a song.

"An eighteen-year-old kid came to me in about 1956," Lowery remembered. "He had written three verses of a song. It had a country ballad feel to it. I listened to what Rick Cartey had done and told him that he was on the right track. As he left I kept reminding him to 'think young.'

"He played the song for his girlfriend, Carole Joyner, and she came up with a chorus line that started, 'Young love, our love, filled with true emotion.' From there Rick finished it out and brought it back to me. I recorded it and put in on a record with a song called 'Oooh-We.' I sent a copy to Ken Nelson at Capitol and Steve Sholes at RCA. Ken passed on 'Oooh-We.' but said he kind of liked the other side. Steve bought 'Oooh-We.' and rejected 'Young Love.' Judging from the reaction we were getting in Atlanta, I thought that RCA had made a good move."

A few weeks later Ken Nelson placed another call to the music publisher. Capitol's A&R man informed Bill that he believed "Young Love" had real hit potential. He suggested that Lowery meet him in Nashville in a couple of weeks. Ken was going to be there for a Sonny James recording session.

Sonny had been with Capitol for just three years, but he had been in the music business for almost all of his life. He was born in Hackleburg, Alabama, in 1929, and his given name was Jimmie Loden. The Loden family had a band that toured the Southern fair circuit. Jimmie was just four years old when he made his professional singing debut. By the time he finished high school he had become an excellent guitar player and poised showman. Finishing a stint in the Korean War, Loden returned to the tour circuit as a solo act. After a series of radio gigs, he was signed by Capitol in 1953.

Since signing Jimmie, now known by the name with which he would gain fame, Ken had been trying to connect the singer with just the right song to launch a big-time career. Nelson had come close. "For Rent" had made the top ten, but James had not been able to go any higher with his next two cuts. Now, as 1956 was starting to slip away, they needed a hit.

Sonny was convinced that "You're the Reason I'm in Love" was the perfect song. He liked the way it fit his voice, and felt that it had national play potential. When Ken auditioned "Young Love" for the singer, James shook his head. He wasn't impressed.

"When I went up to Nashville for the session," Bill recalled, "I found out that Sonny didn't like the song at all. Now I had known Sonny for some time and I liked him a lot. I thought he liked me too. He must have because he told me that he was going to cut 'Young Love' simply as a favor to me and Ken. While he was convinced that 'You're the Reason' was going to be the hit that came from that session, he was willing to do our song too."

"I really didn't like the song at first," Sonny admitted. "The night before we cut it I went back to my hotel room and added my arrangement. I reworked it to where it featured my guitar and the repeat harmonies of my backup group, the Southern Gentle-men. I also reworked it where I broke the syllables in the pattern that I had used on other songs. At that time I felt it was very important to have a style that, even if the disc jockey didn't identify who was singing the song, the people could still tell by the sound. I thought the guitar and the Southern Gentlemen set us apart.

"When we cut the record I had the drummer just use a straight brush going through the whole song and we only used my guitar, that simple drum, and a bass fiddle. Pete Wade then came in and did a little lead work in the middle. Yet even when we got done with it, as simple as it was, I asked Ben Peters if he thought that it was too pop."

Capitol shipped Sonny's cut of "You're the Reason I'm in Love" in November. Ken Nelson made sure that "Young Love" was placed on the record's flip side. Then the label let the disc jockeys decide which song was the "A" side."

"I thought with the new arrangement," Sonny explained, "that 'Young Love' could be a hit. I never dreamed that it would do what it was going to do. No one did."

"A few weeks after the session Sonny called me in Atlanta," Lowery said with a laugh as he remembered their conversation. "He told me that it looked like he had been right. He said that 'You're the Reason' was going to be a big hit. I asked him why he thought so. He informed me that in Dallas the song was really hot.

"I laughed and told him that was news to me. Then I added, 'Here "Young Love" is going crazy.' The truth of the matter was the record-pressing plant couldn't keep up with the demand. I had never seen anything like it."

On December 22, 1956, "Young Love" appeared on the country charts. Two weeks later the single hit the rock list. By the first of the year the song Sonny didn't like had knocked "Singing the Blues" off the top spot. Sonny's first #1 would remain there nine weeks. With that, James was suddenly a potential force in Nashville. His label was now going to have to stick with him for the long haul.

Meanwhile, the debut of this new country act and his record on the pop charts had caused quite a stir. "Young Love" was deemed such a great song that a young movie star was rushed into Dot's studios to cut it. Tab Hunter's "Young Love" was released just weeks after Sonny's version. By the middle of January it was a race to see which cut would make it to the top of the charts first. The country boy beat the movie star by one week. Then Tab knocked Sonny out of the top spot and held it for a month and a half. It would be the movie star's only major hit, but James would record a total of twenty-three #1 country singles, and over his career place forty-three songs in the top ten.

It is no secret that Sonny James quickly came to love the high school love song that launched his career. Without "Young Love," Capitol might have given up on the singer before he ran off sixteen straight chart-toppers in the late sixties. Bill Lowery's music publishing company loved "Young Love" too. Not only did it sell well in 1957, it never stopped generating interest and royalties. It continued to be redone, and landed on both pop and country charts several more times between its original release and its latest appearance in 1989. Maybe the only semi-sad note concerning "Young Love" was that Rick Cartey and Carole Joyner didn't experience it. They broke up not long after the song was completed. No need to feel sorry for them. Theirs was a teenage crush that really paid dividends.

1957
Bye Bye Love

Written by Boudleaux Bryant and Felice Bryant

A year into the rockabilly craze many were waving bye-bye to country music. Some had gone so far as to cede the genre over to the kids. The acts that were doing so much damage on the pop and country charts—Elvis Presley, Jerry Lee Lewis, Sonny James, and even to a certain extent Marty Robbins—didn't seem to care enough about traditional hillbilly sounds to save them. Yet in the midst of all these Southern males who rocked both major charts, two brothers emerged who brought old-style country harmonies to new Nashville-penned songs.

Don and Phil Everly came from a family which had a deep rural music tradition. Their father had been one of the primary influences on a young Merle Travis. Their parents, Ike and Margaret, had been singing country music on radio for a generation. Migrating from Kentucky in the mid-forties, this husband-wife duo had become the anchor and identity of KMA radio in Shenandoah, Iowa. Their sons were brought up with the traditional country style of picking and singing. When the boys were still in grade school they would perform with Ike and Margaret both on radio and stage.

In the mid-fifties when their sons finished high school, the older Everlys retired from the music business, and Don and Phil moved to Nashville to try to take the family country music tradition to the next level. Thanks in large part of their father's contacts, the boys didn't go through many lean times. Almost immediately they made meal money playing local clubs. Eventually their close harmonies caught the eye of several labels and promoters. Cadence was the record company which first stepped forward with an offer.

At about the same time Don and Phil were making their move to Nashville, Boudleaux and Felice Bryant were preparing to make a move to the suburbs. Boudleaux, who had been named for the Frenchman who'd saved his father's life in World War I, was born in Georgia. By the time he finished high school, the boy was not only a classical and jazz violinist, he also played piano, bass, and sousaphone. Throughout his late teens and early twenties he performed with symphonies, jazz bands, country groups, and pop combos. He excelled in chord structure and harmony. With one one-nighter after another, it was harder on him than any physical labor he had ever done. Yet he loved music too much to quit the long road and even longer hours.

While working a gig in Milwaukee at the Schroeder Hotel, Boudleaux met a young woman who was employed by the hotel as an elevator operator. It was love at first sight, and within five days they had become Mr. and Mrs. Bryant and had left Milwaukee.

"When he was gone somewhere to play," Felice remembered, "I would get bored. So I would just write little songs."

While she didn't have the formal music training of her husband, Felice had grown up in a family which sang Italian folk songs and played instruments by ear. Felice had a natural feel for music and she also had a gift for composing poetry. The union of her innate strengths bore fruit in her songs.

Boudleaux had also been writing for some time, and when he finally discovered that his wife was a better tunesmith than any of the musicians with whom he worked, be began to spend his Sundays writing with Felice. After a while he thought that some of their stuff sounded pretty good.

"We had eighty songs," Felice recalled, "and so we began to write letters seeking a publisher. Most of those letters were returned unopened. Finally I asked Boudleaux, 'Don't you know anybody?' He wrote Arthur Godfrey and sent him a song called 'Country Boy.' Godfrey liked our material, but he wanted all publishing rights and co-credits as a writer."

In the meantime the couple had gone back to Cincinnati, where they made contact with an old musician friend from their Detroit days who advised the Bryants that they should allow him to contact a new publisher in Nashville. His name was Fred Rose.

The friend, Rome Johnson, called Rose, and he too expressed interest in the song "Country Boy." Suddenly the two were at a crossroads. They had heard of Godfrey, but not of Rose. With the urging of Rome Johnson, they signed a contact with Rose.

By 1956 the couple had composed scores of chart songs including "Out behind the Barn," "How's the World Treating You," and "Midnight." The royalties from these and scores of other hits had brought them their first taste of financial freedom. They could now live many of their dreams, and one of the most important was building a home. They chose a wooded lot in Old Hickory and hired a construction crew.

"One day, while driving out to inspect the builder's

work," Felice explained, "Boudleaux looked over at me and said, 'I've just got the greatest idea for a song for Johnnie and Jack.' He then sang me the chorus. I told him that it was good, and I began to harmonize with him on what he had written. When we got to house the we kept it rolling and finished the song.

"A few days later we showed it to Johnnie Wright and Kitty Wells. They told us that they already had enough songs for their album. So that was that."

Cadence, an up-and-coming label, was going to add a country corner to their recording stable and "Bye Bye Love," in addition to several other Bryant songs, was sent to the label's Archie Bleyer. Bleyer would be in charge of picking the music for their three country acts. Among that trio was the Everly Brothers.

Archie picked "Bye Bye Love" for the Everlys and the rest is history. Employing the same country harmony style they had used since childhood, the boys recorded "Bye Bye Love." Their version had a slightly upbeat tempo, and didn't use a fiddle or a steel guitar, but it was still a very country-sounding cut. As it was shipped to both country and pop radio stations and outlets, Cadence and the brothers crossed their fingers and hoped that disc jockeys and fans would respond.

"Bye Bye Love" hit the country charts in May 1957, and began a steady climb. Two weeks later it appeared on the rock charts. In mid-July the Everlys celebrated when their first record hit the top of the country playlist. It would hold #1 for a total of seven weeks. On the rock side Don and Phil would peak at #2. Their very country-sounding song had become a crossover hit, so a host of acts, including honky-tonk's Webb Pierce, rushed to cover it.

"Bye Bye Love" set up the Everlys for even bigger things later in the year. For their second single the brothers again chose a Bryant cut. "Wake Up, Little

Susie" topped both national charts at the same time. Boudleaux and Felice then penned "Bird Dog," "Devoted to You," and "All I Have to Do Is Dream" for the brothers. Over the next four years Ike's boys would become teen idols and the hottest brother act in show business. Screaming girls would greet them at live shows and their many national television appearances. Kids everywhere would be singing their songs. And a lot of the credit for this success and acclaim had to go to the songwriting Bryants.

At the same time the Everlys were selling millions of records, their country harmony style was heavily influencing four lads from Britain. The Beatles would later admit that much of their sound came from trying to imitate Don and Phil's special vocal blends. A host of other groups and singers borrowed from the boys too.

Because of the major exposure the brothers received in the late fifties and early sixties rock/teen market, it now is usually overlooked that the Everlys'

best charts numbers were earned on country playlists. Unlike so many others acts of this period who changed their sound to appeal to the broader rock base, Don and Phil simply did what they had always done. With their simple acoustic guitar licks, their rural harmonies, and their straightforward arrangements, all of their hits reflected their rural roots. This seemed to be proven as their biggest hits were later revived by other artists. When "Bye Bye Love," "All I Have to Do Is Dream," "Devoted to You," "Cathy's Clown," "So Sad," "'Til I Kissed You," and even "Lucille" reappeared as hits, they were revived by country acts and appeared almost exclusively on country charts. Thus, at a time when the young new acts were being accused of ruining country music, the Everly Brothers took country music's influence and spread it around the world. Along the way they also helped Felice and Boudleaux purchase a few more dreams and earn a ticket to country music's Hall of Fame.

1957
Great Balls of Fire

Written by Otis Blackwell

Otis Blackwell grew up a long way from the country and even further away from Nashville, but this once-poor black kid from Brooklyn, New York, nevertheless had a profound effect on Music City. The songs that he created dominated the country and rock charts in the middle and late fifties. Through his compositions a host of performers earned the title of star.

Otis got his first real taste of music as a floor sweeper in a motion picture theater. Between performing his various duties, the teenager had the opportunity to listen to cowboy stars sing western music on the silver screen. He was quickly drawn in by the singers, especially Tex Ritter. Soon Blackwell began to teach himself enough piano to write a few cowboy ditties for himself. Otis expanded his writing from there, and by the time he reached twenty he had a record contract.

As a blues singer Otis began to make the rounds of the city clubs. A few nights in smoky noise-filled bars quickly convinced him that pressing clothes in a laundry was far better than trying to make music over the moaning of loud drunks. With a sour taste in his mouth, he stayed away from the music business for two years. Then, as his laundry job began to grow old, he stopped and took stock of his future.

"Rock 'n' roll had just got to moving," he explained a decade later, "and I found out that I could make as much as fifty dollars a week writing songs. So I quit

the cleaners and joined Goldy Goldmark of Shalimar Publishing."

Not long after Blackwell had settled into his new profession, Goldmark excitedly told the songwriter that they had just gotten a huge break. It seemed that RCA and Elvis Presley were interested in "Don't Be Cruel." There was a catch. In order for it to be recorded, Blackwell would have to give Elvis fifty percent of the song. Still innocent, Otis agreed and waited to see what would happen. As it would turn out, that half of "Don't Be Cruel" cost Blackwell millions of dollars. That song would become the biggest record of the rock 'n' roll era. Yet Otis didn't bemoan what he had lost. Rather he reveled in what he had gained. Over the course of the next few years Presley would place a long list of Blackwell originals on the top of the charts. Through Elvis, the songwriter's career became well established.

"Don't Be Cruel" was still riding the charts when Presley walked back into the old Sun Studios to catch up with Sam Phillips, Johnny Cash, and Carl Perkins. Perkins had just finished a session, and he took the time to introduce Elvis to a new kid who was working as a session pianist. The young man's name was Jerry Lee Lewis.

Lewis had grown up in Louisiana learning how to play and sing at an Assembly of God Church and a black honky-tonk. Over the years Jerry Lee had mixed those two musical styles to the point that his wild piano pounding had gotten him expelled from a Bible college. For a while in the early fifties he had sold Bibles and sewing machines door to door. Then he formed a band and began to play teenage dances. Too eager to wait to be discovered, the polite but extremely confident young man had come to Memphis to see what was going on at Sun Studios. Jerry Lee felt that he could sing rockabilly as well as anyone. After a while, Sam Phillips agreed.

Much like Hank Williams, Lewis had been influenced so heavily by black music that it had become a natural part of his style. Much like Elvis, Jerry Lee used this musical style even when he did hymns or straight country tunes. With his almost unequaled piano skills, Lewis had the ability to take those religious and hillbilly standards to places where Presley had never gone. Elvis might have had the capability of threatening middle-class white America with his stage show, but Sam Phillips sensed that Jerry Lee could frighten those same people out of their wits with his stage antics and brash attitude. It was soon obvious that Lewis was to Presley what the Rolling Stones would be to the Beatles. For a while this image would make him a star. Eventually it would also all but ruin his career.

Jerry Lee's first release for Sun was "Whole Lotta Shakin' Goin' On." No one was surprised when the single jumped onto the rock charts in July 1957. What surprised everyone, including Lewis, was that the rockin' number hit the country playlists in the middle of June. While "Shakin' " was to freeze at the third position in pop, the country fans would take the song all the way to the top.

Needing a follow-up for Jerry Lee's debut single, Sam Phillips turned to the same man who had already knocked out a couple of hits for Elvis. The producer called Otis and asked for something wild. Blackwell had just the right thing.

Over the course of his first two years of writing, Otis had begun to realize that he could get inspiration from almost anywhere. He had once purchased a bottle of Coke, dropped it, picked it up, and watched it fizz. From that simple episode he got the concept that would lead to "All Shook Up." For Jerry Lee's next cut Blackwell reworked the same idea, about a pretty woman really getting to a man, only this time he used an old saying as the hook line, "Goodness gracious, great balls of fire."

With his rollicking piano style, "Great Balls of Fire" was tailor-made for Jerry Lee. Phillips pushed it out the door as quickly as he could record and press it. The single was being shipped while "Shakin' " was still hot on the charts. "Fire" hit in December and made a simultaneous run up both major charts. It pegged at #2 in pop, thus becoming Lewis's highest-charting rock 'n' roll effort, but "Great Balls of Fire" didn't stop on the country side until it knocked Marty Robbins's "The Story of My Life" out of #1. It would remain Jerry Lee's biggest hit until fifteen years later when he was in the middle of his transformation to a full-time country singer.

While Jerry Lee's own penchant for scandal would kill his rockabilly career and stall his country revival, Otis Blackwell would continue to score on both country and rock charts for decades. Dolly Parton, Conway Twitty, the Judds, and more than a dozen other stars would join Jerry Lee Lewis and Elvis Presley with major country hits penned by the Brooklyn songwriter. Four decades after he first made his skills known, the man who had had more than one thousand songs recorded and had accounted for record sales in excess of 185 million, was still affecting the charts. In 1988 Otis even moved his base of operations to Nashville because that was where most of his songs were now being recorded.

Going back to its infancy, country music had been influenced by black writers and musicians. Jimmie Rodgers learned much of what he later shared on his records from blacks. Hank Williams too owed a great deal to the African-American influence. Yet the first black man to really cash in on what was going on in Nashville was Otis Blackwell. He might have been from the heart of New York City, but he understood the essence of what it took to write a song that black and white Americans would love. His skills were some of the most powerful behind-the-scenes shapers of rockabilly, a music that revolutionized the way Nashville did business. Blackwell's writing opened up country to a new generation of fans. His magic touch is still being felt today. Goodness gracious, didn't he shake things up!

1958
Pick Me Up on Your Way Down

Written by Harlan Howard

Harlan Howard seemed to be born to write songs. As a child growing up in Detroit he listened with his parents to *Grand Ole Opry* and fell in love with the music of Ernest Tubb. Blessed with a wonderful ear, he could pick up the "Texas Troubadour's" melodies easily enough, but sometimes young Howard couldn't remember all the words. When this happened, he didn't resort to humming or mumbling. He simply wrote his own lyrics. As he sang these new words to Tubb's time-worn melodies, he dreamed of joining his hero in Nashville. But Michigan was a long way from Tennessee, especially for a poor boy.

Using three or four chords and an old guitar, Harlan continued to expand his writing skills as a teenager, and then later when serving a hitch in the Army. He got ideas for his songs everywhere. Sometimes a concept came from something somebody said. Other times inspiration might hit in the form of something he had seen at school, on the streets, or even during mess duty. And throughout this time, every chance he got, he would grab a ride to Nashville to listen to his favorite country acts live at the Ryman. He would also spend his spare hours knocking on doors and trying to make contacts in Music City, but invariably he would return to his Army base with little to show but empty pockets and tired feet.

Upon completing his military service, Harlan worked factory jobs in Detroit, Arizona, and finally Los Angeles. Still writing, he impressed Johnny Bond and Tex Ritter enough to have them buy a few of his original compositions. Yet neither performer did anything with Harlan's songs. By and large, like most young aspiring talents, Howard found a lot more dead ends than helping hands, a lot more reasons to quit than continue. Yet he never gave up. As if it were therapy, he continued to write about almost everything he observed.

One night, while hanging out in a smoky West Coast honky-tonk, Howard finally received his biggest break. Ironically, this wonderful opportunity came in the form of a lovers' spat.

"I was watching a couple fussing at this club," Harlan recalled. "After they had fought for a while, the girl walked off. When she did, the man hollered after her, 'Well, you can just pick me up on your way down.' I must have thought about that fight and that line for about a year before I sat down to write the song."

It only took the assembly-line worker just a few minutes to transform a lovers' quarrel into a country music classic. But even though "Pick Me Up on Your Way Down" came together in less time than it took for the couple to fall apart, Howard still didn't have the contacts to connect it with people who could turn it into a hit.

"Not long after I had written 'Pick Me Up on Your Way Down' I was talking to a friend of mine in

Nashville," Howard remembered. "The song came up and he asked me to mail him a copy. This friend worked at Pamper Music, and told me that he would plug it for me along with a couple of his songs. I had never heard of Pamper, but I trusted him and so I mailed the song to him."

True to his word, the friend went to work for Howard. Over the course of the next few weeks "Pick Me Up" made the Music City rounds. It finally ended up on the desk of a golfing buddy of Ray Price. The works of most unknown writers usually collect more dust than interest, but not in this case. For some reason this demo got played.

Charlie Walker was a San Antonio disc jockey who had a strong background as a country musician. One of the nation's favorite on-air talents, he wanted to become a recording star in his own right. Decca had given him a shot in the mid-fifties, but his "Only You, Only You" had stayed on the charts for just two weeks. In early 1958 he convinced Columbia to give him a second chance. Relying on almost fifteen years of experience spinning hits on the radio, Charlie picked out Harlan's composition as a potential winner.

Columbia released Walker's version of "Pick Me Up on Your Way Down" in late fall. The label was convinced that it was destined to be a big record. Harlan Howard was a bit more skeptical.

"I had never heard of Charlie Walker," he laughed. "I sure wanted the song to be a hit, but I wasn't very confident at that time."

"Pick Me Up on Your Way Down" rode the country music charts for the remainder of 1958 and a good portion of 1959. It stayed at #2 for four weeks, and launched Charlie Walker's recording career. More importantly, it opened the door for a man who was to become and still remains one of the industry's most successful songwriters.

"I wasn't ready to quit my job," Harlan admitted, "At least not after that first hit." But "Pick Me Up's" success did give him a great reason to keep writing. Within a year Harlan Howard would finally make his boyhood dream come true. He would move to Nashville, and in doing so he would reshape the city of his dreams with a writing career that after more than four hundred songs is still going up!

1958

City Lights

Written by Bill Anderson

On August 27, 1957, a nineteen-year-old University of Georgia student sought refuge from the heat and humidity which had invaded his small bedroom apartment at Commerce's Hotel Andrew Jackson. Climbing up a flight of steps that led to the building's roof, the young man plopped down in an old well-worn chair and took in the view. Tired from a long day of classes and a hard evening shift as a disc jockey, his body and mind craved sleep. Yet on this particularly clear night, as the young man noted the beauty of the millions of stars that blanketed the heavens, rest was the last thing on his mind. After hours of spinning the hottest country records, there was music in his head and it had energized him. Taking his well-worn guitar, the man looked across the city's skyline and began to play.

As Bill Anderson strummed and studied the few lights that blinked at this late hour, a thought came to him. As he glanced again to the sky and then back to the city streets, inspiration struck like lighting. Pulling a WJJC envelope from his pocket, he began to jot down his thoughts with a pencil. These random thoughts would radically change his life's course.

"You know there weren't a half a dozen lights in Commerce at that time," Bill recently explained, "and yet those lights grew in my mind to 'a great white way.' Commerce became a huge city. Then in the seconds verse I looked to the skies and thought, 'Did the God who put those stars above make those city

lights?' Within a few minutes I had completed the song.

"My dad said much later that he knew that I had a writer's imagination if I could look at Commerce and write about a great white way."

On that night Anderson was not only a visionary, he was a bit of a philosopher. He saw beyond the small town where he lived and walked through places he had never visited. In contrasting the draw of a sinful world of bars and honky-tonks to the purity of a heaven awash with bright lights, he summed up the everyday battle for man's soul. His latest composition was a moral ode that raised questions about the evil and temptations a country boy faced when he left his home for the city streets. He was painting every mother's worse nightmare.

Sensing he had something special, Bill made a recording of the song in a nearby television studio and shipped it to Bob Tanner at TNT Music in San Antonio, Texas. Anderson had found TNT by writing to almost every publisher in the country hoping to land a home for his compositions. Bob Tanner was the only one who'd responded. TNT had released Bill's first two efforts on their own label. Still, because Tanner had not made any money on Bill's first efforts, he was ready to simply pass on "City Lights." Then Anderson saved the deal by saying the magic words: "I'll pay if you press a few records off my own recording." The promise of money was the key as Tanner went to work, putting one of Anderson's other demos, "(I've Got) No Song to Sing," on the flip side.

As a disc jockey Bill rarely played "City Lights" on his show. At the local dances he noted the kids going crazy for "No Song," so he figured his best shot was with the rocker, not the ballad. Fortunately, Charlie Lamb, a music reporter, happened to listen to "City Lights" when he reviewed the copy Anderson had sent his way. Lamb thought it was a powerful piece of work and took it to Chet Atkins. Chet was, at that time, RCA's A&R man. He reviewed it, also liked what he heard, and passed "City Lights" along to Dave Rich. Rich cut the song and the label released it. Even though Anderson was thrilled to have a big-time cut, the single failed to make the playlists. But even if he didn't make any money from the venture, just getting a Music City recording was a dream come true for the college student.

Bill's composition would have probably died there if Ernest Tubb and Ray Price hadn't made a date to play golf. Riding in a car equipped with a radio, the two country music stars caught the Dave Rich cut one of the few times it ever made the airwaves. Tubb commented that it sure did sound like Price's kind of song. Ray dismissed the veteran's remarks, but Ernest wouldn't quit hounding Price.

" 'City Lights' is just your style," Tubb prodded. "You could have a huge hit with that. If I were you I would cancel whatever it was I was about to release and cut it."

A week later Price took Tubb's advice and went into the studio. To set the mood, Ray actually gave his people a pep talk just before they cut the song. He told everyone to imagine that they were in Las Vegas, it was cold, and they had just lost everything in the casino. Then like a football team charging onto the field after the coach's pregame speech, the fired-up

session players walked into the recording studio and laid down the tracks. The mood was perfect, and they came up with a real winner.

Price's record was released in early summer, just about nine months after Bill had climbed to the roof of the Hotel Andrew Jackson and penned it. "City Lights" put Anderson on the charts for the first time in mid-July, and on October 20 the song hit #1. Price's recording would hold that position for over three months. Ray would even cross over and make some noise on the pop side too. In the midst of the youth and rock explosion, a quiet song had not only become the year's biggest country hit, but had opened Nashville to a college boy from Georgia.

Maybe one of the most remarkable things about this cut of "City Lights" was that besides giving Bill Anderson his big break, it also gave another legendary songwriter/performer a golden opportunity. On the flip side of Ray Price's "City Lights" was "Invitation to the Blues." The writer of that cut was an old friend of Anderson's, Roger Miller.

Price's recording turned on "City Lights" for the music community. Time and time again it was cut. In 1975, eighteen years after it peaked the first time, Mickey Gilley would again bring "City Lights" back to the top spot. Over the years everyone from Mel Tillis to Ivory Joe Hunter to Debbie Reynolds has cut the Anderson classic.

Two decades after Bill Anderson wrote "City Lights" he had become known as one of Music City's best songwriters. Over four hundred different Anderson songs have been cut, and many of then have passed the point of being hits and become classics. As a performer the soft-spoken college man has charmed audiences around the world, landed on the major playlists more than eighty times, and cut five records which have topped the *Billboard* chart. He has won almost as many awards as he has written songs. Yet maybe the most meaningful professional tribute came in the late seventies when the city of Commerce, Georgia, erected a marble monument on a downtown street just a few steps from the old Hotel Andrew Jackson. The writing etched in the granite read, "Bill Anderson, Country Music Hall of Fame Songwriter, Wrote His First Hit, 'City Lights,' in Commerce, Georgia."

Not far from where the monument was placed is one of the community's city lights. Bill Anderson's work has been spotlighted thousands of times in hundreds of ways, but probably none is quite as appropriate as this one.

1959

Heartaches by the Number

Written by Harlan Howard

When one examines Harlan Howard's life's work of more than four hundred recorded songs and hundreds of millions in record sales, when one observes as the composer seems to magically pull fabulous phrases out of the air and then generate new melodies on the spur of the moment, it might look as if Harlan writes everything easily and quickly, that his genius just explodes in creative rushes. But in truth, what may have seemed to take this master tunesmith only a few moments to create was more than likely years in the making.

The fact is that Harlan Howard seems to "find" songs in places other people never look. He could look at the same thing every day and never see it the same exact way twice. His perspective is both unique and refined. While he was in the Army he was "inspired" by everything from medal ceremonies to warehouse inventories. In civilian life old men on street corners and children constantly gave him new ideas. And even though he didn't jot down a new composition for every unparalleled moment he witnessed, he never seemed to forget any of them. These scenes were somehow vividly filed in his memory just waiting for the right moment to be shaped into a musical story.

"A lot of my songs had been written in my mind," Harlan explained, "long before I finally put them on paper. I just thought about them until they came together easily."

In 1959 Howard was still just another factory worker who had written hundreds of songs while composing just one hit, "Pick Me Up on Your Way Down." While there was nothing quite as important to Harlan as songwriting and he was thrilled with his Charlie Walker release, he wasn't going to let it go to his head. This little bit of moonlighting success wasn't about to get him to quit his day job. He was mature enough to realize that one hit did not a songwriter make. He knew that in order to move to Music City he would have to prove that he could follow up his first recorded effort. Thanks to the contacts made by "Pick Me Up," he soon got the chance.

"Ray Price was a good friend of Charlie Walker's," the songwriter recalled, "and one night he called me at home in Los Angeles. He told me that he was about to record a new album. He said that he wanted to record one of my songs and wanted to know if I had anything."

Harlan thought for a few moment before modestly replying that he had two or three that might fit into "The Cherokee Cowboy's" style. A pleased Price ended the conversation by asking the songwriter to put them on tape and rush them to Nashville.

One of the demos Howard cut was a hurting song which owed its inspiration to his days in the military. It was this almost-decade-old idea which would stand out on the demo tape.

"Everything in the Army was by the numbers," Howard remembered. "From the time we got up until we went to bed we were always doing things that way. So I had gotten to thinking about a song that used numbers. I was trying to combine it with a standard song idea. I started with, 'Heartache number one was when you left,' and just continued from there."

When Ray Price heard "Heartaches by the Number" he knew that his call to Los Angeles had not been wasted. This song had the perfect feel for both his voice and the late fifties market. In the studio he felt sure that this was a hit. Columbia agreed, and released the song as a single in May. It stayed on the charts for forty weeks. "Heartaches" became Price's fifteenth top-ten single, topping out at #2. Yet what Ray had accomplished with the song paled in comparison to what Guy Mitchell was able to achieve.

The Detroit-born pop singer had often used country music as a vehicle for his own career. In 1956 this product of Mitch Miller's band had garnered a #1 single by covering Marty Robbins's hit "Singing the Blues." So few were surprised that five months after Price had released his country version of "Heartaches," Mitchell recorded the song and spun it onto the rock charts. In spite of competition from a host of hot rock 'n' roll acts, "Heartaches by the Number" stayed on the hot-play one hundred for twenty-two weeks, eventually claiming #1 for two weeks.

Price's hit had helped Harlan establish his relationship with Nashville, but it was Mitchell's recording that had finally given the songwriter the financial security to quit his day job and move to Music City. Once there he would soon welcome Hank Cochran and Willie Nelson to little Pamper Music. In a brief span of time these geniuses would turn out some of the most unforgettable songs in the history of country music and make the small company one of country music's greatest treasures.

"I was lucky," Howard modestly states when attempting to explain why he has been able to continue to write hit songs for four decades. "I came along at the right time. I grew up listening to country music in the era when it was filled with so many great talents and so many great songwriters. I was exposed to this and it taught me how to write."

Yet there is more to the songwriter's accomplishments than he cares to admit. Like few others, Harlan has allowed his total life experience to become a funnel for his creativity. He has drawn upon everything from his poor days as a child to his work on a factory line. He continued to walk the streets and got to know the common people long after he had earned his fame and fortune. He never lost the drive that began when as a child he first made up words to Ernest Tubb songs. For almost forty years Harlan Howard has shared his genius with the common people by writing some of history's most unforgettable songs, with a list of hits that goes on forever. Country music has been made far richer by Harlan Howard's efforts.

1959
The Battle of New Orleans
Written by Jimmy Driftwood

"The Battle of New Orleans" is probably the only hit song ever inspired by a need to motivate a grade school class. James Morris had grown up in the Ozark tradition of playing music and writing poetry. Driftwood, Morris's nickname since birth, was from a family of guitar- and fiddle-playing "hillbilly" singers. Not only did the Morris clan compose much of what they performed, but most of their instruments were homemade. They were therefore as much craftsmen as musicians, and they were proud of both of these talents.

For the first half of this century, music, hard work, and hard times were the common ties for most of the Arkansas backwoods people. Of those three, only music consistently produced real joy and relief. For Driftwood and the rest of the Morris family, it was always a primary focus in their lives. A day never went by that they weren't playing, singing, or studying music.

Unlike most of the locals, Driftwood left the hills long enough to journey to Conway, Arkansas, and earn his college degree at Arkansas State Teachers College (now University of Central Arkansas). In the midst of the Great Depression he then returned to his roots to teach. By 1936 Driftwood was an underpaid and overworked twenty-nine-year-old Snowball, Arkansas, schoolteacher trying to get his sixth-grade pupils interested in history. No matter what he at-

tempted, books, pictures, or reports, they didn't respond. Then, in a moment of real inspiration, Driftwood drew upon self-penned poetry as a way of sharing the world's most important events. It was this history, set to a poet's rhythm, that first captured the students' interest while also teaching them something they had once not wanted to learn. Placing more historical odes to music, Driftwood discovered a teaching aid that really worked. He used it time and time again. Hence, to the teacher, his poem "The Battle of New Orleans," set to an old square dance fiddle tune, "The Eighth of January," was simply another in a long line of motivational classroom tools.

For the next two decades Driftwood took his historical songs with him wherever he taught. His students also took them with them as they fanned out across the area, region, and nation. By the mid-fifties the songwriter had developed a certain degree of respect and esteem from the folks living in the hills and hollows surrounding the towns of Timbo, Mountain View, and Snowball. He was also becoming well known in school districts throughout the Ozarks. Yet no one, especially Driftwood, dreamed that his work would ever be anything more than a student learning stimulator.

In the mid-fifties Porter Wagoner and steel guitar player Don Warden got together at Red Foley's *Ozark Jubilee* television show in Springfield, Missouri. These two savvy "hillbilly" musicians had been around the music industry long enough to realize that songwriters made music publishers a great deal of money while often keeping little for themselves. In order to cut out the middleman, Wagoner and Warden formed a publishing company. Initially the business's sole purpose was to publish Porter's compositions. Yet within a year the duo saw a need for growth, and Don was beating the backwoods looking for new songwriting skills.

In 1957 Don's old friend Hugh Ashley told Warden about a songwriting teacher with a great deal of untapped talent living in the Ozark backwoods town of Timboe. The publisher jotted down the writer's name and hometown and promised his friend that he would give him a call. A few days later Warden sought out Driftwood's telephone number. He found that there was no listing for a Jimmy Driftwood or a James Morris. As the publisher would discover, Driftwood had never obtained a phone. Warden then tried writing Driftwood in care of general delivery. A few weeks later he received a reply. The teacher informed the publisher that he had written a few songs and that he wouldn't mind playing them for Warden at a future date.

Warden wrote back and asked Driftwood to put some of his songs on tape and send them to his office. The teacher answered explaining that he didn't have access to a tape recorder. He wondered if he could visit Don in Nashville and play the songs for him in person over the next school holiday. Through a series of letters the two agreed on a date.

During their initial Nashville meeting in a hotel room Driftwood played Warden almost everything he had written. By and large Don was at best mildly impressed, but he was not moved enough to make any offers. As the publisher was getting up to leave, Jimmy began fiddling around with "The Battle of New Orleans." As he listened, Don smiled and sat back down on the bed. Within a hour Warden had hatched a plan to get the schoolteacher a recording contract.

Chet Atkins at RCA thought enough of Warden's endorsement and Driftwood's songs to place twelve of the teacher's compositions on an album of folk music. Yet the label had little success marketing the final product. Everyone agreed that it was good stuff, but there was simply no niche for it in the market of the times. It seemed that Driftwood's music was too folk for most of the country radio stations and too country for the pop playlist. It also contained the words "damn" and "hell," both being banned by most respectable programmers. Finally, after much lobbying from RCA and Atkins, WSM began playing "The Battle of New Orleans" occasionally, but only in the middle of the night.

Johnny Horton, a former Baylor University basketball player and geology student, was driving back from a late-night small-town concert gig when he caught the song on his car radio at 2:00 A.M. The next day he called his label, Columbia, and told them he wanted to record it. At this point Horton was just another *Louisiana Hayride* rockabilly performer who at best was a regional star with just the bare minimum of a national following. His main claim to fame was based on the fact that he had married one of Hank Williams's widows, Billie Jean.

While Columbia didn't mind spending a bit of time fulfilling Horton's wish to record "The Battle of New Orleans," releasing a version of the former teaching aid as a single was a risk. Frankly, the label wasn't sure it would be worth the effort or money. Traditionally folk or story-type songs had not done well in the country music market. Since Elvis's rise, traditional steels and banjos had also taken a backseat to a more bass, electric guitar, and drum-driven sound. Within the previous year rock 'n' roll standards like "Great Balls of Fire," "Bird Dog," and "City Lights" had all been huge country hits. "The Battle of New Orleans" thus went against every facet of the current market trend. Yet with Horton's urging, Columbia agreed to release the song as a single. No one expected what was to follow.

From the day "The Battle of New Orleans" hit the airwaves radio stations' request lines lit up. By mid-summer the song had climbed to the top spot in both country and pop music. It would ride those charts for almost half a year. Ultimately it was the biggest song of 1959, one of the twenty-five top songs of the first five years of the rock 'n' roll era, and would make Johnny Horton into a national sensation. It would also spawn a number of historically based hits for a host of recording stars. These cuts included "Johnny Reb" and "Sink the Bismarck" for Horton himself. While it may not have changed the classroom teaching methods of history teachers, "The Battle of New Orleans" did give rise to a new folk-driven sound in both country and pop music.

Even before Horton's version of "The Battle of New Orleans" took off, Jimmy Driftwood returned to the Arkansas hills to resume writing songs and teaching school. Over the course of the next twenty years he would compose a number of hits for artists such as Eddy Arnold, tour the world as an entertainer, join the *Opry*, become known as one of the foremost experts on American folk music, and get a telephone. Four decades after his song hit the top of the charts and almost sixty years after he had first performed it for a sixth-grade class, he was still performing "The Battle of New Orleans" and winning new fans to his kind of hillbilly folk music.

Life wasn't as kind to Johnny Horton. The dynamic singer would hit #1 one more time with "North to Alaska" before tragically dying in a car wreck on an East Texas bridge. Though his complete catalog of recordings is not large, his records are still selling at a steady clip. In 1986 Dwight Yoakam launched his Bakersfield honky-tonk sound with a version of Horton's first hit, "Honky-Tonk Man."

1959
El Paso

Written by Marty Robbins

Marty Robbins observed many times that if he had just been born a little sooner he would have spent his life as a cowboy. He loved horses and guns, camping out and driving cows. He was an outdoorsman who loved to challenge himself and nature. Yet by and large the Arizona native had failed to reveal his love for the range during his first six years in music. His hits and his writing reflected more modern concerns ("A White Sport Coat"). It was only when he sang the theme to a 1959 Gary Cooper movie, *The Hanging Tree*, that he first delved into a western sound.

Later that same year, as a result of riding down the road listening to the radio, he began to consider writing lyrics and music to a western story. His inspiration had come from Johnny Horton's "Battle of New Orleans." This Jimmy Driftwood-penned composition seemed to prove to Marty that the public had a craving for finely crafted historical odes. If this formula could work for a song about a war that few even remembered studying in history class, then maybe it could be used to tell a tale of the Old West. After all, a lot more people knew a great deal more about Billy the Kid than Andrew Jackson!

In a sense Marty's timing couldn't have been better. More westerns were a part of network prime time than at any time in television history. *Bonanza* was the nation's favorite program, and a dozen other horse operas such as *Gunsmoke* and *Wyatt Earp* were gallop-

ing not far behind. Even the kids tuned into cowboy shows each day after school, as well as on Saturday morning. Willie Nelson would later write that his "heroes [had] always been cowboys," and this generation of baby boomers was echoing his thoughts each day with the toys they bought, the shows they watched, and the games they played. The kids of the late fifties were completely caught up in Annie Oakley, Roy Rogers, the Lone Ranger, and a dozen other cowboy stars. To Marty it seemed only logical that every generation would love a song about the Old West.

Robbins had driven through El Paso, Texas, several times during his tours. He often stopped in the community, getting to know its people and its history. While visiting, Marty had fallen in love with the mix of Mexican and American cultures which gave the area such a unique atmosphere. So it was not unusual that as he began to write his western answer to "Battle of New Orleans," he placed the border city and its musical sound at the center of his tale.

For his story line inspiration Robbins reached back to his youth. His grandfather had been a cowboy. He had lived the life of a rover and cowpuncher. As a child Marty had heard the stories of range wars and cantina fights firsthand. Sorting through his memories, the songwriter began to work out a tale of a cowboy, a beautiful Mexican maiden, and a mean gunslinger. By the time he finished, Robbins had composed a tragedy of Shakespearean proportions. As he was soon to find out, he had also written a song which few people wanted to touch.

In both country and pop music there had long been an unwritten law which read, "No record company will release a single that it is any longer than three minutes." Record label executives and producers had long felt that a long song simply wouldn't gather an audience. They were convinced that the public wouldn't sit still and listen to anything that ran over the three-minute limit. Furthermore, if a release had too many lyrics, the audience couldn't and wouldn't care to follow the story line. The rule for both ballad and up-tempo releases was to keep it short, keep it uncomplicated, and make it repetitious enough that the tune and words could be learned in a matter of a few quick plays. Marty's latest composition broke all the established rules.

The singer probably wouldn't have even fought to have the song recorded and released if Johnny Horton hadn't done so well with "Battle of New Orleans." That song, complete with banjo, was tearing up both the country and pop charts. Fans of every age were buying it. Using the success that Horton had garnered as his springboard, Marty finally convinced Columbia to give "El Paso" a try. With this hurdle clear, Robbins was faced with an even larger stumbling block.

Marty's cut sounded nothing like anything he had ever recorded. Accompanied by very simple Spanish-flavored instrumentation with Tompall & the Glaser Brothers providing the harmonies, "El Paso" seemed to fly in the face of the two things which were then driving country music hits—rockabilly and shuffle-beat honky-tonk music. Besides that, the song was four minutes and twenty seconds long. To many disc jockeys this was an eternity. It was simply too long to program. Besides that, the story was depressing.

Robbins argued that his live crowds loved it and that the story line was tragic, but not depressing. He believed that audiences would strongly identify with the cowboy and his undying love for his sweetheart. Marty pleaded for the radio programmers to just give him a chance. He believed that if they did play the song, then it would draw in new listeners to country stations.

Columbia shipped "El Paso" in the fall of 1959. It reached stations just as "Battle of New Orleans" was losing its grip on the country and pop top spots. In country, the Johnny Horton single was being replaced with "Waterloo," a Stonewall Jackson historical ode. Robbins felt this again worked to his advantage. If Jackson could score with a song that traded off a European war, then Marty knew that the market was ripe for his cowboy ballad.

Just after Christmas, the song which Marty had been told would never find a home on radio hit the top of the country playlist. It would hold #1 for seven weeks. Even more remarkably, it was soaring on the rock charts too. It would hit the top spot in pop music in January, and remain in that position for two weeks.

Back in the studio Robbins cut another cowboy balled, "Big Iron." It too would find the top ten later in the year, but the new single couldn't match "El Paso's" numbers. Over the course of his long and powerful career Marty would have three records which would have more successful rides on the country charts than this western ballad, but none would be so identified with the singer as "El Paso."

In 1976 Robbins wrote a follow-up to his most famous hit. After viewing El Paso from the air he scribbled the words to "El Paso City." The song was very little but a rehash of the original, but that didn't seem to matter to country music fans. They were still hungry for more of Robbins's western style. By July, Marty had placed the single at the top of the charts. It was his first #1 in five years.

"El Paso" has grown into more than a song. It is now a part of history. Like "Tumbling Tumbleweeds," Marty Robbins's ballad has come to represent the West itself. The fact that the song's events were fictitious is no more important than the fact that the tumbleweed was a Russian thistle that didn't even arrive in the American West until the final decade of the last century. Robbins's epic captured the romance of the range like no other song ever had or probably ever will. With its unique story line, "El Paso" conjured up images of how people wanted their West to be, and continued the marriage of country music and cowboys that had begun with the Sons of the Pioneers.

1960
He'll Have to Go

Written by Joe Allison and Audrey Allison

One of country music's most memorable and success-ful songs was inspired by a husband's phone call to his wife. As Joe Allison checked in at home, he found himself straining to hear each of his wife's words. Au-drey's soft voice simply wasn't carrying over the line. After a few minutes of asking her to repeat what she had just said, Joe told Audrey, "Please talk louder and put your mouth closer to the phone." She did, and he had no problems after that.

When the songwriter got home that night, he found a single line written in longhand on an other-wise blank piece of paper. He recognized the hand-writing as his wife's, and as he read the sentence he realized that it had come from their phone call: "Put your sweet lips a little closer to the phone." By simply changing "mouth" to "lips" and phrasing it as if two lovers were having a very intimate conversation, Au-drey Allison had begun what was to become one of Music City's most beloved ballads. As Joe studied the solitary line he was overcome by its direct beauty. Not even bothering to ask why Audrey hadn't finished the lyrics she had started, the man picked up a pen from the table and began to add his own ideas. Within min-utes Joe had completed what his spouse had begun and composed the music. When Audrey read it over she knew that their "He'll Have to Go" was a won-derful song.

In many ways team songwriting is often a strange

endeavor. If Audrey hadn't rewritten something her husband had told her, then Joe would have never been moved to compose the rest of the song's lyrics. So while most of the actual labor may have been his, Mrs. Allison's inspired first line triggered everything else. Neither of them could or would have written the song alone, but together they combined to create a bit of musical magic.

"He'll Have to Go" ended up at RCA, where Chet Atkins reviewed it. The guitar player was in charge of turning out country hits, and he was convinced that Joe and Audrey's new song had #1 written all over it. Yet, just as it took a special combination of talent and effort to write "He'll Have to Go," it was also going to take Atkins marrying the composition to just the right voice to make it a hit. The ballad cried out for a singer who was smooth and assured and could produce a pop sound that would play well in the country mar-ketplace. Chet didn't have to look very far. He already had the man signed with his label.

Jim Reeves had backed into country music star-dom. Like Roy Acuff, Reeves had dreamed of playing major league baseball. A top-flight pitching prospect, Jim made it a lot further than most. The good-looking Texan had left the University of Texas baseball squad to play for a St. Louis Cardinals farm team. While starring in Lynchburg, Virginia, Reeves injured his leg beyond repair making a slide into second base. As they carried him off the field, the young man sensed that he was going to have to find something else to do.

Using his God-given deep voice, he polished his diction and gained employment as a radio announcer. While he was occasionally cajoled into singing a few songs on the air, Jim did not consider himself to be a singer. He was a radio personality who someday wanted to own and manage his own station. Jim worked throughout the late forties in Henderson, Texas, then moved east into a bigger market. While announcing for a Shreveport station, Reeves was approached by Abbott Records. They wondered if he would like to cut a record or two. Thinking of it as a way to make a few extra dollars, Jim agreed and recorded several sides. One of them, "Mexican Joe," unexpectedly made the national charts. What happened next shocked the radio announcer. By May 1953, Reeves's throwaway little single had actually climbed up the playlist and knocked Hank Williams's "Your Cheatin' Heart" out of country music's top spot.

With a suddenness that even he couldn't comprehend, Jim was forced to go from announcing to performing. Reeves quickly put together a band, joined the *Louisiana Hayride*, and rushed back into the studio to see if he could catch lightning in a bottle twice. Jim did just that as he and the Abbott label scored a second #1 with "Bimbo." Five chart releases later RCA signed Reeves away from the local label and the singer became a part of the *Opry*.

Reeves would have no problem scoring hits for RCA. Early on he topped the charts with "Four Walls," one of 1957's biggest songs. His "Billy Bayou" also hit the top spot the next year. Many of his records were also doing well on the pop side, and with his smooth voice RCA was beginning to look for material that would make the star a bit more cosmopolitan and even more successful in the pop market. In late 1959 Chet Atkins knew he had found just the ticket with

Joe and Audrey Allison's simple song about a phone, a man, and a jukebox. Jim, who by now had a publishing company, agreed.

"He'll Have to Go" was released in early winter, and not only climbed up the country playlist, but all the pop lists too. In February the song began a fourteen-week stay at country's #1 position. At that same time the record was enjoying a three-week rest in pop's #2 position. Within a few months of the session that captured this hit, RCA had sold over three million copies of the record. Staying on the country charts for thirty-four weeks, "He'll Have to Go" then traveled overseas and topped charts in Europe, Africa, and Australia. A year after the Allisons' song first hit the playlists, Jim had become the biggest country music sensation in the world. Touring the globe, Reeves was often mobbed like a rock or movie star. A man who had once backed into country music was now fronting the charge in the worldwide growth of that musical genre.

As Reeves grew hotter and hotter, many in country music began to question if the Texan was really a country act. His critics claimed his voice was too smooth and his records sold too well in the city. Besides, he liked to dress in tuxedos and perform in concert halls. Jim even used the English language like a Southern aristocrat. Yet the patrons at the Opry never turned their backs on the singer, and neither did the millions of his fans who bought more and more of his music. There is no telling how many records he could have sold if he hadn't lost his life in a 1964 plane crash.

To many, Jim Reeves was an icon to show just how far country music had come. While Eddy Arnold had won a host of city slickers over to rural music, Reeves had made even more inroads. Thanks in large part to this Texan, it was no longer a sign of bad taste to buy a country album or admit that you liked country music. At a time when the rockabilly acts were turning a lot of country music's older fans off, Reeves was there to turn them back on. He assured these old-timers that the rest of the world might be going to rock, but he was going to stick with love songs. Yes, country music was evolving, but Jim seemed to prove that this change wasn't all bad.

Jim Reeves's biggest hit, "He'll Have to Go," captured the singer, his remarkable voice and style, better than any of his eighty other singles. Today, more than three decades after his death, "He'll Have to Go" is not only still selling, but has become one of the twenty best-charting songs of all time. As time has proven, the only thing wrong with Jim Reeves's accidental rush to stardom was that he had to go far too soon. He brought country to city and then the world, and after he died most of his fans stuck with the musical style which had made him a star.

1960

Please Help Me, I'm Falling

Written by Don Robertson and Hal Blair

Hank Locklin was born in Florida in 1918. By the age of six he was playing a guitar, picking cotton, and singing songs. Three years later the instrument had been repossessed, but Hank's love of music didn't wane. He would eventually buy another guitar and begin to play dates in the local area. The Depression got in the way of his career plans, forcing the teenager to leave home and work in WPA programs. Locklin took his guitar with him, and as he toiled on projects for Uncle Sam, he continued to play dances and small clubs. He would scrape by in this fashion until the Japanese bombed Pearl Harbor.

Completing a service hitch during World War II, Locklin resumed his career, migrated to Louisiana, and became one of the first regulars on the *Louisiana Hayride*. By the late forties he was a regional radio personality, had earned a Decca record deal, and was making more money than he had ever made in his entire life. The fact that his "star" income barely placed him in a lower-middle-class lifestyle showed just how far the singer had come since his days on the farm. For Locklin, a product of dire poverty, even the eighteen dollars a week the *Hayride* paid its stars was high cotton.

Hank's deal with Decca produced no hit records, and a follow-up contract with 4 Star often staggered, scoring far more downs than ups. Finally in 1953, Locklin scored a #1 record with "Let Me Be the

One." His nasal tenor was now recognized throughout the hillbilly world, and Hank was invited to join the *Opry*. This would lead to a meeting with Steve Sholes and a better record deal with RCA. Yet in spite of these positive moves, Locklin's record career didn't explode. Seven years later he had made the national playlists just four times, with no record climbing any higher than #3.

In early 1960 Hank hadn't made a chart appearance in two years and his record career appeared dead in the water. He was still popular in his native Florida and with *Opry* fans, but it looked as though the forty-two-year-old singer would be lost in the youth movement that was so dramatically changing country music. In particular his value as a recording artist appeared to be completely dead.

At about the same time Locklin had last produced a hit, master songwriter Don Robertson was playing with lyrics and music that had a straight country feel. He was attempting to compose a song centered around the idea of a man who was trying hard not to fall for a woman he shouldn't love. Several times Don had endeavored without success to finish the number. Sensing that he had something special but didn't know what to do with it, he took the number to several other writers. None of them were interested in what Robertson had started, so the writer filed it away and began working on other concepts.

A year later he was writing with Hal Blair. Blair, like Robertson, had made a lot of house and car payments by knowing what it took to build a good song. As the two California tunesmiths went over each other's ideas, Don pulled out the unfinished song that began, "Please help me, I'm falling in love with you."

Robertson's lyrics could have been the story of Blair's life. Hal had actually fallen in love with someone he shouldn't have. He had even written about this experience in "One Has My Name, the Other Has My Heart." As Blair read Robertson's lyrics out loud, he began to give Don his insights. In a manner of a few minutes the two writers had completed the song which they titled after its first line, "Please Help Me, I'm Falling (In Love with You)."

Taking the completed number into the studio, Don decided to cut a demo not only using his skills on piano, but for the first time contributing the vocal as well. In an effort to give the recording a very country feel, he also used a new piano style on which he had been working for years.

"I was trying to imitate a banjo slide on the piano," Robertson explained. "The style sounded like nothing I had ever heard. When Hill and Range Publishing sent it over to Chet Atkins, Chet called me and spent more time talking about the piano style than our song. He even asked me to teach the technique to his RCA session player."

Atkins may have been especially interested in Don's new piano lick, but he was also impressed with "Please Help Me, I'm Falling." Chet took it to one of the label's hottest acts, Jim Reeves. Reeves listened to it for three weeks and then turned it down. The song then found its way to Hank Locklin.

RCA needed a hit for the Florida singer and the Robertson/Blair piece seemed a perfect fit of subject and style. Putting Hank in the studio, the company cut "Please Help Me, I'm Falling." Released in late winter, the record landed on the chart on March 7, 1960, and RCA knew from the immediate response that this was going to be a big single. Yet even they failed to understand just how big. Within days record plants were pressing day and night just to keep up with sales. Locklin's "Please Help Me" needed no help at all locking onto the top spot in May. The song would not release its hold on that position for fourteen weeks. In a year that only saw five songs hit #1, Hank's was the biggest. The man who had, at best, a very mediocre recording career beat out other chart-toppers by Ferlin Husky, Marty Robbins, Cowboy Copas, and the man who had originally passed on the song, Jim Reeves.

While "Please Help Me, I'm Falling" was a monster hit, it failed to do much for Locklin's American career. Recording for another nineteen years, he never again hit any higher than #7. Only two of his follow-up recordings even landed in the top ten. Yet while mostly ignored in the United States, Hank would go on to become one of Europe's biggest country music stars. In Ireland his tenor voice made him a legend. Much of the successful introduction of country music to Europe was thanks in large part to his efforts and the worldwide success of "Please Help Me, I'm Falling."

While being recorded scores of times, the Blair/Robertson classic would hit the charts on three more occasions. The most successful of these belonged to Janie Fricke in 1968. Skeeter Davis also drew on the inspiration of the song to record a big hit in 1960. Davis's "(I Can't Help You) I'm Falling Too" served as an answer to Hank's plea. Skeeter rode this version of the song to #2. Davis's only song that would become a bigger hit was "The End of the World" two years later.

Based on a love affair that couldn't be fulfilled,

"Please Help Me, I'm Falling" set the stage for country music's reach to invade foreign markets. It would later become a catalyst in a successful Mc-Clellan, Florida, mayoral race for Hank Locklin. It also would help guitar man Chet Atkins establish a new country piano style. But that's another story that has to do with another song and another super talent.

1960
Tips of My Fingers

Written by Bill Anderson

By 1960 Bill Anderson had moved to Nashville and become an important player in the songwriting community. Living in a small apartment, the rent paid with royalty checks, he had set up a tiny table and a manual typewriter in the living room and tried to work on a regular schedule composing new material. At this point it was his writing much more than his performing career that was making his living. For this reason most country music fans didn't have a firm idea as to who Bill Anderson was, but those folks looking for inspired material did.

Between regular fits of inspiration, Bill hit the road and began to introduce himself to more and more fans. At fairs and in schoolhouses he performed before audiences that numbered from the hundreds to the thousands. Unlike many entertainers, Anderson stayed late after every show, signing autographs, posing for pictures, trading stories, and winning new friends. Already known as one of the nicest writers in Music City, Anderson was well on his way to earning a reputation as one of most personable live acts in the business.

Bill had signed a recording contract with Decca soon after Ray Price had taken "City Lights" to the top of the charts. Anderson's first cut, "That's What It's Like to Be Lonesome," had gone to #12. He had followed "Lonesome" with "Ninety-Nine" and "Dead or Alive." If neither of these songs sounds familiar, it

is because they failed to score big numbers on the charts. They were forgotten not long after they were released. As he entered his third year with Decca, Bill had proven that he could write hit songs, but he still hadn't proven that he could sell the ones he recorded.

At about the same time that Bill was penning "I Missed Me," a future hit for Jim Reeves, an idea came to him that seemed both inspired and jinxed. Anderson had realized that "I let you slip right through my fingers" was a killer hook line, but for weeks he couldn't seem to come up with a way to make it fit with anything else. He worked on the song regularly, but he couldn't turn the corner that allowed him to finish it.

"Writing is a combination of inspiration and sweat," Bill explained, "and 'Tips of My Fingers' had a lot of sweat in it before I was finished writing."

After a month of "arts and crafts" work, the talented songwriter began to feel satisfied with "Tips of My Fingers." He had come up with a follow-up for the hook line. With that line the rest of the song had followed in fairly rapid order. Now that it was completed, the real dilemma came to the forefront. Should he demo it and allow someone else to have the big hit, or should he use this latest creation as his next release? He opted for the latter.

Owen Bradley and Decca needed a song that would crystallize Bill's career as a performer. The producer and the label felt that Anderson had all the right tools to become a star, but in spite of these positives they also wondered if the public would ever discover him. As he struggled to get that first big record, Bill couldn't help but remember Dave Rich, the man who had initially cut "City Lights." RCA had been convinced that Rich was going to be a star, but his career had never taken off. Another songwriter who was having the same problem landing a hit record was Willie Nelson. Like Nelson, Anderson was far from ready to give up singing. Still, Bill knew that he might never become the performer that he wanted to be. Too many things over which he had little control seemed to be working against him.

Decca shipped "Tips of My Fingers" in late spring. The record took off much more quickly than any of Bill's other releases. Some figured that the singer/songwriter's long nights on the road and many hours put in visiting with local disc jockeys were finally paying off. Others simply believed that Decca was putting a bit more work into this single. Yet the record's success was probably just due to the genius evidenced in the final product. "Tips of My Fingers" had been worth the weeks of effort. It was a masterful story of lost love. This composition fully exposed the emotion and depth of Bill's writing. The fact that his voice reflected all the song's pain and anguish in such a simple but stirring manner caused people to be drawn to the recording more each time they heard it. Thus there was really very little mystery why "Tips of My Fingers" lingered on the charts for more than half a year and stayed in the top ten for several weeks. As time would prove, it was just that good.

With "Tips of My Fingers" Bill's recording career was placed on the main road to success. Within two years he would place five songs in the top ten, and his "Still" and "Mama Sang a Song" would hold the top spot for seven weeks. He was now more than just a writer, he was a star. Yet while he was moving on to

pen and record a host of other tunes, "Tips of My Fingers" was still being kicked around the studios.

In 1963 Capitol introduced their newest act, a young guitarist named Roy Clark, to the world. Clark's first cut placed him solidly in the top ten. That single was "Tips of My Fingers." Three years later Eddy Arnold used the Anderson classic to hit the charts for the ninety-third time. Arnold's version would peak on the charts at about the same time Eddy was elected into the Country Music Hall of Fame.

In 1975 Jean Shepard used "Tips of My Fingers" to win a place on country music playlists for the thirty-eighth time. Besides these single releases, scores of acts in and out of Nashville placed Bill's song on albums or used it as a part of their live shows. Amazingly, with each new rendition, the song sounded as good as it had in 1960. Rather than having time claim it as a victim, "Tips of My Fingers" seemed to remain forever fresh.

Steve Wariner had been making his mark in Nashville since 1978. The Indiana native had worked with Dottie West and Chet Atkins before striking out on his own. In the mid-eighties he had scored six chart-topping songs in a span of just two years. Yet by the nineties some were predicting that his career had bottomed out. The hits had quit coming and Steve and his longtime label, MCA, had even parted ways.

Arista Records gave Wariner a second chance to spread his wings and bring his own style and talents to their label. Using that freedom he recorded "Tips of My Fingers." Released in early 1992, it would become his biggest hit in four years, riding the charts for twenty weeks and matching Eddy Arnold's earlier cut by peaking at #3.

"Steve really did a fine job on the song," Bill noted with pride.

More importantly for Wariner, he didn't let the opportunity which Arista had given him slip through his fingers. He nailed a classic, proving that there was still a lot of life in both him and the song.

Some call the sixties the "Decade of Bill Anderson." Surrounded by some of the brightest songwriting talents in country music history, Anderson stood among the giants and produced hit after hit for both himself and scores of other acts. Modest, unassuming, and seemingly unfazed by his own talents or success, Bill spent so little time seeking out praise and honor that his contributions have sometimes been overlooked. Maybe it was his quiet nature more than his singing style that earned him the nickname "Whisperin' Bill." Yet one glance at the *Billboard* charts in the ten-year period after the first release of "Tips of My Fingers" reveals that Bill Anderson didn't let many good ideas slip through his hands. Almost every week during that decade one of his songs was anchored in the top ten.

1961
I Fall to Pieces

Written by Harlan Howard and Hank Cochran

In music there is a long list of performers who become known as one-hit sensations. For a brief instant in their lives a song and a style come together at just the right moment to rocket both to the top. Then, after a few concert appearances and a short time in the spotlight, the luster fades and they never again catch the magic.

When Patsy Cline came out smoking in 1957 with her monster hit "Walking after Midnight," a host of critics and fans believed that the sultry brunette would quickly become Nashville's newest "gal sensation." The bluesy "Walking after Midnight" quickly shot up the charts and stayed at #2 for two weeks. Blessed with a powerful voice and strong personality, this anything-but-demure Virginian looked like she had a sure shot at stardom firmly in hand. She was the perfect woman to charge through the door which Kitty Wells had knocked down in 1952 with "It Wasn't God Who Made Honky-Tonk Angels." Yet four years later Cline had landed on the charts just one more time, and her "A Poor Man's Roses" didn't even make the top ten. Though no one really understood why, she hadn't put together a follow-up. In Music City being a dynamic presence on stage wasn't enough. In a business where records drove careers, Patsy, an *Opry* favorite, desperately needed another hit.

Singer/songwriter Hank Cochran was in similar straits. Living from hand to mouth as a song plugger for Pamper Music, he was attempting to come up with a hit so that he could move his family to Nashville from California. Scraping by on less than ten dollars a week, depressed and lonesome, Cochran really did feel as if his whole life and his dreams were falling to pieces. Ironically, it was this haunting realization that would dramatically change his mood and his situation.

Cochran stopped by one day to visit with Harlan Howard. Harlan, whose stock was on the rise, was more than happy to encourage the young man. When Hank mentioned the concept of a song built around the line "You walk by and I fall to pieces," Howard offered to sit down and work with him. With that simple concept in mind, the first half of "I Fall to Pieces" fell together in a matter of minutes. Hank then left, hoping to put it on tape later in the day. As Harlan reviewed what they had written, he felt it was a little too short.

"I got singing it after he left," Howard recalled, "and I determined it just wasn't long enough. I went back to work and got the second half."

The lyrics and tune of "I Fall to Pieces" were sad, mournful, and filled with all the anguish that had engulfed most struggling songwriters' lives. It was a mighty ode to rejection and heartache. But at the time, Harlan doubted that it was a hit.

"To me it was a good song," he remembered, "but it was right in the middle of fifteen other songs I had just written. I can't say I thought it was a hit."

Working on a limited budget, the two got Harlan's wife, singer Jan Howard, to cut a demo record in Pamper's converted garage studio. Then Cochran began taking it, along with a number of other songs, from label to label to drum up interest. In retrospect it might seem surprising that they got no takers. After numerous rejections, they did find a lone supporter.

Owen Bradley, at the time a producer for Decca, loved the song. He assured the folks at Pamper that his rock 'n' roll sensation Brenda Lee could turn it into a smash hit. At that time Brenda was pop music's hottest female star, and royalties from her record sales would do a great deal for Hank's bank balance. It would probably even make Cochran's career. For a few days it seemed as if "I Fall to Pieces" was going to put everything together for him. Then everything did fall to pieces.

Instead of jumping at the opportunity to record the song, Brenda Lee passed. It was "too country" for her. After Lee turned thumbs down, so did a host of other Decca stars. Men thought it was a woman's song and the women just didn't like it. Still, Bradley believed in the commercial potential of the composition, so he turned to someone who really needed a hit, Patsy Cline.

Without hearing it, Patsy assured Bradley that she would record the number. After all, she had been told that it was a great woman's song. Then, upon listening to the demo, she abruptly changed her mind. In no uncertain terms she informed the producer that she didn't like anything about it. She didn't care if Owen rearranged it or rewrote it, she wasn't going to record it. Once again Cochran's dreams had been dashed. It must have seemed that the song was cursed.

Yet Bradley could be as stubborn as Cline. He con-

tinued to push even while she continued to say no. This titanic battle of wills might have continued if outside forces hadn't stepped in. Decca's New York executives were convinced that this would be a good vehicle for Cline. In a phone call they informed Patsy that they were tired of her selling just ten thousand units per single. They wanted a hit of major proportions and this song was her chance. With their tone and wording Cline could have decided it was her "last chance." It is really doubtful that the label was tired of supporting her, but they were ready for her to record something they thought was commercial. Left with no real choice, the singer finally relented to Decca and Bradley's judgment and joined the producer in the studio.

Owen Bradley was not going to take any risks with the song. If he had his way "I Fall to Pieces" would become a breakout hit. To insure this he brought in Nashville's best session players. For the harmonies he made a deal to get Elvis's backup group, the Jordanaires. Finally, in order to take advantage of Patsy's real strength, voice and style, he slowed the tempo down. Now the singer was free to depart from the demo and interpret the song's lyrics and melody in her own way.

When Patsy begin to sing, there was magic in the air. As her deep, pure voice echoed the lyric's emotions, Bradley knew that his instincts had been right. There were smiles all around. When the final take was over and they had nailed it perfectly, heads were bobbing up and down. Then as the playback came over the speakers, most of those in the studio were awed. Even Cline had to admit that it was special. Still, as the session ended and she left for the evening, she refused to acknowledge any affection for the song. The Cochran/Howard composition may have won over everyone else, but not her. At least not yet.

"Owen Bradley told me that they might not even

release the song," Hank Cochran explained. "Decca just didn't have much faith in Patsy. The only way that they were going to press the single was if they got five thousand advance orders. Hell, a best-seller sometimes didn't get more than thirty thousand back then. I knew we were in trouble. Patsy and I went up to Cincinnati to see Pat Nelson, who worked plugging songs for my publisher, Pamper Music. He and Patsy convinced the biggest radio station to [play] the record. Patsy could really charm you when she wanted to, so then she met the local distributor—the person who ordered the records for the whole area—and sang 'I Fall to Pieces' for her. That day the distributor ordered five thousand copies. Now Decca suddenly believed in the song, put the plants to pressing the record, and shipped it to all the stations and outlets. Publicity got to working on it too!"

"I Fall to Pieces" was released in April 1961. It become Cline's first #1 single, landing at the top and staying for two weeks. It remained on the country music charts for an incredible thirty-nine straight weeks.

"When the song really hit strong," Hank recalled, "Patsy had been in a bad car wreck. It almost killed her. She was in the hospital with her head wrapped with bandages. She could barely see and she sure couldn't read. I came in to see her with the reports. I told her, 'You got yourself a pop hit, girl.' She couldn't believe it. I think she thought I was just fooling around. When she finally got a good enough look at the numbers, she just laid back and said, 'Damn!' "

"I Fall to Pieces" stayed on the pop charts for ten weeks, topping out at #12. Yet more importantly than the chart success and record sales, "I Fall to Pieces" had quickly made Patsy into one of the nation's best-loved talents. She was now identified as a song stylist in the fashion of pop stars Peggy Lee, Patti Page, and Brenda Lee. No woman in country music had ever been so recognized. She was undeniably country music's brightest new talent and on the fast track to becoming a legend.

"I Fall to Pieces" has been recorded hundreds of times since Patsy took it up the charts. It has become a standard for female singers around the world. On its own the Cochran/Howard standard deserves a special place in country music history. It is a beautifully written testament to heartache and lost love. Yet without the marriage to Patsy Cline's style and voice, there seems little doubt that "I Fall to Pieces" would have missed realizing its full potential. Of course without "I Fall to Pieces" the world might have never really come to know the vast talents of Pasty Cline. More than thirty years later the song still works, and more than three decades after her death Cline is still selling records and winning new fans.

1961
Walk On By

Written by Kendall Hayes

Kentucky songwriter Kendall Hayes was having a problem with one of his compositions. There was something missing, but he couldn't put his finger on just what it was. The title "Walk On By" was a killer. It seemed perfect for the country market and the lyrics were well written, yet in spite of that, no one was interested in recording it. It was very much a song he couldn't sell.

"Kendall was one of the most wonderful men I ever knew," recalled music publisher Bill Lowery. "He was a delight to work with. He had put together several things for us that had done pretty well too. But he just couldn't seem to get folks interested in 'Walk On By.' It needed a hook that it didn't have, and Kendall just couldn't come up with it."

By 1960, Atlanta-based Lowery Music had opened a Nashville office to plug their songs and find new material. Gary Walker was running the office, and would check in with Bill on an almost daily basis. The outgoing Walker had a knack for being able not only to plug good material, but also to recognize promising new artists and songwriters. Walker was one of the reasons that Lowery Music was doing so well in both country and pop music.

"One day Gary called me," Bill remembered, "and he told me that he had a line that would work well with Kendall's song. Gary thought we could add 'wait on the corner,' and 'Walk On By' would become one of the best cheating songs we had in our catalog. If we could rework it with that one line he thought we could place it. After I hung up with Gary, I called Kendall. He agreed that we might have just found the key to finishing 'Walk On By.'"

After Hayes had completed rewriting his song, Bill Lowery called Shelby Singleton, the A&R man for Mercury in Nashville. Most of the phone call consisted of pumping the Lowery catalog, including the newest thing Kendall had written. A few days later Shelby received a demo of "Walk On By" and played it for Leroy Van Dyke.

If any artist in Nashville needed a hit it was Van Dyke. In a four-year recording career for two different labels, the Missouri native had placed just one song on the charts, his debut single, "The Auctioneer." That self-penned hit had leapt into the top ten in 1957, hung around for just two weeks, and then disappeared. After that, Leroy had been shut out. But while the singer and his new label wanted to find a big record, Van Dyke knew that he wasn't going to starve to death if all his country music dates dried up.

In a very real sense, Van Dyke was one Music City artist who didn't have to depend on each new song and personal appearance. Unlike most, he had something to fall back on. Leroy was a former journalist with a degree in agriculture from the University of Missouri. An auctioneer, he had also once been assigned to the Intelligence Department of the United States Armed Forces during the Korean War. Good-looking, bright, and well schooled in a wide variety of fields, he had a host of jobs waiting for him if he decided to ditch a musical career that had begun as nothing more than a hobby.

A guitar player, Van Dyke had spent a part of his time in Korea entertaining his buddies. It was during this time that he and Buddy Black wrote "The Auctioneer." The song gave Leroy an opportunity to show off one of his growing list of professions. The composition brought not only smiles from those who heard it, but also encouragement from a host of top brass who thought their man should try to sell his composition. After being discharged, Leroy took that advice and sold "The Auctioneer" and himself on *Arthur Godfrey's Talent Scouts* television show. Van Dyke won first place that night and was rewarded with a Dot recording contract. Now, four years later, Mercury Records was trying to restart his career and place him back on the charts. Bill Lowery was hoping that they would accomplish this with the Hayes song, but things didn't pan out again.

While Van Dyke agreed with Shelby that "Walk On By" was a good song, neither of them felt that it was strong enough to be a lead single. After cutting it, they put it on the "B" side of Leroy's newest release and forgot about it. That might have been the end of Kendall's best work, if not for Lowery Music. While Van Dyke and Singleton were plugging the heck out of the "A" side, Bill Lowery and Gary Walker were pushing "Walk On By."

"We pitched 'Walk On By' to all of our radio contacts," Bill said with a laugh as he recalled his company's counter-intelligence work. "Mercury was telling them to play one side and we were telling them to play the other. After a while we began to win and 'Walk On By' took off."

For the first time in fifty-five months Leroy Van Dyke found himself on the charts in September 1961. Shockingly, it was a "B" side that had placed him there. The artist and Mercury were even more amazed as "Walk On By" began to take the long stroll toward the top. In just three weeks the Hayes composition had gone from being a throwaway to the #1 song in the nation. Leroy's record would hold the top spot for an incredible nineteen weeks.

"Once we had a hit in country," Lowery explained, "we went to work on the rock 'n' roll side. We finally convinced a few disc jockeys to put it on their playlists and 'Walk On By' began to make some noise on pop stations too."

As Van Dyke's song held strong in country, it moved into the pop numbers in November. Against strong rock entries by the teen idols of the day, the country cheating standard held its own for three months, peaking at #5. The Mercury presses were overwhelmed just trying to keep up with demand.

"Walk On By" lingered on the country playlists for thirty-seven weeks, and for a short while made Leroy one of the nation's hottest acts. Running back into the studio, the singer cut a follow-up number that capitalized on his biggest hit's cheating message. "If a Woman Answers (Hang Up the Phone)" would also work its way into the top ten.

Gary Walker had no idea just how much his one line, "wait on the corner," would mean to both the song and himself. "Walk On By" would go on to become one of the top ten country music records of all time. It would also be far and away the top hit of 1961 and the top-producing song released between 1960 and 1995. It not only made Leroy Van Dyke's career, but also made Kendall Hayes's too. But overwhelming success did create problems.

"One of Kendall's biggest concerns centered around what he needed to do for Gary Walker," Bill recalled. "Kendall talked to me about how he should reward the man who had come up with the line that had made his song. I left that up to him. Later I found out that he gave Gary one quarter of all the royalties on "Walk On By." Not bad for contributing just a single line. Of course without that line, the song would probably have never been a hit."

Over the years a host of different artists have charted with the Hayes classic, but none has been able to follow the success of the original release. By the same token, Leroy Van Dyke could never follow his top recording either. Van Dyke never again ruled the charts.

There are songs and people whose talents shine brilliantly but briefly. Such is the case with this artist and this song. "Walk On By" was a failed effort that found life through a four-word editing suggestion. The record was a "B" side that was supposed to drift into obscurity, but through hard work earned a shot to compete in the marketplace. It was a straight country record that found great acceptance on the city's pop playlists. In a very real sense "Walk On By" is the rags-to-riches fable that validates the American dream of the underdog overcoming all odds to make it to the top. Passed by time and again, when polished it became the diamond that one could walk on by.

1961
Last Date

Written by Floyd Cramer, Boudleaux Bryant, and Skeeter Davis

Traditionally the piano had not been considered a country music mainstay. The instrument had long ranked well behind the guitar, fiddle, and steel as an important ingredient for a country band. While some progressive bands like the Texas Playboys always carried a keyboard player, most groups let ivory-ticklers find work in gospel, blues, or jazz. When Chet Atkins brought Floyd Cramer to Nashville to work RCA recording sessions in the fifties, this concept changed dramatically.

Cramer was born in 1933 in Shreveport, Louisiana, but grew up in the small town of Huttig, Arkansas. Floyd began to show an interest in music at a very early age. Before he entered first grade he was picking out tunes on the family piano, and by the time he hit high school he was known as the community's best musician. With only a bit of local club experience, Floyd was hired at eighteen by the *Louisiana Hayride*. This was the beginning of what was to become one of the most successful piano careers in entertainment history.

At the *Hayride*, Cramer not only played for all the artists who needed a piano for their live weekend performances, but often joined them in the studio or on the road. Between 1951 and 1955 Floyd traveled or recorded with, among many others, Hank Williams, Faron Young, Jim Reeves, and Elvis Presley. His solid work didn't go unnoticed by the music industry's ex-

ecutives. Chet Atkins, then heading up RCA's Nashville studios, came to know Floyd and his arsenal of keyboard talent when the young man accompanied Jim Reeves and other *Hayride* stars in studio sessions. Impressed, Chet arranged for Cramer to move to Nashville and play for the RCA sessions. Within a year of arriving in Tennessee, Floyd was the hottest studio musician in Music City.

Touring from time to time as a solo act, Floyd won rave reviews and was asked to join the *Opry*. By the late fifties, along with Atkins, Cramer was one of the two session players who were recognized not only by the performers, but also by country music fans. Yet it was the development of a certain piano style that was to make Floyd a star.

Songwriter and pianist Don Robertson had tried a new playing technique on a demo he had sent to Chet Atkins for review. Chet was fascinated by what Don had done in "Please Help Me, I'm Falling," and played the record for Floyd. Cramer shrugged, sat down, and easily mimicked Robertson's blended piano method. It seemed that Atkins's ivory sideman had been fooling around with a similar style for years. He had just never had a reason to play it when he was in session work.

"It is really a slurring of certain notes," Cramer explained. "It is kind of like what Maybelle Carter did with her guitar."

Chet saw commercial possibilities for the sound and signed Floyd as an artist. He then urged the pianist to come in with a song that would properly display this new country keyboard sound. It just so happened that Floyd had already created just such a tune. The song didn't have any lyrics, but with its sad, mournful melody line, he thought it would be the perfect number to use as his single debut. It was only after Atkins gave Cramer the approval to cut the composition that Floyd stopped to consider a title.

"I came up with 'Last Date,'" Floyd would tell his friends, "because the whole thing sounded sad and so final. It just seemed to fit a last date situation."

Released in the fall of 1960, Cramer's solo piano debut worked its way onto rock charts in late October. It would spend fifteen weeks on the pop side, peaking at #2 and holding that position for a month. Ironically, Elvis's "Are You Lonesome Tonight," a song which featured Floyd's playing, kept the pianist from recording his first #1.

Country jocks were slower to pick up on the piano instrumental. The reason may have been based on the prejudice that the keyboard was not a true country instrument. Yet a week after rock fans had begun to request Cramer's slide-note style, country fans jumped on the bandwagon too. Lingering on the playlists for four and half months, "Last Date" ended its run just out of the top 10 at #11.

The haunting melody which Cramer had written challenged scores of songwriters who wanted to fit words to the instrumental. The first to give it a try was Skeeter Davis. Floyd's record had been out just a few weeks when the RCA artist brought Chet the lyrics she had written to go with Cramer's music. Sensing the possibilities, Atkins called in famed songwriter Boudleaux Bryant to rework Skeeter's draft.

"Boudleaux tried to finish what Skeeter had started," Felice Bryant remembered, "but he was having problems. He wanted to start fresh, but she didn't want to give up her own lyrics. Finally, Chet just kind of put the two together. Boudleaux didn't like the final result at all. He didn't think the two different versions fit together and made any sense."

Bryant may have not liked it, but the public did. They gave Skeeter a three-month chart ride, and her "My Last Date with You" finished at #5 in early 1960. Even though Davis's country numbers had been better, in most country fans' eyes "Last Date" remained Floyd's song. Everywhere he appeared, he had to close his show with the sad melody.

At about the same time that Davis was working up her first draft of words for Cramer's song, a rockabilly star got the same idea. Just like most recording artists, Conway Twitty had known Floyd Cramer for some time. When he heard the piano master's "Last Date," Twitty was moved to write words to it also. When Davis beat him to the recording studio, Twitty sat on his version of "Last Date" for twelve years. In 1972, after having played it for Floyd and receiving the composer's blessings, Twitty released "(Lost Her Love) On Our Last Date." This third rendering of the song took "Last Date" to its first appointment with #1.

More than a decade later, Emmylou Harris recorded the Cramer/Twitty version again. When she released "(Lost Her Love) On Our Last Date" in 1983, Harris had not scored a chart-topper in three years. It took three months for this interpretation of the old piano standard to rise to the top. It seemed that just like Cramer's unique playing style, his classic composition never goes out of style.

Going back to Al Stricklin, the inventive piano pounder for the Texas Playboys; Moon Mullican, the King of the Hillbilly Piano Players; Del Wood, *Opry's* Queen of Country Ragtime; and Jerry Lee Lewis, rockabilly's frantic piano pounder, country music has recognized a solid and diverse group of keyboard masters. Yet before the emergence of Floyd Cramer, the piano was a country music novelty to most traditionalists. Its place in the genre was small and somewhat unimportant. Cramer, with his unique sound, as well as his work on thousands of studio sessions, put the ivories on the Music City map and took the dust off old uprights. In 1960 Floyd's "Last Date" earned the keyboard an overdue date with destiny and became the national anthem of the country piano.

1961
Hello Walls

Written by Willie Nelson

When Willie Nelson arrived in Nashville in the early sixties, many wondered if the singer/songwriter would fit in. Willie looked like he belonged. In those days the small Texan wore his hair short, slick, and precisely combed, dressed in nicely pressed suits complete with white shirts and thin ties, and wore boots that were spit-shined. Yet underneath this all-American cover was a man who was already a bit of a rebel. The independent nature that would someday make the man a major star was, at this time, evident only in his songwriting.

If anyone was the product of hard times, it was Willie. Born in Fort Worth, Nelson had grown up poor in tiny Abbott, Texas. Raised principally by grandparents, Willie considered himself a farm boy, a child who liked the solitary loneliness found in cotton fields and along country roads. Yet while living in the sticks, he was also drawn to the sounds of the city. Through the radio he came to know and love not only Ernest Tubb and Bob Wills, but the music of the big bands, tunes from Hollywood and Broadway shows, the jive of jazz ensembles, and the feel of black blues.

By his teens, Nelson took his fascination with music a step further. Learning a few chords on an old guitar, Willie began to sing and play at local events. It made little difference to Nelson if the group that needed him was a polka band, a hillbilly group, or a blues quartet. He just loved to perform. After a hitch in the

Air Force, he drifted throughout Texas and even up the West Coast in search of both a dream and a place to play. It was in Houston where he finally began to make his mark in clubs and earned his first few dollars as a songwriter. Strapped for cash and with a family depending upon him for support, Willie sold one of his first compositions, "Family Bible," for $50. A year later the song became a national hit, making its new owner thousands of dollars in royalties. Meanwhile Nelson had almost nothing to show for it. Yet this first best-seller did prove that he could write, so Willie packed his family and his bags and moved closer to the action.

Arriving in Nashville, Willie Nelson cast his lot with the likes of Hank Cochran and Harlan Howard and began writing for Pamper Music. Sitting in the publishing house's main office, an old windowless garage, Willie began to call upon his eclectic background and compose songs that had a much different feel and pace than anything else coming out of Music City at that time.

"I remember meeting him at Tootsie's," recalled Cochran. "We used to gather there, pass around a guitar, and play the latest things we had written. This new guy was there and he had some of the best songs I had ever heard. After he finished playing, I introduced myself and asked, 'Who are you with, Willie?' He told me, 'I don't write for nobody. Nobody wants me.' I told him to come to Pamper Music the next morning and play his stuff for our talent guy, Hal Smith."

"I'll come if somebody can give me some money for gas," Willie explained.

"I gave him the money for the gas," Hank remembered. "The next morning he came and played his stuff for Hal. Willie had already told me that he had a wife and three kids and needed at least fifty dollars a week to live on. That was what I was making and I had already had a couple of good songs. When I told Hal what Willie needed, he informed me that if we signed this new guy, I wouldn't get a raise. I thought about that for a moment, then said, 'I'm getting by now, let's do it.' So we got Willie a contract with Pamper."

As was evident from the beginning, Willie was an artist more than he was a commercial writer. He didn't really write what he thought was going to sell. Instead he wrote what he felt. When he composed he didn't rely on straight country chord patterns or tried-and-true lyric formulas. He would blend his country concepts with jazz, blues, and even big-band sounds. The results were often so different and so unique that it took a really good ear to "see" the songs' potential.

One of his early Nashville efforts that no one wanted had been inspired by the room where he wrote. One afternoon as he struggled to come up with ideas, Nelson began to think out loud. As Willie would later tell his songwriting buddies, "I just looked up and said, 'Hello, walls.'" The song about a lonely man who had no one but an unfeeling house to share his heartache grew from that simple concept.

"I was in the studio when Willie came up with the idea," Hank Cochran explained. "He said, let's write it, and I was ready to get started. Then I got called into the office, which was an old house a few steps from the garage-studio, for a phone call. When I came back to the studio just ten minutes later, Willie had already written the whole damn thing."

Nelson pitched his "Hello Walls" to everyone who would listen to him, and to a man they all turned him down. Most felt that it was quirky and almost comedic. They didn't believe the seriousness of the message would get through to the audience. Depressed, Willie gathered with friends at Tootsie's Orchid Lounge in downtown Nashville.

"Willie was there," Faron Young recalled, "and he tried to sell me a song. He needed money and he offered to sell me something called 'Hello Walls.' I listened to him sing it and said, 'Hell, that ain't bad.' But I wouldn't buy it. I did promise Willie that I'd record it later. He told me that he needed the money now, so I gave him a four-hundred-dollar loan."

Young was in the midst of the hottest phase of his long career. A *Louisiana Hayride* veteran, he had a smooth style that had first infatuated radio and record fans in 1953. In a span of eight years the singer had produced thirty-five chart records and three #1's. His 1958 version of "Alone with You" had spent thirteen weeks anchored at the top of the *Billboard* chart. One of Nashville's hardest-working stars, in the mid-fifties Faron had spun his good looks and easy charm off and made several western movies. Yet even as his star rose higher and higher, the singer never lost touch with his humble roots or his desire to help others. When he was in town, he was on the streets meeting the fans and spending time with new talent. Not long after Willie had arrived from Texas he and Faron had become friends.

Good to his word, in early 1961 Faron took Willie's unique ode to a man so lonely he talked to an empty room into the studio. Young cut "Hello Walls" with a very personal approach. Though his voice was as smooth as it had been on his ballads, there was an almost spoken quality about his rhythm when he sang

Nelson's song. Faron's arrangement therefore seems to draw the listener into the plight of this poor lost soul. While putting the song's message out for all to hear, Young's phrasing also made the song's lyrics very easy to learn and sing. By the third or fourth time someone heard "Hello Walls," they were either singing with Faron or answering along with the backup vocals. This participatory quality became infectious and within a month of hitting the charts, Nelson's strange song's lyrics had been learned and were being sung by millions. The piece no one wanted was going to be a hit.

"Hello Walls" charted in mid-March and topped the charts on May 8, 1960. It would ride at #1 for nine weeks and remain on the country playlists for over half a year. Surprisingly, "Walls" would also cross over to the rock lists. The number would peak at #12 and spend almost a quarter of the year on rock 'n' roll turntables. Young had never seen anything like it, and neither had Willie.

Even before the royalty checks began to roll in,

Nelson found himself in demand. Pamper Music was getting a host of calls wanting to know if Willie had any new material. Parody songs based on "Hello Walls" flooded the market. Jokes also seemed to spring up everywhere. Within a year Liberty Records had even offered Nelson a record deal and he was a regular guest on many of the nation's best-known country-music television shows. Though still fifteen years away from real fame and fortune, with Faron's huge hit Willie had laid the foundation for future stardom.

Not long after Nelson received his first very sizable royalty check for "Hello Walls," the songwriter ran down Faron Young. With a smile reaching from ear to ear, Willie handed the singer $400. When Young inquired what the money was for, Nelson reminded him of the loan. Pushing the cash away, Faron laughed and told Willie, "You don't owe me a thing. If anybody owes anybody here, it's me that owes you." A lot of singers would soon owe Nelson for their hits too!

1961
Heart over Mind

Written by Mel Tillis

Songwriter, singer, comic, and musician—Florida-born Mel Tillis had become all of those things by his twenty-fifth birthday. His compositions had scored hits for some of country music's greatest stars including Ray Price and Webb Pierce. He had spent time as the lead vocalist for Bob Wills and His Texas Playboys and opened for some of the greatest acts in entertainment. A songwriter since his teen years, he had overcome a serious speech impediment on his way to industry-wide songwriting recognition and a writing contract with the Cedarwood music group. It seemed as if his career was charmed. Then, just when it looked as if things were really going to take off, the bottom dropped out.

Mel and his manager got into a dispute over song profits and royalties. A long court battle followed, and Tillis's career was put on hold. Months dragged by and with all of his music earnings tied up by courts, Mel had no way to provide for his growing family. Sadly, he packed his bags and he and his wife and kids left Nashville and headed back home to Pahokee, Florida.

Tillis's speech problem had been no real detriment in plying his trade as a songwriter—as long as he was speaking from a prepared text or singing, the stutterer had a constant rhythm to follow—but it was a different story in the real world. Blessed with a clever wit and eager personality, he was an engag-ing, good-looking man with a suitcase full of charm. Yet more often than not, this was overlooked as soon as he opened his mouth and began to stutter. The stammering made a bad impression before Mel's personality had a chance to shine through. Because of this, many doors were rudely shut in his face. First he was closed out of the business he loved by a judge, and then he was pushed aside because of other people's false judgments. It seemed no one was willing to give Mel a fair shake.

Tillis finally convinced the owner of Harries Cookies to give him a shot. It seemed Mel's fortunes had changed when the snack company agreed to try the unemployed songwriter as a salesman. They gave him a uniform, a truckload of cookies, and a brand-new route. His job was to take Harries into virgin territory. In other words, Tillis had to sell this product to store owners and managers who had never before placed it on their shelves. As Mel would soon discover, for a man who had problems expressing himself, this was going to be a herculean challenge.

"I worked for three weeks and didn't sell one cookie," Mel remembered. Mainly he just drove from town to town, store to store, and after he failed to make a sale, tried to keep himself from getting discouraged by singing in his truck. In the face of all of his problems, staying positive was almost as tough as selling the cookies.

"I kept telling myself, 'Mind over matter,'" Tillis recalled. "Soon those words turned over in my head and became heart over mind."

With a new song title rebounding in his head, the cookie hawker drove toward his next stop, using his few spare moments to himself slip into his old vocation. Soon he was cruising through Miami humming an original shuffle-beat four-by-four dance melody.

"Heart over mind, worried all the time" were the first words Tillis fitted into the new tune. The remainder of the lyrics quickly followed. Over the next few days Mel continued to compose in his truck. As the missed sales added up, so did the finished songs. By the end of three weeks he had added "One More Time" and "No Love Have I." With those three tunes in hand, he turned in his uniform and keys and headed back to Music City.

Mel was able to quickly sell "One More Time" to Ray Price. It would hit #2 on the charts in 1960. "No Love Have I" also found a home with Webb Pierce. It would also jump into the top five that year and many years later be recorded by Gail Davies and Holly Dunn for hits. In 1961 Price finally recorded the first of the cookie truck trilogy, "Heart over Mind." Though not as big as "One More Time," this swing tune did make it to #5 on the charts.

Throughout the sixties Mel juggled songwriting and performing. He had more success with the former than the latter. "Ruby, Don't Take Your Love to Town" and "Detroit City" proved that Tillis was one of Music City's most gifted tunesmiths. Yet even as good as his writing was, it seemed as if Tillis's chance at performing stardom was slowly slipping away. Country music was beginning to evolve from hard country into the middle-of-the-road pop sound of Glen Campbell and Lynn Anderson. This country-rock movement also welcomed former rockabilly stars like Conway Twitty and Jerry Lee Lewis. Mean-

while, the old-timers who had recorded Mel's past efforts were now either being pushed aside or, like Ray Price, had switched to a much softer sound. The honky-tonk/Texas swing-dance songs were fast becoming a part of the past too. Most industry movers and shakers considered the Tillis style to be outdated.

From all appearances it seemed that the critics were right. Mel had been recording for almost eight years with only nominal success. His self-penned "Who's Julie" had made Kapp Records some money in 1968 by climbing to #10, but couldn't climb any higher. He'd followed that with two more songs that had only moderate chart success the next year. As country headed into an even more pop-oriented direction with songs penned by the likes of Rhodes Scholar Kris Kristofferson, chances for Tillis scoring big on the charts seemed very remote. Then, just when every judgment again appeared to be turning against him, the singer dusted off an old friend.

"Heart over Mind," with its dance-flavored beat, combined all of what Mel knew best. It was a basic song of heartache and misplaced love set to a beat that Hank Williams, Hank Thompson, or even Bob Wills would have recognized. This number was not anything like the music of the day's hot songwriters, Jimmy Webb and Joe South. It had none of the polish or shine. Yet in Mel's mind it had been hit material once and could be again. In a world filled with formula songs, he believed that "Heart over Mind" stood apart. If his instincts were proven wrong, then Mel would either have to develop a new sound and style or be relegated to the second tier of country acts. For Tillis the performer there was a great deal riding on this cookie truck composition.

Released in May 1970, "Heart over Mind" surprised everyone by quickly shooting up the charts and passing more contemporary tunes by the younger balladeers. It would peak at #3, two places higher than

Price's 1961 version had. It was Tillis's biggest hit to date, and it awoke a listening audience to his type of music. Overnight, after over a decade of hard work, the song's success made Mel a major player in the recording business and left both the public and disc jockeys wanting more of this "new" sound. He was able to give it to them too. Keeping his supposedly outdated shuffle-beat intact, he would score more than twenty times in the next decade (most of these were released on MGM), and would top the charts six times. From out of nowhere he would eventually vault into one of the top-twenty-five-charting acts in country music history. Besides his work on stage and in recordings, for which he would win the Country Music Association's Entertainer of the Year award in 1976, Tillis would also branch out into comedy, acting, and writing. As he constantly moved forward and met every new challenge with child-like enthusiasm and energy, his growth was amazing. Yet he also remained true to the old country sound he had heard as a child. Tillis the superstar was still unsophisticated and honest.

Dr. Bill C. Malone, one of country music's foremost writers, researchers, and scholars, would call Tillis's "Heart over Mind" "one of the great performances of the modern period." As one listens to Tillis and the Statesiders smoothly work through the number, the simply crafted work stands as a monument to what can happen when a truly great song meets a truly great singer. In this case Mel Tillis was the sum total of both parts.

"Heart over Mind" is one of the few releases of the late sixties and early seventies which belongs to no one era. Like most of Tillis's material, this composition is as much at home in 1995 as it would have been in 1945. As he now performs in his own Branson theater, time has had little effect on Mel. Fads may come and go, but real style remains. Unlike other country music veterans whose music seems to have been born in another age, Mel's is still fresh and alive. Given time, another generation will probably discover the remarkable man's unadorned genius.

1962
Wolverton Mountain

Written by Merle Kilgore and Claude King

Merle Kilgore's bio reads singer, guitarist, songwriter, disc jockey, actor, and manager. In his five decades in entertainment, he has not only seen it all, he's done it all, and usually done it very well. A product of Oklahoma, but raised in Shreveport, Louisiana, Merle has often said that his real roots were planted in the Arkansas Ozarks. His mother and grandmother had been born in those mountains, and most of his relatives called those wooded lands home.

Kilgore played guitar as a child, landed a position as a disc jockey while still in high school, and bought into a radio station when he was in college. In his spare time, he wrote songs and performed at talent shows, fairs, and dances. By the time he turned eighteen in 1952, he had already written a classic, "More and More," that would become a #1 hit for Webb Pierce.

Moving his talents to the *Louisiana Hayride*, Merle not only sang, but became the top accompanist for many of the show's best-known acts. A master showman, he was a crowd favorite. Outgoing, Kilgore made friends easily, and soon found himself on the road with the likes of Faron Young, Webb Pierce, Jim Reeves, and Elvis Presley. As Merle churned out a long list of hits, including "It Can't Rain All the Time," "Johnny Reb," and "Everybody Needs a Little Loving," his musical successes called him away from his college studies. As a songwriter he approached the

sixties as a hot commodity, but he wondered if he was ready to try it as a solo entertainer in Nashville.

"In 1959, I took some time off and drove up to Arkansas to visit with my uncle and aunt," Merle recalled. "I didn't know if I should give up my radio career and all the other things I had worked so hard to get, just to move to Nashville and try to make it there. I wondered if that was too big a risk. I trusted my Uncle Clifton a great deal and visited with him about my situation."

Merle's Uncle Clifton lived on the same mountain where Kilgore's mother and grandmother had been born. There was a peace, as well as sense of belonging, that Merle felt when he walked the long trails and studied the picturesque vistas of Wolverton. Here the pace was slow and the people were honest. It was the perfect setting not only to reflect on life, but also to gain insight and inspiration.

"As I spent time on the old place," Kilgore explained, "I began to think about the mountain and my uncle's life. Grabbing my guitar and a pen, I wrote a song that I called 'Clifton Clowers' [his uncle's name]. When I finished it, I went looking for my uncle. I found him out in a cane field making sorghum molasses. He wanted to know what I had, so I just sat down and played him my song. When I finished, he smiled, then told me, 'You just wrote yourself a hit!'"

Confident that everyone else would have the same

reaction as Uncle Clifton, Kilgore raced back to Shreveport and played it for one of his best friends, Johnny Horton. Horton listened to "Clifton Clowers," shook his head, and said, "That is probably the worst song I have ever heard."

Kilgore was taken back by Horton's response. Usually Johnny had loved his material. Still, he didn't give up on his latest inspiration. The songwriter simply went looking for someone else with a record contract. The next singer Merle ran into was George Jones. Merle played it for Jones. This time Kilgore didn't even finish before George cut in. "I hate mountain songs," he said. Again and again Merle tried, but no one wanted to take a chance on Kilgore's song.

In 1960 Merle would finally move to Nashville. With him, Kilgore brought his guitar, his songs, and his uncle's blessings. Quickly landing a recording contract at Starday, Merle managed to chart with three songs. None of the records established Merle as a solo act, so Kilgore went back to songwriting and opening for better-known acts. He also began to dabble in acting.

"I got a call one day from Tillman Franks," Kilgore remembered. "Tillman had managed Johnny Horton. When Johnny had been killed in a car wreck, he had picked up another Shreveport boy, Claude King."

Merle knew all about King. Claude had been a local sports star when Kilgore had entered high school. After college, King had returned and become a popular folk singer. He was a solid performer who had scored big a couple of times in 1961 for Columbia.

"Tillman told me that he was going to do a folk-style album with Claude," Merle explained. "Folk music was really hot at that time, and they thought they might cash in if they found the right songs. Franks then inquired if I remembered a mountain song that I had once played for Johnny Horton. I replied that not only did I remember it, but the best that I could recall, Johnny had loved that song."

Merle dug up "Clifton Clowers" and took it over to Franks. Claude King listened to it and thought it had some potential.

"Claude wanted to make a few changes," Merle recalled, "and I told him to go ahead. He tinkered with the words a little. When I found out that he was going to cut it, I gave him half of the songwriting credits for doing this new arrangement."

One of the most noticeable changes King made was the song's title. No longer was it "Clifton Clowers." He had retitled it "Wolverton Mountain." Released in mid-spring of 1962, the song shot up the charts. In June it grabbed the top spot, and held that position for nine weeks. In pop music it also made a strong showing, topping out at #6. "Wolverton Mountain" would become the biggest hit of King's career. Yet the fact that it would become the most important country folk song of its era paled when compared to its power to capture the imagination of millions of people worldwide.

"It was crazy," Merle recalled. "Suddenly the state of Arkansas was being flooded by calls from folks all over the world wanting to know how they could get to Wolverton Mountain. My uncle was not only receiving scores of phone calls and letters, he did interviews with media from all over the world. He had his picture taken with thousands of tourists. The song made him a celebrity and created a rush of traffic up U.S. Highway 65 for years."

Clifton Clowers would continue to live on Wolverton Mountain for the rest of his life. When he died at 102 in 1994, newspapers all over the world ran his obituary. His nephew, Merle, would tour the globe singing, acting, and lecturing. Merle would also become the manager for a man who had been on the verge of stardom for years, Hank Williams, Jr. With

Merle's help, Hank Jr. would became a huge star in his own right. The CMA, which had already recognized his songwriting skills, would honor Kilgore as the Manager of the Year in 1990.

The song which Merle wrote about his uncle warned, "They say don't go on Wolverton Mountain." Yet it seemed few people took these words seriously. "Wolverton Mountain" was revisited scores of times after Claude King first took audiences there. Bing Crosby cut the song, as did Nat King Cole and Louis Armstrong. Hank Williams, Jr., would even include a reference to it in one of his own hits. And yes, Merle Kilgore still occasionally goes back to Wolverton Mountain in order to find a little peace and a lot of inspiration.

1962

Crazy

Written by Willie Nelson

When Faron Young topped the charts with "Hello Walls," and even crossed the recording over to the rock 'n' roll playlists, songwriter Willie Nelson, the man everyone in Nashville had once thought a bit crazy, suddenly found his career extremely hot. It seemed that everyone in town wanted to cut one of Willie's songs, and his demos were being ordered by scores of different studios, managers, and stars. When Nelson walked into Tootsie's, all the patrons gathered around him to see what Nashville's newest genius had written lately.

Patsy Cline was no exception. She too grabbed Nelson whenever she got a chance and begged him to share some of his latest ideas. The very first time she heard Nelson's "Funny How Time Slips Away," Cline fell in love with it. She had a recording session coming up and Patsy just knew that the Willie song had to be a part of it. She called the writer to arrange a meeting. Things didn't turn out the way the singer had planned.

Billy Walker had known Willie since their days in Texas. The singer had even put Nelson up at his house when Willie had first come to town. When Willie had needed someone to cut demos, Walker had stepped in. Billy had even sung the vocal on "Funny How Time Slips Away." When his label, Columbia, heard Walker's version of the Nelson composition, they opted to recut it and release it. It had been eight years since Billy had managed a top-ten record, and the label thought "Funny" might give the man's career a big shot in the arm.

Cline was infuriated when she discovered that Billy Walker and Columbia had beaten her to "Funny How Time Slips Away." She needed a follow-up to her classic "I Fall to Pieces," and she wanted it to have the ability to cross over on the pop charts. She urged Willie to allow her to cut "Funny" too. The songwriter owed far too much to Billy to let that happen, so he declined. Then the ever-polite Nelson, addressing the hot female vocalist as "Miss Patsy," told her that he had a bunch of other songs that were hits back at the office. If she wanted to record one of his numbers, Nelson assured her that he would save one for her.

At about that same time Billy Walker had entered the room, and he reminded Willie about another song that Walker had cut a demo on. The two men agreed that Cline's voice was perfectly suited for the piece, so they raced off to retrieve it. Patsy practically went crazy as she waited for the men to return with their song.

Willie had written "Crazy" very soon after coming to Nashville. When he had first pitched it, the song had failed to generate any interest. So Willie had pretty much set the song aside to collect dust. Occasionally he would try to sell "Crazy," but finding a home for the number was not his passion. Yet at the moment when Patsy and her producer Owen Bradley were hot for a hit, this was about all the young Texan had to offer.

"Crazy" didn't have any special story behind it. The song had fallen together in a writing session. Yet even though the number's words were apparently tied to no special event in Nelson's life, they did seem to reflect a great deal of what he was having to deal with upon his entry into the world of Music City songwriting. Poor, alone (his family had stayed in Texas until Willie could make enough money to bring them to Tennessee), talented, but unappreciated, Willie had to be aware just how crazy he was for sticking it out in the music business. In almost a decade of work he had very little to show for his troubles. He loved entertainment, but it didn't seem to express any affection for him. In a very real sense, even if it was unintended, "Crazy" reflected Willie's relationship with his profession.

When Nelson and Walker played the song for Cline, she couldn't believe it. She thought it was one of the worst things she had ever heard. This wasn't a ballad, this was a song where the singer spent most of the time talking to the audience. She flatly rejected "Crazy," and then asked Nelson what else he had.

What Patsy hadn't realized was that she had heard "Crazy" just a few weeks before. Her husband Charlie Dick had gotten a copy from Willie when the two of them had stopped in Tootsie's for drinks. Charlie had practically worn the record player out playing the demo over and over again. His wife had gotten so tired of the "stupid damn song" that she had threatened to break it into pieces. It was only when Charlie played it again that night that she realized that she had rejected "Crazy" not once, but twice.

Nelson's song would have probably gone back into storage and collected more dust if not for Owen Bradley. The Decca producer liked "Crazy" and he was convinced that it was perfect for Patsy. He informed her that she would be recording the Nelson effort. She told him that she wouldn't. Much as they had with "I Fall to Pieces," the producer and singer went back and forth with their arguing. Finally, Bradley pulled rank. Because of a car wreck, Cline hadn't been able to record for months. Owen pointed out that she needed to have a solid session filled with good records and he wasn't going to let her act like a spoiled brat and miss recording what he thought was a great song. Left with no choice, Patsy listened to the demo and began to pick up the lyrics.

In the studio Owen allowed Cline to tinker with the song. She tossed out Willie's unique phrasing and sang it in her own style. She also tried to smooth the song's meter. Yet because of the pain created by her broken ribs, she was unable to really soar the way she was used to when recording her lead vocal. After several hours of work, she quit without putting together a satisfactory cut. When the star went home, Bradley laid down all the other tracks figuring he would catch Patsy's vocal when she felt better. Within a week Cline had come back in and overwhelmed the producer with a brilliant version of "Crazy."

When Willie heard the final product, he was blown away. He would tell those at Tootsie's, "It was magic!" Even three decades later Nelson would still proclaim that recording of that song as "the favorite of anything I ever wrote."

In one take Patsy had made "Crazy" hers. Released in mid-fall, the song steadily climbed the playlists. It landed on the pop charts on November 6. A week later it would arrive on the country side. Her biggest rock cut, "Crazy" would peak at #9. In the country listings Cline would manage to spend two weeks at #2. "Crazy" marked the fourth time Patsy had charted, and with the record's strong showing on both major playlists, she had become a major star beyond the borders of Music City and country music.

With royalties taking care of his bills, Willie was now finding it a bit harder to produce top material. As he would later reflect, "It is not easy to write when you're not hungry." Certainly Cline's "Crazy" had bought Nelson a few meals, but more important, it had secured him a place as one of the era's greatest songwriters. After "Hello Walls" and "Crazy," no one in Music City thought that Willie was insane.

1962
She's Got You

Written by Hank Cochran

"I Fall to Pieces" had established both Patsy Cline as a singer and Hank Cochran as a writer. Patsy, now over the injuries suffered in the automobile accident that had nearly killed her, was back on the road and drawing record crowds. Hank, basking in the glow of not only having written one of Pamper Music's biggest hits, but also having discovered the publishing company's hottest new writer, Willie Nelson, was also in demand. Nashville's finest recording artists wanted to know if he had anything they could record. Yet in spite of being responsible for one of Music City's biggest records, and being labeled a "hit-maker," Hank found things were still tough.

Cochran was living on just $50 a week, his draw from Pamper. He had given up his raise so that the company would have the means to sign Nelson. The royalties from his compositions wouldn't start coming in for another year. Hank could see that he would be in the chips soon, but that didn't help him much right now. With just enough money to get by, the only thing the writer could really do was sit in the studio and write songs.

"Patsy had been after me to write her another song," Hank recalled. "I tried, but I just couldn't come up with anything she or her producer, Owen Bradley, liked. She had just had a big hit with Willie's 'Crazy,' and I really wanted to write the next single, but it just wasn't working."

Patsy called Hank almost daily to see if the writer had any new things for her. Each day the response was always the same. As the time for Cline to go back into the studio approached, it looked as though Cochran would strike out.

"When you start to think about where the inspiration comes from for writing a song," the songwriter explained, "the only real answer is the Man Upstairs. One minute you don't have an idea in the world, and then the next, bang, it just hits you. Suddenly you are writing down lyrics that just seem to fall out of the air. That is the way it had always been with me, and I knew it was the same for most of the other writers I worked with. Something would happen, it would trigger an idea, and then what had been so hard for so many weeks would be so easy."

With the pressure of Patsy's upcoming recording session looming over him like a black cloud, Cochran was practically living in the studio. Sitting at an old desk, he would scribble down ideas on paper, then after hours of fruitless work, pitch them in a trash can.

"I remember this one afternoon so well," Hank recalled. "Several of us writers had been at Pamper, in the back in the studio, and we had been guitar-pulling and writing. Around five or six o'clock, everyone started to drift towards home. I decided to stay, hoping that the solitude would help me come up with some new ideas. I had been there by myself for a while and

I was still shooting blanks. When pacing didn't jog any new ideas, I sat down and started looking around at the little room. There were no windows, and the furnishings were stark. There just wasn't much to see. Then I leaned back in my chair and pulled open the desk drawer that was right in front of me. The first thing I saw was a picture. Just like that, the idea came to me."

"I picked up a pad and wrote, 'I've got your picture, the one you gave to me,' and from that point it all fell together."

After weeks of working long hours trying to come up with anything, in just a few minutes Hank knew that he had come up with something very special. The tune came as quickly as the lyrics had. Singing it to himself, the writer felt confident he had written a Patsy Cline hit. Now the question became, what would she think? After all, Patsy hadn't liked either "I Fall to Pieces" or "Crazy."

"I got to a phone—at that time we didn't have one in the studio—and I called Patsy at home," Hank remembered. "As soon as she picked up I hollered, 'I got it! I got you a hit song.' She quickly replied, 'Well, bring the SOB over here, and on your way pick up a pint of whiskey.' I slammed the phone down and ran out to my car."

Cline and her husband Charlie Dick lived clear across Nashville from Pamper's Goodlettsville office. Just getting to their house was going to take Cochran the better part of an hour. But in order to pick up a pint of liquor he was going to have to drive past Patsy's and into the next county. At the time that was the nearest place that wasn't dry.

"When I finally got there," Cochran recalled, "we opened the bottle and took a sip. Then I played it for her. As I sang it, she started crying. Then I started crying too. After a few more sips and a few more times through the song, she told me, 'You sure have written the SOB.'"

Picking up the phone, Cline called Owen Bradley. When the producer answered, the singer was her usual straightforward self. "Hank's got it. That no-good SOB has found the song we need." When Bradley heard the new piece the next day, he agreed. It was one of the first times the producer and singer had ever been satisfied with the same song.

Cline recorded Hank's composition just before Christmas 1961. It had taken just two cuts to get it right. "She's Got You," the song inspired by a photo left in a desk drawer, was released early the next year.

"It seems funny now," Hank laughed, "but when they shipped 'She's Got You,' I was scared to death. I thought, my God, she's had two monster songs in a row. What if this one flops?"

"She's Got You" charted the first week of March. Three weeks later it was the #1 song in country music. It would hold the top spot for five more weeks. Once again Cline slipped over onto the pop charts, this time taking the Cochran song to #14. In a recording career that embraced several classic performances, "She's Got You" would go down as Patsy's biggest hit.

Just six months after Patsy had topped the charts, Hank Cochran had his own record deal with Liberty. His first single, "Sally Was a Good Old Girl," would make it to the top twenty. Yet while Hank's recording career would place him on the charts several more times, it was his genius as a songwriter that would make him a Nashville legend.

"I still have problems talking about Patsy," Hank acknowledged as he looked back more than three decades. "I still get real emotional when I think of her. She meant a lot to my career, but even more to me as a friend. Without her I probably wouldn't have made it to where I am."

Hank Cochran pulled the concept for "She's Got You" out of an old desk drawer. His wonderful composition about lost love and painful memories has been recut countless times. Loretta Lynn, one of Cline's close friends, even took it to the top of the charts in 1977. Yet in his mind, as well as the minds of millions of fans, "She's Got You" will always be Patsy's song. Hank wrote it for her. Except for a heart full of memories, a few precious recordings, and some treasured photographs, "She's Got You" is now all Hank has left of the friend he loved so dearly.

1962
Don't Let Me Cross Over

Written by Penny Jay

Carl Butler sang in a manner that reminded folks of Roy Acuff. With his heavily accented twang and rural church-singing style, he would have been right at home on the *Opry* in the thirties. Yet Butler was still in a Knoxville, Tennessee, grade school then, and wouldn't even make it to Nashville until a decade after Acuff had become a big star. With one possible exception, it seemed that Carl would always arrive just a bit too late to achieve real stardom.

An accomplished musician and performer while still a high school student, Carl put together his own band during World War II and worked both clubs and dances. By the time he turned twenty in 1947, the singer had already sung on three radio stations and had a large following in the Smoky Mountains area. His name had also become well enough established to earn Butler an invitation to join the *Opry*.

In Nashville, Carl began to write songs for some of country music's more successful acts, tried to expand his own recording career, and took a little time off to fall in love. Pearl Jones had been raised in Music City, and had absorbed a great deal of knowledge about country music. A solid singer who had appeared in many amateur productions, in her first decade of marriage to Carl she was content to be a housewife. During this time the only places she used her vocal talents were at family get-togethers and in church.

Throughout the fifties Carl attempted to shape himself into a recording star. Though he was able to continue to compose hit songs for other acts, Butler couldn't seem to ever find any acceptance on the charts for himself. A great deal of Carl's problem centered on timing. While his unabashed hillbilly style made him an *Opry* favorite with the older crowd, it wasn't commercial. The record buyers were into honky-tonk and rockabilly, and these were styles that Butler couldn't and wouldn't play. Stuck in an out-of-date rut, he was dropped by Capitol, and even though Columbia added him to their roster, the label couldn't produce a hit for him. Carl began to sense that he might have been born a generation too late.

About the same time that Carl Butler was wondering if he would ever have a song appear on the *Billboard* playlists, Penny Jay was on a Midwestern tour. Penny was in much the same position as Carl. While the singer could make a modest living entertaining before small groups in little venues, she couldn't get the break that would take her to the big time. As Penny rode along toward another show in another high school gym, she got an idea for a song that would eventually open the charts for Carl Butler, as well as open the door to a new kind of country music recording.

Penny would later recall that she had been watching the yellow stripes that marked areas where you couldn't pass. These no-passing zones were so much a part of the back roads and highways that connected small rural towns that no one ever thought much about them. Yet on this day Jay would not only notice them, but use them for a song title idea. Starting with that simple concept of not crossing a line that led to a sinful affair, she built a very moralistic number about a person caught on the verge of cheating for the very first time.

In that era female vocalists didn't record cheating songs. It would be another decade before radio and the public would accept their women having feet of clay. So in order for "Don't Let Me Cross Over" to make any royalty money, the publisher and Penny knew that they were going to have to find the right man to cut it. Upon hearing it, Carl Butler had an even better idea.

In 1961 Carl had finally placed one of his songs on the charts, so Columbia was ready to let the singer record a hard-country follow-up. When he chose "Don't Let Me Cross Over," the label gave it their approval. What really surprised them was the singer's insistence that this would make a solid duet song. Butler wanted to pull his wife out of the kitchen and have her harmonize with him on the cheating number. He reasoned that the fact that they were happily married would negate any negative reaction caused by the song's lyrics.

The "Don't Let Me Cross Over" that Carl and Pearl cut was a plaintive, pleading song. In their vocal inflections, accentuated by their heavy mountain twang, listeners seemed to sense that this couple was actually dealing with not wanting to fall into a sinful affair. Maybe it was because of the Butlers' hard and often harsh country style, but the pleading lyrics began to come alive. It had been years since a record had captured this kind of emotional anguish. That was probably the reason that the song took off.

"Don't Let Me Cross Over" jumped on the playlists on December 8, 1962. The record knocked Hank Snow's "I've Been Everywhere" out of the top spot just three weeks later. Carl and Pearl's debut duet would then hold #1 for eleven weeks, and remain on the charts for just under half a year. Named by many polls and organizations the song of the year, "Don't Let Me Cross Over" became the first mixed duet to make it to #1. Though it was strictly rural country in style, the Butlers' hillbilly hit even crossed over onto the pop charts for a few weeks in 1963. In an age when the smooth styles of Jim Reeves and Marty Robbins sold records, the Butlers defied the odds and created a monster.

Carl and Pearl Butler would record a dozen more duets, but only one would make the top ten. So in reality the couple's contributions to country music sales were limited to their first release. Yet the Butlers' influence on country music was profound. With the success of "Don't Let Me Cross Over" other labels began to seek out duet acts and record them. Eventually the mixed duet would become a staple of most record companies' catalogs. The fallout created by "Don't Let Me Cross Over" would thus lead to much more successful recording teams like Porter Wagoner and Dolly Parton and Loretta Lynn and Conway Twitty. It would also create a niche for songs specifically written for close male/female harmonies.

"Don't Let Me Cross Over" would make the top ten two more times. In 1969 Jerry Lee Lewis and his sister, Linda Gail Lewis, took it to #9. A decade later RCA brought Deborah Allen into the studio and had the young woman cut it with the late Jim Reeves. This electronically manufactured duet worked its way up to the tenth position.

An old Southern saying declares that it doesn't make any difference if you are the best, only if you are the first. Dozens of country duet teams have probably been much more talented than Carl and Pearl Butler, but the couple's crossover hit not only was the first, it remains the biggest.

1963
Six Days on the Road

Written by Earl Greene and Carl Montgomery

In the forties folks from around Stevens Point, Wisconsin, would turn out in droves every time they heard that young Dave Dudley was going to be featured. He was one of the best performers the small community had ever seen, and everyone thought that some day this high school sensation was going to make it to the big time. The whole town was sure that Dave was going to be a star. At that time his best record was 15 and 3.

Dave Dudley, who would eventually score time and time again on country music charts, was a six-foot-two-inch star baseball pitcher in his youth. While he may have played a little guitar on the side, no one seemed to notice. They were all much more interested in his fastball and curve. When Dave's future was talked about in beauty parlors or taverns, the locals laid bets on when he would make the major leagues, not when he would sing on the *Opry*. In 1949 Dudley was well on his way to making himself the Pride of Stevens Point when an arm injury cut him down in the minors.

Dudley came home from Texas not knowing where to head next. Baseball had been his life. His entire identity has been wrapped around his ability to strike other men out. By getting hurt he had shattered not only his own dreams, but the hopes of an entire town. In postwar America playing in the major leagues was about as good as it got. Now it seemed that when local

folks talked about Dave, they always began each observation with the words "what if." Yet the former baseball star knew that he couldn't live on past glory. In order to pay the bills he was going to have to find something else he could do well.

A chance visit to a radio station gave the young man an opportunity to revive an old talent. A friend remembered Dudley's guitar playing and wondered if he would like to perform live on the local station. Dave hit a home run his first trip to the plate, and fan mail poured in at such a rate that he soon had his own show. By 1953 Dave had a trio, and he began a seven-year stretch of playing clubs across the northern tier of the United States. In 1960, just when it looked as if he was going to get a record contract that would take him to Nashville, Dudley was hit by a car and almost lost his life. In bed for six months, he eventually worked his way back into radio and some performances in the area around Minneapolis, but his second chance at the big time had gone the way of the first. The "what ifs" were again coming back to haunt him.

At the time that Dudley was striving to regain his strength, Earl Greene and Carl Montgomery were driving a semi-trailer up and down the East Coast. Their Robbins Floor Products run was six days long. The drivers left Tuscumbia, Alabama, either Sunday night or early Monday morning and didn't return until Saturday afternoon. After cleaning up, the men then would head down to a local club and play country music. After a night of playing, they would return to their rig and head back north with a fresh load of product.

On a run to Pittsburgh the two men shut down the radio and began to talk about how long six days really was. As they visited about their hard work and lousy hours, one of them said, "You know, six days on the road would make a great song title." Inspired, the drivers used truckers' lingo and began to piece together a song that told the story of a trucker's life. From the ICC to ten forward gears to popping pills to stay awake, their composition began to capture the real feel of the road. It wasn't just a song, it was the autobiography of every man who had ever made a long haul. By the time Greene and Montgomery returned home on Saturday, they were ready to deliver a finished product to folks at the local club.

"Six Days on the Road" made the rounds in Southern honky-tonks before being carried north by the men who drove the big rigs. Eventually the song found its way to Minnesota and into the hands of a now fully recovered Dave Dudley. Buying time at a local studio, the disc jockey cut a version of the Greene/Montgomery truck-driving song. When Dave hit the road for a series of dates in North Dakota, he gave a number of copies of the recording to a friend. In his spare time the man worked area truck stops and diners convincing the owners to put "Six Days on the Road" in their jukeboxes. Dave's record quickly became a favorite and area radio stations began to clamor for it.

Soma, a local label, picked up the song and filled the orders by simply printing more of Dave's own cut. When that small label was unable to handle orders, Golden Wing stepped in and cut more. With no national publicity, with no press agents working phones,

without the benefit of a label with which disc jockeys and fans were familiar, "Six Days on the Road" suddenly was traveling coast to coast and border to border. All the while, Dave Dudley was working obscure little clubs in small towns unaware that he had a potential hit on his hands. By the time he returned home, truck drivers had made his song their national anthem.

On June 1, 1963, Dave's homemade cut of "Six Days on the Road" made the national charts. Pushed by the demand of truckers and the disc jockeys who served them, the song climbed up playlists like a sixteen-wheeler with a deadline and a load of perishables. Before it finished delivering the goods, this song's run would last a total of twenty-one weeks, two of those sitting at #2. Overnight, after working small-town clubs for thirteen years, Dave Dudley was a star.

Mercury saw the potential for the trucker's deep voice and signed him to a long-term contract. Forming a band known as the Roadrunners, Dudley hit the road playing the most important dates of his life. Several times he rolled up and down the Eastern Seaboard, and six days out on the road was now a short haul. Over the course of a decade-long solo career Dudley would become a *Grand Ole Opry* regular, play thousands of dates, and score with a wide variety of songs touching on themes from the game of pool to the war in Vietnam. Yet it was his first hit, as well as songs like "Truck Drivin' Son-of-a-Gun," that would instantly identify him everywhere he went. Dudley was the "King of the Truck Stops," and it was the truckers who would always think of him as one of their own.

Over the years truck drivers have remained some of country music's most loyal fans. Roy Acuff, Hank Williams, Marty Robbins, and Patsy Cline kept these hardworking men company on long nights when the road was lonely and the drive was hard. Probably more than any other single group, truckers identified with the performers, the men and women who hit the road traveling from town to town, setting up only to tear down and move on again. Ted Daffan had struck a chord with the drivers in the early forties with "Truck Driver's Blues." Alabama, Jerry Reed, and others would pay tribute to truckers through songs like "Eighteen-Wheeler" and "East Bound and Down." Yet the song which has continued to mean the most to this group, as well as the record which the public has embraced as the definitive truck-driving song, is "Six Days on the Road." Even now, the former baseball pitcher from Stevens Point is still considered country music's truck-driving man.

1963
Detroit City

Written by Danny Dill and Mel Tillis

"I was looking for a follow-up to a hit song I had written called 'Tupelo County Jail,'" Mel Tillis remembered as he thought back to his early days as one of Nashville's hottest songwriters. "Webb Pierce had had a big hit in 1958 on my song 'Tupelo County Jail,' and so I naturally began to think along these same lines. I eventually fleshed out my idea and took it to Owen Bradley at Decca. My new song's first line was, 'Last night I went to sleep in the Tupelo County Jail.' Owen listened to it and shook his head. He looked at me and said, 'Hell, Mel, write songs about someplace other than Tupelo. You've already done that. Write a song about Chicago or someplace.' I took my idea along with his criticism and left."

Tillis drove straight to Cedarwood Publishing. Mel was a staff writer for the music company which had been founded by Webb Pierce and spent a part of each day there. After he arrived, Tillis climbed a flight of stairs and sought out his honky-tonk singing boss. Pierce was in his office, but he was in no condition to write. The singer and a friend had been partying all night long and weren't ready to stop. Pierce even suggested to Mel that he quit writing and join them. Tillis declined and wandered around the office until he ran into another house songwriter, Danny Dill.

"Danny had been out on the road," Mel recalled,

"and I told him what Owen had observed about my new song. He listened, thought for a second, and then told me about something he had observed when he was playing bars in Detroit a few years before. He noted that a lot of the old Southerners who had left home to make good money in the auto plants were so homesick that they drank away their paychecks in bars. The story that Danny told me was a sad, depressing commentary on how some country boys just couldn't adjust to city life. Using my original melody as a base, we set about writing a song to fit Danny's story. It didn't take us any time to finish it. Now at least I could take the song back to Owen and prove that I could write about someplace other than Tupelo, Mississippi."

Bradley liked what Dill and Tillis had done with Mel's "Asleep in the Tupelo City Jail." The producer had just signed Nashville session player Billy Grammer to a record deal, and thought the song might be perfect for him. Quickly running one of Music City's most famous guitar men into the studio, Owen produced a song that he decided to title "I Want to Go Home." It was shipped the last month of 1962 and made the charts in early 1963. For five weeks Grammer's cut tried to climb the playlists, but it could reach no higher than #18.

While "I Want to Go Home" failed to convert many country music listeners, one man who was impressed with the song took it upon himself to re-make it into a hit. Chet Atkins was probably the most respected musician in Nashville. He exercised power at RCA which could make or break careers. Chet had spent most of his life building people up, not tearing them down, and when he heard "I Want to Go Home" was looking to make another man into a star. In 1963 he would use the Dill/Tillis piece to take this new act on his first trip into the top ten.

Bobby Bare had been raised in tragic circum-stances in rural Ohio. His mother died when he was five, and his sister was then placed in an orphanage. His father often worked menial low-paying jobs just to provide for what was left of his family. At fifteen Bobby had to leave school to get a factory job. He also moonlighted as a farm worker. Money was so scarce that Bare made his first guitar out of a coffee can, string, and an old piece of wood. Singing and playing in what little spare time he could find, he eventually formed a band and made enough money to leave home and escape to California. Still desper-ately poor, Bare sold one of his songs for just $50 (later this tune, "All American Boy," would be recorded by Grandpa Jones and hit the charts) be-fore going into military service just to get enough to eat.

When Bare left the service in the early sixties, he migrated to Nashville and eventually caught Atkins's ear. Folk songs were coming on strong in both the rock and country divisions of RCA, and Chet thought that Bobby might just be the man to bridge the gap between country and folk and score hits on both sides of the charts.

In 1962 Bare landed on playlists with "Shame on Me," but it was not a hit. For Bobby's second cut Atkins wanted to find something stronger. He needed a song where Bare could show off his sincere delivery and strong plaintive voice. When Chet heard Grammer's "I Want to Go Home," he knew he had found just the right composition for his boy.

RCA didn't want disc jockeys to ignore Bare's record the way they had Billy Grammer's first ver-sion of "I Want to Go Home." Therefore, to make this record seem brand-new, they retitled it "Detroit City." Many radio programmers and fans never made the connection between the first failed record and Bobby's new one. Those who did quickly forgot it, as the Dill/Tillis piece immediately took off. Stay-ing on the charts for eighteen weeks, it not only hit #6 in country, but moved over onto the rock charts and landed in the top twenty. A little later in the year "Detroit City" would also win a Grammy. Bare fol-lowed "Detroit City" with a number of crossover folk classics, the best of these being "500 Miles Away from Home," but the song which made him a star remained the fans' favorite.

It is doubtful that Danny Dill or Mel Tillis real-ized the real formula that they exploited when they wrote "Detroit City." They knew that the song had a hook of a Southern boy caught in a strange and for-eign world, but at that time they probably didn't know just how many men and women were going to identify with that situation and those lyrics. America was in the midst of a massive urbanization. Folks who had known nothing of city life were now mov-ing into a world of mass transit, apartments, and de-partment stores. The sounds of nature had been replaced by noise compounded with more noise. The cities had jobs, but they didn't give folks from the hills and hollows much in the way of peace. Hence, these migrating former farmers dreamed of fishing, hunting, and sitting under a tree watching life crawl by at a rather slow pace. They wanted out, but there was nothing at home for them. The only way they could provide for their families was to put up with a life they hated. As Dill had observed, many of them couldn't cope with their new lives and turned to booze.

On another level "Detroit City" represented the story of the expansion of country music. With the invention of the phonograph and radio, hillbilly folk music had left its regional home and begun to be heard in other areas. During the Depression and World War II, this music was taken by displaced Southerners across the nation. In spite of this extension of influence, even into the fifties country music was basically considered a Southern rural musical expression. With the industrialization of America this changed dramatically as rural families from all over the country migrated to better-paying jobs in the city. This move spread and anchored rural Southern music in every city in the nation and led to the first national country radio explosion. Music was one of the few things left to millions of homesick folks that could bring them any comfort. Thus its new urban popularity opened up first the airwaves and later the nightclubs and dance halls to the genre.

Written as a follow-up to an earlier hit, inspired by the plight of men in smoky bars, "Detroit City" became more than just another country music song. Long before "Okie from Muskogee" was adopted as an anthem for forgotten middle Americans, the Dill/Tillis composition gave a voice to social dilemma created by a changing nation. As cities grew, crime, depression, and addiction soon followed. Three decades later those problems have escalated and the feelings of being trapped and confined are still haunting urban life. Today, even more than then, a lot of folks are dreaming about going home to the country and leaving their problems behind. Some of them have even done it.

1963
The Night Life

Written by Willie Nelson

Willie Nelson had migrated to Houston in the late fifties. He played in clubs by night and worked at the Buskirk School of Guitar during the day. The man who would one day be Nashville's hottest star made his spending money by teaching kids to play guitar. Ironically, the man who hired Willie, Paul Buskirk, realized when he hired him that Nelson didn't know that much about the guitar and even less about teaching. Still, Paul's gut told him to take a chance on the clean-cut young man. Given time, the investment might just pay off.

When Nelson wasn't working with a pupil, he became one, taking lessons from the owner. Over a period of a few months Buskirk taught Willie scores of licks and chords. As the two of them worked to improve Nelson's playing, Paul began to sense that this young man was very talented. He only hoped that he could keep him around for a while.

During these long days and even longer nights, Nelson saw little of his family. When he wasn't at the school, he was driving across town to work five or six sets at one of several different local night spots. The smoky clubs, often filled with lonely drunks and aimless dreamers, quickly became as much a home to Nelson as the address where he received his mail. The patrons came to know the outgoing singer, and Willie came to not only recognize the regulars, but to know them as friends.

Nelson was developing his unique style of phrasing lyrics, hitting words on off beats, then pausing in a manner that was meant to prompt listeners to reflect on what the young man was saying. Yet more often than not, the patrons could care less about Willie's technique or his penchant for soft touching ballads. They just wanted to hear a good old Webb Pierce or Lefty Frizzell standard. So most of the time that is what they got. By and large the only person who seemed to care about what Willie was thinking was Paul Buskirk.

Because of the great potential he saw in the young man and the confidence he showed in him, Willie began to look upon Buskirk as a mentor. Over time the fledgling songwriter even began to share some of his writings with the man. Paul assured Nelson that he liked what he heard, and encouraged him to keep at it. Willie did, using what little spare time he could find to scribble down lines of verse.

One night on the way home from playing in a club, Nelson began to reflect on his wild and crazy life. On the streets he noted the people that normal folks never saw. There were winos and junkies, hookers and pimps, street workers and loners, cops and hoods, and lonely drifters who used the night to cover their sadness. With steam rising from drain shafts and wastepaper blowing down dingy streets, the nocturnal Houston was a world unto itself.

The vivid portraits which Nelson observed in the

late night hours served as the inspiration for a very special composition. Written easily and with little effort, Willie told the story of his life, "The Night Life," in a blues vein. The lyrics Nelson chose transcended description and rose to life as images on the canvas of a simple and free musical score. Dark, foreboding, depressing, and dramatic, the song presented the total scope of how the songwriter saw his and thousands of other lives. It also underscored how Willie had chosen this existence, that this eerie world had become his, and how he really wanted to stay in these surroundings for as long as he could.

As brilliant as Willie's effort on "The Night Life" was, the writer didn't have the contacts to get it published or recorded. It may have been his best work, but it could do nothing for him. The people who watched him at the club would much rather hear "If You've Got the Money" over a slow blues ballad anytime. In the sense that he had been able to so expressively expose his heart and soul in a song, "The Night Life" was special. But all of the magic that had gone into the writing didn't pay any bills, nor did it get him any nearer the big time.

While Willie might have thought that his latest effort had little real-world value, Paul Buskirk thought "The Night Life" was luminous. Like its writer, he wasn't sure if there was a market for the song, but he recognized that this was a very special effort. When Willie had inquired if Paul wanted to purchase all rights to the number, the guitar school owner made an offer of $150. As a bill of sale was signed and money changed hands, Willie was sure that he had gotten a much better deal than Buskirk.

Over time Nelson would finally make enough contacts to get to Nashville and begin to write at Pamper Music. Soon after his former employee left Houston, Buskirk, who had also purchased all rights to Nelson's "Family Bible," would eventually inter-

est others in Willie's early compositions. "Family Bible" would become a country hit twice in 1961. Two years later Paul would finally get a record deal on "The Night Life."

By 1963 Willie Nelson had become one of Music City's hottest and best-known song scribes. He had given Patsy Cline, Faron Young, and a host of others long chart rides with his compositions. His phone was continually ringing and he could not keep up with the large demand for his songs. With Nelson's reputation at its highest, Buskirk finally convinced Columbia and Ray Price to cut the blues song. Price's voice was perfect for "The Night Life," but neither he nor the label seemed to believe that the song had a commercial country sound. Paul was disappointed when his Nelson composition was released on the "B" side of "Make the World Go Away." In spite of not receiving its just due, "The Night life" still managed to earn a top-thirty finish. While the royalties would more than pay for his original investment, it was hardly the payback for which Buskirk had hoped. Ah, but the night wasn't over yet.

"The Night Life" was a strange kind of song. At first people seemed to pass it off as just another of Willie's quirky efforts. But given time, the number worked on people. While Price's recording didn't generate much heat upon initial release, the song's fire didn't completely die either. Soon Ray found that fans would request it at all his shows, and as he began to do more live versions of the Nelson blues effort, other acts began to pick it up for both album and single cuts. Three decades after its poor initial showing on the *Billboard* charts, "The Night Life" has created numbers that almost match the scope and genius of the song's magical lyrics. More than thirty million copies of the song have been sold and over seventy different artists have cut it. It has floated out of country and become a standard in blues, pop, rock, big-band, orchestra, and even elevator music. The royalties generated by "The Night Life" make it one of country music's biggest moneymakers. The song has made Paul Buskirk rich. And all Willie received for his contributions on this masterpiece was that first $150.

Looking back on what he had given up, Nelson reflected to a group of writers, "So what? I needed the hundred and fifty dollars a lot worse then than I do the millions now." That is a logic and an attitude that only a person of the night would fully understand.

1963
Act Naturally

Written by Johnny Russell and Vonei Morrison

As the sixties began, Johnny Russell was a young man living in Fresno, California. A singer who had won a long line of talent shows and was now working small clubs in the area, he had a reputation larger than most who had just seen their twentieth birthdays. Even though he was based on the West Coast, folks in his native Oklahoma were well aware that the entertainer had talent far beyond his years. Yet as important as his music was, there were times when Russell just wanted to forget the smoky nightspots and twanging guitar and go to a show with his girl. That was exactly what he had planned for a summer night over three decades ago.

"I got a call from some friends of mine in Oklahoma," Johnny explained as he thought back to that fateful day. "They were doing a recording session in Los Angeles and they wanted me to come down and help them. There was no getting out of it, so I had to break a date with a girl I had been seeing. When she asked me why I was going to L.A., I answered. 'They are going to put me in the movies and make a big star out of me.' We both laughed."

Russell didn't laugh for long. As he thought about the concept of being brought to Hollywood and made into a movie star, he began to play with a hook that could make the joke into a country love song. When he came up with an idea he thought would fit, he began to play with lines and mesh music to his new concept.

"I wrote the song that day," the songwriter remembered, "and I even tried to teach it to the boy we were recording. The problem was that he couldn't ever learn it. So I just brought it home with me. I was doing some recording at the time, and I sent a copy of it to my producer. He told me that songs about the movies weren't making it, so he turned it down too."

Johnny couldn't understand why his unique "Act Naturally" was not grabbing any attention. It seemed perfect. Yet as he continued to show it to folks in the business, time and time again he was told to go back and write a song about heartbreak, not a gimmick number like the one he was trying to plug.

"I really thought 'Act Naturally' was a fresh approach about talking about being in love," Russell explained. "I believed that it was unique enough to work, but I couldn't find anyone else who did. No matter how hard I tried, I just couldn't get anyone interested in it."

At that time Johnny was writing songs with a young woman named Vonei Morrison. When Russell finally played "Act Naturally" for Vonei, she fell in love with it. She thought it would be a natural for Buck Owens. Because she worked with Buck on a regular basis, she was sure that she could get him to record it.

"Vonei and I had an agreement during that time," Russell recalled, "that whatever we wrote, both of our names would go on the song. So now that I had showed her my old song, I also gave her a writing credit on it. We made an acetate of five of our songs, including 'Act Naturally,' and Vonei gave them to Buck."

As Russell waited to see what Buck thought, he went back to club work. When Vonei finally called him several weeks later, the news wasn't good. Of the five songs they had placed on the demo, Owens had only liked one. The number he'd liked the least was "Act Naturally."

Unknown to Russell or Morrison, Don Rich, one of Buck's most important band members and his tenor backup singer, liked "Act Naturally" a lot. Whenever the band went on the road, Don kept singing or humming the song. Eventually Buck began to hum it too.

"I was in Eureka, California, singing at a hotel club one night when I got a call from Bakersfield." Russell couldn't help but laugh as he remembered the night. "When I picked up, Buck was on the other end of the line and he asked if he could record 'Act Naturally.' I told him that it was fine with me. I later found out that he already recorded the song that day and just wanted the publishing rights. I was more than pleased to give him the rights in order to get the song recorded."

Buck Owens was probably the hottest thing on the West Coast since Spade Cooley and Tex Williams. He had made Bakersfield, California, Nashville West, and his unique blend of honky-tonk music sung with an Oklahoma twang (he had actually been born in Texas and raised in Arizona) had been making noise on the national playlists for about two years. Three of his singles had even climbed to #2 on the charts. Yet the top spot had eluded him, and many were predicting that Owens would not become a real star until he moved his operation to Music City. Johnny Russell's song was about to change all of that.

Recorded early in the year, "Act Naturally" hit the charts in May. The composition that everyone thought was too offbeat to work moved quickly, claiming #1 in June and holding that position for a month. All told the single spent over a half a year on the major playlists.

Johnny Russell was thrilled. Suddenly publishers were calling the twenty-three-year-old writer wanting to know what new things he had written and if he had anything for certain artists. He also found himself working nicer clubs and getting feelers for record deals. Yet as good as things seemed, they were about to get even better.

In 1965 the Beatles were finishing what was to become a best-selling album. They needed one more cut to complete the session. Paul McCartney astutely noted that with Ringo Starr's soaring popularity, maybe he should cut a number where he sang instead of just supplying the drums. As he stepped out from behind his instrument, the guys asked Starr what he wanted to do. Those gathered were expecting something from Buddy Holly or Elvis Presley, maybe even an old Chuck Berry standard. Ringo floored them all when he announced, "I want to do Buck Owens's 'Act Naturally'."

Recording the number in straight hillbilly style, the world's hottest rock group laid down the tracks to one of country music's most straightforward twang songs. British accent and all, it came together as if touched by magic, nicely putting the final touches on a rock album that would later sell millions of copies around the world. The song would remain so much a part of Owens's and Starr's identity that some twenty-four years later Ringo would join Buck and cut a duet version of "Act Naturally." Their cut lingered on the country charts for four months.

"Act Naturally" was the song which established Buck Owens as a country music power and Johnny Russell as a songwriter. Russell would go on to pen several major hits and record the barroom favorite "Rednecks, White Socks, and Blue Ribbon Beer." Buck would become one of the ten most successful country music recording acts of all time and place almost one hundred songs on national charts. That song that they combined to make famous would not only light up the charts, jukeboxes, and airwaves for years, but would also find its way into movie soundtracks and television scores. Even now "Act Naturally's" spopularity continues to amaze not only its writer, but a host of folks who once turned it down.

"One day not long ago," Russell explained, "I was at the Royal Gardens Hotel in London, England. As I ate my meal, Mick Jagger of the Rolling Stones walked in, sat down, and ordered. As he waited at the table beside me, he noted a cap I was wearing. Printed on the cap was the word Nashville. Mick inquired if I was in the music business in Nashville. I told him that I wrote songs. He asked if I had written any that he might know. I replied that the Beatles had cut one of mine. He then asked which one, and I began to tell him that Ringo had had the lead vocal on 'Act Naturally.' Before I could finish the title Jagger grinned and began singing the song. He knew it all.

"That night I was working a music festival when the promoter called me over to meet the famous English ballad singer Roger Whittaker. He had recorded a worldwide hit with 'The Last Farewell.' When Roger found out who I was, he began to sing 'Act Naturally.' No matter where I go, everyone seems to know it. I am still surprised at how many people tell me that the first song they ever performed in public was "Act Naturally.' "

Probably the best move that Johnny Russell ever made was breaking a date and going to Los Angeles to work a recording session. That short trip to the big city inspired a song that has naturally become one of country music's most endearing classics. "Act Naturally" may have been written in Fresno, but even in Hollywood it couldn't have been scripted any better.

1964
Together Again
Written by Buck Owens

Buck Owens rode into 1963 on the heels of his first #1 single, "Act Naturally." In late summer he released what was to be his biggest hit, "Love's Gonna Live Here." The father of the Bakersfield music movement was a thirty-six-year-old sensation whose California honky-tonk sound had seemingly come out of nowhere to control a good portion of Nashville's chart action.

In spite of being hung with a West Coast label, Owens was a Texas-born product. A native of Sherman, in the Depression Buck had migrated with his family to Arizona, and the boy would split his youth between his native and adopted homes. A high school dropout, Buck held a number of menial jobs in his late teens before taking his musical talent west. By the time he reached twenty-one he had not only become a solid guitar player, but had a steady job with a nightclub band. By the mid-fifties he had worked his way into a Los Angeles recording studio as a session player for the likes of Sonny James, Tennessee Ernie Ford, Faron Young, and Wanda Jackson.

During his days of session work Buck often tried to convince the A&R men that he had what it took to sell records. He was rejected time and time again. This pattern was broken only when a producer told him, "Owens, we got plenty of singers. What we need are songs."

While Buck continued to work sessions and play clubs, now he also began to write songs. By 1956 his compositions had caught the eye of Ken Nelson at Columbia. Nelson reviewed all of Owens's new stuff, and the more he listened to the songwriter, the more he liked the singer. In 1957 Ken began to work with Owens, signing him to a record deal. Two years later they first hit the national charts.

One of the things which had sold Ken Nelson on the kid was that he had a style that was all his own. Raised on Texas swing and cowboy music, Owens had fallen in love with rockabilly when that craze had controlled the country charts. To these three diverse musical styles, the singer added a western honky-tonk nasal vocal style that was more melodic than Webb Pierce and not as harsh as Lefty Frizzell. While all of these areas of influence could be heard in his work, none seemed to dominate. It was an even mix that was unique to Buck. The style later became known as the Bakersfield sound, and was the foundation for the music of Merle Haggard and Dwight Yoakam.

As a songwriter Owens knew his singing strengths and weaknesses extremely well. His compositions thus were written with one voice in mind. Therefore only a few of his hits would be redone by other artists. Typical of his work was "My Heart Skips a Beat." With a constant joyful drumbeat setting the rhythm and Don Rich's high tenor harmonies, the song literally jumped off a radio. In songs like

"Love's Gonna Live Here," "I've Got a Tiger by the Tail," and the aforementioned "My Heart Skips a Beat," it seemed that Buck was eternally grinning his way through each word. He didn't seem to be feeling the song's message as much as he was experiencing the happiness of making money with music. Everyone who watched him seemed to sense that there was a lot of mischievous little boy inside Owens. For that reason it was very hard to take him seriously on or off stage.

One of his self-penned hits that seemed to reflect a much deeper Buck was "Together Again." When he composed it, Owens immediately dismissed it. He had written the number in just a few minutes, and maybe because it had taken so little effort, he couldn't see the song's real merits. "Together Again" spoke of the joy of reclaimed love in an almost prayerful manner. Its simple mesaage was wrapped in a melody that seemed almost better suited for a song about heartbreak, not love rekindled. With its mournful music set against its happy message, it reminded the listener of just how much it hurts to lose someone you love. Yet it also spelled out that this deep anguish is what made getting together again so wonderful.

Buck tossed "Together Again" on the "B" side of "My Heart Skips a Beat." Nothing was expected of the ballad. Yet a week after the "A" side landed on the charts in 1964, "Together Again" followed. "My Heart" would hit #1 first in May, and "Together Again" would then surprise its writer by knocking its record mate out of the top spot in June. Both songs would spend more than half a year on the country charts.

The song that Owens had tossed aside as a loser was now one of his biggest winners. Yet the man with the happy face and sly grin didn't seem comfortable singing "Together Again" on stage. It always looked as though he was a bit uneasy having to stand still and be so serious about love.

In 1976 a onetime opening act for Gram Parsons was looking for a song that would take her to the top of the country charts. Emmylou Harris based her operations out of California and recorded for a West Coast label, but she really felt at home in Music City. One of the purest voices in music, because of her rock background and West Coast ties Harris was considered an outsider in Nashville. She could understand the industry's fear, but it was her rock associations that had led her to Music City. Before he died Parsons had gotten the singer hooked on real country music. Gram had pointed out that in rock the music's message was often secondary, while in country it was almost always primary.

From her study of country music Emmylou had come to treasure the way that "Together Again" told a love story without coming off as corny or superficial. She felt that her strong but sweet voice could take a song like this and add a layer of rich fabric to the message. While Buck had made the song a hit, Harris sensed that there was still a lot left to exploit and expose in this number. In the studio Emmylou would take the song and paint a magnificent picture from those wonderful words and that soaring tune with her rich country phrasing.

Reprise released Harris's version of "Together Again" in early 1976. With her voice drifting along like a bird in flight, the song traveled up the chart throughout late winter and early spring, landing at #1 in April. It was Emmylou's first chart-topper, and would lay a foundation for a career that is still going strong.

Emmylou felt as if "Together Again" had been written for her, and as it turned out, so did Buck Owens. Buck loved Harris's record, and really came to realize the real power of his composition when he heard her sing it. The writer was so moved by Emmylou's rendition of "Together Again" that he went back to work on the song. Three years later Owens and Harris recorded a top-twenty hit entitled "Play Together Again Again." In 1984 Kenny Rogers and Dottie West would take the original up the country music playlists.

Often overlooked and neglected, his influence many times dismissed without much thought or consideration, Buck Owens is one of country music's most important stars. He hit the top of the charts twenty-one times, held the #1 position for eighty-two weeks, and is ranked as one of country music's ten most successful recording artists. A television star and a songwriter, he not only forged a new sound, but also was responsible for bringing country music to a legion of new converts. His honest approach and easy smile won him millions of fans. Yet his most lasting and impressive work may have been one whose potential not even he could foresee. "Together Again" became a hit in spite of Buck Owens and will always be around to remind us of the man's genius.

1964

Once a Day

Written by Bill Anderson

Connie Smith had grown up poor and abused. She married and had children at a young age, and except for a little singing at local shows, the Ohio housewife had little time for anything except housework, cooking, and keeping up with her kids. In those rare times when Connie did get out of her house and away from the seemingly endless routines created by motherhood and marriage, she would often use the precious moments to sing at a local fair or in a stage show. These occasions spent under a small-time spotlight energized her. She found that singing songs in front of an audience lifted her almost as high as having one of her babies say, "I love you, Momma."

Smith was in her early twenties when she won a local talent contest near Columbus, Ohio. On one of the days away from all her responsibilities she had sung a Jean Shepard classic, "I Thought of You." As she shaped the song in her unique, inflective, powerful style, one of Nashville's most respected young men sat in the audience and intently listened. Patsy Cline had just died, and she had been the dominant female vocalist of the day. Most young women were trying to sound like either Patsy, a hot newcomer named Loretta Lynn, or the "Queen of Country Music," Kitty Wells. Yet, this pretty, blue-eyed blonde didn't sound like any of these country music stars, nor was she the image of pop stars Lesley Gore, Brenda Lee, or Connie Francis. Her style was

as singular as she was beautiful. Leaning back in his chair and taking in the way Smith wrapped her voice around each word, Bill Anderson thought he might have just found the next great girl singer. His gut-level instinct told him that she was "really something."

Connie hadn't expected to meet and visit with Bill that day in August 1963. After all, the man had written scores of hits for other people, and was now carving out a recording career of some note on his own. Surely Anderson wouldn't have time for a small-town contest winner. So Connie couldn't believe it when Bill approached her and told her that he thought she should come to Nashville and give the music business a shot. She didn't accept his words as the truth until he called again in March, brought her down to Music City, and arranged for her to sing on Ernest Tubb's post-*Opry* radio show.

Even after Smith made the trip and performed on WSM, the young mother still didn't expect to ever find stardom. She was just satisfied to have had the experience that Anderson had given her. Back at home there were diapers to be changed, dirty dishes to be done, clothes to be washed, and food to be cooked. This was what her life had been, and she expected that this would be the way it would always be.

"I was knocked out by Connie," Bill Anderson explained as he remembered back to first hearing her in

August of 1963. "She has such a big voice for such a small person."

While Anderson had Smith in town he cut a few demo tracks, and took them to Owen Bradley at Bill's own label, Decca. The singer sold Connie hard, but Bradley was convinced his stable was full. He had Loretta Lynn, and just didn't want or need to fool with another girl singer.

After Owen turned him down, Bill went to RCA. Chet Atkins took a listen and liked what he heard. He confirmed what Anderson already knew: This girl could really sing. Then Chet dropped the hammer.

"I have already got three girl singers, Dottie West, Skeeter Davis, and Norma Jean," Atkins explained. "I can't get enough material for them right now. How am I going to find songs for another girl singer?"

Taking a deep breath, Anderson took the plunge. "If you will sign Connie, I will promise you that I will write the material for her."

With that promise in hand, Atkins passed his blessings on Smith to RCA. Within a few weeks the unproven housewife found herself signing a contract with the city's largest major label.

As if she were wearing glass slippers, Connie returned to town in July and walked back into a recording studio. If Anderson could come through with a hit for the pretty blonde, this would be one of the most remarkable stories in Music City history. Without a hit, it would rank alongside a thousand other stories of false starts and shattered hopes.

His reputation on the line, Bill had sometimes worked all day and all night trying to come up with material for Smith's first release. His first efforts proved solid. "I'm Ashamed of You" and "The Threshold" were both good cuts, but they weren't as commercial as what Anderson thought they needed for a hit debut record. Continuing to toil long hours,

he came up with the cut that seemed inspired by his burning of the midnight oil.

"Once a Day" has one of the best hook lines the master tunesmith ever conceived. It was obvious to everyone at the session that the chorus was not just a classic bit of verse, but country heartbreak at its finest. Connie Smith sang it with so much conviction that even the writer knew that he had married the perfect singer to his latest effort.

RCA shipped Connie Smith's "Once a Day" in August. The request lines lit up immediately. No one even knew who this young new singer was but they couldn't wait to get her record. Customers came into stores simply asking for that "Once a Day" thing. When the clerk would ask who the artist was, more often than not no one could remember Connie's name. It was simply unheard of that any female singer could have this kind of success out of the box.

"Once a Day" hit the charts in late September, and by Thanksgiving Connie had moved Buck Owens out of the nation's top spot. Smith would hold #1 for eight straight weeks, and remain anchored on the charts for more than half a year. "Once a Day" would be the first time a female artist had ever had an initial release hit the top of the charts, and would also become the first time a woman had ever claimed country music's most successful chart record for any given year. And how it would change that young woman's life!

From appearing at PTA meetings in Ohio in the spring of 1964, Connie would be in Hollywood making guest appearances with Jimmy Dean and Lawrence Welk. From listening to the *Opry* on the radio in June, in October Smith would be sharing the bill with stars she had once just dreamed of meeting. From being a housewife whom few people knew, she would quickly become a Nashville personality who could draw hundreds at a record store autograph session. It was overwhelming.

"It may have happened too fast," Bill explained as he looked back on the circus days surrounding Smith's first release. "One day this beautiful young woman is just a wife and a mother, and the next she is one of the hottest acts in Nashville. She simply didn't have time to adjust."

Connie actually began to feel guilty. She didn't think she had paid her dues. She became somewhat embarrassed by all the fuss and attention. In a very real sense the sudden fame scared her. Yet with her movie-star looks and powerful voice, she would continue to turn out one-of-a-kind records for years to come. When her records quit scoring, it was because she backed away from her career to get back in touch with her children and herself. If she had felt the drive to continue, there is no telling how far she would have gone. Still, even in semi-retirement she wasn't forgotten.

In 1993 a national magazine reviewed a collaboration album by Dolly Parton, Loretta Lynn, and Tammy Wynette by posing the question, "Where was country music's best voice, Connie Smith?" Three decades after America first heard her, Smith remained one of the most unique and powerful voices in the industry.

"Once a Day" made Smith a star and kept Bill Anderson out of Chet Atkins's doghouse. Since Connie's release, only one record has ever held the top spot as long as this single. No female vocalist has ever claimed #1 for as long. Yet the scope of what Connie Smith accomplished with her first recording has now been all but forgotten, but it seems that the singer is comfortable with that too. A longtime *Opry* member, Connie knows that at least once a day someone somewhere remembers her first historic moment in the spotlight and requests the song that was her ticket to fame.

1965
King of the Road

Written by Roger Miller

Country music has been blessed with a number of geniuses. The industry has also had its share of eccentrics. Yet in more than seven decades of serving up entertainers and performances there has been only one man who took his eccentricities and his genius and put them together in a way that somehow made sense to millions while also leaving everyone wondering, "Where is this guy coming from?"

Roger Miller was one of the most unique talents to ever find the Music City spotlight. A product of Fort Worth, Texas, orphaned before his third birthday, he was raised by relatives in Erick, Oklahoma. Like so many who would gain stardom in Nashville, he was a victim of the Depression. Poor, undereducated, forced to go to work before he had entered his teens, Miller grew up in a world that was both hard and unfair. World War II broke out when the boy was five, but even as the economic state of many farm families improved, Miller's life changed little. When the fighting ended and the nation embraced real prosperity and growth, Roger still lived in a world that was filled with blighted hopes and unreachable dreams. Yet somehow, through even the bleakest times, the boy joked, laughed, and smiled.

After years of ranch work and some time spent on the rodeo circuit, Miller found a steady paycheck, plenty of food, and brand-new clothes in the Army. For the young man who had grown up eating turnips and dehorning cows, the military was a walk in the park. Overjoyed to be in a place where he had everything he needed, Roger often picked up a guitar and sang off-the-wall songs to make some of his homesick buddies laugh a little. This performing talent was soon noticed, and earned the young man a transfer to Special Services, where he was "forced" to play with an Army hillbilly band. Writing much of the outfit's material, picking up drums and fiddle as well as his guitar, Miller was not only the group's star, he was their happiest member. He had never dreamed that life could be this good. Roger now had more than he had ever had and everything he had ever wanted.

Discharged in the mid-fifties, Miller found that the real world was not nearly as accepting of his humor or his whimsical view of life. With an elfish grin he talked himself into and then out of a number of jobs before thumbing his way to Nashville. Working as a bellhop, he began to write a few songs and meet other struggling writers. He received a lot of tips, but no offers, and for a while it looked like he would spend his life carrying other people's bags.

Ray Price finally picked up on Miller's talent and placed the songwriter's "Invitation to the Blues" on the flip side of "City Lights." It was ironic that Roger's first successful effort at songwriting was backing Bill Anderson's initial hit composition. Anderson and Miller had known each other for a couple of years and had often traded ideas. Now Nashville had noted their talents at the same time. Roger took that as a good sign. Of course, he could also take rejection or a disaster as a good sign too!

Thanks to scoring a Ray Price record, Miller would write for Faron Young's publishing company for a while. His work on a host of future hits, including "In the Summertime," convinced RCA to give him a shot at recording. He produced one minor hit for the label, "When Two Worlds Collide," before moving on to Smash. It was here that he would find real success.

There was little doubt that Roger was talented, but to many it appeared that he was also crazy and prone to wasting time on compositions that were written just for laughs. While "normal" scribes spent days perfecting serious songs, Miller was often content to while away his time writing things that made no sense. More and more his work seemed to have no commercial value. Many of these Miller products were so strange that they made novelty songs seem downright serious. More often than not, even those who called him a genius also labeled the young man a flake.

Somehow Smash saw a method in the madness and caught onto what country music had missed. When Roger toured, those who bought tickets to his show liked Miller best when he made them laugh. In many ways he was a stand-up comedian who delivered his jokes in lyrics and music. His skewed point of view always seemed to score points, particularly with the younger crowd. Without even knowing it, Miller had invented a type of funny folk music. Sensing that there was some value here, the label thought that it would be worth the risk to release one of Roger's most unique songs.

"Dang Me," complete with a bizarre nonsensical chorus line and a mostly dialogue-driven verse, somehow became a major hit. It stayed at #1 for five weeks in 1964. It also made rock's top ten. The equally strange "Chug-A-Lug" and "Do-Wacka-Do" also climbed the charts that year. Partly singing, partly talking, mostly laughing, the poor boy had become a star whose royalty checks could now buy him anything he wanted. This sudden crazy success would also give Miller a chance to finally be taken seriously.

When writing his fourth Smash single, Roger called upon two of his own life experiences. The first was the poverty that had been at the core of his first twenty years. The other was the strange gypsy lifestyle which he had lived as both a songwriter and an entertainer.

In his first years out of the Army, Miller had held down countless jobs for as many as "a few days at a time." He had lived in cheap hotel rooms, run-down rent-houses, and rusting mobile homes. He had bummed countless cigarettes and gotten by many days on catsup sandwiches and watered-down coffee. Yet in the midst of all this, Roger had never lost his smile or his sense of humor. Like an innocent child, he'd turned even the worst day into an adventure. During that time he had also discovered that there was a sense of power in running your own world and depending upon no one else. In Miller's mind, the fact that he was really beholden to no one made him rich. And now, as he was fielding offers for his own network television show and putting more and more money in the bank, he realized that he had been just as wealthy and more in control of his life when he had been struggling. "King of the Road" was his story, a serious song that dealt with poverty in an upbeat fashion.

Roger's ode to independence, set in stark depression, somehow made people feel good. The melody had a grace, and the lyrics floated in such an easy manner that folks would sing them without even realizing it. To country fans who had grown up in the Depression, "King of the Road" represented "their good old days." To younger folks, whose desire for adventure and freedom was stymied by the realities of having to make a living and take care of a family, the song described their longings. To Smash Records this little ditty was solid gold.

The song went #1 just five weeks after it first appeared on the charts. "King of the Road" would hold that position for five more weeks, and stay on the playlists for twenty. On the pop side it would become Roger's best-charting single, working its way up to #4. "King of the Road" would lead Roger to five Grammys and countless other awards. Just a year after recording his first hit record, Miller had become country music's most visible national star.

Over the course of the next three decades, Roger Miller's songs would be learned and sung by adults and children everywhere. Millions who cannot remember their anniversaries and who have never bought a single Roger Miller record can sing every word of "Dang Me," "England Swings," "Kansas City Star," "You Can't Roller Skate in a Buffalo Herd," and "King of the Road." Miller would use his songwriting and performing skills to gain notice as an actor, a humorist, and a Broadway composer and star. Before his death in 1992, he would be recognized around the world as one of the brightest talents of modern music. He could do it all.

Hank Williams left the world with songs of heartaches that made fans want to cry. Merle Haggard gave the world songs that celebrated the sacrifices of the workingman and the downtrodden. A long list of great writers have defined love in countless ways. Roger Miller left us with something not nearly as dramatic, but maybe far more meaningful. He gave the world a smile because he knew that a smile, accompanied by a whimsical outlook, made all of us feel like royalty.

1966
Don't Touch Me

Written by Hank Cochran

Some songs don't start trends, don't establish careers, don't win all the major awards, but stand out simply on their merits as an incredible marriage of inspiration, talent, music, and lyrics. Hank Williams's "I'm So Lonesome I Could Cry" was one of these special songs. So was Willie Nelson's "The Night Life." In 1966 another Hank, Hank Cochran, created another such masterpiece. Cochran's "Don't Touch Me" has stood the test of time like few other works. Hauntingly beautiful, poetry set to meter, this composition merits particular praise for the exquisite manner in which it relates its story of love, doubt, and commitment.

"It is amazing where ideas come from," the song's writer emphasized. "You can get them from anywhere. I guess that is why I have always believed that real inspiration comes from heaven. It is just like a window suddenly opens up and you can see just how to write.

"In 1966 I was trying to make it as a recording artist and working a lot of shows. I was doing a show at a Minnesota club. A manager and I were running around one day and we passed a mental institution. He began to tease me. 'We had better hurry up or those folks will come out and get you,' he had joked. That went on for a while, and then the talk got a little more serious. We began to wonder what we would do if someone decided we were crazy and placed us behind those walls."

What had begun as teasing had now turned into a rather sobering concept. Thinking about what it would be like to really be locked behind bars with people looking at you as if you were insane made Hank uneasy. When he spoke again, his voice was more reserved.

"I told the guy that I would sure hate for them to catch me and put me in there. But if they did, and then they started to try to help me, I would tell them that I wouldn't let no one touch me if they didn't love me. As we drove along I got to thinking that I had just come up with a hell of a song idea."

While he finished his week in Minnesota, Hank worked on the song, but he just couldn't seem to get satisfied with the final result. When his gig ended, he hopped a plane and headed for New York. Cochran was dating a twenty-five-year-old singer who was working with Porter Wagoner. The songwriter wanted to use his schedule break to spend a few days with her before he was forced back on the road.

Jeannie Seely, Hank's new girlfriend, was a Pennsylvania native who represented a new breed of female artists. A music veteran, on stage since she was ten years old, Jeannie was more city than country, more North than South, and had a good head for business. When forced to, this was one woman who would take matters into her own hands. She was creative and tough, and these assets made her very attractive in Hank's eyes.

Talented and outgoing, Seely had written songs on the West Coast before coming to Nashville in 1965. Ernest Tubb used her on his show for a short while. Then she replaced Norma Jean on Wagoner's tours. At about that time Monument Records decided that Seely might have some value as a recording artist and signed her to a contract. When she started seeing Cochran, she was looking for something to use as her first single.

"By the time I got to New York," Hank recalled, "the song idea that had come from that trip by the mental institution was eating me alive."

Cochran's frustration with the ballad might have been caused by the song's message. He was falling for Seely, and he had some reservations about getting seriously involved. He was coming off a divorce and didn't want to ever go through anything that painful again. In a sense the very words he had written explained this fear so eloquently that he might have been afraid to so expose his heart to Jeannie and the world.

"One night while Jeannie and Porter were working I got real drunk," the songwriter admitted. "After their show, when I was trying to explain my condition, I began to talk about this great song idea I had and how I had been working on it. Porter wanted to hear it. I tried to sing it for him, but I was too drunk to even play the guitar. I finally taught Jeannie how it went, and she played the guitar while I sang it. She and Porter thought it was fabulous. Up until that point I hadn't known if 'Don't Touch Me' was good or not. When they confirmed that it was all right, the boiling inside me stopped. I guess it just wasn't going to leave me alone until I shared it with someone."

Monument's Fred Foster had already informed Jeannie that as soon as she came up with a good song, he wanted to record her. Sensing that this was it, she called the producer and told him to set things up. Meanwhile, a sober and happy Cochran made a trip to Chicago to appear on a local television show.

"I was feeling good now," Cochran recalled, "and I was really excited about the song. Buck Owens, who at that time was the hottest thing going, was also on the show with me. During a break, I played 'Don't Touch Me' for him. He went crazy."

"I want that song," Buck had demanded.

"You can't have it," the writer had explained "I have already given it to Jeannie Seely."

"Who the hell is Jeannie Seely?" Owens had returned. "I never heard of her."

Cochran had laughed, then slyly added, "You will as soon as this song comes out."

"Dammit, Hank," Buck had replied. "Do you know how hot I am? Do you know what I could do for that song? If you let me have it you know that it will be a big hit."

"I can't," Cochran had admitted. "I made a promise to Jeannie, and I am going to make sure that she gets the first cut on the song."

Monument pulled Jeannie into the studio when she returned to Nashville. Fred Foster put together a solid recording of Hank's new song, then quickly pressed and shipped the record. Released in March, it was on the charts in mid-April. It was almost unheard of for a new act to get that kind of early chart action. Owen Bradley at Decca noted those early numbers with great interest.

Bradley immediately knew that "Don't Touch Me" was what was pushing the new artist. The producer had always liked Cochran's work, and sensed that the song was one of the best things he had ever heard. Owen quickly hatched a plan and met with one of his newest singers. Wilma Burgess had just put "Baby" into the top ten. She needed a follow-up. The producer and the recording artist decided to cut Seely's new record. Then they were going to make a rush shipping in order to try to beat Jeannie's recording up the playlist.

"When Wilma Burgess covered it," Cochran remembered, "we were concerned for Jeannie. Decca was a much bigger and a much more influential label than Monument. The way they were promoting and pressing records, we could see they were trying to beat Monument with distribution."

Using his own money, Hank hired a couple of men to start plugging the Seely cut in the big markets. This worked in most places, but not in Chicago. The stations stayed hot on the Decca release and ignored Jeannie's. Decca had a foothold, and now the two songs were fighting it out for the smaller markets. By late summer the war was over and Seely had won. Wilma managed to climb to #12, and then tailed off. Jeannie had finished at #2. She held the position for three straight weeks.

"Having two versions of the same song going head to head kept Jeannie from getting a #1 record on *Bill-board*," Cochran conceded, his voice still revealing a slight bitterness. "Still, she did go to #1 on the other two national charts. So I got a couple of BMI awards for the song."

Hank and Jeannie got more than a second-place record and a pair of awards. "Don't Touch Me" won a Grammy for the best performance by a female country artist in 1966. It also took Seely on her lone ride up the pop charts. Over the course of the years Hank's ballad has been cut more times than even he can remember, and has become one of the industry's most performed songs.

"You know, even though we were fighting Wilma's cut," Cochran said with a laugh, "'Don't Touch Me' would have still made #1 in *Billboard*, except for one small thing. When Jeannie was a #2 and about to make her move up Buck Owens came back to haunt me. His 'Think of Me' jumped over us and kept us locked in second. The day it happened Buck called and reminded me that if I had let him have 'Don't Touch Me' I would have topped the charts. After he got done laughing I told him, 'I am still glad I didn't give it to you.'"

1966
Flowers on the Wall
Written by Lewis DeWitt

In 1955 Harold Reid joined Lew DeWitt, Phil Balsley, and Joe McDorman and performed before just a handful of people at a Methodist church in tiny Lynhurst, Virginia. This performance was the debut of a group that would eventually come to be known and loved as the Statler Brothers. In the mid-fifties, long before they considered "What Ever Happened to Randolph Scott" or remembered "Elizabeth," the guys were called the Four Star Quartet and their most requested song was "Have a Little Talk with Jesus." Slowly at first, the four high school friends would add more gospel standards to their act and build themselves into one of the area's best-known local gospel groups. Yet there wasn't much money to be made in Sunday services or church socials, so by 1960 the group had dissolved. Missing the good times with friends and the opportunity to harmonize, Reid reformed the quartet as the Kingsmen a year later. Harold's brother Don replaced McDorman, who had left to find a real job in the real world.

While the Kingsmen generally performed the religious standards wherever they worked, financial concerns necessitated their singing any kind of music that would put money in their pockets. So while the Kingsmen were a straight gospel quartet on Sunday, during the week they performed country, pop, and rock music at conventions, dances, and banquets. The more they played in the secular world, the more in-terested the guys were in developing their sound to fit the songs that people requested.

The Kingsmen's gospel role models were the Blackwood Brothers. In rock the guys could emulate the sounds of the close-harmony doo-wop groups such as the Crew Cuts. But in country there were no groups to look to for inspiration. Except for a very few harmonizing family acts, hillbilly music relied heavily on lead vocals, with groups only being used for chorus accompaniment. With no pattern to follow, the Kingsmen simply worked out their own arrangements of songs that were written to be sung as solos.

Country music's failure to develop quartet-style groups seems strange. With the genre's close tie to church music and hymns, and with the hardcore country music fan usually a product of a Protestant shaped-note hymnal, all-day singing, and a dinner-on-the-ground environment, it would have seemed so natural that a harmony-type sound would have evolved from gospel to country during the early period of hillbilly music. Yet it didn't happen. Even in the early sixties when the Kingsmen began to draw some regional interest in the Virginia area, record companies ignored the boys while giving auditions to a host of different solo acts. Much like church and state, there seemed to be a country music law that kept gospel quartets and country music segregated.

The Kingsmen might have never found the warm

Music City spotlight if it hadn't been for Johnny Cash. Cash first caught the group in 1963. As he watched them work a small-town crowd, he was impressed with not only their sound, but their ability to charm a country audience. A year later when Johnny put together one of the first big country music package shows, he thought of the Kingsmen again.

Cash already had the Carter Family signed to tour with him. He had also convinced his old Sun Records buddy Carl Perkins to come along. Yet he needed something else to bring a big-time show to small-town America. That something could turn out to be a quartet who could do gospel and easily turn a country standard too. To evaluate his theory Cash managed to get the Kingsmen booked as his opening act for a single show. After watching the crowd's reaction to the group, Cash asked the quartet to join him. Within days the guys were playing before thousands instead of hundreds.

Being on the road with Cash provided the group with enough money to quit their real-world daytime jobs. It also presented them with a new problem. In Virginia everyone knew who the Kingsmen were. Now they were performing in front of people who didn't know them personally and who assumed that they were the rock group who had just scored with "Louie, Louie." In order to separate themselves from the other Kingsmen, the group picked a name off a tissue box and became the Statler Brothers.

After the boys got their stage and road legs, Johnny Cash used his power at Columbia to wrangle the Statlers a record deal. The studio was far from enthused about their new act, and had no idea how to promote them. The Brothers weren't a gospel quartet, they weren't a folk harmony act, and they didn't sound like anything that had ever placed much on country charts. Where was their niche? Besides, only two of them were brothers. For a while the label did

little publicity on the group, and simply recorded the guys enough to keep Cash happy. It therefore was no surprise that the first Statler records bombed. If the boys were going to have a hit record, a great deal of the responsibility for creating that hit would be theirs.

By 1965 the Cash road show was drawing bigger crowds than any other country music act. The reason for this appeared to be the interest Johnny was generating with the young folk/rock crowd. In order to win these new country music converts over to their style and sound, the Statlers began to perform a few folk numbers. The warm response these songs received set Lew DeWitt to thinking. Maybe he could write an original song that would combine the quartet harmonies with a folk-type lyric coupled to a country beat.

The idea that would become the group's first hit song began to take shape in a hotel. While on the Cash tour the group stayed in a room with flower-covered wallpaper. Grasping on the quirky things people do when they are bored, DeWitt thought about how long it would take to count all the flowers in the room. From there he noted other ways that musicians passed time on the road. All around him were people who were avoiding watching the clock slowly tick off the minutes by playing cards, smoking cigarettes, and viewing television. Using a country beat and a driving bass that sounded a great deal like the one Cash had employed on his early hits, Lew composed a song based on his observations. A bit later the Brothers polished DeWitt's work and cut it at the Columbia studio.

The record label sensed that "Flowers on the Wall" had a real possibility of making a dent in the pop charts. This song of a hopelessly one-sided love affair was somewhat similar to many of the things the Kingston Trio and Peter, Paul and Mary were doing. Columbia believed that with a little luck and this song, the Statler Brothers might be marketed as a folk group and erase some of the red ink that had been run up on their first recordings.

Releasing "Flowers on the Wall" in August, the label watched hoping that the song would make the pop top forty. Columbia was disappointed when the rock charts failed to welcome the record. Yet things were not all bad. In late September the Statler Brothers landed on the country playlist for the first time. What was even more surprising was that there was a bullet beside their single. With a steady pace, fueled somewhat by Johnny Cash's road show's popularity, "Flowers on the Wall" worked its way toward the top of the charts. The Brothers would eventually stall out, but not before they had held #2 for four straight weeks.

Buoyed by interest from the country fans, folk listeners began to demand that rock stations play "Flowers on the Wall." In December the song appeared on the rock charts. Nine weeks later it had worked its way to #4. Now, instead of counting flowers on the wall, Harold, Don, Phil, and Lew could think about counting royalty payments in the mail. Besides establishing their recording potential and making a little money, "Flowers on the Wall" also won them a Grammy.

It would take five more years for the Statlers to find their niche and country music to fully accept their quartet sound. During this period the guys would struggle with a number of different styles and approaches. In 1970 their "Bed of Roses" made them legitimate hit-makers and caused a host of other quartet acts to think about making the move to country. Some tried for a few months, then raced back to gospel. In 1976 the Oak Ridge Boys made the move, won a legion of fans, and recorded a long list of hits. Between them, the Statler Brothers and Oak Ridge Boys have placed more than 110 songs on the country music charts.

It took a long time for the gospel-quartet sound to find a place in country music. It took a very headstrong, stubborn, and talented group to break down the barrier between the two closely related musical forms. When the Statlers bridged that gap, America not only gained a great new sound, but discovered a group that would compose some of country music's most unique songs. Over the years the Statler Brothers have made a great impression on a genre that once didn't even know what to do with them. In 1966 one strange little song gave their group their big break, and now an even better method of killing time than counting the flowers on the wall would be trying to remember all the Statlers' hits.

1966
You Ain't Woman Enough

Written by Loretta Lynn

Loretta Lynn's life is among the best-chronicled in country music history. Her millions of fans can recite her story line for line and verse for verse. Her humble beginnings, her early marriage, her days spent raising children when she was still a child herself, her first tentative steps into country music, her close friendship with Patsy Cline, her rise to superstardom, and the Hollywood movie made about her life are the major elements of Lynn's stranger-than-fiction biography. Much like George Washington, Davy Crockett, or Babe Ruth, this daughter of a coal miner has somehow stepped beyond her life's station to become something more than what she ever was or intended to be. At the same time, Lynn has never ceased being the real person who escaped poverty around the same time she first appeared on the *Opry*. Bigger than life, she is also seen as a representation of the everyday blue-collar woman.

Loretta was born in Butcher Hollow, Kentucky. She was married when barely a teenager and began her career by working local talent shows, fairs, and honky-tonks. Her husband, Mooney, served as manager, driver, promoter, and baby-sitter during her lean early years. The couple often drove from town to town to just visit with disc jockeys and pass out her first record. Within a year of this mostly personally financed promotional tour, Lynn was signed by Decca and America's latest Cinderella tale was born.

In many ways Loretta would emulate her hero and friend Patsy Cline. Yet Lynn would never become so absorbed by Cline's personality and charm that she would lose her own. Simple, direct, homespun, Loretta would eventually rise to the top of the country music charts but she wouldn't make it overnight.

From the start, she was as much restricted by popular attitudes of the day as any other female singer: She was the decoration on a man's show; she was expected to let men make her decisions; she was asked to believe that women singers just weren't as important as their male counterparts and would never sell as well. This is the way that Nashville was, and it was the way that most insiders expected it to remain.

While other female acts might have acquiesced to these unwritten rules, Lynn didn't. Soon she was defying the men and picking her own material, writing her own songs, and building a fan club that would rival and eventually surpass that of all the mighty men on Music City labels. Carefully, but boldly, she stepped out and demanded not only to be heard, but to have a real voice. Once people began to listen, she took up a banner that would make her one of America's best-known women.

Through hard work, from 1962 through the middle of 1966, Loretta became one of the dominant female singers in Nashville. Her concerts slowly built into reunions. Fans who had seen her ten times would return again, not just to hear her sing, but to stay afterwards to visit with the star. The "Blue Kentucky Girl," as some were calling her, was affecting country music's faithful at the grass roots. She wasn't on par with the successful male stars, but she already had seen more chart action than Patsy Cline.

As her fame grew, so did Lynn's assertiveness. She might not have had much formal education, but she had a lot of common sense. She knew that she could identify with the women who became her audience and bought her records a lot more than the men could who were running her career. Against those men's advice, she began to write songs that articulated a woman's view. She began to sing about, subtly at first, abusive relationships, cheating, scheming, drinking, and lying. As her confidence grew, so did her courage. By mid-1966 she was both loud and bold, and her messages were no longer veiled.

In a world where women normally sang only about love and broken hearts, Lynn put on the gloves. "You Ain't Woman Enough" blatantly announced her intentions for both life and career. It also signaled the beginning of a new era for female country music singers and their fans.

"You Ain't Woman Enough" was in many ways like Loretta's other self-penned records—it was inspired by a real-life experience. Early on, when she was touring small honky-tonks and fairs, women would come on strong to her husband, Mooney. Night after night, she would watch from the stage as ladies of all ages made advances toward her man. In a very real sense, Mooney and her kids were all she had, and she wasn't going to lose either one without a fight. So rather than take this treatment and smile, Lynn challenged each invader face-to-face. At 5'2", the fiery singer proved time and time again that she was not just petite and pretty, she was also tough and strong. She didn't just hold her own, she won.

"You Ain't Woman Enough" gave voice to her many battles and her own strong will. Through her simple words she told thousands of women that they didn't have to be bullied anymore, that they could stand up and fight for what was theirs, and that no one—including their husbands—was going to walk on them anymore. In each line and verse of her new composition, Loretta demanded that women had a right to take charge.

"You Ain't Woman Enough" entered the charts in early 1966. It was Lynn's eleventh single for Decca. Jumping on the playlists in June, it would push up the ladder until mid-August. Loretta's song stalled at #2 for two weeks, unable to crawl over David Houston's "Almost Persuaded." Houston's ode to the temptations of cheating with an appealing young woman flew in the face of the message Lynn was preaching in "You Ain't Woman Enough." While Houston may have won this skirmish, Loretta had far more firepower. She would win the war.

After twenty-three weeks on the charts "Woman" faded. Yet even when the song had made its final playlist bow, the effects of Lynn's powerful declaration were still felt. Loretta's next single voiced another overdue women's issue: amorous drunk husbands. "Don't Come Home A'Drinkin' (with Lovin' on Your Mind)" would land Loretta in the top spot for the very first time. It would also provoke enough controversy to be banned in several cities for being so vociferous with its message. It would not be the last of Loretta's records to create controversy or be banned.

Over the course of her next fifty singles, Lynn would make her pitch for women's rights time and time again. Through her writing, she expressed what most women had long thought but had been afraid to declare in public. Lynn lobbied against abuse, adultery, and alcohol long before they were popular issues, and she sided for birth control and assertive wives. Once the Kentucky-born performer opened the door to this forum, all the men in Music City couldn't even begin to close it. Lynn's direct, issue-oriented songwriting led other women to sing songs which expressed many of the real interests and fears concerning modern women.

With her views, Lynn became an icon for women everywhere. Even though her country twang and simple manners should have endeared her only to the southern working class, Hollywood and New York embraced her as well. Lynn was featured in stories in every major magazine and became a voice for the women's movement. Other experts may have been able to quote vast statistics and point out gross injustice, but with her "I've-been-there" approach, Loretta spoke far more clearly to the issues.

In many ways Loretta Lynn was country music's first recognized political voice. Even though the songs which established her as a real star were based on personal experiences, Lynn's lyrics spoke directly to millions of women who had suffered silently for years. Her talent as a performer notwithstanding, it was her writing which took an uneducated woman from the far backwoods and made her into one of this nation's most respected women. With her message, Lynn inspired not only her fans, but women everywhere to speak out and be heard. And those who were still too timid to do so had Lynn's music to do it for them.

Lost in the glow of a Hall-of-Fame career and hidden by the myth and legend that has grown out of Loretta's own traumas has been the real impact and influence of this female pioneer. This important facet first became evident with "You Ain't Woman Enough" and steadily grew through "Don't Come Home A'Drinkin'," "Woman of the World," "I Wanna Be Free," "Rated X," "The Pill," and "You've Come a Long Way Baby." Without Lynn's unadorned honesty, who knows how long it would have taken country music, or even the country in general, to face up to the power and needs of women.

1967
There Goes My Everything

Written by Dallas Frazier

In 1952, when he was just twelve years old, Dallas Frazier won a talent contest sponsored by country music performer Ferlin Husky. Husky was so impressed by the Bakersfield, California, child that he took him on a summer tour. Dallas charmed audiences with his singing and poise. He also impressed musicians with his talents on a wide variety of instruments including guitar and trumpet. When still in his teens, Frazier put together a band and became well known on the West Coast while performing on Cliffie Stone's "Hometown Jamboree" television show. Most figured that he was well on his way to a long and rich career in country music. Yet by the time he had completed high school in 1958, his association with country music consisted of little more than a few photographs and some wonderful memories.

It was the comic pages which probably kept Frazier's music career from ending altogether. As the teenager read a strip about a group of prehistoric misfits, a concept for a song began to come together in his head. Within a few months Gary Paxton and his Hollywood Argyles had recorded Dallas's "Alley Oop," and the novelty number became one of 1960's biggest hits. Unfortunately for both the group and the songwriter, Dallas couldn't come up with a follow-up.

Within three years Frazier had drifted up the coast to Portland and dropped out of the music business. He had gotten married, put away the toys of his youth, and was getting on with a life in the real world.

"I wasn't pursuing the business at all," Dallas remembered, "but when Ferlin Husky came through town on a tour, I went to see him. He was an old friend and I just wanted to visit."

During the visit, Husky, who owned two of country music's biggest hits, "Gone" and "Wings of a Dove," urged Dallas to get back in the music business. The singer thought that Frazier was wasting his God-given talents. To emphasize just how strongly he believed in the young man, Ferlin offered Dallas a songwriting job in his publishing company. It took nothing else to convince Frazier to make the long move.

Immediately upon arriving in Music City, Frazier began to work long hours putting words and music together. He didn't know if this move was going to prove successful, but he vowed that if it wasn't it wouldn't be for lack of effort. For immediate inspiration the songwriter looked at the lives of the people he knew best. In the case of what was to become his biggest hit, that inspiration came from observing his mentor.

"The idea for 'There Goes My Everything' came from Ferlin's life story," Dallas recalled. "He had just gone through a divorce and he was hurting badly. As I thought about how he felt, the song came together very quickly. Maybe it was because I was so fresh, so new to Nashville and the music business, so full of boldness and daring, but it seemed to just fall out of the air."

The bold and daring Frazier played the number for Husky at his first opportunity. The songwriter was very proud of this effort, but maybe because it hit so close to home, the singer opted only to include it in his next album. He made no plans to release it as a single. Still, this work seemed to prove that Ferlin's faith in Dallas was well placed. He patted him on the back and urged him to get back to his desk.

In a very real sense, "There goes my reason for living, there goes my everything," the song's unforgettable and now immortal first line, was all but forgotten as both singer and songwriter went back to work. Ironically, Husky would never again score a #1 hit, while Frazier would quickly strike gold several times.

Three years passed before a former construction worker who was approaching his fourth decade noticed the old Husky album cut. Jack Greene was a one-timer drummer and guitar player with Ernest Tubb. It was the Texas Troubadour himself who had pushed Greene out on his own and helped him land a contract with Decca. Still, even with the legendary Tubb's backing, up until 1966 Jack had spent a total of just seven weeks on the charts. Then he released his version of Ferlin's album cut.

Catalog #32023, better known as "There Goes My Everything," raced to #1 on the country charts and stayed there for seven weeks. It even cracked the top one hundred on the rock side. Less than a year after the all-but-unknown Greene cut the Frazier tune he would win the Country Music Association's "Male Vocalist of the Year" honor, join the *Grand Ole Opry*, and become one of the era's most consistent hit-makers. The song that made Jack Greene a star and put young Dallas Frazier solidly on the songwriting map would also become a standard for every up-and-coming male and female vocalist. Frazier himself used it as a springboard to go on and compose scores of classics, including "Elvira" and "Mohair Sam."

"There Goes My Everything" would have probably been a huge hit for Ferlin Husky had the singer and his label, Capitol, released it as a single. It might have even revived his flagging career. As it was Ferlin missed his shot to be identified with the classic. Since Jack Greene's release, the CMA's 1967 Song of the Year has been recorded countless times. Elvis scored a hit on it twice. And over three decades after he wrote "There Goes My Everything," it is still making money for its writer, now Rev. Dallas Frazier. It has become the classic that literally fell out of the air and will linger on the lips of country music fans forever.

1968
Mama Tried

Written by Merle Haggard

Merle Haggard could have been a John Steinbeck invention. Merle certainly would have made a perfect anti-hero for one of the great writer's American epics. A product of a poor migrating Okie family, Merle was born in a junked boxcar that his father had converted into a house. He was raised in Bakersfield, California, or as many of the locals called it, Oklahoma West. Raised in a strict Church of Christ household, the boy grew up singing hymns with his mother, Flossie, and yodeling Jimmie Rodgers's songs with his father, James. Almost destitute, but always proud, the family often lived from meal to meal. Yet by the time young Merle turned nine in 1946, it seemed as if things were getting better. The economy had improved and good times appeared to be ahead. Then James died.

While she held down a job, Mrs. Haggard kept her baby boy on a tight leash for the next few years. In retrospect it was probably too tight. In his early teens Merle rebelled, began to skip school, and became involved in juvenile crime. Sent to a boys' home, he escaped and drifted full-time into petty crime. From there Merle moved into theft, hot checks, fencing stolen goods, and grand theft auto. He was in and out of local jail and knew all the area judges by sight. Worse yet, they knew him too. If Merle hadn't been run down and placed in prison in 1957, he very well might have died a violent death while committing even more serious crimes.

Sentenced to a stretch in San Quentin, Haggard again mixed with the wrong crowd. Trouble followed him even behind bars. A week in solitary confinement finally gave him an opportunity to evaluate his life. A later visit with a death-row inmate who was eventually executed forced Haggard to look deeper at what he had become and redirect his energy into more productive ventures. Released in 1960, Merle swore that he would never again see the inside of a prison.

For the ex-convict things on the outside were tough. Haggard's salvation was the emergence of Bakersfield as the West Coast center for country music. Following in the steps of Buck Owens, Merle worked construction in the daytime and played music in local honky-tonks and bars at night. By the mid-sixties, performing had become his full-time occupation and Haggard was one of the area's best-known singers.

Capitol Records took note and signed Haggard just five years after his prison release. Immediately Merle began to sell a few records and develop a national following. Many of his early compositions reflected his own life's situation, and their stark honesty seemed to appeal to an ever-growing audience. In 1966 Merle tasted the top-ten three times, landing his first chart-topper with "The Fugitive." A series of #1 efforts followed in 1967–68 including "Branded Man," "Sing Me Back Home," and "The Legend of Bonnie and Clyde." Except for the ode to the Depression-era robbery team, each new release appeared to mirror moments of Haggard's own life.

By 1968 Merle's fame had grown to the point where Hollywood came calling. Not only did they want Haggard to join Dick Clark and Robert Walker in the movie *Killers Three*, they also wanted the singer to write a song for the film. Drawing much more from his own life than the script, Merle painted an unmitigated picture that showed what could have happened to him if he had not pulled away from a path of crime.

On the surface "Mama Tried" was the story of a boy who celebrated his twenty-first birthday in prison. Convicted of a major offense, the young man had no chance of gaining parole. Just when his life should have been starting, he was staring at the prospect of never again tasting freedom. A normal writer might have stopped the story here, but Haggard was no normal writer. He presented all sides of the story no matter how personally painful they were.

In "Branded Man" Merle exposed the shame of living as an ex-con. In "The Fugitive" he expressed the fears of running from men who were someday surely going to catch him. In "Sing Me Back Home" he related what it was like to feel the emotions of death row. All of these experiences had been vital parts of his life. In each of these songs the singer drew vivid pictures that detailed shame, exhaustion, loneliness, and anguish. In "Mama Tried" he put his prison years in a fabric that almost anyone could understand by telling the story through two sets of eyes.

When Haggard composed the song's chorus he touched upon the pain and heartache he had caused his own mother. It was the loving woman's wasted efforts that brought the prisoner the deepest shame. It was the fact that she had so wanted him to go right that weighed the heaviest on his heart. Her unanswered prayers brought more tears than any punishment ever could. The convict could carry the weight of a court's judgment, but the fact that he had let his mother down caused deeper disgrace than he could bear.

Merle had been forced to take a few liberties while working out the lyrics to "Mama Tried." The songwriter had never been under a life sentence, and even in the depths of three years in San Quentin, he knew that he would have the chance to again taste freedom. But the emotion that ran through each of the song's verses was real. Framed perfectly with a simple musical line, the song went directly from Merle's heart to the listener's. It was a musical tribute to a mother whose efforts had been appreciated, but rarely acknowledged. Without meaning to, with "Mama Tried" Haggard had touched millions of sons and daughters who, while they might not have ever spent time in jail, somehow fell short of living up to their mothers' efforts. This was their song too!

Released in the early summer of 1968, "Mama Tried" hit the *Billboard* numbers in late July. By the last week in August, Haggard would own the playlist's #1 position. His "Mama Tried" would hold the top spot for four weeks. In a career that saw Merle chart more than one hundred singles, this autobiographical number would rank as his second most popular.

About the time that "Mama Tried" topped the charts, critics were beginning to call Haggard a genius. He felt uncomfortable with almost all forms of praise, and tried to pass this compliment off as pure hogwash. While the genius label may have unnerved him, the title "Working Man's Poet" probably pleased him a great deal. That is what he really wanted to be, a voice for the common man.

Because he was such a great and powerful entertainer, Merle Haggard is far underrated as a songwriter. He is a complex individual, and the honesty he shows when he writes exposes a great deal about his many facets. Early in his career what seemed to come through the loudest was a need to unburden himself of his guilt, as well as the anguish he brought into other people's lives. With the fanatic and heartfelt response to his songs, the American people pardoned Haggard long before the state of California. Looking over a career that produced such a great wealth of material, one senses that Flossie Haggard realized that all of her efforts and sacrifices were worth it too.

1968
Stand by Your Man

Written by Tammy Wynette and Billy Sherrill

Virginia Wynette Pugh never knew her father. He died when she was still a baby. Shuttled between relatives for much of her youth, what she did know was poverty and hard luck. Music offered her relief from life's problems, and the young girl immersed herself in both playing and singing. By the time she reached high school in the late fifties, she had gained some measure of local fame in the rural Itawamba County, Mississippi, area where she lived. Tammy might have continued to pursue music at this juncture if she had not gotten married and moved to Tupelo. Within just a few years, she was running a house, tending two children, and singing little except lullabies.

The tragedy that haunted her youth would follow Tammy Wynette for most of her life. She was pregnant with her third child when her first husband left her. To compound the situation, right after a move to Alabama, Tammy's new baby was born prematurely and suffered severe medical problems. Running up huge bills, Wynette eventually nursed the baby to health. Then the mother of three worked long hours in a beauty shop to pay off her debts.

It was the doctor bills, as well as the high cost of raising three children without a husband, that led Tammy to audition and win a spot singing on a local radio show. This moonlighting job positioned her to work dates in area clubs. These gigs grew to the point that by the mid-sixties Wynette was playing honky-tonks throughout the South. When she landed a guest shot on the Porter Wagoner television show, she thought she had it made. Yet even though several record labels interviewed Wynette at that time, none offered her a contract. Disappointed, Tammy returned to her home in Birmingham.

On her next trip to Nashville in 1966, the struggling mother dropped by unannounced at CBS Records. Billy Sherrill, the label's top producer, was in, but his secretary was out. Boldly the singer introduced herself and gained an audience. Billy was impressed by both the woman's tenacity and her talents, and signed Tammy to an Epic Records contract. Sherrill soon realized he had gotten a much more valuable package than he first realized. Wynette was not only a good singer of heartache songs, but she could write them too.

Tammy's third record, a duet cover of "My Elusive Dreams" with David Houston, hit #1 in 1967. The singer scored her first solo chart-topper later that year with "I Don't Wanna Play House." In mid-1968 she took Bobby Braddock's and Curly Putman's classic "D-I-V-O-R-C-E" to the top of the charts. That song made her one of the nation's best-known new talents, and even crossed over to the pop charts. Yet it would be her next single which would place Tammy the songwriter and singer on the way to superstardom and music immortality.

One of Nashville's best-known stories centers on the birth of "Stand by Your Man." Billy Sherrill had come up with the song's title months before he shared it with Wynette. The only reason the producer presented his idea in August 1968 was the need for another number to finish out a recording session. Taking out a scrap of paper, he showed Tammy the concept idea that was to hatch their collaboration. Then they pulled out a blank piece of paper and a pen and went to work.

Tammy would tell her friends that the song "just came to me." It came fast too. She and Sherrill spent less than a half an hour composing both the words and music for what was to be Wynette's signature number.

In a way, "Stand by Your Man" stood diametrically opposed to the kind of music that Loretta Lynn was then composing and releasing. While Lynn was demanding that women take a step forward and let their voices be heard, Tammy was playing to the more modest housewife. Her new song let it be known that it was all right to be submissive and supportive.

This anti-feminist theme would play well in the Bible Belt. The single was also a perfect follow-up to "D-I-V-O-R-C-E." In the first hit Tammy didn't want to give up on her marriage. In "Stand by Your Man" she was going to do whatever it took to make sure that her love kept her marriage glued together, no matter how much she had to sacrifice.

The song was so well crafted and Tammy's performance so solid that "Stand by Your Man" probably couldn't have failed even without promotion. In this case, everything seemed to be working in its favor. What was to become one of the era's hottest movies, *Five Easy Pieces*, picked "Stand by Your Man" for its soundtrack. This was a dream come true for the Epic publicity machine, as it gave Wynette's music a whole new audience and positioned her to become Loretta's

most formidable challenger. It also gave the song a chance to score on pop radio stations.

"Stand by Your Man" hit the charts in October. A month later the record sat atop the *Billboard* country playlists and was beginning to make a move in rock music. "The Queen of the Country Heartache" was about to become the hottest act in Nashville. "Stand by Your Man" would hold the #1 position in country for three weeks, and its nine-week run on the pop side would end just one step into the top twenty. The back-to-back hits of "D-I-V-O-R-C-E" and "Stand by Your Man" would set the table for sixteen straight top-ten finishes and fourteen #1's in the next eight years. Though she was never as wildly revered as Loretta Lynn, Wynette's records would actually score far better.

"Stand by Your Man" would have a chart life even longer than Tammy's. Recorded countless times, the straightforward country standard would become a hit in soul, rhythm and blues, rock, and country several times. It would be sung by men, women, and groups. It would inspire a #1 hit for Ronnie Milsap, "I'm a Stand by My Woman Man," and become a part of a 1992 Presidential campaign debate. It would also become the theme song for a women's movement that stood against the Equal Rights Amendment and other feminist programs. Embraced by the conservative wing of the Christian Right, it still serves as a political standard today.

Certainly Billy Sherrill and Tammy Wynette never intended to put the singer in the middle of a three-decade-old political fire. Yet by doing so, "Stand by Your Man" placed Tammy right in the center of the national spotlight. She was news, and became more than just another country girl singer. Like Lynn, she had risen above the era's other female artists and now stood on somewhat equal ground with the hot male acts. Unlike Loretta, in her next releases

Wynette would steer clear of controversy and go back to the heartbreak and loving themes that were the usual fodder for Music City's gal singers. Yet with the almost cult status of "Stand by Your Man," Tammy would never again be just another girl singer, and her stature would demand that country charts make room for two powerful women—and they did.

Ironically, in real life it was the crusading Lynn who stood by her man. Through ups and downs, Loretta and her husband rode out their union. Tammy went through several husbands before she could find one she could stand by. Nevertheless, the country music fans forgave Wynette for all her failings and always demanded she sing the song which had come to define both her and her career. Almost thirty years later she is still riding the wave created by "Stand by Your Man."

1969

Okie from Muskogee

Written by Merle Haggard

Merle Haggard might have very well grown up on the streets of Muskogee, Oklahoma, if the Depression hadn't forced his family to leave for California just a few years before the singer's birth. As it was, Haggard felt as if he knew the area and its people thanks to the stories he heard not only from his immediate family, but also from a host of other Okies who had migrated to the Bakersfield area. So even though by birth Merle was a Californian, by culture and home environment he was also an Oklahoman. If he ever forgot this fact, there was a host of folks around him who reminded him and needled him at length about his Dust Bowl roots. Even after he had escaped poverty and became a show business legend, it still seemed as if a long line of people thought he and folks like him were little more than trash. Even in the so-called enlightened years of the Kennedy and Johnson presidencies, the country didn't forgive or forget very quickly.

As Johnson gave way to Nixon, the nation seemed to grow even more cynical. The civil rights movement and the Vietnam War had drawn broad lines between races and generations, and millions from a confused generation of baby boomers rebelled against society and their parents by getting involved in drugs, sex, and alternative lifestyles. The once-unthinkable was now everyday life as whole sections of cities were set on fire, students were shot by National Guardsmen,

draft cards were burned in front of courthouses, and mass murderers were killing movie stars just for thrills. No one could make sense out of this cultural revolution, and few were trying. In America's heartland, folks were just scratching their heads and thanking God that things were simpler on the farm.

It was in these times when Merle Haggard rode his songs of the workingman and common people to the top of the charts. In constant demand, Haggard spent most of the year riding a bus from gig to gig. His travels took him hundreds of thousands of miles, and with fans in the Farm Belt as well as on college campuses, Merle and his band got to see their country's confusion and pain up close and firsthand.

Just outside of Muskogee one day the group was locked in a political discussion when someone joked, "I bet that they don't smoke marijuana here in Muskogee." The always observant Merle agreed, and then began to list a long line of other things that they probably didn't do in central Oklahoma. Before long Haggard and his drummer, Roy Burris, were scribbling down their observations on paper and setting them into verses. Within twenty minutes the duo had finished a song entitled "Okie from Muskogee." They thought of their final product in terms of a novelty number, but it was destined to become so much more.

"Okie from Muskogee's" message and guts came

from the trials and tribulations of modern American news stories, but the title was more a tribute to Haggard's father. James Haggard might have had to give up the family farm, pack his few possessions on an old truck, and migrate west. He might have been looked down on, labeled white trash, and ridiculed for most of his life. He might even have been forced to take jobs that no one else would lower themselves to do, and turn an abandoned boxcar into a home for his family, but he never lost his self-respect and never quit being proud to be an American and an Okie. To the old farmer there was no shame in either. The man died poor, but proud to be who he was.

In his newest song, Merle finally got to proclaim what his father had long felt but had never been granted a forum to announce, "Yes, I am proud to be an Okie. And even if America has done me wrong and kicked me around a bit, I am proud to be an American too." With that proclamation spun off the song's obvious displeasure and distaste for what was going on in a rebellious society, the singer gave voice to the then-unnamed silent or moral majority. As Haggard would soon discover, "Okie from Muskogee" would prove to be one of the most astute marketing moves of all time.

Recorded in the studio, the song was released in late summer and found its way to the *Billboard* list in early October. As Haggard began to plug the number in concerts, he quickly realized that he had made a mistake. The crowds had so embraced "Okie" that Haggard came to believe he should have cut it in a live setting. Making a call to Capitol producer Ken Nelson, Merle got the label to recut and repress a version of "Okie from Muskogee" taped at a concert and ship it to stations. Soon the first studio version was buried by the live version. It was the latter which ruled the top of the country charts from November 15 through December 13.

Surprisingly, the rock charts also embraced Merle's ode to redneck America. The song would climb into the top forty on some playlists. In the South, "Okie" would actually make the top ten.

There is little doubt that a long list of Haggard compositions are far better crafted than "Okie." This simple song does not contain the artistry of "Today I Started Loving You Again" or "Hungry Eyes," yet no Merle song had ever meant as much to as many as "Okie." Timing had a great deal to do with the popularity. Certainly the song would have made little sense in the late fifties, and it probably would have been dismissed if it had come out in the late eighties. Yet by talking about middle-American family values in 1969, the song hit home with its message. This was a song that millions were willing to hang their hats on. By buying this record and singing this song they could vent their rage and disgust with hippies and draft dodgers.

Sensing the commercial possibilities fanned by "Okie," Haggard wrote another, even more spirited pro-American song, "The Fightin' Side of Me." Ending his shows with these two flag-raising banner hits sent some crowds into a patriotic frenzy. At times the fervor that was exhibited at these concerts scared even Merle. And even though his booking fee had tripled since "Okie" hit the charts, Haggard quickly became uncomfortable being draped in the flag. He was a solid American, but he had no interest in becoming a political lightning rod.

With "Okie" having generated endless invitations to the Nixon White House, a shelf of CMA awards, and five-figure fees, the song looked to be a ticket that Haggard could ride for years. Yet even while the song was still in solid rotation, Haggard began to back away from its message. Merle separated himself from a wide number of groups who wanted to use him and his music for their own brand of Americanism. Stepping out front, Merle voiced his own concerns about racial problems and social programs. More often than not, his thoughts were far more liberal and tolerant than the thoughts of those who had so embraced his "Okie." Haggard also wouldn't make a stand supporting the Vietnam War. While he praised the men who fought it, he refused to acknowledge that he understood why American troops were being asked to give their lives for this cause. Back in the studio, Merle returned to writing songs with a more common and individual theme, compositions that asked questions that provoked personal thought and introspection, not political action or flag waving.

"Okie from Muskogee" would become Merle's all-

time best-selling single. It would also become the song that defined his career. He and "Okie" would always be inseparable. Yet Haggard himself was far more complex than his song indicated, and while "Okie from Muskogee" first gave voice to a counter-counterculture movement that reached its zenith in the mid-nineties, it was never meant as a political statement. To Haggard it was a fun piece that allowed him to revisit a place his father had held dear. "Okie" was never really meant to be any more. Yet when it took the nation by storm, Merle found out firsthand the kind of power country music now possessed. In a move that tells a great deal about the man's character, it was a power he never sought to abuse or misuse.

1969
Statue of a Fool

Written by Jan Crutchfield

Country music is generally ignored by most college music departments. The genre is considered to have standards that are far too low to be studied alongside Bach or even Stephen Foster. Yet at Nashville's Belmont College, the music theory department does spend some time reviewing what it takes to make a solid country song. Each semester students listen to and dissect some of Music City's finest compositions and biggest hits. What they are taught is that Jan Crutchfield wrote the "perfect song" in the early 1960s. Crutchfield's "Statue of a Fool" is the standard by which all other songs must be judged.

Jan and his brother Jerry Crutchfield were raised in a rich musical heritage in Paducah, Kentucky. The boys grew up in a family whose listening interests ranged from classical to gospel, from jazz to hillbilly. In the Crutchfield family the only thing more important than listening to or singing music was studying it. Before they reached their teens, the boys knew music history all the way back to the dawn of the popular age in 1890. This education would prove invaluable when Jan later decided to try his hand at writing.

"I was eleven when I first got involved singing with a gospel group," Jan remembered. "We did a lot of things in the Blackwood Brothers style. But that wasn't the only kind of music that interested me. That was the heyday of radio. I listened to big bands and

Opry, and even turned on jazz and blues. I liked it all."

After singing in high school, the Crutchfield boys came to Nashville and joined Chet Atkins at RCA. It was while singing with the Country Gentlemen in the fifties that Jan began to branch out and write songs. While it would be a long hard road to personal success, Jan soon found himself in the company of a pretty elite group of folks. Most of them are now songwriting legends, but at that time they were all starving to death.

"In the early sixties there just weren't that many writers in Nashville," Crutchfield explained. "There was a lot more money in pop, so the writers were on the coast. Even if you did write a country hit, it didn't make you much money, so things were tough. Yet those days were special. We would gather around a table and sing our new songs for each other. There would be folks like Hank Cochran, Harlan Howard, Willie Nelson, Bill Nelson, and a few others, and we would all be passing a guitar around. If they would have set off a bomb in that room, it would have wiped most of the talent in Nashville completely out."

Jan's career took longer to materialize than that of most of the writers he knew. This was not caused by a lack of talent or seasoning. Rather, it was because he was successful in other areas of the business. Over the years he was a song plugger, a performer, a manager, and a director. The fact was that Jan was so involved in every area of his music, that he had less time to work on his songwriting craft than most of his writer friends.

"While I did write some standard three-chord songs," Jan explained, "I also used multi-chord ballads too. Faron Young, Ray Price, Brenda Lee, and Wilma Burgess were among the few artists in Nashville who would cut songs that had multi-chord arrangements at that time. Faron cut my 'Down by the River' and put it out in 1963. It was a hit. Wilma Burgess earned a #1 record with 'Tear Time.' I considered myself a ballad writer, and when Perry Como recorded my "Dream on a Little Dream" it was a huge thrill."

While he was making a living with his writing, Jan's compositions were either being overlooked or recorded in markets outside country music. This was very much the story of the piece that Belmont would call the perfect country song.

"I wrote 'Statue of a Fool' in the early sixties," the songwriter recalled. "It wasn't a country idea and I didn't consider it a country song. In my mind it was just a ballad. I can't say where the idea came from other than I knew the statues that I saw in public places were all put there to remember very famous people. Washington, MacArthur, and others were all honored in this way. I thought why shouldn't there be a statue of a guy who has been a loser in love. A statue of an idiot. A guy who had it all and threw it away. To me this seemed like a commercial idea, and so I wrote it."

The major labels in Nashville didn't care for Jan's latest ballad. Ultimately "Statue of a Fool" was cut in Latin America and by blues groups. Country music ignored it until Jack Greene became a huge star.

Jack had first uncovered the Crutchfield song just after it had been written. When Decca had signed the singer in 1965, Greene dusted off his copy of "Name It after Me," and took it to Owen Bradley. Owen didn't think it would play in the country market at that time and turned it down. The singer simply filed Jan's piece away and waited for the right time. In 1969, after Jack had topped the charts on five different occasions, he brought the idea back to the producer.

"At that time Owen told me he loved the song," Jan recalled, "but he thought it was just too pop. He let Jack record it, but Owen then planned on just letting it sit. He wasn't going to put it out. Nobody at Decca wanted to release it."

Greene wouldn't give up on the old tune. Changing the title to "Statue of a Fool," he once again begged Decca for a single release. When they refused, he pointed out that he was about the hottest thing they had and they had better make him happy. To shut the singer up, the label relented, all the while telling him that Jan's piece would ruin his career.

"Statue of a Fool" hit the country charts in May, and surprised everyone except Greene by hitting #1 in July. It held the top spot for two weeks and remained on the playlists for eighteen. After collecting dust for years, the Crutchfield tune now had a host of producers and artists wondering why they hadn't cut it when it had first been pitched to them in 1961.

"Brian Collins zipped right up the charts right after that in 1974," Crutchfield said with a laugh. "I couldn't believe it had been recut as a single and I didn't even know who Brian Collins was. His version made top ten. After that I got a bunch of album cuts."

That second trip up the charts shocked the writer, but the biggest surprise was yet to come. Beginning in 1987, Ricky Van Shelton ran off a string of #1 hits. He also won a host of CMA awards, including Best Male Vocalist and Entertainer of the Year. Two years after he first topped the charts, he was the hottest act in Nashville and the Girt, Virginia, product had gotten to the point where he had a great deal of say in what he sang and what Columbia released.

One night at a concert, Shelton's producer, Steve Buckingham, noted the fans' wild response to a ballad which Ricky had tossed into the show. Buckingham asked the singer about the song. Shelton told him that it was a Jan Crutchfield original. Steve tracked down the writer's office number and gave him a call.

"That was a shocker," Crutchfield admitted. "Ricky's producer called me and told me that Rick did 'Statue of a Fool' in his shows. I thought that was great, but I couldn't believe it when the producer then told me that he had never heard of my song before that night. Anyway, he informed me that Ricky was going to cut it. Though I was still having problems comprehending that the guy had never heard Jack Greene's version of 'Statue of a Fool,' I was excited about the record. Ricky not only could sing, but he knew how to shape a song. He also had great respect for real music."

Ricky Van Shelton took "Statue of a Fool" for a chart ride that lasted one half year. The single spent two weeks at #1 and went gold. The album that was spun from the single eventually earned platinum status. Jan couldn't believe that magic had struck again.

"I believe that true writers are born," the man who has written scores of pop and country hits observed. "I also believe that to be a good ballad singer you have to be a good person. If you aren't a good person, I don't think you are built out of the right stuff to really touch emotional chords and reach people's hearts. If you don't care about people, you can't write anything that is going to mean much for very long."

By those standards, Jan Crutchfield is a writer who also must be a very good person. His songs have not just hit the charts, they have come back to score again and again. Jan's sad portrayal of the world's greatest loser, the ballad that for years was considered too pop for a country release, has now been called by scholars the "world's most perfect country song." "Statue of a Fool" has received this recognition because of its haunting message set inside a complex but straightforward arrangement and because it has heart.

"Once you have heard a song," the writer explained, "it should tell a story and paint a picture. If it does you will remember the message."

Maybe it is that philosophy that has made Jan Crutchfield's work so unforgettable. Certainly if they ever build a statue of this writer, it won't depict a fool.

1970
Rose Garden

Written by Joe South

Joe South, Mac Davis, and Tony Joe White represented a new generation of songwriters. Raised with rural Southern and Western country music, the men were also exposed to the freedom and vitality of rock 'n' roll. As country song scribes they drew from much different sources and perspectives than Music City's older writers, and the subjects of many of their efforts centered on social problems such as war, hunger, and prejudice.

South, an Atlanta-bred writer, took his craft very seriously. He looked upon each of his compositions as "three-minute novels." In that brief time span he wanted to tell a story that would linger in the listeners' minds long after they had forgotten the tune. A perfectionist, South labored over his efforts and polished his final product like gemstones. In 1969 Joe wrote and recorded "Games People Play." It was a folk/rock tune whose purpose was to expose the hating and prejudice passed from one generation to the next. In his next hit, "Walk a Mile in My Shoes," South took the role of a singing preacher whose musical sermon demanded that people look at their own lives and set things in order there while keeping their noses out of other people's business. In an industry awash with records like "Yummy, Yummy, Yummy," Joe was attempting some pretty heavy stuff.

Idealistic, passionate, and very private, South remained true to his own beliefs in everything he composed. Unlike many writers, he seemed to write for the pure enjoyment of writing and seemed to care little about the monetary rewards that might follow a hit song. He didn't want fame either. Joe South's satisfaction seemed to come when his message rang true.

When he penned "(I Never Promised You a) Rose Garden," Joe had once again turned inside. He knew that as a performer he lived a very unstable life and that the chances of giving a spouse everything she desired was an unrealistic dream. What he tried to say in his song was that when compared to love, the material things didn't matter. Matters of the heart were what really made people rich.

South's publisher, Bill Lowery, recalled, "We knew then that it was really a good song. Much like the things that Joe had done before. We didn't have any problems finding people to record it either. But none of us expected it to be a huge country hit."

South put "Rose Garden" on an album. Then Billy Joe Royal, another Atlanta country rocker, recorded "Rose Garden." Royal too kept the song an L.P. cut. Between his own version and Billy Joe's, South earned a few small royalty checks. Soon a few other male singers placed it on albums, and sales inched up.

"We didn't really think of it as a single," Lowery recalled. "We certainly didn't believe that it would ever be cut by a female artist. What we didn't realize was that Columbia producer Glen Sutton had a woman who was begging to cut it."

Lynn Anderson had purchased Joe South's first album, *Introspect*, when it had been released in 1969. Even before Billy Joe Royal had cut "Rose Garden," Anderson had wanted to rework the lyrics and try it on the country market. At Chart Records she had failed to convince anyone that it was a good song for her. Yet after successes at Columbia with songs like "Rocky Top," folks began to listen to Anderson. Of all the folks at the label, producer Glenn Sutton had the best reason for trying to keep Lynn happy.

Sutton and Anderson had married the previous year, and as he worked with his wife in 1970 to find material for her next Columbia album, he listened as Lynn played the old Joe South recording. Glenn didn't like it and didn't think it was right for Lynn, but she wouldn't give up. At the office and at home Anderson hounded Sutton. Eventually he gave in and worked up a version of the song for an album cut.

At that time Columbia considered the young and pretty Anderson to be one of country music's breakthrough acts. She had initially charted while still in her teens, and she had used her status as a regular on the *Lawrence Welk Show* to create a large audience for her music. One of the first country music stars to work on Bob Hope overseas tours, she was a pinup favorite of soldiers in Vietnam. Sexy, energetic, and all-American, Lynn seemed to have just the right ingredients to challenge Connie Smith and Loretta Lynn. With the right mix of product and publicity, the label felt that Anderson could become the most popular female singer in Nashville.

Knowing what was expected from his wife, producer Sutton didn't want to risk having a bad chart showing with what he considered a weak song, and that was just how he viewed the South tune. He was even more convinced that "Rose Garden" was a loser when they took the song into the studio. It flat didn't work. The tempo, the words, the phrasing, none of them fit Lynn's style. Sutton was ready to simply toss it out, but Anderson insisted they continue to massage it until they got it right. They changed it to an early sixties country rhythm and rewrote a few of the words, and then the musicians hit "Rose Garden" again. This time the performance seemed passable, so they moved on to other numbers.

"When they initially played it back," Bill Lowery explained, "they almost shelved it. It seemed flat. Yet rather than give up on it, Glenn went back into the studio. He had some strings in-house that day for another recording, so he used them. It was unheard of in those days to add strings to a country record, but he overdubbed them onto 'Rose Garden.' When he mixed everything together he began to believe that the song had potential."

Lynn Anderson's "Rose Garden" was now much different from the Joe South original. While Glenn had grown to like the song, the producer still didn't feel it was worthy of unleashing on the country market. Yet Columbia's president, Clive Davis, did. He wanted "Rose Garden" to be Anderson's next single. Davis also felt that it should be shipped to both country and pop outlets. The executive believed that this song was a standout hit.

There was little doubt in Sutton's mind that "Rose Garden" was going to stand out. The single sounded nothing like current country hits such as the "The Fightin' Side of Me," "My Woman, My Woman, My Wife," or "Run, Woman, Run." Nor did his wife's single seem to fit in with rock hits like "Venus," "Let It Be," or "ABC." For all practical purposes, this release had all the signs of a disaster in the making. If that were the case, they would have time to regroup with one of the other cuts from their session.

Shipped in the late fall of 1970, "Rose Garden" took off as if it had been shot out of a cannon. Flying up the country charts, the single knocked "Coal Miner's Daughter" out of the top spot the day after Christmas. It would stay #1 for five weeks and earn the classification as the year's biggest single. On the rock side Lynn's hit would enter the charts in December, climb to the third position, and then hang in the top one hundred until almost April. Not only would the single sell a million copies, so would the album. With appearances on almost all of television's variety and teen shows, Anderson was one of the hottest stars in the country. Her "Rose Garden" was also one of the best-known country records ever.

"You know," Lowery mused, "we never thought of 'Rose Garden' as a country song. We had no idea it would be one of the biggest hits in the history of country music. That song has now been cut in every genre of music."

Much of the pop-country sound that was so successful in the country music of the seventies and early eighties can trace its roots to "Rose Garden." Because of that song's success, lush arrangements, strings, and pop arrangements would soon become a part of even Loretta Lynn's records. Considered a curse by many traditionalists, the sound that was spawned soon after Anderson topped the charts opened country music to a rash of new acts and great talents. Among them would be Tony Joe White, Mac Davis, and Joe South. The pop evolution also created a larger market with more dollars for labels, stars, and songwriters and more choices for fans. Not everything in this move would ultimately be sweet, but not even the country music industry was ever promised a rose garden.

1970
Hello Darlin'

Written by Conway Twitty

A number of great country music artists have been largely overlooked by those who hand out awards and honors. These forgotten men and women have toiled just out of the superstardom spotlight, while racking up numbers that revealed them to be the legitimate fan favorites. In some cases these performers simply had a mean streak that created a political backlash against them. In other cases it was their moral problems that shut them out at the awards ceremonies. But a few individuals simply got left out for no reason at all. With their extraordinary numbers, their immense talents, and their decades of hard work, they should have been crowned royalty time and time again. Instead they were overlooked by just about everyone except their fans.

Conway Twitty was just such an entertainer. In his three decades in country music he placed almost one hundred singles on the charts. He also spent an amazing fifty-two weeks at #1. He was a former rockabilly artist, and his country fans were some of the industry's most rabid. Yet in spite of all his chart-toppers and monster hits, the CMA never recognized his individual efforts. The only major awards Twitty ever received were for his duet work with Loretta Lynn.

Born in Mississippi and raised in Arkansas, Twitty learned to play guitar while in his teens. A solid baseball player, he considered working his way up through the minors, but the military draft got him

first. After a military stint, he came back home and began a career in country music. Starting in local radio, Harold Jenkins, his given name, worked dances and clubs hoping to make it to the *Opry*. Then he was knocked off his feet by Carl Perkins's "Blue Suede Shoes."

"I remember his saying," childhood friend and president of Conway Twitty Enterprises Hugh Carden recalled, "I can do that. I sing that kind of music."

Reworking his sound and his band, he became a rocker and landed a record deal with MGM in 1958. After a few false starts, the singer, now renamed after towns in Arkansas and Texas, recorded the self-penned "It's Only Make Believe." When the record didn't immediately take off, and after a year of playing seven nights a week on the road, Twitty quit the business and began to work on the family farm. Without the singer's knowledge the song became a huge rock hit, holding down the top spot for two weeks in 1958. His record label literally pulled him off a tractor and got him back on the road. He would remain there for the rest of his life.

In the late fifties rockabilly efforts usually did better on the country charts than they did on the pop sides. For some unexplained reason, Conway's "It's Only Make Believe" never crossed over into country. The song which kept the future Nashville star in music would only earn its status as a country hit when it was covered by Glen Campbell in the seventies and Ronnie McDowell in the eighties.

A short series of rock hits followed "It's Only Make Believe," but things dried up in 1961. Despite work in films and numerous television appearances, Twitty couldn't recapture the magic of his debut single. MGM eventually cut him loose in 1965. It turned out to be the best thing that ever happened to him.

In 1966 Twitty reinvented himself as a country act and began a television show based out of Oklahoma. His half-hour program was an immediate regional hit, and in 1967 Conway found himself in syndication. For the second time his star was on the rise. Liking Twitty's new sound, Owen Bradley and Decca Records came calling and signed the singer, now thirty-four, to a contract. His first five releases did little, but starting with "The Image of Me," Twitty would find his niche in the upper reaches of the charts. His first #1 would come in 1968 in the form of "Next in Line."

Conway would meet a lot of his old rock 'n' roll fans on the country concert circuit. It seemed that many of them simply made the move to the genre at about the same time the singer did. With these core fans forming his new support base, Twitty began to roll out hit after hit and build a huge grassroots following. Then, in 1970, after working his way up the ladder for four long years, he landed a monster that would not only make him a country music star, but would also fully establish the sound that defined him as a singer.

Twitty had written "Hello Darlin' " over a decade before he recorded it. The song, like scores of others, had been conceived, composed, and then filed in a big box. At the time there was no market for country in his repertoire, so the singer had simply forgotten about it. Needing material to fill hot-selling country albums in the late sixties, Conway dug out the old box

and began going through it. One of the first things he came across was "Hello Darlin'."

"It was never going to be recorded," Hugh explained. "Conway had just written the lyrics on a piece of paper years before. He only pulled the song out because Owen Bradley needed one more number to finish the session. Hence, it was a fluke."

Twitty played "Hello Darlin' " a few times for the producer and the band before trying to cut it. After listening to the number, Owen brought in an electric piano for a slightly different sound. The producer felt that the instrument gave the composition a fuller feel, but there was still something missing.

"Owen then suggested to Conway that he speak the song's first two words instead of singing them," Hugh explained. "When they did that, they made history. The song moved from being just an album-filler to having the feel of a great single."

"Hello Darlin' " proved an immediate favorite on the concert circuit. Twitty's largely female audience really took to the singer's emotional rendering of the song. Decca noted this response and decided to release it even as Conway's "That's When She Started to Stop Loving You" was still climbing the charts. It hit the market in late April, and it became quickly apparent that Conway had struck a chord with the disc jockeys and the radio audience with this new single. It took Twitty just two months to race up the playlists to the top position. "Hello Darlin' " knocked another old rockabilly star, Sonny James, out of #1 on June 6, 1970. Conway would ride the charts for five months with this almost-forgotten classic. For a solid month Twitty would own #1.

For most of the remainder of his unbelievable career, Conway would choose songs that displayed the grit and emotion of "Hello Darlin'." His songs would speak directly to women, and his voice would emphasize words in a way that revealed a softer side of this macho man. No one would ever do this any better than Twitty. And his long line of unique hit love ballads gave proof of the special gifts he brought to a song. "Hello Darlin' " was the beginning. From there Conway ruled the charts with songs like "Fifteen Years Ago," "She Needs Someone to Hold Her (When She Cries)," "Linda on My Mind," "You've Never Been This Far Before," "Slow Hand," and a score of other classic ballads all cut in the same style as "Hello Darlin'."

Five years after he took "Hello Darlin' " to the top of the charts, Conway got a chance to take the song even higher. NASA called the singer. It seemed that Brigadier General Thomas P. Stafford, commander of the Apollo spacecraft that would be docking with the Russian Soyuz vehicle, wanted to take Conway's "Hello Darlin' " with the American crew into outer space. The only catch was that he wanted Twitty to recut the song in Russian.

"Conway met with the chairman of the Russian Language Department at the University of Oklahoma," Carden explained. "They worked together for several days translating the song into Russian and then teaching Conway the proper pronunciation of each word. When he got it down, he recorded it in Russian and gave it to General Stafford. When the two spacecrafts docked in 1985, the Russian version of 'Hello Darlin' ' was playing. Conway thus signaled the linkup."

In Russian Twitty's best-loved tune was called "Privet Radost." There was no official word if it made the USSR's top ten, but it did become a part of both U.S. and Soviet History.

Conway Twitty would go on to record thirty-six consecutive top-five singles, none of which would be recognized with a major award. Before he died in 1993 he would become the fourth most successful country music recording artist of all time. Yet there was no place for him in a hall of fame and no long row of gold statues presented in his honor. It seems his top award was the enthusiastic response he received every time he said, "Hello Darlin'." In the long run, the loyalty and love of his millions of fans were probably all the recognition Conway really wanted anyway.

1971
Help Me Make It through the Night
Written by Kris Kristofferson

Kris Kristofferson was born into a world that should have guaranteed that his life would be spent far away from the Nashville spotlight and involved in something much deeper than spinning out hit records. Most figured that, instead of winning Grammys, he would be striving for the Pulitzer Prize or being nominated for the Medal of Honor. And instead of ragged and casual denim, it was usually thought that his clothing of choice would be Army green. Yet forecasting what Kris will do next is like trying to predict the weather. Just when you think you know how to do it, a wave of instability blows in.

Kristofferson was born in Texas in 1936, the son of a career Army Air Corps officer. As was typical with military brats, he moved several times during his youth, and it was during these moves that the straight-as-an-arrow Kris discovered Hank Williams, Hank Snow, and the *Grand Ole Opry*. Even though he was one of the few kids of the period who openly embraced hillbilly music, Kristofferson didn't dream of performing. During his high school days his loves were writing and athletics. He excelled at both. In 1958 his ability to write won him a trip to England as a Rhodes Scholar.

The intellectual Kristofferson earned a degree from Oxford, but rather than follow the logical course of further academic study or teaching Kris joined the Army. For the next five years he flew helicopters and played music in local clubs. Then he received a call to join the faculty at West Point. His country wanted him to teach English to its future leaders. His life seemingly mapped out, Kris visited Nashville on a two-week leave. As he took in the sights along Music Row, the soldier met a few songwriters and performers, sang some of his compositions for these men, and promptly resigned his commission. Within months the pressed uniforms and G.I. haircut were gone and the scruffy Kristofferson look was born.

The year 1965 was an eye-opener for the young man. While a lot of people told him he had great promise, no one seemed to care much about giving him a break. After a series of menial jobs, a marriage breakup, and no luck getting a recording contract, Kristofferson went back to flying. Along the Gulf Coast he flew helicopters for oil companies. Though he loved to take to the air, he missed the companionship of the creative scribes who walked the streets of Nashville.

Roger Miller offered Kris a second chance in music in 1966. The pilot quickly turned in his wings and made the trip to California. Working with the talented Miller was an illuminating experience. Like Kristofferson, Roger walked not just to a different drummer, but to an instrument that no one else could hear. Watching Miller carve his own path and seek his own dreams gave the former Army flyer a lot of confidence. Then, when Roger recorded Kris's "Me and Bobby McGee," the relationship also gave Kris his first big break. With royalties coming in, the songwriter could now concentrate full-time on his craft.

In 1969 Kristofferson returned to Music City with a track record and the backing of established stars like Bobby Bare and Johnny Cash. He was poised to take off. Cash recorded a song that Kris had given him some time before entitled "Sunday Morning Coming Down." That single would make it to the top of the charts. Yet it was a second hit that would really establish the Rhodes Scholar's name on Music Row.

Since he was an avid reader, a student of great men as well as great entertainers, it was not unusual to find Kris absorbing a book on war one day and a biography of a musician the next. The man had an unending thirst to learn. His inspiration for the song that would fully establish his career and be called his masterpiece actually came from Old Blue Eyes himself. Frank Sinatra had often said that if he didn't have a woman with him, he would take a bottle to help him make it through long and lonely nights. When Kris read the story, it gave him a concept for a country song. During his first hiatus from Nashville, as he flew helicopters in the Gulf of Mexico, he fleshed out the idea while sitting in the cockpit of his chopper. It would be several years before he found a home for his newest creation.

When the demo of Kris's Sinatra-inspired composition made its Nashville rounds, one of those listening was a California product who had reversed the classic *Grapes of Wrath* exodus. Sammi Smith was born in the West, but grew up in Oklahoma. Performing for most of her life, she moved to Nashville in 1967, and almost immediately landed a recording gig with Columbia. When her first three singles did nothing the label cut her loose, and Smith was picked up by Mega Records in 1970. Her first record there also failed to gain much attention. Then she happened upon Kris's "Help Me Make It through the Night."

Many in Nashville were surprised that Sammi would cut the song. To most people it seemed a bit racy. The lyrics indicated a relationship that was not blessed by a marriage license or even the bonds of love. Smith disagreed. She simply saw it as a beautifully written plea for understanding and comfort. Because there was no real line drawn that admitted that she was really cheating (a taboo that major labels had yet to break), Mega let her cut it.

Smith beat Bobby Bare, who had also fallen in love with the song, into the recording studio, and shipped her version of Kris's composition in the winter of 1970. "Help Me Make It through the Night" hit the charts in December, and fought its way up to #1 in February. The single would linger on the charts for five months, and remain at the top for three weeks. It was a runaway favorite for CMA's Single of the Year in 1971.

"Help Me Make It through the Night" also did well in pop music. Smith took the song into the top ten. Two years later Gladys Knight nailed a new version of Kris's classic. Gladys, who could have been a great country singer, placed the song in *Billboard*'s top forty for six weeks in 1972.

Sammi's single established Kris as one of the new generation of great songwriters. Other college-educated scribes, such as Larry Gatlin, would follow in his footsteps. Kristofferson would soon score again with compositions such as "Why Me, Lord" and "For the Good Times." Yet there seemed to be a wanderlust in his soul that kept him from concentrating on just one facet of his life. Just when everyone along Music Row wanted a Kristofferson number on their next album, the writer decided to give acting a try. Over the course of the next few decades Kris would drift in and out of town, but few folks seemed to ever get a feel on where he would next use his genius and his energies.

Meanwhile the songs he wrote during the late sixties and early seventies continue to come back again and again. "Help Me Make It through the Night" would become an Elvis concert standard and a 1980 hit for Willie Nelson. It was a song that even Old Blue Eyes would come to know and love. It has been recorded scores of times in almost every musical genre and in several languages.

Kristofferson's long-term contribution to country music has been hotly debated. Some give him credit for opening the door for college grads, yet Bill Anderson had done that a decade before the arrival of the Rhodes Scholar. Others point to Kris as Nashville's first brush with the counterculture that was so

much a part of rock music, but in all honesty Music City began dealing with this youth-driven musical form back in the fifties. So maybe Kris's real contribution was a new way of dealing with old story lines. In his lyrics he seemed to reveal a cowboy's love of freedom and a drifter's lack of commitment to relationships. His own honesty and frailties were exposed openly in his words, and he also dealt with his weaknesses without being ashamed. In his lyrics he admitted that he needed a God, but he also desired the gratification that only a lover could give. What Kris Kristofferson really brought to songwriting was a more complex way of trying to deal with emotions. He opened the door to exploring new ways of writing about making it through both days and nights.

1971
Kiss an Angel Good Mornin'

Written by Ben Peters

When RCA premiered its newest country music artist in the mid-sixties, the company decided to work publicity in a rather strange manner. They didn't send out any pictures with their new male singer's bio and they didn't put the entertainer's photograph on his initial album cover. While the company gave a detailed description of the man's love of baseball and his ability to sing a country song, the label didn't describe his physical appearance at all.

It is therefore ironic that Charley Pride's first hit was entitled "Just Between You and Me," because that is just how RCA treated the matter of the singer's race. The label didn't mind telling folks that their new singer was tall, dark, and handsome. They just didn't go into any details about how dark.

In all ways other than race, Charley Pride seemed to be the ideal candidate for a career in country music. Born dirt poor in backwoods Mississippi in the late thirties, Pride had grown up loving country music. He listened to the *Opry* each week, and was especially drawn to Hank Williams. He also liked the *Louisiana Hayride*. In spite of warnings from friends and family that singing hillbilly music wouldn't get him anywhere, the boy continued to learn the songs of the white rural South. Charley even bought a guitar when he was a teenager and began to play his favorite country numbers, trying to imitate the artists as best he could. Most of his peers thought he was crazy,

and many told him so. But that didn't stop Pride from singing country music, even if no one would stop and listen to him perform. All things considered, except for baseball, music was the love of the young man's life.

Besides Hank Williams, Pride's other hero was Jackie Robinson. When Robinson broke baseball's color line, it gave twenty-year-old Charley a new dream. No longer would he have to limit his baseball ambitions to just the Negro leagues. Now he could set his sights on becoming a star in the major leagues. With a new passion, he set to work. He wanted to be the best baseball player who had ever walked the earth.

Working his way through the Negro leagues for almost a decade, Pride finally landed with a mixed-race minor league organization in 1960. With his guitar in tow, he headed to the Helena, Montana, farm club. Singing to entertain both his teammates and the local baseball fans landed him a part-time job in a night club. He was soon playing before packed houses. Yet even though his music career seemed more promising than his baseball, Pride didn't give up on the game until 1964. He knew it was time to quit when the New York Mets didn't feel he was good enough for their sorry team. Already in his mid-thirties, Charley hung up his spikes. But he was concerned. Without baseball, what would he do?

Red Sovine encouraged him to get back into music, and even brought the young man to Nashville. Impressed with his talent, Webb Pierce made a demo. One label liked Pride's sound, but wanted him to dress funny and call himself George Washington III. Charley refused to dishonor or cheapen himself or his race. If that was what it took to break into country music, then he would go back to Mississippi and work at hard labor.

Chet Atkins got ahold of Pride's demo tape and played it for the A&R men at RCA. They loved the man's sound. When they all agreed that the label should make a deal with this fine singer, Chet informed them that Charley Pride was black. For a few moments there was silence. Then one man spoke up.

"He's great, and I think we ought to take a chance." The others quickly agreed.

RCA signed him, and then had to figure out what to do with Mr. Pride. As their early press releases proved, the label was going to be very cautious. They realized that they were handling dynamite.

When Charley had idolized Jackie Robinson and what he had done in baseball, he'd had no idea that he would be called upon to break a color barrier that seemed even more imposing. In the midst of voting-rights marches and sit-in protests, as well as the integration of scores of schools, stores, and restaurants, Pride marched into country music. With some members of Congress predicting race wars throughout the nation, it was understandable why his own label didn't want to share what made their new star so very different from any other country act. It is a wonder that Chet Atkins even had the courage to sign the singer.

Each time Charley Pride walked out to meet an audience for the first time, there was a shocked hush followed by polite clapping. Because of RCA's publicity, even after several hit songs, it wasn't common

knowledge that he was a black man. Only when Charley smiled and said, "I guess this wasn't exactly what you were expecting," did the whispers cease. Then, as he took the microphone and sang his songs, the enthusiasm built until fans wouldn't let him leave the stage. By 1968 no other act wanted to follow him. In 1969 he began a run of six straight #1 singles. Then in 1971 he became the Country Music Association's Entertainer of the Year. The man whose face was once not even shown on an album cover was now the genre's most recognized man.

At about the same time Pride was taking over the mantle of reigning royalty in country music, Ben Peters was taking a drive in his car. Peters was fast becoming one of Nashville's top writers. A music veteran, he had played in rock bands as a saxophone player before joining the Navy. He tried his hand at writing while in the service, and eventually worked his way to Nashville. He slaved at his craft for more than two years before he sold a composition. It was only after Ben landed a job running a small music company that things began to take off for the songwriter.

"My wife and I had just become the parents of our daughter," Peters remembered, "and Angela was about the most special thing in my life. That little girl had really made a mark on me. I couldn't leave the house without kissing her and saying good-bye. I didn't know that I could love anyone so much.

"After I left the house one morning, I was driving down the interstate thinking about one-on-one positive relationships. I felt so great about life, about being a parent and about my wife. I couldn't imagine being any happier. I really felt blessed. As I drove along thinking about all those things, I began to write a song around my feelings and emotions."

One of the first lines that came to Ben was "Kiss an angel good morning." After all, that was what he did every day when he picked up his daughter. The song almost wrote itself from that point. Within two months of Ben's morning drive, the demo of "Kiss an Angel Good Mornin'" found its way into producer Jack Clement's hands. When Charley heard it, he couldn't wait to get into the studio to cut "Angel."

Pride's positive response to the song was based on his relationship with his own wife. The love that Charley felt for her and for the way she had supported him through a two-decade struggle in baseball and music was all expressed in this song. This was the kind of positive country music he wanted to continue to do. Pride's desire would work out well for Ben Peters as the singer would go on to cut more than twenty of Ben's compositions.

RCA released "Kiss an Angel Good Mornin'" in October. A few weeks after Pride had accepted his Entertainer of the Year trophy, the song entered the charts. On December 4 the single would hit the top of the charts and stay there for five weeks. It also became a top-twenty rock hit. In a career that has

spawned more than sixty chart singles and twenty-nine #1 singles, "Kiss an Angel Good Mornin'" would be Pride's top seller and become his signature song.

Probably no entertainer ever made a career choice that would have seemed more inappropriate than Charley Pride. His sister's early warning of, "You'll never make any money singing like that," would have seemed to be very sage advice. Yet Charley Pride ignored race and prejudice and considered only what he felt in his heart. With a strong marriage and positive outlook to anchor him, he remained true to himself and became loved, honored, and revered in a world that should have closed its doors to him. Without saying anything, he opened up people's minds and short-circuited old ideas. As the first black man to walk the country music stage as a star, Charley not only represented himself and his race well, but became an icon that everyone in country music was proud to embrace. "Kiss an Angel Good Mornin'" stands out as Pride's best song, while Charley stands out as one of country music's greatest acts.

1971

The Year that Clayton Delaney Died

Written by Tom T. Hall

If country music has a Mark Twain, it is probably Tom T. Hall. In Nashville he is known as "The Storyteller," and it does seem that his songs stand apart from most because they speak poetically of normal life and normal people in a manner that reminds one more of e.e. cummings than Ernest Tubb. There is a child-like quality about his songs, evident in both their innocence and direct, simple story line. But while Tom's compositions may appear simplistic, they are really built in layers, with each piece of fabric revealing a little bit of Hall's own life experiences.

Born in Kentucky, Tom began to play guitar toward the end of World War II when he was just eight. His was not an idyllic life. His mother died when the boy was just eleven, and his father was injured and forced to quit work a few years later. By sixteen Tom had left school, gone to work in a factory, and formed a band which played backwoods schoolhouses and small fairs. At that time his main goal was to have a group where everyone got to dress alike. Hall's band ended up on radio, and it was there that Tom's real show business career was born in earnest. A few years later he was the area's top disc jockey and making fairly good money, but at twenty-one he grew restless. He wanted to see the world. About the only way for a poor boy to manage that was to join the Army. In 1957 he did just that. Three years later Tom had been a lot of places, seen

a lot of things, and thought he knew what he wanted to do with the rest of his life.

For a while he went home and spun records as a disc jockey. He then bought a store. Finally he went to college, where he worked toward a degree in journalism. Still dabbling in music, Tom sent a few of his compositions to Nashville. That was the beginning of something that would become very big.

By 1965 Hall had left college, worked several different clubs, and won a songwriting contract. He seemed on his way to penning major hits. Then reality kicked in. The songs which Hall wrote were much different from those the established writers were turning out. Like Roger Miller, Tom's stuff was considered a bit too off-the-wall for the big artists. While a few of his tunes found homes, most gathered dust. Finally, against Hall's own desires, Mercury decided to let the songwriter sing his own stuff. Beginning in 1967 Hall charted consistently. His "A Week in the County Jail" even topped the playlists in 1969. Yet by and large, Tom still considered himself a songwriter. That was what he really wanted to do. Touring and working the road just didn't have much luster to "The Storyteller."

In 1968 Jeannie C. Riley put Tom T. Hall on the map in a big way. Recording an ode that Hall had written about a P.T.A. meeting he had once attended, the petite vocalist took both the country and pop playlists by storm. The breakout hit of the year, "Harper Valley P.T.A." would generate more airplay and more money than all of the writer's other songs combined.

Still riding the wake created by "Harper Valley P.T.A.," Hall pulled out another memory from his past. It was the story of a man whom Tom had known as a boy.

"He was my childhood hero," Hall admitted. "He was a solid guitar picker and I met him when I was first starting to play. He moved from Kentucky to Ohio to work clubs when he was still a teenager. He was doing pretty well, but he got sick and was forced to come home. He died when he was about nineteen or twenty."

That young man had impacted Hall in a very strong way. Tom didn't just write the line "I remember the year that Clayton Delaney died," he remembered it vividly. He was eight or nine and had just been given an old Martin guitar when Tom met Clayton. Clayton was in his early teens and knew a lot about playing and singing. Tom was impressed with Clayton's picking, but what impressed him more was the older boy's great independence and style.

"Clayton would take the hit records of the time," Hall recalled, "and he would sing them his own way. He didn't imitate anyone, he just tried to be himself."

The man who inspired "The Year that Clayton Delaney Died" was not really named Clayton Delaney. Hall had veiled the late guitar picker's legacy by using two street names in the song, but the real Clayton's style did strongly impact the young Tom. Several years later when Hall began to work clubs, he too sang familiar songs but in his own style. He even wrote in his own style. Like Clayton, Hall did everything he could to be true to himself and his own feel for music.

When Tom T. recorded "The Year that Clayton Delaney Died," no one would have confused Hall's easy-going vocals for Ray Price or Johnny Cash. The songwriter let his music do the talking. His first and foremost rule was that nothing got in the way of the lyrics. He didn't want any fancy guitar riffs, dramatic backup vocals, or sophisticated instrumentation. He didn't even allow his own vocal to stand out. Only the song's message was important. It was the story he was trying to sell, not Tom T. Hall.

His writing, in this song and all his others, reflected Tom's own introspective view of life. He wrote about things he knew and wrote them from a perspective that was uniquely his. In his mind these "stories" were important slices of his life. He wanted them to be poetic and informative, as well as entertaining. He wanted to draw people in because they were curious and were hearing something unusual. He didn't want to just come up with a new twist on looking at a subject. He wanted to write a whole song that made people say, "Gosh, I never have heard anything like that before." He wanted his words to paint pictures. And like Clayton, in his writing and his performing Hall remained first and foremost true to himself. Being commercial was the last thing on his mind.

Released in mid-summer of 1970, "The Year that Clayton Delaney Died" hit the charts in July. As it began its steady climb up the playlists, the singer discovered that this record was going to be a commercial as well as a personal artistic success. For most of the summer Hall worked his way toward the top, and in mid-September, twenty-three years after Tom's mentor and idol had passed away, "Clayton Delaney" gave the singer his biggest hit. Claiming the top spot for two weeks, the record remained anchored on the charts for five months.

Clayton Delaney probably died of lung cancer. His death was slow and painful, and the young man passed away without ever having fulfilled his dreams. Yet his legacy lived on in another young man whom he inspired. Tom T. Hall took the most important lesson Clayton taught him to heart, and he became an influential writer and performer because he sought his own way of expressing his music. In a sense, both Tom and Clayton made it to the warm spotlight at the same time. That seems appropriate because Hall always said that it was Clayton Delaney who had bought his ticket for the big show.

1972

Delta Dawn

Written by Alex Harvey and Larry Collins

She was just thirteen years old. A blond little girl blessed with a big woman's voice. A whirlwind of energy, she was already a show business veteran who knew Las Vegas as well as the small towns that dotted much of the New Mexico, Arizona, and Nevada deserts. She loved to sing, and would tell anyone who would listen that she was going to be a star, but her first real entertainment gig found her acting in a Robert Redford movie. In so many ways she was already an adult, but in so many other ways she was still a junior high girl.

When her father first brought her to Nashville, no one knew what to do with her. In Music City a girl singer meant someone between the ages of twenty and forty. After all, Loretta Lynn was a grandmother and still called a girl by most folks. Child stars were something that the industry didn't want or need. Songwriters didn't write songs for kids, and logic said that bible-toting women and beer-drinking men weren't going to buy tickets to watch a teenager perform. The record executives, talent scouts, and producers who did meet Tanya Tucker would admit to her father, Bo, that the girl was good, but that there just wasn't any place for her in country music.

Tanya and her family didn't give up. Back in Nevada they worked the local talent shows and talked their way onto country music bills. The blond dynamo impressed Ernest Tubb and Mel Tillis, but

neither of these men could do much more than give her a guest shot in their road shows. Tanya was impatient for fame and fortune, but every move she made seemed to be blocked by Music City insiders saying, "No kids wanted here." Finally, Buddy Killen, a producer at Columbia, listened to Bo's little girl and wondered if Tanya couldn't be the country version of what Brenda Lee had been in rock some fifteen years before. Signing her, Buddy brought the teenager into the studio.

The producer soon found that not only did Tanya have a strong voice, she had an equally strong will. She didn't want to sing songs about little-girl things. She wanted to wrap her lungs around something that Loretta would sing. Killen knew that while this youngster had the talent to sing anything, the challenge was going to be finding something that both he and Tanya agreed was right for her voice and age. If it hadn't been for the work of a very spiritual songwriter, they might have never uncovered the right piece of material to launch what was to become one of country music's most remarkable careers.

Alex Harvey had grown up in Haywood County, Tennessee. His father had owned a small country store on an old dirt road way back in the sticks. Alex had often played around the old building, and he knew all the folks who came to purchase groceries and dry goods by name. There was a host of characters the boy saw every day, but there was one woman who really stood out.

"There was a black woman who had lived in this area all of her life," Alex remembered. "Her family had owned the land around our store since just after the Civil War. I used to watch her walk down the old dusty road. She was dressed in layers of clothes and would always be singing a song in a language I didn't understand. In one hand she would pull an old bush she had cut down, and she would always let that bush drag behind her. Some folks thought that she was really spooky, but I was fascinated with Molly Deberry.

"When I got a little older and a little bolder, I asked one of the older black men about Molly. I wanted to know why she was the way that she was. He told me a story that just set my mind a-reeling. It seemed that Molly had once swollen up with a tumor. The doctor had come and removed it, but Molly had never regained any joy. She thought that somehow during the operation or illness evil spirits had settled in her. She therefore would walk away from her home each day to try to lead the spirits away. She would sing in tongues so the Devil couldn't understand her and the spirits would be driven out. The bush she dragged along behind her she used to wipe out her tracks so that when the evil spirits began to look for her again, they wouldn't be able to find her trail."

For as long as Alex knew Molly, she never got rid of her spirits. By the same token, Harvey could never shake her image out of his mind. But soon the boy was too busy to play around the store or to follow Molly. Harvey's father fell ill and Alex had to help his mother take care of him.

"After my dad got sick," Alex remembered, "my mother never seemed happy. It was just like she was waiting for someone to come along and take her problems away from her. When we would go to church, I would look at her and wonder if there was someone

in her past who she thought she should have married. Then, as the congregation would sing 'Will There Be Any Stars in My Crown,' I would think about just how many stars my mother had earned with her love and devotion to my father and me."

The images of his mother and Molly would haunt Alex Harvey for years. Long after he had gotten into music and begun to write songs, he would often pause and reflect on the hot summer days of his youth back in Tennessee. Yet never in all that time did he try to put his thoughts to music. Then one night in California, the past revisited him in a very special manner.

"I was partying with Larry Collins and the members of Buck Owens's and Merle Haggard's bands. There were eight of us in a hotel room and we were just passing around a guitar and singing songs. After a while most of the folks either fell asleep or left. Soon I was the only one who was still awake. I didn't consciously think about anything, I just started playing the guitar. I got into a real spiritual mood, almost in a trance, and then I started singing words. I began to connect thoughts and places. I thought about my mother's childhood home in the Mississippi Delta and how her favorite time of the day was dawn. From there I combined her story and Molly's. I didn't even realize what I was doing then. It was years before I discovered that the tune I had written was a lot like 'Will There Be Any Stars in My Crown.'"

The first person who heard Alex's "Delta Dawn" was Larry Collins.

"He thought it was a great piece," Alex remembered. "At the time I didn't figure it would be a hit, so I gave Larry half of it."

Several people, including Alex, cut the song, but the first major performer to note the tune was Bette Midler. She was so moved by the song's passion that she performed it several times on the *Tonight Show*. Barbra Streisand was the next entertainer to be captured by "Delta Dawn's" spell. She went so far as to lay down the instrumental tracks, then backed out of recording it when she discovered Midler had already cut it. Barbra should have gone ahead. Bette's "Delta Dawn" was released as a "B" side on her "Boogie Woogie Bugle Boy." With Streisand's tracks in-house, another performer, Helen Reddy, would eventually step up and record Alex's passionate ballad, but that was not until months after Buddy Killen gave it to Tanya Tucker.

Tanya was not very impressed by the song when she first heard it. After a while, it began to grow on her. When she finally used her big-girl voice to stylize it, Tucker really warmed up to "Delta Dawn's" lyrics and music. When Tanya cut the song, she was about the same age as when Alex had lived the experiences which inspired it. In a sense, it was one child's gift to another.

Released in the spring of 1972, Tucker's first single hit the charts in May. For the next seventeen weeks it fought its way into the top ten, as well as crossing over to the pop playlists. With "Delta Dawn's" hit status under her belt, Tanya, seasoned with years of stage work, was ready and waiting to wow crowds. Over the course of the next five years "The Texas Tornado" would be one of the most successful acts in country music. Then, after a brief fling with rock styles, she would come back to Music City again and dominate the charts from 1986 through the mid-nineties.

Alex Harvey doesn't really know what ever happened to Molly. She might have just wandered along that old dirt road until she died. Most folks in Haywood County have forgotten her too. Yet "Delta Dawn" keeps the old woman alive at least in Alex's mind. When he passionately sings the song, he is transported back to days of childhood innocence and curiosity. This is a trip the writer never tires of taking.

1973
The Midnight Oil

Written by Joe Allen

By the late sixties country music songs had spoken openly about almost every aspect of life. Drinking had both been praised and damned, as had cheating, first love, drugs, war, and religion. Yet even after breaking so many former taboos with lyrics that brought so much of what used to be hidden out into the light, one line had not been crossed by a Nashville female vocalist. Women singers could bemoan their men cheating, but those same gals could never participate in this sinful lifestyle. Country music women had to maintain their virtue in the face of any abuse that was dished out to them by the male sex. As Tammy Wynette would so wonderfully phrase it in her 1968 hit, you had to "stand by your man," but you never got to run around on him.

During this era, producer Billy Sherrill, who had helped write "Stand by Your Man," sensed that it was time for a woman to broach the forbidden pain and pleasure of cheating on a spouse. Yet he knew that he had to be careful. The young woman who sang of cheating must be almost angelic in both appearance and lifestyle. To have the audience fully accept the song, they must realize that the girl singing it didn't really mean it.

At about the same time that Billy was considering blazing a new trail, Joe Allen was writing a typical cheating song. Little did he know that his lyrics were soon to produce a top-ten hit for a woman.

"I had been writing for years," Allen explained, "but I had worked my way into the business as a session bass player for stars like Don Williams and Waylon Jennings. I would pitch my songs to the folks I worked with or be inspired to write songs that seemed to fit their style. In 1969 I had been playing with a concept that I called "The Midnight Oil" for a while."

"Certain lines came to mind as I put the song together," Joe remembered. "I knew I had a good starting point when I came up with, 'That call was from the office and I guess I have to burn the midnight oil again.' I also liked the idea of when the man was putting on his hat and boots, he was 'putting on the one who really loved him.' "

While the song's title would be tied into the opening line, in a much deeper sense it represented the guilt that the man couldn't wash off when he was cheating on his wife. This stain was a powerful allusion, and drove Allen to continue working on the concept. He sensed that there was something very unusual and special in his concept.

The ironic touch that ran throughout the lyrics seemed to play well with those with whom Allen shared "The Midnight Oil." Satisfied he had something that was worth pitching, the Waco, Texas, native took it to Billy Sherrill.

"I believe that Billy was and is a genius," Joe flatly

stated. "He listened to "The Midnight Oil" a few times and then told me he liked it for George Jones. Then, after he listened to it a few more times, he said that he felt we should change a few words. He wanted to make it into a woman's song. So things like hat and boots became 'while I'm putting on my makeup.' In short order my song had switched genders." Never doubting Sherrill, Allen left the producer's office confident that his song was going to find a home.

With the perfect vehicle for a female artist, Billy played the demo for one of his newest stars. Barbara Mandrell had been working for Columbia since 1969. During that time the tiny Houston-born dynamo had landed on the charts a few times, but had earned only one top-ten record. One of the most talented showwomen in the business, Barbara needed a major hit to separate her from a pack of other pretty faces who were trying to get a break.

"When Billy played the song for me," Barbara recalled, "it still had the original words. Billy told me that he had first picked it out as a George Jones hit. Then, after listening to it a while, he'd determined that it would be perfect for me. He showed me the new words, and I liked it a lot. I wanted to record it. At the time I didn't even consider the fact that it was a cheating song and that traditionally women didn't cut records like this."

The producer couldn't have picked a more atypical woman to record "The Midnight Oil." With her all-American cheerleader energy and her straight-arrow image, Mandrell appeared nothing like a woman who would run around on her man. All the publicity that had already been circulated on Barbara spent a great deal of time pumping up her Christian values, the roles her family played in her band and career, and how her children and husband were the most important things in her life. The fact that everyone in the world seemed to know that she wouldn't cheat made

Ms. Mandrell the perfect person to break down the final female taboo.

A few at Columbia voiced some reservations about "The Midnight Oil." While they admitted that Barbara had really nailed it in the studio, they thought that some radio stations would back off playing the number. These reservations were similar to those of publicity people who had handled "One Has My Name, the Other Has My Heart" some two decades before. That song had been ignored by some radio stations for several weeks, but eventually the fan requests brought all stations on board. Sherrill thought that the few stations who backed off "The Midnight Oil" at first would play the record when they saw that this was no real issue.

A few folks were also worried that this single might give church groups another opportunity to complain about the mixed messages coming from country songs. A few years before, the religious community had been aghast when Conway Twitty took a woman further than she had ever been before. While some stations had cut the Twitty single from their playlists after the protest, the publicity generated by those who had complained had actually enhanced sales. History again seemed to prove that Barbara's song would not just survive a protest, but would prosper because of any group's organized efforts to ban it.

Some on the inside also wondered if this kind of song might ruin or taint Barbara Mandrell's career. Sherrill could easily answer this rumbling by pointing out that Ms. Mandrell was still much more of a live draw than a recording star. Her last few releases had done very little and if she didn't get a hit soon, she wasn't going to have much of a career to ruin.

Ignoring all the naysayers and fretters, Columbia finally shipped "The Midnight Oil" in mid-summer. On August 18, 1969, it climbed on the charts. Though a few stations did shy away from the cheating song, very little negative press was generated. By and large, thanks in no small part to Barbara's pristine image, the song was given a chance to live on its own merit. By late fall "The Midnight Oil" had climbed into *Billboard*'s top ten and would even make #1 on a couple of other music lists. The timing for Sherrill's move was proven right. Barbara Mandrell had a legitimate hit and a taboo had come crashing down.

Over the time since the release of "The Midnight Oil," women have been given equal song time to cheat on their men, and scores of females have garnered big hits with the theme. Songwriters have also been able to pitch slipping-around compositions to artists of both sexes. In a very real manner, the song opened a large creative door and a host of folks benefited, none more than Barbara. Some of Ms. Mandrell's biggest hits would center on the theme of a woman gone astray. Even though the future Country Music Association Entertainer of the Year didn't know it at the time, "The Midnight Oil" paved the way for "If Loving You Is Wrong, I Don't Want to Be Right," "Married But Not to Each Other,"and "Midnight Angel." In a sense, cheating made Nashville's "Straight Arrow" a recording star.

1974

I Will Always Love You

Written by Dolly Parton

Jan Crutchfield says, "Songwriters are born, not made." And if anyone was born a songwriter, it was Dolly Parton.

Dolly came into this world in 1946. Raised in the backwoods near Sevierville, Tennessee, she was composing songs before she could read or write. At that time Dolly's mother would listen to each new rendering and transcribe the toddler's simple compositions on old scraps of paper. When she was ten the blue-eyed blonde was playing her tunes on an old Martin guitar. By the time she finished high school she was drawing attention far and wide, for her figure much more than her music. That was the way it would be for Dolly throughout her life. People would be so caught up by her exquisite face, beautiful eyes, and Barbie-doll shape that they would often overlook her amazing musical talents.

Just a few weeks out of high school, Parton left the Smoky Mountains and traveled to Nashville. She fully expected to make it big in country music. Already shrewd and seasoned, the young lady used her looks to get through doors and then proceeded to amaze folks with her mountain soprano and self-penned songs. Within six months Dolly had a record deal and was getting a songwriter's draw from a publisher.

Fred Foster and Monument Records had a tough time figuring out what to do with Dolly. Nashville was used to women with strong, throaty voices. Dolly sang more like a child. For years the company tried to get Parton to develop a new style. Nothing they tried seemed to work. Finally the company released "Dumb Blonde" in 1967. It and a follow-up, "Something Fishy," did little, and the label reasoned that Dolly just didn't have what it took to become a force in country music. They dropped her. Parton suddenly found herself a former recording artist who wasn't having any success getting others to record her songs.

Dolly's big break came because of a marriage. Norma Jean, the girl singer on Porter Wagoner's very popular syndicated television series, was getting married and moving to Oklahoma. Porter had heard some of Dolly's compositions, liked her style, and thought her look would work well with his audience. He hired Parton and convinced his label, RCA, to offer the struggling singer/songwriter a contract.

For the next seven years Porter and Dolly would be a mainstay on both television and the tour circuit. With Wagoner's guidance and the exposure she received on his show, Parton began to generate interest. As Wagoner had realized, once people saw Parton, they couldn't seem to forget her. She made a big impression. Beginning in 1970, Dolly also started to make an impression on the charts. The singer took several of her own compositions to the top of the playlists. By 1974 Dolly had grown to be a star in her own right and felt stifled by her business relationship with Porter. She wanted to go beyond hawking Breeze detergent and appealing to just a country crowd. Dolly needed to grow, but Wagoner didn't want to tamper with a formula that was generating so much money.

Dolly once told *Billboard* magazine that songwriting kept her sane. In 1973, as she was trying to find a way to cut herself loose from the Wagoner show, she often thought she was going crazy. This was not going to be an easy parting. Porter wasn't going to let her go without a fight. The anguish and pain that were going to result from the split would be worse than most divorces. The wounds inflicted in the legal battle would take decades to heal, and the scars would be evident long after the two performers had publicly made up.

Parton began to write remarkably sad songs. The war that was raging between her and her mentor had caused her to review her entire life. For weeks Dolly dredged up every one of her life's tragic episodes. She thought about the funerals of loved ones, illnesses, and even broken high school romances. With these memories constantly bombarding her, she penned a plaintive love ballad entitled "I Will Always Love You."

Dolly took the song to producer Bob Ferguson, who agreed that this was probably one of the best things she had ever written. In an almost magical way, Parton had spun the fragile lyrics around a very simple lead line. Her voice, falling and then soaring, brought all the necessary emotions to the monumental work. Direct, straightforward, and honest, "I Will Always Love You" was filled with hidden messages about the complexities of Dolly's current situation. As she left Porter, Dolly hoped that he would realize just how much she knew she owed him. In a way, this song was a thank you for the break Wagoner had given her. It was also her good-bye.

"I Will Always Love You" was released in the late winter of 1974. During its fifteen-week chart ride it would check in at the top spot for one week in June. Other Parton releases had been bigger hits, but there was something about this song that registered with both the singer and her fans. "I Will Always Love You" seemed to reveal a Dolly without all the show business trappings. Folks inside and outside the industry were always wondering who Dolly really was, and many thought they had captured the elusive real person in this ballad. So strong was this song's message that Dolly would use it as a closer for her concerts as well as for her own syndicated television show.

"I Will Always Love You" would have remained one of Parton's most requested numbers even if RCA hadn't released it again in 1980. Dolly was in the midst of making *The Best Little Whorehouse in Texas* when it was decided that the film needed an additional song for Dolly's character, Mona, to sing to the Burt Reynolds character, the local sheriff. With the hectic scheduling and frantic pace of filming, Parton had no time to write anything new, so she reached into her trunk of oldies and pulled out "I Will Always Love You." Everyone agreed that the song worked perfectly in the scene.

Even though the movie was one of the year's biggest flops, Dolly's remake of her ballad covered familiar ground on the country charts. This time "I Will Always Love You" took a nineteen-week trip, hitting #1 in October. Dolly's release also spent a few weeks on the pop charts. When the two records are taken together, this haunting ballad is Parton's most successful song.

By becoming the first record to ever top the charts at two different times by the same artist, "I Will Always Love You" had already made history. Yet Dolly remained unfazed. She had an agenda. She didn't want to be just the most successful star in Nashville. She wanted to be recognized as one of the world's biggest stars or go bust trying. So she wasn't spending much time following the country charts, as she had her eyes on movies, television specials, and spectacular live shows. With smart planning and superb marketing, over the next decade she fulfilled most of her ambitions.

By the late eighties and early nineties new artists had displaced most of Music City's established stars, and Dolly Parton was one of the few "old timers" who could still get play time on country radio. Former superstars and hit makers like Barbara Mandrell, Loretta Lynn, and Tammy Wynette couldn't drum up much interest from labels or disc jockeys. But Dolly still made noise. This power came because she had become bigger than country music. Dolly's face and figure were known by hundreds of millions around the world. Yet it was an old song that soon proved that her songwriting talents exceeded even Dolly's own massive stardom.

In 1992 pop and soul music's dynamic Whitney Houston needed a number to become the theme for her motion picture debut in *The Bodyguard*. What the singer wanted was something that would properly display one of the world's most magnificent voices. With some of music's best composers vying for this shot, the singer rejected the hot new choices and picked Dolly's "I Will Always Love You." Thanks in part to the hit status of the movie, but more to the marriage of composition, talent, and arrangement, Houston put the song on top of all the major charts except country. This new version of "I Will Always Love You" reigned for so long it even passed Elvis's "Don't Be Cruel"/"Hound Dog" as the most popular single in the history of modern music.

Many thought that when Whitney hit the top with the Parton standard that the song would never again be cut. Yet Dolly herself had other ideas. While she spoke fondly of Houston's treatment of her self-penned hit, the country singer/songwriter still considered "I Will Always Love You" as her own theme song, and she wanted to make sure that the world associated it more strongly with her than Whitney. So in the summer of 1995 Dolly headed back into the studio to cut a new version of what had now become a country and pop standard. This time she invited Vince Gill to join her, and for the first time the song was cut as a duet.

On August 26, 1995, Dolly returned to the stage of the *Grand Ole Opry* for the first time in five years. Her old mentor, Porter Wagoner, introduced her to a full crowd and a national television audience. Dolly sang "Jolene" and then brought out Vince Gill. She knew that she had the audience on the edge of their seats and let them sweat for a few moments as she talked about her new album. She then debuted a song which was destined to become a monster hit for the fourth time. The audience rose to their feet and demanded that Dolly and Vince come back and do it again. Giggling, Dolly agreed and asked Wagoner to join them. "I Will Always Love You" once again proved to be solid gold. As Dolly found out that night and when the cut was released a few weeks later, this is a song that is so good it will probably become a hit again long after Whitney, Dolly, and Vince have quit singing.

Dolly always said that she dreamed of becoming Cinderella. All made up with a lot of places to go, Parton has toiled most of her life building an image that was crafted for the spotlight. Yet image could only take her so far. The reason she finally went farther than any other country act was because of her sheer talent and drive. Dolly's God-given gifts were never better displayed than when she wrote "I Will Always Love You." I guess, just like that August 1995 *Opry* crowd, we will always love Dolly too.

Amarillo by Morning

Written by Paul Fraser and Terry Stafford

In 1964 an Amarillo-born singer/songwriter made his first appearance on the pop charts with the classic rock 'n' roll ballad "Suspicion." When people initially heard it, most thought that it was Elvis's latest hit. As a matter of fact Presley had cut the number in 1962 and put it on his *Pot Luck* album, but RCA had never released the song as a single. When Terry Stafford covered it for Crusader Records two years later, "Suspicion" became an instant hit.

Stafford couldn't find a follow-up to his first chartbuster, and soon faded from the rock music scene, but he didn't get out of the business. Basing his operations out of California, the former singer not only wrote for other acts, but worked in films and television as an actor. In 1969, Buck Owens took Terry's "Big in Vegas" up the charts, and the songwriter began to think about returning to his roots. By 1973 he had signed a country record deal with Atlantic and was trying to make his mark in Nashville.

At about the same time another old rocker, Paul Fraser, was offered a chance to earn a draw from writing. Needing the steady money and tired of the road tours, Paul took the job, settled down in Los Angeles, and met Terry Stafford.

"Terry and I began to write together," Fraser remembered. "It was the early seventies and we were both going through some changes. I had been con-

tacted about writing a musical score for a film, so we began to work on that each morning. We were pulling ideas from wherever we could find them, but we weren't producing anything that was really special.

"One night Terry called me at home. He had been watching television and a commercial for a delivery service had just run. It got him to thinking. This commercial guaranteed they could get your package to places like Amarillo by the next morning. I don't know why Terry was so caught up by that idea—maybe it was because he was from Amarillo—but he wanted to write a song around that concept."

Stafford and Fraser decided to meet the next morning and devote some time to the new idea. Yet Paul couldn't wait that long.

"The song just started to work on me. I sat down at the table and over the course of an hour wrote the whole thing. The next day, Terry came in and liked what I had done. He took it to Atlantic Records and they cut it for the country market."

Beginning in late 1973, the six-foot-four-inch Stafford hit the road plugging his latest single. Shy and introverted, Terry proved to be a better scribe than country music performer. Stafford's cut of "Amarillo by Morning" was solid, the singer's voice was perfect for the rodeo ballad, but Terry didn't like working the live crowds. He would have rather been home writing. In spite of this, "Amarillo" lingered on the charts for fourteen weeks and managed to reach thirty-one for a high-water mark.

"At that time," Paul recalled, "Terry and I didn't realize that the song had become a big record in Texas. Long after it left the national charts, bands down there were playing it at all the clubs."

One of those who heard the fans' requests for "Amarillo" each night was a young man from Pearsall, Texas. George Strait had learned to play guitar while serving a stint in the Army in the early seventies. A college graduate with a degree in agriculture, George helped form the Ace in the Hole band while in school. The group quickly earned a solid reputation throughout southeast Texas.

Ace in the Hole played Texas music. With fiddles and steel, Strait and company were producing a sound that was nothing like what was being generated by Nashville. Heavily steeped in Bob Wills and Lefty Frizzell, the group soon caught the eye of a man who had given George Jones his first break. Pappy Dailey owned a Houston record label. George cut "Ace in the Hole" for Daily's D Records, and saw the song do well in Texas. When Nashville failed to notice, Strait considered leaving music. He probably would have returned to ranching if it hadn't been for an old contact.

Erv Woolsey had managed a club where George's band had once played. Now a promotions executive at MCA, Woolsey got Strait an audition. Though the label questioned if this Texas swing sound would work with the modern audience, they signed him. A year later the singer produced a #1 with "Fool-Hearted Memory."

MCA thought that Strait would do better if he moved away from the honky-tonk swing that was so much a part of his stage show. George resisted. A compromise was struck. If Strait would cut the pop-oriented "Marina Del Rey," the label would let the singer record "Amarillo by Morning." "Marina" was released first and worked its way into the top ten. MCA executives then waited for "Amarillo" to bomb. It didn't.

"Amarillo by Morning" took a seventeen-week chart ride, peaking at #4. Throughout the Southwest the record was treated with rave reviews from fans and disc jockeys. In Texas it almost became a Lone Star anthem. A host of veteran country stars stood up to applaud the number. They were so glad to have what they considered real country music back on the charts. The record's success gave George the power to fuel his career with the kind of music that he had played in his early club dates. Now every concert and recording session felt like a trip home.

The swing brand of country music that had been all but forgotten since the early fifties was suddenly back in a big way. A host of bands emerged playing not only old Bob Wills standards, but new songs built on the same sound. Strait himself would ride high with "Does Fort Worth Ever Cross Your Mind," "The Cowboy Rides Away," "All My Ex's Live in Texas," and a host of other hits that the Texas Playboys would have been only too glad to have recorded in the thirties and forties. Largely because of this style of music, the country dance craze hit nationwide. Suddenly country bands were looking for fiddle players and songs that folks could two-step to. With his new old-fashioned country sound, the good-looking Strait would lead the way and become country music's most consistent draw for the next decade.

"It is kind of funny," Paul Fraser observed, "the song that had so much to do with bringing the Texas sound back was written by a couple of old rockers and inspired by a commercial." You have to wonder if all this would have happened if Terry Stafford hadn't thought about a package that absolutely had to be in Amarillo by morning.

1975
(I'd Be) A Legend in My Time

Written by Don Gibson

There are many songs which spend years waiting to have just the right artist discover them and take them to the top of the charts. There are some compositions that are so good that only a superstar can do them justice. There are even a handful of songs which are so well written that each new generation claims them as its own. But there are only a few songs which move past hit status and become legends in their time. Don Gibson's "(I'd Be) A Legend in My Time" is one of those songs.

Gibson had gotten the idea for "(I'd Be) A Legend in My Time" as he rode down the long highway between Nashville and his Knoxville home. To kill time he had been listening to the radio while leafing through a magazine. On several different stations he heard Bobby Darin's "Dream Lover" and "Mac the Knife." About the fifth time one of these records roared out over the speaker, Don came across an article profiling the singer. Interested in finding out more about the hot teen idol, the songwriter began digging into the text. About halfway through the piece Don came across a quote that caught his attention. He even stopped to read it out loud to the car's driver, fellow Acuff-Rose staff writer Mel Foree.

"Listen to this," Don had said, "that rock and roller Bobby Darin has an ambition of becoming a legend in his time. He is something, isn't he!"

Gibson, who had worked so long and so hard just to get into the spotlight, was a bit put off that a brash young man barely out of his teens was talking about becoming so big that everyone would notice him before they even looked at anyone else. The rocker's statement stuck so deeply in Don's gut that even after he got home he couldn't help but think about it.

"A legend in my own time, indeed!"

Rather than continuing to fume over Darin's gall, the songwriter began to work with the idea. Soon Gibson came up with a tune to go with the hook line, "I'd be a legend in my time." Over the course of the next few days he fleshed out and polished the complete story of a man who would become a living legend by losing at love's crazy game. Though it was simple and made up of only a verse, a chorus, and a bridge, Don thought it had potential. Laying it aside, he vowed to cut it during his next session.

In 1960 Gibson recorded "(I'd Be) A Legend in My Time," but rather than release it as a single, he simply used it as an album cut. Over the course of the next fifteen years the Gibson-penned song would appear on dozens of albums and be sung in countless concerts, but for some reason no one ever released it as a single. Despite this fact, it seemed as if almost everyone in the business knew all the song's words and could play it from memory. Country music fans also had embraced it as if it were a hit, often calling radio stations and requesting "(I'd Be) A Legend in My

Time" over current playlist songs. In one of the strangest of musical quirks, "(I'd Be) A Legend in My Time" had become a standard without ever spending one day on the hit parade.

In 1974 a twenty-eight-year-old blind singer from North Carolina began to make a mark in country music. An outstanding pianist, he had grown up listening to blues and rockabilly, and his first records had made noise on the big-city blues charts. In a career-shaping moment, a young Ronnie Milsap was playing around between sessions in Memphis. While he was singing an old rock standard, a man approached Milsap, told him how good he was, and then advised that he stop trying to sound like Elvis Presley. Ronnie would later discover that the critic had been Elvis himself. Three years before the King's death, Milsap would hone his personal style to the extent that Presley's own label, RCA, would sign the blind singer to a recording contract. Rumor had it that Elvis was thrilled.

When it came to coming to Nashville, Ronnie's timing was perfect. With the advent of new stars like Eddie Rabbitt and Barbara Mandrell, country music had urbanized. The sound was much more middle-of-the-road than hillbilly, and because of this, former rock 'n' roll fans were becoming country converts. Milsap's style was an ideal mesh for this new growing audience. His first release, "I Hate You," made the top ten. Three releases later he took an Eddie Rabbitt-penned song, "Pure Love," and hit the top of the charts. He followed that monster with another chart-topper, "Please Don't Tell Me How the Story Ends." Now being called country's Stevie Wonder, Milsap was selling out concerts and on the quick path to superstardom.

For his second album Ronnie wanted to cut his favorite Don Gibson song. Milsap loved "(I'd Be) A Legend in My Time," and he felt that with a little tinkering he could reshape it into something that sounded enough like his other two hits to make some noise on the charts. Using a 4/4 beat, instead of the original's 3/4, he converted the song into a Milsap masterpiece. Everyone who was in the studio as Ronnie polished his work knew that this was going to have to be a single. When Ronnie finally recorded the song, ending by pushing the final "time" seemingly off the scale and out of the room, the place erupted. Tom Collins, the session's producer, smiled and nodded his head in approval. The old song was going to be a hit again, they agreed.

Most of those in the Milsap session swore that "(I'd Be) A Legend in My Time" had been a hit several times before. Yet when RCA searched the charts for press-release information, they couldn't find it. After several more searches, it finally became clear that the song had never been on a chart. They couldn't believe that Milsap would be the first to cut a single on this classic.

RCA released "(I'd Be) A Legend in My Time" in early winter. The song raced up the hit lists and peaked at #1 in late January. The new album, which carried the single's name as its title, also did well too. By October, Ronnie had two more hits spun from the same session and was attending the Country Music Association awards show. Milsap's effort would win Album of the Year.

Ronnie used the "(I'd Be) A Legend in My Time" album and hit songs from it to become country music's most electric star. His concerts were love fests and his showmanship made him as popular as country music's up-and-coming sweetheart, Barbara Mandrell. His long and golden ride would signal the real power of this new brand of country music.

Over the next five years Milsap would record most of his thirty-five #1 singles and cross over to the pop charts on many occasions. He would win the CMA's

Male Vocalist of the Year three times, and in 1977 he would take home Entertainer of the Year. A pacesetter and role model, he inspired as much in victory as any of those who had ever walked the *Opry* stage. When he accepted his award as the genre's top entertainer, Milsap thanked and praised his wife. As Ronnie smiled, many in the audience choked back tears. Watching from a mobile home, a starving songwriter named R.C. Bannon listened to Milsap's speech and then sat down and wrote what was to become one of Ronnie's biggest hits, "Only One Love in My Life."

Even if Bobby Darin died without knowing it, Don Gibson, Ronnie Milsap, and country music owed him a great deal. Darin's style has made him one of rock's most enduring performers. After his death at age thirty-seven in 1973, the singer didn't fade away like a long list of other teen idols. Today Darin's name is well-remembered, he has been voted into the Rock 'n' Roll Hall of Fame, and his old hits have been revived in rock, country, and blues. And though he still isn't quite a legend yet, the song he inspired sure is.

1975
Before the Next Teardrop Falls

Written by Vivian Keith and Ben Peters

The Hispanic influence had been a part of commercial country music almost since the beginning of the genre. In the twenties Bob Wills was using Mexican musicians in his band and borrowing heavily from the music of their culture. Much of the western sound made popular by Gene Autry, Roy Rogers, the Sons of the Pioneers, and a host of other cowboy singers had a distinctive below-the-border influence not only in its melodies, but also in its phrasing, harmonies, and instrumentation. In the second generation of country music's evolution, Marty Robbins and others pulled heavily from the Hispanic culture for both inspiration and sound. Over time these Anglo artists put the Mexican brand on almost every facet of country music, but especially the western sound. Still, the origin of these contributions, as well as some very talented artists themselves, was usually buried or forgotten.

It wasn't until the seventies that Hispanic artists slowly began to emerge at the major-label recording studios. The first to have a lasting impact on country music playlists was a young man from Sabinal, Texas, Johnny Rodriguez. In 1973, when he was just twenty-one, the singer became somewhat of a teen idol as he reeled off three straight #1 records. He would remain a solid hit-producer for the next decade, with "Ridin' My Thumb to Mexico" ranking as his most successful release.

By and large Rodriguez was packaged by his label as a Latin romantic. Nashville viewed Johnny as a country music sex symbol, and used him in much the same way Hollywood had long used its Hispanic movie stars. In most cases Johnny's roots were ignored, and the songs which Rodriguez recorded were basic middle-of-the-road country compositions packaged with an Anglo sound.

In 1974, Huey P. Meaux, a producer for Dot Records, was recording a rhythm and blues album with a thirty-eight-year-old portly singer from San Benito, Texas. Baldemar G. Huerta had served a three-year prison term for marijuana possession in the early sixties, had drifted to New Orleans for a time after his release, recorded rock music for several different labels under a host of names, and never produced a hit record. Now working under the handle of Freddy Fender, the singer had immersed himself in the blues, something he had experienced firsthand.

Fender had completed all except one cut of his newest album, and was digging for that final number when the producer offered a quick solution. It seemed that sometime before, Meaux had laid down the tracks to an old Ben Peters composition, "Before the Next Teardrop Falls," and he had never put a vocal over the accompaniment. To save some time and money he suggested that the singer simply fill out his sides with the old standard.

Fender didn't want to cut "Teardrop" because it sounded too country. He backed away until the producer charmed him by explaining how much the song needed Freddy's style and voice. Impatient to finish the project, the singer made a date to cut the Peters tune. In the meantime, Fender translated the lyrics into Spanish. When he put his vocal on the tracks, Freddy sang the second verse in the language of his people.

"The first time I knew it had been cut again," Ben Peters recalled, "was when I got a call telling me that "Before the Next Teardrop Falls" had been number one in parts of Texas for a couple of months. It hadn't hit the national charts, so I simply hadn't heard about Fender's record until then."

Fender, who was working the Southwest, was as surprised as Peters with the song's initial success. Freddy had dismissed "Teardrop" within a few minutes of recording it. He had also been surprised and a bit dismayed when Dot had chosen to release it. While he liked having a hit, even if it was on a country song, Freddy knew that a minor regional seller didn't make much difference in anything except area bookings. In this case he didn't figure it would even do that. After all, who was going to book a Mexican blues singer into a legitimate country honky-tonk? So like the song's writer, Freddy rejected the record's initial numbers as a fluke. As both men would soon find out, this record wasn't going to die without a fight.

"My secretary, Vivian Keith, had given me the title for the song back in the sixties," Peters remembered. "I had written 'Before the Next Teardrop Falls' soon after that. Duane Dee cut it in 1967 and had it going pretty good. He had moved it to #44 before he got drafted. When he went into the service he quit working the song and it died. After that it was recorded more than forty times in the next six or seven years. All of the cuts were placed on albums. I don't guess I

ever thought it would be a single again. Then came Freddy's cut."

On January 11, 1975, "Before the Next Teardrop Falls" crawled into the top one hundred. Resting at ninety-six, it was on life support, in no danger of earning a bullet, and seemed to be nothing more than a product of the regional push for the song in the Southwest. Yet the next week it was still there, moving ever so slowly up the playlist. By the third week it had picked up a lot of steam and was being added to almost every major market's rotation.

The sudden surge of "Before the Next Teardrop Falls" caught everyone by surprise. Dot had to press more records just to fill the orders during the song's initial bottom-of-the-chart run. Now that Fender's country single was a legitimate hit, the factory really had to go to work to catch up with demand. Freddy was also having to adjust. Magazines wanted to interview him and country honky-tonks did want to sign him. To harmonize with his new country fans, the singer was even having to work up new material. He quickly discovered that there was a long list of Hispanic-style songs in country music catalogs.

"Before the Next Teardrop Falls" hit the top of the country charts on March 15, 1975. It would hold the position for two weeks. All told, Fender's single would ride the playlists for more than four months. In an instant Freddy had gone from an unknown and unappreciated Hispanic rhythm and blues singer to one of the hottest commodities on the country music market. "Teardrop" was so strong in country that the singer even found himself on the rock charts in March. In late May, Freddy would have the distinction of knocking Earth, Wind and Fire out of the #1 spot in pop music. Less than five months away from playing in dirty cantinas for a few hundred dollars a week, Fender was now entertainment's freshest new sound. He was overwhelmed.

Freddy's next single, "Wasted Days and Wasted Nights," would also earn him a gold record and a spot at the top of both the country charts and the rock charts. He would follow these first major hits with a long list of remade pop and country classics. Most would chart very well.

What probably created the Fender magic was his own insistence on cutting songs in Spanish and English. The use of both languages on almost all of his recordings not only made him the pride of the Hispanic community, it also gave him instant recognition and respectability with Anglo country music fans. Even though his name had been changed, Freddy never quit being Baldemar G. Huerta, and that honesty, combined with a great voice, made him a star. In 1976, when Fender lent his talents to the classic western ballad "Vaya Con Dios," he not only nailed the song, he finally brought to light just how much his own people's culture had impacted country music.

In October of 1975, "Before the Next Teardrop Falls" was named Country Music Association's Single of the Year. It was an honor that Freddy Fender had never even considered claiming. The singer had always figured that he had a better chance of walking on the moon than being honored on the hallowed pines of the Grand Ole Opry. Suddenly, two decades of recording and performing frustration were erased and his smile lit up the Nashville night as the moon never had.

Today, twenty years after scoring a long string of hit records as a solo act, Fender is a devoted country music addict. He joined the Texas Tornados band in 1990, and is bringing the real sounds of traditional Tex-Mex music to country music fans. Comfortable in Nashville, New York, or El Paso, Fender has not changed his look, his act, nor his enthusiasm for music. In Spanish and English, Freddy has left his mark on country music and opened the door for a host of other talented acts.

1978

Mammas, Don't Let Your Babies Grow Up to Be Cowboys

Written by Ed Bruce and Patsy Bruce

In 1975 things weren't working out the way that Ed Bruce had always planned. By now he figured he should have been a star. He had been paying his dues for more than half his life. Ed was thirty-five years old, had recorded for Sun Records just after Elvis had left that studio, had charted six times with three different record labels, had a solid core of fans in the business, had opened for some of country music's hottest acts, but hadn't been able to turn out any hits. His wife, Patsy, had been able to get the singer/songwriter some work in commercials to help pay the bills, but in those roles Ed felt as if he was just marking time by making money off his speaking voice. For almost twenty years folks who should know about such things had told him that he was talented, yet in spite of this, Bruce the entertainer just kept coming up short.

Frustrated, Ed turned his emotions inside out and began to write a very autobiographical song that had "Mammas, Don't Let Your Babies Grow Up to Be Guitar Players" as both the title and the hook line. The first verse and the chorus summed up Bruce's feelings about his own life. Yet after weeks of trying, he couldn't come up with another verse. It was as if there was nothing more to say. How much lower could he get?

"I think he was embarrassed that the song was so autobiographical," Patsy recalled. "He had worked out the first part of it so quickly as he drove down the freeway, and then maybe because it hit him that he was sharing his own story, he couldn't finish it."

As Patsy looked over Ed's song she suggested a subtle but monumental change. She felt the song was solid, but it needed something different than guitar players as the hook. After all, except for the two or three thousand undiscovered guitar players walking the streets of Nashville, there weren't that many who could relate to a broken-down instrumentalist whose life had fallen far short of his dreams. Besides, most of those who could relate didn't have the money to buy their next meal, much less a record.

"I suggested that he go with 'Mammas, Don't Let Your Babies Grow Up to Be Cowboys,'" Patsy remembered. "It seemed so natural. Cowboys were the Knights of the American Round Table, the childhood heroes of most country music fans, and the most romantic of all the country's legendary figures. At that point, with that image in mind, we sat down and finished the song."

For a while Ed, who was between record deals, thought about pitching the song. It certainly had sales potential. Yet rather than give it to someone else, the songwriter first took it to United Artists hoping that they would like the song so much that they would sign Bruce to a new contract. The ploy worked, and in late 1975 Ed's cut of "Mammas, Don't Let Your Babies Grow Up to Be Cowboys" was released. By simply staying on the charts for fourteen weeks and topping out at the fifteenth spot, it would become the singer's most successful record. Still, with those weak numbers it couldn't be considered a legitimate hit, and Ed was very disappointed. When his next release failed to make the top thirty, he was right back where he had started. Time was running out and he still couldn't get any higher up success's ladder.

A couple of years later Patsy had put "Cowboys" pretty much out of her mind and was going about her management business. While her husband's recording career was pretty much stuck, Ed was being called for more commercials. So the Bruces were living pretty well and getting by without having bill collectors knock on their door. In real-world terms, they were settling in to a middle-class life. That suddenly changed when, while attending a tea party, Patsy received a phone call.

"Ed tracked me down, called me, and was real excited," Patsy said with a laugh. "He just couldn't wait to inform me that Waylon Jennings had cut 'Mammas, Don't Let Your Babies Grow Up to Be Cowboys.' Of course I was thrilled too. It was worth being called away from the party."

With the outlaw movement going strong, Buddy Holly's old band member was cashing in in a very big way. Waylon's "Luckenbach, Texas (Back to the Basics of Love)" had not only put the already hot singer in high gear, but made him a national star whose career plans included Hollywood as well as Music City. Jennings's next cut, "The Wurlitzer Prize," had done almost as well as "Luckenbach," earning the star his sixth #1 single in four years. Now it seemed that Way-

lon's only problem was finding material good enough to follow the songs with which he had already scored. To have someone like Jennings pick and cut "Mammas, Don't Let Your Babies Grow Up to Be Cowboys" was a dream come true for Bruce.

"Mammas, Don't Let Your Babies Grow Up to Be Cowboys" had all the right elements to be a big Jennings hit. It felt so right as Jennings cut it. Still, as Waylon listened to the playback, it seemed that the arrangement was missing something. Jennings discussed it with his producer, and even called Ed back and talked to him about how the song just seemed to be a little flat. Both of them wondered what would make it jump off the record. Waylon decided to try some new background vocals and informed Bruce he would get back to him later when he believed the song was right. The backup vocal the singer decided to try consisted of bringing an old friend into the studio. Using Willie Nelson's unique harmonies, Jennings recut the song as a duet. Now, with Willie's voice being added to the tracks, Waylon thought that the record sounded complete. He called Ed back and gave the songwriter something about which he could really be excited.

Just two years before they had joined efforts on "Cowboys," Jennings and Nelson had scored the CMA Single of the Year with "Good-Hearted Woman." The Ed and Patsy Bruce original seemed to have that same kind of appeal. The more Waylon and the folks at RCA listened to it, the more they were convinced that this needed to be the first single released off the *Waylon and Willie* album.

"Mammas, Don't Let Your Babies Grow Up to Be Cowboys" appeared on the charts in January 1978. It climbed steadily up the playlists for two months before knocking Margo Smith's "Don't Break the Heart That Loves You" out of #1. For the next month the Bruce-penned ode to the classic American hero would hold that position. Before the year was out "Mammas, Don't Let Your Babies Grow Up to Be Cowboys" would also win a Grammy.

Ed Bruce, who had labored in obscurity for so long, was now recognized as an authentic cowboy star. The song, a favorite around the world, had put him on the map. MCA stepped up to give him a new record deal, and NBC signed him to appear in a weekly television series. Almost in his fifth decade, Ed had been discovered.

"It is remarkable what that song has meant to both of us," the now-former Mrs. Bruce explained. "It really put Ed's career at another level and helped me too. Yet one of the most remarkable things about 'Mammas, Don't Let Your Babies Grow Up to Be Cowboys' is not what it did for us personally, but how much the song meant to so many other people. Tom Brokaw of NBC news once told me that it was his favorite song. So have senators, house painters, movie directors, and garbage collectors. It is a song whose audience seems to cut across all lines and ages."

Even at its release this wide acceptance of what had once been a song that told the story of guitar players was evident as "Mammas, Don't Let Your Babies Grow Up to Be Cowboys" crossed over to the rock charts. This single, so very country in nature, pushed up to #42 in pop at a time when hard rock was blasting away most of the competition.

The outlaw music and style that had made Waylon, Willie, and the boys stars would ride strong for a couple more years and then fade away. The group movement, starting with Alabama, would lead to its demise. Yet the song that seemed to characterize this Texas-based country counterculture period remains as well known as any icon of the era. In a sense "Mammas, Don't Let Your Babies Grow Up to Be Cowboys" has become a part of the American myth, just like the lonely life it celebrated. It has grown well past a frustrated guitar player's look at his own life.

1979
The Devil Went Down to Georgia

*Written by Charlie Daniels, Tom Crain, Taz Digregorio, Fred Edwards,
Charlie Hayward, and Jim Marshall*

Charlie Daniels has been kicking around music for almost all of his life. The North Carolina fiddle player had begun his career in the early sixties as a rocker and songwriter. He even scored during that period when one of his compositions, "It Hurts Me," became a gold record for Elvis Presley. Yet in spite of penning a hit for the King, by and large Charlie's country roots mixed with his rock-driven sound did not earn him many friends in the music industry. The West Coast seemed to think that the big man was too country, and Nashville didn't have a clue as to what to do with him. Creative and independent, the immensely talented Daniels refused to change his style to fit the current music mood, thus joining a few other country rockers out on the music world's fringe. He would starve in that land of limbo for many years.

Tired of going it alone, in 1971 Charlie formed a group that would embrace music as he felt it. The Charlie Daniels Band would hit the road, touring with a wide mix of country and rock sounds coming together in a style that was distinctively their own. Once again no one knew what to do with Charlie Daniels. Record executives didn't even know what to call the band's sound.

Talent couldn't be ignored forever, and in 1973 the band landed a record contract with Kama Sutra. This was not the country music label of choice, but with a large bank of hot rock stars, the company did have the resources and contacts to make folks in pop music sit up and listen to an electric fiddler player and his strange mix of musicians. In May 1973, Charlie's first chart single, "Uneasy Rider," hit playlists and climbed to #9 in rock music. Roaming in very unfamiliar territory, Kama Sutra also managed to push it to #67 on the country side. Two years later the label would release Daniels's "Texas" and take that single into country's top forty. Still, the company with a Buddha as their logo was a bit lost in the Bible Belt. The label really didn't relate to country disc jockeys or fans. Besides, Kama Sutra was much more interested in the big money to be found in rock royalties than they were in country's smaller profit margins. Sensing that the Charlie Daniels Band was more a country act than a rock-driven band, they allowed Epic Records to sign them. Buddha thus left the country charts, and few seemed to notice.

Epic may have been a strong country music label, but they really didn't know what to do with the group either. Charlie's sound was just not right for the standard country market. It was too frantic and hard. Some even thought it was hippie music. After Daniels's first few releases went nowhere, the company might have let the band go, but Hank Williams, Jr.'s, surging success changed their thinking.

Hank Jr. had "found" himself in 1972 with the #1 single "Yellow Roses." Since that release his songs had gotten progressively harder. Seven years later his music was drawing hordes of former rockers to his concerts. By opening up his style to include these younger folks, Williams had created a fan base which spent more money at concerts and on records. This fan base also seemed more rabid than the normal country mix. Williams had tremendous sway over them and they picked up on his suggestions. If he said to party, they did. If he told them to check out a new act, they did. And when Hank acknowledged that one of the best country rockers in the business was Charlie Daniels, and backed this claim up by using the band leader on his recording sessions, several thousand fans began to listen to the Charlie Daniels Band.

Coming into the studio with the rush created by country fans finally discovering his sound, Charlie sensed that the timing was right to make a real impact on the country charts. While he had not changed his style, it seemed that Music City was opening up a bit and beckoning to include his freer kind of instrumental-driven music on radio playlists. So, Charlie reasoned, if he was ever going to be a recording force, it was going to have to be now.

"We were in the studio cutting the *Me and My Reflections* album," the big man remembered. "I felt that we needed a fiddle song to round out the album. At that point we had kind of hit a wall, so I decided to take a two-day break and then come back and finish the session. Over the break we rehearsed and I thought a lot about finding just the right fiddle tune."

As Daniels considered his recording options, for some unexplainable reason his thoughts drifted back to his days as a grade school student. He remembered a poem that had fascinated him entitled "Mountain Whippoorwill." The Stephen Vincent Benet piece talked about the Devil and temptation. Using that as his theme, Daniels updated and reworked the idea into the beginnings of the ultimate fiddle song. This time Satan and little Johnny would face off with bows, not harps.

"I have always believed that the very best things happen off the cuff," Charlie explained. "So I got the band together and we just wrote the melody as we felt it and fit the words to it."

Perhaps this Woodland Studio session was one of the most enthusiastic recording days in music history. With Charlie heating up his bow and telling a story in a way that actually reflected an urgency that only facing the Devil could drum up, the musicians came together and laid down the tracks on one of the greatest country lyric-led instrumentals in modern history. "The Devil Went Down to Georgia" was so special that Epic immediately realized that it was going to be the next single. As good as the other songs on the album were, there could be no other choice.

It was released in late spring, and the country charts gave way to the "Devil" in late June. By August 25 the single had climbed to the top of the charts. The song also drew a strong following on the rock charts, peaking at #3. When the CMA held its awards show in October, "The Devil Went Down to Georgia" pulled down the Song of the Year award. After years of just being a fiddle player, now Charlie Daniels was a big star.

Charlie Daniels would never again hit *Billboard*'s top ten. His songs would only become solid sellers because of the band's wide appeal with both rock and country markets. Yet his signature song, inspired by a grade school class, would remain a country standard long after its rock fans had moved on to something else.

In 1993 country music fiddler Mark O'Connor revived "The Devil Went Down to Georgia." This time O'Connor would not only put together a great new studio recording of the classic tune, but he would invite in a few old friends to flesh it out for a single and video release. Appearing with Mark would be Travis Tritt, Marty Stuart, and Johnny Cash. O'Connor would also invite one of his heroes, Charlie Daniels, to join him with the fiddle work. A major video hit and a smash single, Mark's version would firmly anchor the Daniels composition as not just a great one-artist recording, but a genuine classic that would join the "Orange Blossom Special" to become an important piece of every fiddle band's musical menu. With his "The Devil Went Down to Georgia," not only did Charlie Daniels give the Devil his due, but he forced Nashville to give Daniels's style of country music its due too.

1980
He Stopped Loving Her Today

Written by Bobby Braddock and Curly Putman

With the exception of Eddy Arnold, no country music artist has spent more time on the charts than George Jones. The Texas native first sang in church, but by the time he returned from Korea, George had taken up performing in clubs and at dances throughout southeast Texas. An old-fashioned honky-tonk stylist, Jones had a much more traditional sound than many of the performers of his day. With phrasing and style closer to Webb Pierce than Hank Snow, Hank Williams, or Bob Wills, George caught the eye of H. W "Pappy" Dailey, a Houston record executive, in 1954. Dailey took the twenty-four-year-old singer under his wing and groomed him for stardom. It didn't take long.

In 1955 Jones scored with the first of his more than 150 chart appearances. The song, released on the small Starday label, started as a regional Texas hit before catching onto the *Billboard* playlists in late 1955. "Why, Baby, Why" would spend fifteen weeks on the national charts, peaking at #4, before being replaced by another Jones offering, "What Am I Worth."

Jones's success on Starday earned him an invitation to join the *Louisiana Hayride*. The Shreveport radio show was then at its peak. Elvis had just left to go on to international fame. Johnny Horton, Faron Young, Jim Reeves, and a host of other up-and-comers were either in the midst of a long ride on the show, or had just been invited to Nashville. At this point there was

magic in Shreveport, and Jones took full advantage of it. This was the stage where unknowns became big stars overnight. With his energy and unique sound George would quickly become one of the *Hayride's* most popular draws.

When rockabilly took over country music, Jones made a living with a string of top-ten honky-tonk songs. Yet he didn't break out and register a major hit until he signed with Mercury. Taking a number that had been written by "The Big Bopper," J.P. Richardson, Jones recorded his first #1, "White Lightning." Two years later he would follow with an even bigger hit, "Tender Years." If the singer had never recorded another song, these two monsters would have established Jones as one of the era's best country acts. As it was, they were simply the foundation for much greater things.

After scores of top ten records, Jones's recording career probably peaked in the late sixties and early seventies. George cut a string of #1 singles, won a legion of new fans with his Tammy Wynette duets, and grew immensely as an artist. As country music fans were quick to point out, it wasn't just Jones's style that set him apart, it was also the emotion that seemed to carry through in each of his performances. George always appeared to feel such great pain that you could hear it when he sang.

By the end of the seventies, Jones had earned a

place as one of country music's great stylists, but he hadn't won many awards while carving out his deserved reputation. Part of this lack of respect and honor could be hitched to his personal life. George would often miss concerts, show up drunk during shows, and get caught in very loud public disputes. The emotion that was so much a part of his songs seemed to spill over uncontrolled into his life. To gain the recognition which he so badly desired, he was going to have to get his private affairs in order and find a song that would display his highly touted vocal skills at their best.

About the same time that George was dealing with the anguish of losing his wife, Tammy Wynette, in a divorce, Bobby Braddock and Curly Putman were combining their immense songwriting skills. Putman had found great recognition in Nashville during the late sixties. His "As Long as the Wind Blows" and "Green Green Grass of Home" were two of the most intelligent and fresh songs produced in the days after Hank Cochran, Harlan Howard, Willie Nelson, and Bill Anderson had begun to release control of the charts. Curly was a songwriter who brought a fresh perspective to his craft. His compositions went beyond simple love. They got into the essence of family, home, and country. Putman was unafraid to tackle any subject, and he usually turned even the most bizarre situations into hit material.

Like Putman, Bobby Braddock brought unique views to the Music City songwriting scene. Bobby, a rock 'n' roll piano player who had come to Nashville as a part of Marty Robbins's band, had first scored big with a song that looked at the most painful aspects of divorce. His "D-I-V-O-R-C-E" would become a Tammy Wynette standard and anchor the writer as a man who could take any situation and milk every drop of emotion from it.

"In early 1977," Bobby recalled, "Curly and I were writing together. He swears that I brought him an idea about a man who so loved his wife that his love only stopped the day he died. I don't remember coming up with the concept, but over the course of a writing session Curly and I put most of it together. I then finished it at home. I thought the song was all right, but I just wasn't very excited about it."

Braddock and Putman were so unimpressed with the number that they almost forgot about it. Over half a year after they had written it, Bobby finally cut a demo of "He Stopped Loving Her Today." When Tree Publishing shopped the song around, the response they got was pretty disappointing. The only artist who was even remotely interested in recording the number was Johnny Russell.

"Johnny cut the song twice," Braddock remembered, "for two different labels, and neither record was released. In a way I could understand why. I kept a diary that rated all my songs. "He Stopped Loving Her Today" just didn't rate very high in my book either. In my mind it just wasn't a hit."

All but forgetting about the song, both writers went on to other things. Their composition would have probably remained undiscovered if Dan Wilson, a Tree Publishing plugger, hadn't come across the Braddock/Putman effort. Dan took "He Stopped Loving Her Today" to Billy Sherrill at Epic. Sherrill thought it could make a great George Jones single, if the writers would just add another verse.

"Billy didn't like the way it ended," Bobby explained. "He wanted us to add a verse where the woman comes back to the funeral. We worked on several drafts, and he kept sending them back for more work. Finally we hit on one he would accept. Still, I just didn't expect much of the song. At that time I had several things I thought were far better."

Bobby wasn't the only one unimpressed. George didn't like it either. In his mind it was too morbid. He couldn't see himself doing a song about a guy who died. It took the producer months to get the singer into the studio to cut it. In early February, when Jones did show up, he wasn't excited.

The first cut failed to impress anyone. Jones's voice was flat and unemotional. All those present could tell that he didn't care for the song or feel its message. Then, just before the second take, the atmosphere changed dramatically.

"L.E. White, a songwriter friend of mine," Braddock recalled, "was in the studio for the session. L.E. told me that the first take just didn't go anywhere. Then Tammy Wynette and her new husband walked into the studio. George watched as Tammy went into the booth and sat down beside Billy Sherrill. It was strange because, where she was sitting, a single light came down and illuminated her face. George Jones seemed riveted to that scene, and when he sang the song the second time, he never took his eyes off Tammy. It was like he was singing every word just for her."

A few days later Bobby Braddock heard that tape. For the first time he realized the power in the song he and Curly had crafted.

"It hit me that this was the perfect marriage of song, singer, and production. Everything on it was so compelling. I sensed at that time that this was going to be a great record." While the writer had finally been impressed, the singer wasn't.

George Jones didn't think the song was worth anything. On the day it was shipped he told his producer that this record was a waste of time. "Nobody will ever buy the morbid SOB," he warned.

Jones's ninety-seventh single hit the charts in May. On July 5, 1980, "He Stopped Loving Her Today" would climb to the top of the playlists. The record would be chosen CMA Song of the Year and would help propel George into the Male Vocalist of the Year. This recording would come to be known as the song that finally got Jones his just due and recognition.

A decade and half after its release, "He Stopped Loving Her Today" had been tabbed several times as the best country song ever written. The British Broadcasting Corporation chose it as the most important song in country music history. A host of other polls have echoed this sentiment. While the debate about its place in songwriter annals will never be completely decided, there can be no doubt that this was the perfect marriage of song and singer. For more than twenty-five years George Jones had needed to find a number that could be a vehicle for his remarkable country sound. "He Stopped Loving Her Today" was that song, and allowed the singer to finally reach his full potential as a song stylist.

1980
Looking for Love

Written by Bob Morrison, Wanda Mallette, and Patti Ryan

It took the combined efforts of two schoolteachers, a publishing veteran, and an unknown Texas club singer to turn out a song which came to signify a new era in country music. In early 1980 these four unique and distinct personalities would be brought together through a song that would become the centerpiece of one of the era's hottest movies. Without "Looking for Love" and the movie *Urban Cowboy* leading the way, the country dance craze which inundated country music in the late eighties and early nineties might never have gained a national foothold.

Like so many college students in the days of Vietnam protests and left-wing marches, Patti Ryan was backpacking all over Europe in 1976 trying to figure what she wanted to do with her life. Nearing the end of her money and travel time, she overheard the Eagles' "Lyin' Eyes" playing on a radio as she hitched a ride to Austria. "I can do that," she thought as she rolled the song's words and melody over again and again in her mind. "I can write music."

There was some foundation for Patti's newfound dream. Her mother was a public school music teacher, and as a teenager Ryan had performed in school bands as well as with several local bands. The fact was that the young college graduate had been around music all her life, and therefore thought she understood the essence of what made a hit. Beyond this very elementary concept and very casual experi-

ence, she had nothing else but enthusiasm from which to draw. Yet as fate would have it, returning to the States she discovered that her older brother had opened a recording studio in Mississippi. He was mainly working on advertising jingles, but he was making contacts in other areas too. Younger sister bugged Chuck until he introduced her to another songwriting wanna-be, Wanda Mallette. Wanda, a local second-grade teacher, and Patti quickly discovered common ground in both their goals and dreams.

As soon as Patti found a job as an art teacher, she and Wanda devoted all their spare moments away from their classrooms to learning and honing the craft of songwriting. After they had progressed to the point where they felt comfortable sharing their collaborations, they contacted Wanda's old high school friend Bob Morrison. Bob had formed his own Nashville-based publishing company, and word was out that he was scouting fresh talent.

"The first batch of stuff we sent wasn't that good," remembered Patti. "Still, he wrote back and told us that he thought we had some potential. He encouraged us to try again. So we went back to work to prepare another package of material."

The two labored together and separately for several weeks on a host of different ideas. Then one day, after reading a children's book, Wanda mentioned a new concept to Patti.

"She told me the very germ of a song," Patti recalled, "and it just wouldn't leave me alone. Going back and forth to grad school night classes at Southern Mississippi I kept thinking about Wanda's 'looking for love' idea. One night I was driving my VW bug through a terrible rainstorm. The wipers were beating out a rhythm as they tried to keep up with the pouring torrents. It was in these moments that I began to really hear the song, and in the middle of the storm I outlined the chorus. As soon as I got home I called Wanda and we quickly fleshed out the rest. It really wrote itself from that point on."

"Looking for Love" was in the second package of songs which Ryan and Mallette sent to Bob Morrison. On his first run-through of their stuff he quickly noted that they had improved a great deal. He had been right. They did have some real potential. He really liked what they had done with the "Looking for Love" number. He felt particularly drawn to the wording, but he believed that the tune didn't sound enough like "Nashville" to sell. He recommended that they get rid of seventh and minor chords. The two women felt strongly about their melody, but they bowed to the pro and let Bob rework it for them. Three weeks later Morrison was shopping the demo.

For the better part of the year "Looking for Love" was welcomed in and then booted out of recording studios all across Nashville. Universally, producers and artists alike didn't like the song. Almost two dozen rejected it outright. Others simply dumped it in the trash without comment. Still, Morrison refused to give up. He forwarded it to a friend on the West Coast. From there it found its way to Irving Azoff, a Los Angeles-based producer/manager who wanted to create a double-sided country music sound track for a film that would be shooting in a honky-tonk named Gilley's just outside of Houston. Azoff tossed the demo in a box of Combine Music material and sent it to the filming location. That was where Johnny Lee entered the picture.

Lee had been a locally popular regular at Gilley's for years, and the film's director wanted to use him in the movie to establish some authentic club background and flavor. Lee's role would be small, a brief background cameo as he performed with his band. Still, rather than assign the song that Johnny was to do, the crew simply gave him the box of Combine demos and told him to pick his favorite. The first one Lee found that he liked was the one Music City had hated, "Looking for Love."

When Johnny cut the record, the film crew literally went crazy. They rewrote an entire segment of the script just to feature the number. In order to make room for "Looking for Love," they even bumped the Willie Nelson/Waylon Jennings effort "Mammas, Don't Let Your Babies Grow Up to Be Cowboys." As the final rushes of *Urban Cowboy* were finally pieced together, the Ryan, Mallette, and Morrison song became the movie's theme, thus causing the rewriting and refilming of the film's last twenty minutes. Meanwhile, Patti and Wanda were completely in the dark in Mississippi. They had no idea that their song had been picked up and that a multi-million dollar movie was being rewritten around it.

"Bob called us one night," Patti recollected, "and he said that he didn't have a lot of information, but they were going to use 'Looking for Love' in a movie that was filming in Houston with John Travolta. I wanted to know more, but he told me that that was all the information he had."

Ryan and Mallette then called a mutual friend in Houston, who told them about Gilley's and the movie that they were filming there. A few weeks later when spring break arrived, the two songwriters packed their bags, got into Patti's VW, and drove all night to

Texas. Conning their way onto the *Urban Cowboy* location set, they walked in just as the crew was filming Johnny Lee singing "Looking for Love."

Urban Cowboy became one of the biggest hits of 1980, beginning the craze that led to the monumental expansion of country music's demographic base and the explosion of country music night clubs. The song launched club singer Johnny Lee's career too. "Looking for Love" stood atop the country charts for three weeks in the late summer, while also climbing as high as #5 on the pop side. The cut also propelled Ryan's and Mallette's careers. "Just Another Woman in Love," a #1 hit for Anne Murray in 1984, followed "Looking for Love." Since that time the duo has turned out a long list of other hits, including "Out of Her Shoes" and "Americana."

So with a song that no one wanted, two women, a fledgling publisher, and an unknown singer started a musical revolution. And in a twist of irony that only Patti Ryan could fully appreciate, the song which gave her her first hit single had been married to the initial inspiration for her taking up songwriting. On the "B" side of the *Urban Cowboy* single of "Looking for Love" was the Eagles' "Lyin' Eyes."

1980

Tennessee River

Written by Randy Owen

In one form or another the four guys who made up the group Alabama had been playing music for over a decade. By the end of the seventies they had worked their way from small gigs around their Fort Payne, Alabama home to being the house band at The Bowery, one of Myrtle Beach's hottest clubs. Though not starving to death, the group was not rolling in the chips either. They didn't have a major record deal, nationally they were unknown, and the timing for a country band making it in Nashville seemed completely wrong. It appeared that the boys were about forty years too late.

The fact was that when country music fans thought of a country music group, they didn't think of four guys playing instruments and singing. At that time successful groups were limited to quartets like the Statler Brothers or the Oak Ridge Boys, and bands were the musicians who played behind the big stars. When asked to name their favorite band, most country fans would just pick the men who backed up their favorite solo acts. Folks like the Strangers or Do-Rites.

The Music City recording industry also thought little about signing country bands. Most producers and executives had never worked with a real band. Groups like the Texas Playboys or Spade Cooley and His Orchestra were just a part of the distant past, a vague memory from a day long gone. Solo stars had

driven country music for decades, and most critics thought individual acts would continue to drive the genre well into the next century. Occasionally a group might manage a fluke hit. That had happened a few years before with the Charlie Daniels Band and "The Devil Went Down to Georgia," but no group would ever have consistent charting power. It just couldn't be done in these modern times. Country wasn't like rock. The country fans wanted their stars one-on-one.

RCA first took note of Alabama when the band took a self-penned song, "My Home's in Alabama," into the top twenty in early 1980. Not only did the fact that a group had scored a minor hit stun the big label, but the fact that an unknown band had been able to land in the top twenty with the small MDJ label was shocking. No one in Music City knew quite what to think. Most just shook their heads and went back to looking for the next great solo act. Yet RCA decided to explore a little more before turning their backs on Alabama. Catching the group in person, watching hardcore country music fans react to the group's country/rock sound, listening to the guys' unique mix of old country and sixties rock influences, the label decided to take a chance.

Using veteran producer Harold Shedd, RCA put the boys in the studio and picked through their music looking for anything that might be commercial enough to place Alabama in the top ten. One of the songs that seemed to give the boys a shot was a Randy Owen-penned tune.

Owen, who was the group's lead singer, had written a song that had been expanded from his observations of trade day in Scottsboro, Alabama. Folks from all over the region had gathered for a First Monday flea market. In amongst the hundreds of booths, everything from antiques to junk would be sold. Bargain hunters, shop owners, and poor folks just looking for good deals would wander the grounds in order to find that certain item that would make their trips worthwhile. Randy sensed a carnival atmosphere in the proceedings, and the song he wrote captured this jubilant spirit.

In order to get to Scottsboro, the trip from Owen's home in Fort Payne took the singer by the Tennessee River and past Lookout Mountain. Working these well-known settings into the song's hook line, he finished out three verses and turned it over to fellow band member Jeff Cook. Cook was the group's fiddle player, and Jeff arranged a hot rocking fiddle bridge that brought the song together.

In the studio the boys cut the song two ways. The longer version was used on their first album. A second "Tennessee River" was cut that dismissed the second verse and tightened the song for the single. The single was shipped just a month after it had been cut, and RCA and the boys waited to see if country radio was ready for a country band.

On the last day in May "Tennessee River" surfaced on the charts. At that time Ronnie Milsap was holding down #1. Less than a month before, pop singer Debby Boone had even taken a song to the top. There would be no confusing what Alabama was doing with either Milsap, Boone, Mandrell, or the now-smooth Ray Price. What gave RCA some hope that this record might make top forty was that the crowd which had made Hank Williams, Jr.'s, Dixie rock so strong might also be caught up in Alabama's sound.

Williams probably did pave the way for Alabama. Yet his music was actually harder than the stuff the boys were playing. Hank Jr. was closer to rock than the new RCA act. Yet because they were a real band, many older listeners initially perceived that Alabama was simply a rock act trying to make it in country music. This was what RCA had feared would doom the group.

"Tennessee River" started slowly. At a time when many records hit their peak within two months of being released, this single was still working its way up the charts at the end of two months. Most at the label were thrilled when in late July the single made it to the top ten. They were shocked a few weeks later when, on August 16, the record went #1. Now, the label wondered, could the group follow their surprising successful debut?

Over the course of the next seven years Alabama would score twenty more #1's. The only two records they recorded which failed to reach the top spot were a special seasonal release, "Christmas in Dixie," and a duet with Lionel Richie, "Deep River Woman." Everything else that they recorded hit the top of the charts. In a little more than a decade, Randy Owen, Teddy Gentry, Mark Herndon, and Jeff Cook would record thirty-two #1's. Not only would they replace the Statlers and Oaks as country's hottest and most loved group, but they would be named Entertainers of the Year on three different occasions.

Through the music of Alabama, a younger crowd began to tune in country stations. There can be little doubt that the huge growth of country radio in the eighties was created in no small part by this group's explosion of sound and popularity. Because of Alabama's success, other country bands began to spring up and groups like Restless Heart, Diamond Rio, Sawyer Brown, and Exile had an opportunity to spin their own sounds on turntables and jukeboxes. While the move toward country groups didn't supplant the solo acts altogether, it did make a huge dent in their control of the genre.

"Tennessee River" dramatically changed the course of country music. The country band, long just a product of local dance halls, would again become a major force. With the move of these young driven musi-

cians, a huge flow of new blood and fans would pour into Nashville-based music. The average age of the country music buyer would move downward as record and product sales spiraled upward. Millionaires were made overnight as the big money suddenly arrived in the country market. Building on their first major release, Alabama resurrected the country band and changed the face of country music more dramatically than anything since Elvis and rockabilly.

1984
Mama He's Crazy

Written by Kenny O'Dell

A thirty-year-old Kenny O'Dell had come to Nashville with a background centered in rock a pop music. O'Dell had begun to sing at the age of nine, and using a Martin guitar as his rhythm partner, he had performed with several bands before he graduated from junior high. In the fifties and early sixties he migrated to California and worked with a host of different stars, including rock guitar legend Duane Eddy. In 1967, after a decade of pitching, Kenny finally landed a West Coast record deal and hit the charts with a self-penned song, "Beautiful People." Bobby Vee also cut Kenny's composition and made "Beautiful People" into a minor hit. When O'Dell's next song, "Next Plane to London," became a top-twenty hit for the group Rose Garden, things looked bright. But rock music was becoming much harder, and soon the Oklahoma musician's talents were falling on deaf ears. When he was offered the opportunity to move to Nashville in 1970 and run Bobby Goldsboro's publishing group, O'Dell jumped at the chance.

In Music City Kenny soon found his niche. Writing such classics as "I'll Take It on Home," "Behind Closed Doors," "Lizzie and the Rainman," and "What I've Got in Mind," O'Dell was getting more requests for his work than he could possibly fulfill. The successful scribe was even given the chance to come back into the studio and record. Now seemingly blessed with a golden touch, there was little doubt that after two decades of searching, the former rocker had found a place where he was dearly wanted.

"In 1981 or early '82," Kenny remembered, "this mother/daughter duo was performing on Ralph Emery's local morning television show. My wife and I thought that they had something on the ball, so we met with them. Even though they didn't have any record deals, I began to work with them hoping that I could write their material and produce them. Naomi, the mother, was really excited about my getting involved."

For the next few months Kenny and the Judds would meet regularly at a downtown office and go over material. Not only was the songwriter trying to get the women a record deal, but O'Dell was also interested in polishing their sound and act. It was tough work, and in spite of a lot of raw talent, Kenny couldn't win anyone over to the Judds' potential. He could realistically understand why. After all, Wynonna was still in high school and had a mouth full of braces, and Naomi, though beautiful, had a track record that consisted of little more than being a mother and a nurse. Though he worked hard drumming up interest in the women, O'Dell couldn't find anyone who was willing to take a chance on the act. Nevertheless, even after months of rejections, Kenny continued to write songs specifically for Naomi and Wynonna.

"One afternoon I took a break from writing and was watching a soap opera with my wife. It was about two in the afternoon, and I became intrigued by the crazy things that were going on in this television show. Grabbing a legal pad, I began to scribble down some lines that came right from the dialogue. One of them, "Mama he's crazy," jumped out at me.

"At that point I actually used the Judds as my inspiration. I imagined what it would be like for a mother to have a daughter dating. In very little time I had put it all together. Then I grabbed my boom-box recorder and guitar and dubbed off a very rough copy of "Mama He's Crazy." The next week I played it for Naomi and Wynonna and we worked up an arrangement for them."

Soon after Kenny had written "Mama He's Crazy" the Judds moved and their weekly sessions ended. Within a few months O'Dell lost track of the mother/daughter duo. He also forgot about the song he had written for them.

Realizing that a music career was a long shot, Naomi had gone back to nursing at the Williamson County Hospital. Working in the ER, the singing nurse came face-to-face with RCA record producer Brent Maher's daughter. She had been admitted following an automobile accident. While checking on Diana Maher's condition, the elder Judd managed to slip the young woman a homemade tape recording of her and Wynonna. A few weeks later Brent Maher himself called and invited the girls to sing for RCA.

After the label signed the duo, Maher worked trying to identify their sound. Like Kenny had before him, the producer kept running into the walls. It seemed that the Judds liked to sing anything and everything, but they didn't have a style that was strictly their own. After performing scores of different numbers, the Judds kept coming back to something Brent had never heard. And it was this unknown song

that came closest to a sound that Maher thought might work on the country charts. When he inquired where Naomi had found it, she told him about their work with Kenny O'Dell.

"Brent Maher phoned me one day and began to talking about 'Mama He's Crazy,'" O'Dell recalled. "He wanted to use the song with a new act he was recording. I couldn't imagine how he had come across the song. I hadn't even done a demo on it. As a matter of fact I couldn't even lay my hands on a lyric sheet. Anyway, when he told me had signed the Judds, I was pleased and told him to go ahead and cut the song."

RCA held "Mama He's Crazy" until after the label got a chance to see how the group's first release, "Had a Dream," would do. When "Dream" went to #17, the organization felt they had a strong chance to make the Judds' next release a hit. Pushing the obliging duo into the studio, the label cut a video based on "Mama He's Crazy's" story line. These images would be the first that millions of fans would ever see of the mother/daughter team.

With a strong record and video, RCA shipped the Judds' new product in early spring. By March the song was climbing the charts and the video had become one of CMT's hottest. In August, Naomi and Wynonna took the song which Kenny had written specifically for them to #1. "Mama He's Crazy" would begin a string of eight straight chart-toppers for the team. Over the course of the next five years the Judds would release sixteen singles, and only two would fail to hit #1.

No mother/daughter duo would have the influence or the following of Naomi and Wynonna Judd. On records, on videos, and in concerts, their ability to sell themselves and their music would be second to none. Overnight they would become entertainment giants, and their special sound would not only set them apart from the other acts of the time, but would defy any attempt at imitation. It is therefore all the more ironic that this family team had once been unable to sell themselves even to a minor label, and that the song that made them superstars would have been lost and forgotten if not for an auto accident. Even the soap opera which inspired Kenny O'Dell's "Mama He's Crazy" wouldn't invent a plot that ridiculous.

1984
Uncle Pen

Written by Bill Monroe

Country music bluegrass legend Bill Monroe never managed a #1 song on any national chart. By the time the hillbilly charts were spun off the pop playlists, Monroe and His Blue Grass Boys had already been regulars on the *Grand Ole Opry* for seven years. It was therefore too late for many of Bill's classic records to have a chance to claim anything but a regional audience. With music moving from the straightforward hill forms of expression to dance music, swing, honky-tonk, smooth ballads, and rockabilly, it was a wonder that Monroe's beloved bluegrass survived at all. Yet a small circle of performers and fans continued to embrace the style which Bill himself had invented. These chosen few managed to keep bluegrass alive, even if had been pushed way out of the spotlight.

Former Monroe band members Flatt and Scruggs managed country's first #1 bluegrass hit in 1963. Yet in all honesty, "The Ballad of Jedd Clampett" was more of a novelty record than a true bluegrass standard. Written strictly as the theme song for CBS's wildly successful *Beverly Hillbillies* the number would have never become a top-seller without the television show's support. While "Jedd Clampett" did open up a tiny pocket of interest in the traditional musical form, it failed to generate a large trend that would bring bluegrass consistently to either the top of the charts or the center of the country music stage. By

and large, except for a later brief surge created by the movie *Bonnie and Clyde,* banjos, fiddles, and dobros had given way to drums, electric basses, and hot Fender guitar licks. In the minds of most performers under the age of fifty, bluegrass was an ancient musical style that was little more than a reminder of the roots of the genre. For all practical purposes it was dead.

Traditional country music had become such an unimportant part of the business that by the mid-seventies some of Nashville's most influential musicians were extremely concerned. They acknowledged that with so few youngsters becoming interested in old hill music, instruments such as the Dobro and banjo might become a part of the past. There just didn't seem to be anyone in the current generation who was taking the time to learn them. With the older musicians passing away, who would be left who could play these acoustical pieces?

Yet even as Music City's traditionalists fretted, deep in the hills of Kentucky a youngster was growing up in the bluegrass tradition, and his hero was none other than Bill Monroe. This young man would come to town in the seventies and find himself looked upon as an old-fashioned picker awash in a Nashville that was enraptured with middle-of-the-road music. Facing tremendous odds, this man would not only create a resurgence in bluegrass music, but would also become one of the biggest and brightest stars in the industry.

Bill Monroe's recording career was pretty much history by the time Ricky Skaggs was born in Cordell, Kentucky, in 1954. Yet this small boy was so hooked on the sounds created by Monroe that he was already on stage singing traditional mountain-style country songs at the age of eight. By the time he was in his teens he had played with Flatt and Scruggs and Ralph Stanley's band. One of his good buddies, fellow bluegrass picker, Keith Whitley, soon joined Ricky and the two worked with several different groups throughout the late seventies. Signing with a small label—the major record companies had little use for a new bluegrass singer—Skaggs cut an album in 1980. By 1982 he had taken an old fifties honky-tonk tune, "Crying My Eyes Out over You," to the top of the charts. In the midst of outlaw music and pop production, Ricky was riding on the far right side of the country music road. Many thought he was driving the musical equivalent of a Model A too, but he would quickly prove them wrong.

Skaggs would follow that first #1 with six other hard-country chart-toppers. In two brief years he had become a star of major proportions, and Skaggs found himself hounded by not only the major labels, but millions of fans. Modest, straightforward, and at peace with himself and his sound, he seemed completely unaffected by fame or fortune, and continued to record songs which reflected his own rural roots. His unbelievable back-road journey to superstardom was completed when he reached back almost fifty years to pay tribute to the man who had invented the music which Skaggs so loved.

Though he was a product of his bluegrass roots, up until this time Nashville had labeled Ricky's music more of a new honky-tonk sound. Thus, Bill Monroe had again failed to receive any just due from the new powers which governed Music City. Therefore it should have been expected that when Ricky picked out Monroe's "Uncle Pen" as his next release, the record company balked. They simply didn't understand what he wanted to do. The market wouldn't buy a recording that sounded so old-fashioned, they argued. Yet to beat this argument and to emphasize just how much he believed in the number, Skaggs pointed to his live crowds' reaction to the old Monroe classic. Still, Sugar Hill held off.

Skaggs had filled out his *Don't Cheat in Your Hometown* album with "Uncle Pen." With no prompting from either the star or the record label, disc jockeys had begun to play the song as if it were a single. Soon requests began to build for the number. Slowly, from one region of the country to another, "Uncle Pen" was generating an audience. People were even buying the album just to get a copy of the song.

Still unconvinced, Sugar Hill bowed to Ricky's new star power and released the straight bluegrass song. It charted in July and moved quickly up the playlists, grabbing #1 in early October. Except for the *Hillbillies* theme, it was the first bluegrass song to ever own that position on the *Billboard* charts. The record label was surprised, Ricky was pleased, and for both public and private reasons, Bill Monroe was extremely proud.

Monroe had written "Uncle Pen" as a tribute for his own uncle, Pendleton Vandiver. Vandiver was the fiddle player who first turned Bill on to music. The old man would play his fiddle jigs for hours and the family would dance and sing to Uncle Pen's music. Monroe would remain close to Vandiver until the man died. Even then, as Bill continued to play the old man's music, it seemed that Uncle Pen came to life night after night on stages, in barns, and at dances where Monroe performed. Eventually overcome with memories, Bill put all of his emotions into a song about the effect Vandiver's music had had on the Kentucky hill people with whom Monroe had grown up. Yet, because bluegrass was never a very commercial form of music, Bill's "Uncle Pen" never found a large audience. Therefore Monroe thought that his Uncle Pen had never been given his just due. In a way the Country Music Hall of Famer thought he had let the old man down.

When Skaggs played "Uncle Pen" he also performed it as a tribute. The man Ricky honored with the song was his own idol, the father of bluegrass, Bill Monroe. Thus when "Uncle Pen" went #1, it gave both Ricky's and Bill's inspirations a chance to shine in the spotlight for a while. It was a long time coming, but the old Kentucky bluegrass finally grew a hit, and thanks to Ricky Skaggs, several more would follow. Seven decades after he played his last dance, Uncle Pen had finally made it to the big time.

1987
Forever and Ever, Amen

Written by Paul Overstreet and Don Schlitz

Don Schlitz had spent some time at Duke University before the urge to try to make it in the music business overcame his good sense. Packing his belongings, he left North Carolina and moved to Music City. Vanderbilt University offered him a late-night job in a computer room that paid the bills. When he wasn't sitting in front of a terminal and punching a keyboard, he had his hands wrapped around a guitar and was plucking strings.

For years Don labored without anyone noting his songs or his talent. Still, a few folks on Music Row kept their doors open to the polite young man. Many in the industry thought he was one of the greatest people they had ever met, but none of those who so wanted him to succeed could offer much more than encouragement. After years of hearing nothing but rejections, for reasons which he often didn't understand, Schlitz never gave up. Trying to pick up what he could learn from friends who had sold a few songs, Don kept honing his craft until his gamble finally paid off.

Another songwriter had showed Don a special way to retune his guitar. Schlitz was fascinated and began to play with the open chording sound. Within hours after he began to play, he picked up a pad and was scribbling down thoughts for a song. In short order he had written a riverboat classic, "The Gambler."

Suddenly Don found himself holding a full house. A host of folks were interested in cutting his new composition. Capitol thought so much of the song that they let Don himself cut it. The numbers weren't that good, a short seven-week ride and a top position of sixty-five, but it did get the songwriter and his work noticed. In late summer Kenny Rogers recorded Don's tune, and what followed was a hit song and a long line of made-for-television movies. After years of losing, Don now found himself holding a winning hand. "The Gambler's" success would make Schlitz one of Nashville's hottest songwriters.

Eight years later Don would team with a young man from Mississippi. Paul Overstreet had also labored almost unknown and unnoticed in Music City for years. Once caught in alcohol's web of confusion, Paul had turned his life around not long before he and Don began to write together. One of the first things they had penned was Randy Travis's "On the Other Hand." Not surprisingly, when that song hit the top of the charts, the hot young singer wanted the team to produce another golden moment for him.

The idea for the song which would become one of the finest written in country's modern age was taken from a combination prayer and exclamation of love. Don's son would often tell his wife, "Mommy, I love you forever and ever, amen." Thinking about the sweet innocence in that childhood message, Don took it to Paul. On a warm evening the two sat out on Overstreet's front porch and began to write.

"We wrote 'Forever and Ever, Amen' by candlelight," Paul remembered. "I was afraid if we turned the porch lights on it would attract bugs. We had to strain to see well enough just to write the words."

One of the song's key lines came from a now-funny but then-embarrassing experience. Paul's wife, Sarah, had been a hairdresser. Once she mixed the wrong solution and accidentally dyed a friend's hair green. Thankfully, the friend forgave Sarah and the two remained close. From that situation, the two scribes came up with a line about "loving me even if I were bald." Within two hours the perfectionists had crafted what they both believed was a sure winner.

Overstreet cut the demo with just a guitar and took it over to Travis's office. The singer liked it as well as the writing team had. Schlitz and Overstreet were now assured that if the song became a single, they would own another hit. After all, for the last year that was all the singer had turned out.

Randy Travis was hot. The Marshville, North Carolina, product had worked his way up through more than a decade of playing small clubs. Often in trouble with the law, he was saved from a possible life of crime by Lib Hatcher. The club owner brought him to Nashville, got him a gig at the Nashville Palace, and pushed Travis and his deep voice into stardom. Seemingly easygoing and good-looking in a rugged way, Randy was a mix of the old Ernest Tubb sound combined with new marketing and promotion. With Warner Brothers packaging him as a modern cowboy hero, Travis was perceived as a too-good-to-be-true, aw-shucks sex symbol. The only thing standing between Randy and climbing to the top of the country music heap was a few more #1's or one very spe-

cial song. When Lib and Randy heard "Forever and Ever, Amen," they sensed that this was that song.

Released in early April, the Schlitz/Overstreet single landed on the charts late in the month. The key element of Travis's *Always & Forever* album, the tune quickly climbed the playlists. In June, Randy knocked Dan Seals out of the top spot. "Forever and Ever, Amen" would hold #1 for three weeks, and take a twenty-two-week ride on the charts. At the CMA awards it would pull down the Single of the Year and secure male vocalist honors for Travis. *Always & Forever* would sell more than two million copies in a half a year thanks in large part to the wonderful first release. Just as Lib and Randy had surmised, this one big song did put the singer at the next level.

Randy Travis would build on "Forever and Ever, Amen" and push six straight records to the top of the playlists over the next two years. Within a year of the "Amen" release, Travis was the most recognized voice and face among the new breed of Nashville superstars. With songs like "Forever and Ever, Amen," his image was so solid that he appealed equally to grandmothers, mothers, and daughters. Even macho men took a liking to him. He spun this chart success off into wildly successful concert tours, movie roles, and television specials. Along with George Strait, Travis was setting the table for a huge country music explosion. Appealing to a large core of fans outside the normal country crowd, Travis had surpassed the success level of every previous country act except Alabama. For four years he was as hot as anyone in the music business, and Travis's success did more than just secure Randy's place at the top.

Paul Overstreet, who had grown up dreaming about becoming a music star, rode the sales of "Forever and Ever, Amen" to a recording contract of his own. Keeping positive songs at the heart of his message, Paul and RCA teamed for several hits in the early nineties.

Meanwhile, while Travis and Overstreet hit the road, Don Schlitz stayed home, wrote more hit songs, and made sure his wife never forgot that he loved her "forever and ever, amen." With the royalty checks still rolling in, it is doubtful she ever did.

1988

When You Say Nothing at All

Written by Paul Overstreet and Don Schlitz

If bad experiences are what great songwriters draw on to compose hits, then Paul Overstreet began to work overtime the day he left his small town home and hit Nashville, Tennessee. He put in long nights at bars playing in bands, all the while living adventures that had killed many a stronger man. When he wasn't on stage or working menial jobs to help pay the rent, he was living in seedy back rooms, picking his guitar, playing with words, and drinking whatever was around. Yet he was surprised when this wonderful new life that he had jumped into headfirst didn't provide much inspiration. It certainly didn't do much to make him a star. The negative lyrics that came out of his head simply matched the negative life that was slowly drowning him. Still, he was stubborn and didn't give up. It took years of wallowing in the mud until one night he came out of an alcohol-induced daze long enough to discover he was alone, unhappy, and with no real hope of achieving a single one of his boyhood dreams.

"On that night in 1984, in an old dim room," Paul recalled, "I looked back on my life and took inventory. I looked back on the things that I thought were important. As I thought about it, I found myself in a real miserable world. Yet the thing that was most ironic about this world was that it was pretty much what I had always designed and wanted. I was living the life of barrooms, booze, and long road trips, and these

were all the things that I thought would make me happy. Now I had discovered that for so many, many years, they had made me miserable.

"As I looked back over my whole life, I tried to find a point where I thought things were exciting, fun, joyful, and peaceful. And what I had come up with were the times when I was in church as a child.

"I thought long and hard about what was the difference between then and now. Then it came to me. The difference was that I had some people who cared about me then, and they were working with me, and they were trying to show me a way to have fun that would not make me miserable the next day. It wasn't like they were asking me to do anything special. It was just a lot of different people being together and enjoying each other."

Overstreet went back to church a few Sundays later; found the answers for his life in an old bible; made some wonderful, honest plain-talking friends; gave up drinking; and met a fine God-fearing woman who was to become his wife. In the process the songwriter found a lot of positive inspiration for his songs.

Like Paul Overstreet, Keith Whitley had grown up wanting to live the life of a country music star. A native of the backwoods Kentucky town of Sandy Hook, Keith began playing guitar before he attended first grade. By his teens he was in a bluegrass group that included Ricky Skaggs. In 1974, at the tender age of nineteen, he had joined bluegrass pioneer Ralph Stanley's band. Nine years later, after working as the lead vocalist in several groups, Whitley moved to Nashville. In his first year Keith landed a recording contract with RCA, and within two years he had married *Opry* legend George Morgan's talented daughter Lorrie.

For a man so young, Keith's public life was one filled with spectacular accomplishments. He was the shining example of what hard work, talent, and drive could do. However, in stark contrast, Whitley's private world had been a lesson in wasted time, energy, and money. When not on stage the young Keith had spent the nights with fast cars, moonshine whiskey, and brushes with death. Many around him had thought that he was either crazy or suicidal. He would drive down country roads at breakneck speeds all the while sipping on a bottle. He had had several wrecks, one that should have killed him on the spot. Yet somehow he had always survived and bounced back to party again. Like a cat, the singer seemed to have nine lives. His friends often questioned just how many he had left.

By the time Keith had gotten to Nashville, he had drunk enough booze to last two or three lifetimes. All those who loved him hoped that a solo RCA deal and a life filled with promise and direction would put the singer on the right track. They knew that Lorrie certainly loved him enough to give him reason to stay sober. Even though he probably didn't know it, there were a bunch of people praying for Keith Whitley.

Whitley's recording built slowly. In 1986 he hit the top ten for the first time. He followed that with several good marks in 1987, and the next year earned a #1 with "Don't Close Your Eyes." With his charisma and smooth voice, Keith was on his way to becoming one of Nashville's biggest stars. He was a great entertainer, and crowds loved him. What he needed was to capture his stage energy and enthusiasm in the studio.

Whitley knew all about the great work of Paul Overstreet and Don Schlitz. He had recorded their "Nobody in His Right Mind Would've Left Her" and "On the Other Hand," but he and RCA had elected not to release the cuts as singles. When the label held back, George Strait and Randy Travis put the songs out and earned #1's. Keith wasn't going to make the same mistake the third time. He was going to find something special that the two writers had done, cut it, then put it out.

The song which would become Whitley's biggest hit was a product of what had been a lousy and uncreative day. After working for hours, Schlitz and Overstreet had come up with nothing. In a sense both Don and Paul had hit the wall, and neither of them could get to the other side to find a fresh idea.

"We were just joking around humming and saying nothing," Paul remembered. "As we tried to find another way to say nothing, it led to the song."

It was funny to consider that having nothing which inspired the writers actually inspired them to compose "When You Say Nothing at All." While Overstreet and Schlitz thought the number was all right, they were not nearly as impressed with their work as Whitley was. He was overwhelmed with the song's overriding theme. In the anguish and sadness, he could hear magic. He wasn't going to sit on this song—he was going to cut it and release it in a hurry. He seemed to feel that this story was his life!

The *Billboard* playlist for the week of September 17, 1988, shows a bullet beside "When You Say Nothing at All." Keith had been right, the magic was there. The single actually went to #61 the first week on the charts. For Christmas, Santa would bring Whitley a #1 record. His record would stay at that position until the second week in January.

Keith Whitley would challenge Randy Travis and George Strait in the spring of 1989. One of these young men was going to nail down a spot as country music's most popular new star. When "I'm No Stranger to the Rain" topped the charts in April, everyone assumed that it would be Keith. RCA and the singer had found the right formula. Pulling out all the stops, producer Garth Fundis was capturing all the young man's life and energy in the studio. With a great song, "I Wonder Do You Think of Me," cut and waiting to be shipped, it looked as if the whole world was at Whitley's beck and call.

On May 8, 1989, Keith Whitley spent the night by himself. His wife was on the road. No one really knows why he began to drink that night or why he drank so much. Most thought his problems with alcohol were all behind him, but on this night they came back. Whitley was found dead just after midnight. His blood alcohol level was five times the state minimum for intoxication and almost twice the lethal limit for the human body. Having every reason to soberly enjoy his wonderful accomplishments, Keith had cho-

sen to drown himself and his genius in a sea of booze. He would never know that he won the CMA Single of the Year and that he would have three more huge hits. At thirty-three his life and work were tragically finished.

Paul Overstreet and Keith Whitley both possessed special gifts that allowed them to touch hearts with their music. While searching for their destiny, both men found themselves lost in a sea of alcohol and bad times. When Paul hit bottom, he discovered the answers he needed at a church. Among a group of new friends, Overstreet found people with whom he felt free to visit and reveal his fears and anguish. In return those new friends would be honest as well as loving. When Keith hit bottom, he told no one about his pain. As a matter of fact, he said nothing at all. He just died. Paul Overstreet knew when he got the word of Keith's death that, but by the grace of God, it could have been him.

1989
Are You Ready for Some Football?

Written by Hank Williams, Jr.

Hank Williams, Jr., recorded his first hit record before he earned a driver's license. Over the course of the next fifteen years Hank Jr. would chart some fifty different times, taking two songs to #1. Yet in spite of this wealth of successful material, he was rarely taken seriously. Music City didn't consider Williams a real talent, only the son of a real talent.

The singer/songwriter had been born Randall Hank Williams. On his own he had decided to change his name, and with the urging of friends and family he played off his God-given talents to ride his father's coattails. It worked too. Playing before thousands who had idolized his dad, Hank Jr. made them laugh, cry, and ante up big bucks for the opportunity to see the closest thing this old world had to the real Hank Williams.

After a while, the grind of living up to the legend got to the son. He was in his thirties, tired of being told what to sing and how to sing it. He was ready to stand on his own and find himself. Rejecting the advice of both his mother and his closest advisors, Hank Jr. began to work on a new kind of music in 1977. It was Southern rock, and it defined this man as the true son of the rebel his father had always been.

In 1978 he was ready to explode and make the real Hank Jr. known to the public. Using his first fifty singles as a platform, Williams went into the recording studio and leapt off into unknown territory. The singer called upon a host of influences in forging his new sound. Some, like Charlie Daniels and Merle Kilgore, were known in Nashville. Others, like Toy Caldwell and Chuck Leavell, were members of the rock movement. After a great deal of experimentation, Williams found a combination that he liked, and then Hank Jr. cut tracks that his label frankly didn't like. This controversial work resulted in the album *Hank Williams, Jr. & Friends.* The new Williams LP scared many promoters to death.

Music City's argument was, "Why change something that ain't broke?" Williams was selling pretty well, had earned a couple of #1's, and was drawing good crowds. But Hank didn't care what folks thought or what they wanted him to be. He wanted to show the world what he liked and who he really was. As it turned out, he almost didn't get the chance. While on a hunting trip in Montana, Williams fell five hundred feet off a cliff. It would be almost a year before he was able to work again.

The release of Hank's revolutionary album was put on hold while the singer recovered. When he finally hit the road again, Williams's new sound caught the industry and many fans by surprise. Most couldn't believe that Hank Sr.'s son would be performing that "rock junk." In many of the hardcore country fans' eyes, this was blasphemy. Things got so bad that more often more customers walked out of many of his shows than stayed. He once started a concert with four thousand paying customers jeering him en masse, and finished that same show with only two hundred people remaining until the bitter end. Yet those two hundred represented what would become a growing core of Dixie rock fans who kept Hank Jr. going.

The song which finally defined this rebel with a cause was "Family Tradition." Playing off his heritage while funneling in his new sound, Hank stood up and proudly declared that he was a lot more like his dad than anyone wanted to believe. As he pointed out, "Daddy wasn't no angel either."

"This was the pivotal song in Hank's career," his manager Merle Kilgore declared. "This was where the world found out who he really was and what his music sounded like. It was also where the industry figured out that this kind of stuff could sell too. Hank Jr. gave them a whole new market."

Over the course of the next few years, few acts were as hot as Williams. He played concert dates in huge arenas just to accommodate all those who wanted to see him. His fans, many of them high school and college students, represented a new generation of country music buyers. His music, brash, bold, and reflecting a man who liked to party hard and long, opened the door for a host of other acts who had once been considered too wild for Nashville. Ultimately, his sound would form the basis for the advent of the country bands of the late seventies and early eighties. Certainly a large number of the kids who embraced Alabama so enthusiastically first got hooked on country through Hank Jr.

During this hot period, George Greenberg of ABC-TV called Merle Kilgore. He had gotten a brainstorm and needed Hank in order to capitalize on it.

"He told me that ABC was getting involved with a new football league [the USFL] and wanted to know if I thought Hank would like to do a really hot song

for the opening. I thanked George for calling, told him that Hank did love both college football and the NFL, but he didn't have much use for the USFL. George thanked me for my time, and we said our good-byes. I forgot about that call until six years later."

In 1987 and 1988, Hank Jr. took home the trophy as the Country Music Association's Entertainer of the Year. His new-style music had earned him eight #1 songs, as well as seventeen others which had landed in the top ten. No country act during the era had done any better. He had won the right to stand on his own.

"I was working in the office one day," Merle Kilgore recalled, "and our phones were ringing off the wall. Hank was big news and everyone wanted him. At that time he was living down in Alabama and was dealing with some personal problems concerning a divorce. We had cut way back on work until we could get all the financial matters straightened out.

"I picked up the phone and on the other end of the line was George Greenberg. George was still with ABC and he had just gotten out of a meeting with the producers of *Monday Night Football*. They had been trying to come up with something special for their twentieth anniversary, and George had remembered that I had told him about Hank's love for the NFL. ABC wanted to know if Hank would write an opening song for the show. I told him that I thought it sounded like a great idea, and I'd discuss it with Hank."

Williams loved the idea as well. Taking his "All My Rowdy Friends" song, he came up with a catch line, "Are you ready for some football?" Hank knew that *Monday Night Football* had actually become bigger than the game itself. The show was now an event. People planned their Monday evenings around it. The three announcers were stars. So Hank played on that theme and reworked the catchy, tough country rocker "All My Rowdy Friends" into something that

ABC loved. They cut several different versions for each of their games. When it premiered, it scored like no theme song ever associated with a sporting event.

Within weeks fans were holding up signs to television cameras asking, "Are you ready for some football?" The phrase "Are you ready?" soon became America's favorite question. Because of the worldwide popularity of *Monday Night Football,* kids around the world who didn't speak a word of English and had never heard of country music could sing all of Hank's football song. It didn't take long for the industry to figure out just how perfect this marriage of sport and country music was.

"Are You Ready for Some Football?" won an Emmy for the best theme song on television in its initial year on the air. This was the first time a country music song had ever been so honored. The theme would come back and win three more Emmys over the next four years. In the football form this song had never been a single, never spent a day on the charts, but it had become Williams's most beloved hit. At concerts Hank's crowds would demand the new version of "All My Rowdy Friends."

In 1993, ABC decided that "Are You Ready for Some Football?" had lost its punch. They scrapped the song in favor of a host of different rock and rap tunes. In a move that surprised the network, the fans rebelled. They wanted Hank Jr.'s song. ABC even discovered that a host of viewers who weren't football

fans had watched *Monday Night Football*'s opening each week just to listen to the theme. When the country music stopped, those viewers had switched over to *Murphy Brown.*

In an unprecedented move, ABC brought "Are You Ready" back in 1994. Hank's song again proved such a powerful marketing and identity tool that ABC invited the singer to perform it at the pregame ceremonies of the Super Bowl. As Hank Jr. sang, fifty thousand people joined in.

In the history of country music "Are You Ready for Some Football?" stands alone with "High Noon" in having captured a special award given completely outside the music industry. Yet even without the award, Hank's song is worthy of recognition because it represents the power of country music in today's society. In a very real sense, the musical form which Williams himself helped expand now belongs not just to the South, but to the whole world. Even on a worldwide basis, country music defines moments, games, people, places, and cultures. It brings folks together and brings out emotion on a larger scale than ever before.

In 1979 Hank Williams, Jr., asked the world if it was ready to listen to the real Hank Jr. Ten years later, the man whom the world had finally accepted on his own merits posed the same question about football. "Are you ready?" And the answer was a resounding "Yes!" Now it is impossible to think of *Monday Night Football* and not remember a country music song.

1990
When I Call Your Name

Written by Vince Gill and Tim DuBois

There are lots of country music singers who have embraced golf as a hobby. It is often said that more deals are cut on the golf course than on Music Row. Yet only one country music superstar had to choose between a career on the links and one in the flood-lights. It was a talented Oklahoman who had earned a powerful bluegrass reputation who had to make that hard choice between drivers and guitars. The fact was that his golf strokes were almost as good as his guitar riffs.

Vince Gill, the son of a judge, had worked early in his performing career with a young Ricky Skaggs. With bluegrass interest at a low, Gill left Nashville before Skaggs hit pay dirt in the late seventies. Vince worked as a guitar picker in Los Angeles for a while, eventually ending up with the country rock band Pure Prairie League.

As he worked with Pure Prairie League, Gill's talents as both a lead vocalist and songwriter grew within the music community. The group's biggest hits, such as the top-ten "Let Me Love You Tonight," came from Vince's pen, but none of these songs were able to do much more than keep Gill's career going. Even with long tours and months on the road, Pure Prairie gave no signs of really taking off. Sensing he needed a new direction to reach his poten-tial, Vince left the rock group and joined Rodney

Crowell's band. At about the same time, his wife Janis was beginning to find fame as a member of the Sweethearts of the Rodeo. While he was with Crow-ell, Nashville began to take note of Vince's work. RCA called and offered him a record deal. The label announced that it had great plans for three new acts, Louise Mandrell, The Judds, and Gill. RCA Nashville predicted all would quickly become major stars.

Though they tried for four years, RCA and Vince couldn't come up with a major record. Most of his songs managed modest chart success, but none made much money for either him or the label. Both the Judds and Louise Mandrell were scoring far bet-ter. By 1988 RCA dropped Gill and concentrated on finding other new acts. Vince would have probably drifted along for years had it not been for Tim DuBois and MCA.

DuBois had long recognized Gill's talent and charm. He thought that Vince was one of the best vocalists in music, but for reasons that escaped DuBois, RCA had not chosen material that made this fact known. Somehow Vince had been turned into a rocker when his voice was made to order for ballads.

"It was frustrating for me to watch Vince not get a chance to break through," Tim recalled. "Here was this wonderful guy with so much talent and he couldn't seem to get a real opportunity to show his stuff."

In an effort to help his friend, DuBois and Vince worked on songs for the singer's first MCA release. Some of them followed a rodeo theme, while others centered on a pop sound. Gill was not going to be limited to one style or theme. Yet as their collaboration continued, one Gill/DuBois number began to stand out.

"When our fields were dry, God provided rain," DuBois explained as he talked about the crowning achievement of their efforts. "We had been working for quite a while when Vince shared the idea for 'When I Call Your Name.' "

Gill and his wife spent so much time apart because of their careers that more often than not when Vince did get home, he was alone. The personal loneliness that Gill felt when he called his wife's name and no one answered just ate at his soul. He told Tim he wanted to find a way to wrap those emotions in a song.

"I feel fortunate to have just gotten a chance to help him on the song," Tim admitted. "Most of the song was his. It just came from inside him, from his life at that time, and I added a bit here and there. I would love to tell a wonderful long story about what inspired the song for me, but that wouldn't be true. It was Vince's inspiration. And when we started writing it was just like God providing rain, the song's words just seemed to fall in place. When we completed it I knew that it was special. Still, Vince had never been able to get a break. Even when I listened to 'When I Call Your Name,' I had to wonder if the public was going to miss this wonderful effort too."

For a while it seemed that MCA was going to miss the Gill/DuBois song altogether. The label picked "Never Alone" as the first release from the session. In spite of having the then-hot Rosanne Cash provide harmony vocals, the single failed to break into the top twenty. Next the label shipped "Oklahoma Swing." The fast-paced dance duet featured country's most popular female star, Reba McEntire. While the single did stay on the charts for half a year, it also failed to make it to the top ten, peaking at #13. Finally, MCA gave Vince a shot to score on his own and tried "When I Call Your Name."

The Gill/DuBois single hit the charts in May 1990, climbing to the second position on the playlist. With Patty Loveless adding harmonies, the single was the year's most requested love song. It probably saved Gill's recording contract, while also making him a major star. Suddenly the world was ready for his sincere vocal style, his tight guitar work, and his bashful good looks. After ten years of trying, he was finally being recognized. Vince Gill had become a household name.

"When I Call Your Name" would win a Grammy and be named the Country Music Association's Single of the Year. Within two years Vince would become the hottest act in country music, winning so many awards that the CMA annual awards fest would become known as the "Vince Gill Show." Out of the sidelight, he had been thrust suddenly into the spotlight, and was making millions of fans in both pop and country circles. Suddenly Gill was living up not only to his dreams, but to others' expectations too. He finally knew that he had made the right choice when he had chosen music over the golf tour.

"When I Call Your Name" was a song whose words fell like rain. Those words made a superstar out of Vince Gill and positioned Tim DuBois to begin the Nashville wing of Arista Records. In their respective positions both men would have profound effects on Music City over the next five years. Yet as big as Vince and Tim had become, their haunting lyrics and melody might just outlive them both. There is a timeless grace which surrounds "When I Call Your Name," and because of that quality, this song will probably become a hit many more times in both country and pop music.

1990
Friends in Low Places

Written by DeWayne Blackwell and Earl "Bud" Lee

Earl "Bud" Lee grew up in Florida playing guitar and dreaming of making it in the music business. His background was not much different from thousands of other dreamers except that he followed his dream. When he had the opportunity he took it. Scraping together enough money for a few months' expenses, Lee left home in 1980, moved to Nashville, and gave songwriting a shot. Once in town, he hit the streets and began to get to know the area around Music Row. Visiting with every songwriter who had ever sold a song, Bud asked questions and tried to pick up pointers on how to write and polish ideas. One of those Lee met and questioned was a Music City legend, Harlan Howard.

"I can't say enough about Harlan," Lee explained. "This guy is a legend. He had written so many classic songs, and yet he still helps the guys on their way up. He doesn't have to do it, he just does. I can't begin to tell you how much Harlan taught me. I may have had some natural talent, but he is the guy who polished my skills. He pulled me up."

When his skills were refined enough to impress the professionals, Bud latched on to a writing contract at Mary Tyler Moore Music. At that time MTM was attempting to make a mark in country music, and they had several acts which were doing very well. Over time the label would be overwhelmed by other companies with more money, but in the early eighties MTM was a pretty good place to be. For Bud Lee it was a great place to start.

"One of the folks I met during my days at MTM was DeWayne Blackwell," Bud recalled. "He was another songwriter who like Harlan, had credits that went back a long time. DeWayne had written songs like 'Mr. Blue' early in his career, and numbers like 'I'm Gonna Hire a Wino to Decorate Our Home' after he came to Nashville. I was real fortunate to have a chance to write with him."

Several years after DeWayne and Bud began to pool their efforts, they joined a couple of other writers for lunch at Tavern on the Row. As they ate the group swapped song ideas, sports stories, and the latest Music City news. When the check came, they all looked to the man who had invited them. He had forgotten his billfold. Another guy didn't have any cash.

"How are we going to pay for this?" DeWayne joked.

"Don't worry," Bud said with a laugh, "I've got friends in low places. I know the cook." Everyone grinned, and then someone pulled out a credit card and picked up the tab.

"DeWayne and I knew at that moment," Bud remembered, "that the line 'I've got friends in low places' would be perfect for a song. Yet other than jotting it down, we didn't do anything else about it then."

A few days later the two decided to celebrate some chart action by buying a new pair of boots. As they shopped, a clean-cut young man from Oklahoma inquired if they needed any help. The friendly employee pulled several different pairs of boots for the men, explaining the pros and cons of each.

"We really liked this guy," Bud admitted. "He was polite and doing everything he could to make sure we got a good deal."

Eventually the store clerk got around to asking just what it was the two men did. When he discovered that they were songwriters, the young man began to tell them about his own dreams. It seems his mother had once sung on Red Foley's *Ozark Jubilee,* and she had even recorded a little in the fifties. He had grown up singing too. In college he'd had some success in clubs. The writers even found out that this was the young man's third try at establishing himself in Nashville.

"He was newly married," Bud explained, "and working as hard as he could. He had already made a few contacts in town, but he knew he needed more. What he really wanted to do was sing on some demos. We told him that we would give him a try. We found out he was pretty good, so for the next few months we used him on a lot of our stuff."

The young sales clerk's name was Garth Brooks. And when Blackwell and Lee got him into the studio, they sensed that there was some good raw talent here. The guy had a smooth voice in the Gary Morris vein. He wasn't really country and he certainly wasn't pop, but used in the right manner, Garth could probably turn some heads and sell some records. Of course the songwriters saw great talent every day, and most of it was never discovered. As much as they would have liked to see this guy score with a label, they knew it would be a long shot.

"A few months later DeWayne and I were at a party celebrating a number-one record for a friend of ours," Bud recalled. "While we were there we got to talking about our friends-in-low-places idea. For some reason, at that very moment, it all started to come together in a song. We looked for a pad or piece of paper, but nobody had one. We ended up writing the entire song on a series of napkins. Later, when we had polished it, we called Garth and asked him if he could cut a demo for us."

When Brooks came by the studio he excitedly informed the writers that he had landed a deal with Capitol Records. They had just produced his first album and he had a single that was going to be released in just a couple of weeks. While Blackwell and Lee were pleased, they also realized that this meant they were going to need to find a new guy to cut their demos.

After Garth finished the session, he walked up to Bud and thanked him for all his help. He then commented on the number they had just cut. "Why couldn't we have done this a few weeks ago when I was looking for material. I love this song." Lee shrugged his shoulders. The two shook hands and Brooks left.

Using the new demo the duo pitched the song to another fresh talent, Mark Chesnutt. Mark liked "Friends in Low Places" and cut it, but the song did nothing. At that point the scribes moved on to other things and forgot about "Friends." Then a year later, Brooks called them back. He was doing his second album and wanted to know if he could use their song. Blackwell and Lee gave it to him and waited to see what would happen.

Working with Allen Reynolds, a Capitol producer, Garth had developed a relaxed, almost casual vocal style that was making him one of the hottest new stars in the business. Thanks to songs like "If Tomorrow Never Comes," he was really connecting with the young fans. On most of his early work, he was even contributing to the writing. Yet when Brooks got ready to record his second album, he wanted to introduce his producer to two guys who had given him one of his first breaks. As Lee would later remark, "I guess he wanted to show his label that he had friends in low places."

Reynolds liked the Blackwell/Lee effort, and decided to make it the showpiece of Garth's second album. While both he and Brooks thought it had hit potential, neither of them could have guessed just how much this song would mean to the singer, the writers, or the expansion of country music.

Released in mid-summer, the single jumped on the charts in August 1990. For twenty weeks it would remain on every playlist in America, becoming the most programmed song of the year. By far Brooks's biggest record, "Friends in Low Places" stayed at the top of the charts for a month. It was the CMA's Single of the Year, and would become the signature song for an artist who would go from selling boots in 1988 to making more than $50 million in 1991.

"When Garth released 'Friends in Low Places,'" Bud remembered, "things got completely out of control. It sold and sold and sold. We couldn't believe it. It certainly made that trip to buy boots worthwhile.

The last report I received indicated that the song had recorded over fifteen million worldwide sales in both single and album form."

"Friends in Low Places" would become the biggest-selling country single of all time. With lavish concerts, double and triple platinum albums, spectacular television specials, and more awards than he could count, Garth Brooks had quickly evolved beyond even the superstar label.

What happened to Brooks, as well as to DeWayne Blackwell and Bud Lee and their song, points to the immense power and popularity of country music in the nineties. Once Nashville and the genre was looked down on by those in rock because country music couldn't bring home the really big money. Many of country music's hottest stars had even tried to go the rock or pop route just to get a taste of large royalty checks and huge concert draws. Brooks's mega-star status put country music on equal financial footing with its old rivals. And just think, it all started with a bad joke, a pair of boots, and a demo record. Or maybe it really started when Harlan Howard stopped to befriend a young Bud Lee and give him some songwriting pointers. I guess you could say that Harlan's friend in low places did all right for himself and the business.

1991
Don't Rock the Jukebox

Written by Alan Jackson, Roger Murra, and Keith Stegall

In 1985 Alan Jackson was just a former construction worker from Newman, Georgia, who had come to Nashville in hopes of landing a recording contract and making it big in country music. Jackson would quickly live the story that thousands of others had lived over the past five decades. He would walk in their steps and have the same doors close in his face. The hard reality of fact smashing his idyllic dreams would hit him in the heart time and time again. For all of his telephone calls and personal visits, over the course of his first few months in Music City Jackson would make just one contact in the business, a short-order cook who sang part-time at the Nashville Palace. That cook's name was Randy Travis, and he was just as frustrated as Alan.

Landing a job as a mail-room clerk for TNN, Jackson had his hands on some of the most important, career-making letters in Nashville. Unfortunately, he couldn't seem to do much more than get his fingerprints on them. Turned down by countless talent agents, Alan found bits and pieces of work at small clubs, banked his check from the mailroom, and thanked the Lord each night that his wife Becky had a solid job as a flight attendant. Common sense would have told him to go home, but the stubborn young man stuck it out.

After more than a year of polishing his songwriting skills, Jackson finally landed a job as a staff writer and made enough money to quit his day job in the cable network's mail room. Forming a band, Alan began to develop his own sound. Yet while old friend Travis was making noise on the charts and appearing on network specials, Alan was working far away from the spotlights in dingy honky-tonks. For three years the situation continued. It seemed that everyone agreed that Alan was good enough to earn a record deal, but no one was ready to make the move and sign him. It appeared that there was just no room for a new hat in the business. On lonely nights as he ended his shows, he would often walk over to a jukebox, see Randy Travis's name, and wish that he could somehow join his old friend. As the nights turned to weeks and the weeks into years, it looked as if it was never going to happen.

In 1989 Arista Records noted the huge growth of country music and decided to open a Nashville office. Tim DuBois, a talented songwriter/manager who had been instrumental in Vince Gill's career, had been hired to run the label's Music City thrust. DuBois quickly used that power to sign Jackson. Tim had noted Alan's voice and stage charisma a few years before, but he had been able to do nothing then. Now, with a label behind him, he was ready and able to mold the young man into a star.

With Arista behind him, the tall Jackson charmed listeners from the start. After releasing several records which played near the top spot for a year, Alan peaked with "I'd Love You All Over Again." Coming off a platinum album and with worldwide star status, he informed Becky that she could finally quit supporting them. Few people had ever gone from being so far out to so far in so quickly.

Becoming Nashville's hottest new act was quite an adjustment. Alan Jackson was now receiving more mail than he used to deliver. His road shows were playing to sold-out audiences filled with screaming women who thought of the happily married singer as country music's hottest hunk. As Alan began to pick up major award after major award, he appeared to be riding a wave of popularity that would never end.

Tim DuBois was well aware that becoming so hot so quickly could spell doom just as easily as it spelled lasting success. Country music now dismissed stars as quickly as it made them. Folks who were hot one day found themselves without a record deal the next. All it took was one bad record for the town and the fans to sour on an artist. Therefore Arista was going to have to release a strong follow-up for Jackson. The next release needed to be a song that would identify him as a lasting force, not just another quick-hitting and suddenly missing star.

"When the band had been on the road," songwriter Roger Murra recalled, "they had stopped in a diner to eat. Alan was listening to the jukebox when one of the band members leaned up against it. That sudden bumping caused the record that was playing to skip a little. Alan liked the song, so he warned the guy, 'Don't rock the jukebox.' He realized immediately that the phrase had real song potential."

Jackson, Murra, and Keith Stegall sat down to work on the "Don't Rock the Jukebox" concept just as soon as Alan returned from his tour. It wouldn't take long for the trio to come up with a final product.

"We decided to tie rock and country together," Roger explained as he recalled the essence of the session. "So we just began to mate things like the Rolling Stones and George Jones. It all came together in practically no time."

Murra, who had been a background player in Nashville since 1972, had a wealth of experience in songwriting. A former member of the *Ozark Jubilee*, the singer/songwriter had already penned such hits as "Life's Highway" and "We're in This Love Together." His talents were well respected by both of the other contributors.

Stegall was also a well-versed country music veteran. Alan Jackson was still in diapers when Keith had formed his first band. By 1980 he had a recording contract and had toured Europe. Yet in his eleven releases for three different labels, Stegall has been unable to score big. By the late eighties Keith, like Murra, had almost exclusively turned to songwriting.

When the trio had completed Jackson's idea, the singer passed it on to Tim DuBois. The record executive liked the composition. He sensed that this just might become the song which could make his rising star into a major player with a very long-playing chart life. Tim booked the studio and while Alan cut the single, the Arista publicity folks went to work supporting the song.

"Don't Rock the Jukebox" was released in the spring of 1989. It jumped onto playlists in May, and rocked its way to #1 in July. Alan would hold the top spot for three weeks, beating all competition for the year's hottest song. "Don't Rock the Jukebox" didn't stop at just being the best-charting single of 1989. It also went gold in just two months, and platinum before the year was completed. Needless to say, four years after Jackson warned his band member about leaning on a diner's jukebox, jukeboxes around the world were still spinning the disk.

Since the forties, country music has seen a rush of

songs which used the jukebox as their central theme. "I'm a Truck-Driving Man," "It Wasn't God Who Made Honky-Tonk Angels," and "Drinking My Baby off My Mind" were three of the biggest to embrace the record-playing machine in their lyrics. Yet "Don't Rock the Jukebox" took the message of all of those songs and moved a step further. In the Jackson classic, the jukebox was no longer a background player, it was the song's star.

"I guess that timing is everything," Murra noted. " 'Don't Rock the Jukebox' was so radio-friendly. Because of that, it rode the crest of a younger generation coming from rock to country. It really mirrored what was happening to country music in real life." And as it rode the charts the song also put the spotlight on one of country music's best friends.

The jukebox had long been a staple at every truck stop and honky-tonk. It was as much a part of country music history as dancing, drinking, cheating, lying, and loving. These colorful music boxes often played the hits first, and usually were still booming them out long after radio had moved onto something else. They have always given and still give the fans the ultimate choice—to literally reach out and directly pick the play that they really want to hear. In an age when the boundaries between country, pop, and rock have become razor thin, "Don't Rock the Jukebox" became the country music fan's ultimate anthem. It gave words to an idea that had been brewing since rockabilly first scared Music City in 1956. It wouldn't be hard to image Webb Pierce, Hank Snow, and Ernest Tubb warning country music fans, "Don't Rock the Jukebox."

1992
Is There Life Out There

Written by Susan Longacre and Rick Giles

When he was a kid, Rick Giles played guitar and often told his folks about his plans to make it in music. They discouraged him, informed him his future in show business would be limited at best, and asked him to set his sights on business. He listened to their words of wisdom, and after finishing his education, moved to Washington, D.C., and became a very successful buyer for a large retail department store. Rick was a yuppie who was on his way up the ladder. Just in his twenties, he was making good money and had a bright future. His parents were justifiably proud.

"I may have been successful," Rick explained, "but I wanted more. I wanted to be the star of the world. Looking back on it now, my ego was really out of control at that time."

Against the advice of everyone he knew, the cocky Giles quit his job to make it in the music business. It wasn't nearly as easy as he thought it would be. For ten years he tried to write and perform. A decade of work produced just one song that charted, a minor rock hit that Rick had penned for a band called Silver. His greatest accomplishment was entitled "Wham Bam (Shang-A-Lang)."

"I was thirty-five and at the end of my rope," the songwriter remembered. "I wondered if there was any hope that I would ever make it in the business."

Rick had fallen a long way since his days in retail sales. He had gone from confident and brash to depressed and doubting. Between 1976 and 1982 he wrote no songs. In the middle of the long dry run Rick met a beautiful, young, level-headed woman in D.C.

"When Pat and I got married," he remembered, "she told me to do one thing or another. I either had to go back into the real world of business or write full time. A New York publisher hooked me up to a co-writer in Nashville, and I got involved in country music."

Rick moved to Nashville and began to make some headway. Getting his feet planted firmly on the ground, he sold some of his material. As he approached his fourth decade, he was no longer cocky, but he was also not in the least depressed. He may not have been the world's biggest star, but Giles had finally found happiness and his writing showed his spirit.

Producing songs like "Jealous Bone," "Wild Man," "A Woman Loves," and several other top-ten cuts, Rick found his skills in demand. At just about the same time he was starting to feel successful, he met a young woman whose songwriting talents seem to mesh very well with his own. In his brasher days he would have refused to work with anyone, but the now-settled Giles gladly welcomed the advice of this fellow scribe. Rick felt he could learn a lot from the woman who had penned "Leave Him Out of This."

"One day Susan Longacre came into the studio with an idea that she didn't feel was commercial, but she wanted to write it anyway," Rick explained. "It was the story of her stepmother. It seemed that after her kids left home, she had lost most of her own identity. As Susan talked, I thought about my grandmother and how she had gone through the same thing. The loneliness and emptiness of that situation really hit me, and the two of us began to play with the idea.

"We wrote the song with weird verses. They had five lines, but in spite of the fact that this wasn't a normally formatted song, it came together quickly. I did a demo and then we started to pitch it."

One of the first artists Rick took it to was a Canadian singer who was just beginning to make her mark south of the border. Michelle Wright liked the song, but her manager didn't think it was a song she should be singing to women.

"Susan and I really felt strongly about the message in 'Is There Life Out There,'" Rick explained, "and we didn't want to change any of the words. So Michelle passed on it. Lorrie Morgan passed too. Lorrie had a real problem with the line 'Is there life beyond my family and my home?' Both singers thought that wives and mothers would really be upset with that question. Still, we wouldn't change it."

"Is There Life Out There" soon found its way to Tim DuBois, who pitched it unsuccessfully to Steve Wariner. From Steve the song traveled over to Starstruck Entertainment and Reba McEntire. "Is There Life Out There" was thrown in with a batch of two dozen other songs being considered for Reba's next session.

"I don't know why I felt this way," Rick remembered, "I had no reason to, but it just seemed to me that the song was perfect for Reba. I was so sure that she was going to cut it that I called Susan and assured her that it was going to be not only on Reba's next album, but it would be a single and it would be a hit."

As Giles would later find out, it was never a sure thing. McEntire was drawn to the song, but she was having problems getting it right. She considered dropping it. Reba finally changed the tempo, played with the phrasing a bit, and came up with a cut that satisfied her. Still, she had questions. It was only later, when they reviewed the whole session, that MCA and the singer agreed that "Is There Life Out There" was going to be the redhead's forty-seventh single.

Reba had grown up in Oklahoma singing with her sisters and brother. A college graduate, she had planned on teaching elementary school. Then Red Sovine heard her perform the "Star-Spangled Banner" at a rodeo and convinced her to give country music a try. A stylist in the mold of Patsy Cline, Reba placed no limits on her music, her career, or herself. Driven and intelligent, she was constantly pushing herself to new levels of performance. Sixteen years after coming to town, McEntire had risen to the status of Music City's dominant female talent.

Reba was one of the first Nashville performers to understand the real power of video. While some established stars were avoiding the new medium, considering it a trashy gimmick, and others simply used filmed concert footage for their video productions, McEntire was making mini-movies. Her videos were not only as affecting as her vocals, they often developed emotional edges that cut even deeper. In "Whoever's in New England" viewers could see how it felt to be the other woman. "Sunday Kind of Love" presented the emotions of homecomings in a fashion long since forgotten in Hollywood. Because McEntire used this creative avenue to its full potential, the release of each of Reba's videos had become an event, and the singer always had folks guessing just what she would do next.

One of the reasons Reba's star had risen so high for so long was that she surrounded herself with bright, talented people. When she needed someone to write a video to match the haunting "Is There Life Out There," she turned to no less than a Harvard graduate.

Alice Randall was intrigued by the message she found in the Giles/Longacre piece. As she went to work on the script, the African-American woman couldn't help but think of her own mother. Alice knew that her mom must have been dealing with the same kind of emotions as Rick and Susan had written about in their song.

"My mother," Alice explained, "went back to school when I was growing up. While she was raising her family, she earned both a college and a graduate degree. So much of what I put in that script was her story. She taught me about literature, and like the mother in the story, my mother knew how much it meant. When we presented Reba's character reading '[I Know Why] The Caged Bird Sings' to her daughter, that was one of my mother's favorite stories. It was like she was reading it to me."

Scripting the video, Alice Randall found herself being magically transported back to her youth. In vivid detail she recalled the measured lessons her mother's sacrifice had taught her. She realized just how much her mother's efforts had been responsible for shaping Alice's own life.

"Mother taught me," Ms. Randall declared, "that education was the one thing that no one could take from you. They could take away your house, your health, your car, and everything you owned, but they couldn't take away what you had learned."

The video of "Is There Life Out There" became one of the most remarkable pieces of film ever shot in Nashville. Using Belmont College for many of the background scenes, the mini-movie cast Reba as mother, wife, and waitress trying to juggle all aspects of her life while working to achieve her dream of going to college. Too old to fit in with the other students, wearing clothes that were ragged and worn, trying to pick up where she left off two decades before, she struggled, but never gave up. In the end she celebrated with her family as she accepted her diploma.

The video was so well done that the preview brought tears to most eyes. Yet if CMT and TNN would have had their way, "Is There Life Out There" would have never aired. The two networks objected to the video's length, well over four minutes, and the fact that it had dialogue mixed in with the music. They wanted it cut into a standard video format. They felt that a video should only present the song, no more.

Reba went to bat to save her best work. Lobbying in print and on talk shows, she forced the cable outlets to give "Is There Life Out There" a fair shot. When CMT and TNN relented and ran the video, they were overwhelmed by viewer response. Within days of the initial airing, Reba was in heavy rotation.

Just weeks after the video and record's release, "Is There Life Out There" jumped on the playlists. The composition which Susan and Rick had determined wasn't commercial, but wrote anyway, would hit #1 in late March. "Is There Life Out There" would spend two weeks anchored at the top spot, and have a chart run that would last from January through June. Yet even more remarkable than the song's strong sales was the effect it was having on thousands of women.

"Not long after the record was released," Reba remembered, "I had women of all ages who were coming up to me after my concerts. They were thanking me because the "Is There Life Out There" video had inspired them to go back to school. Others came up to me and told me that because of that video, they had gotten their GED. There were women in their sixties and seventies as well as young mothers who were stopping to tell me what that video had inspired them to do. I was overwhelmed."

Several different national education agencies estimated that the Alice Randall-scripted video had been the motivating factor for driving as many as forty thousand women back to either high school or college. Some college classes even adopted the song as their theme.

In its original form "Is There Life Out There" posed a question about whether there was anything left for a woman who had raised her children and watched them leave the nest. The song grew into a music video (and later a movie) which not only answered that question in a triumphant manner, but presented a formula for thousands of women who wanted so badly to move out of a place where they felt trapped and unappreciated. Here was a song and a video that came to mean much more than anyone could have imagined.

"Is There Life Out There" accomplished something else important too. It showed the real power of country music video. The new age had arrived, and artists could use this new medium as not only a creative and marketing outlet, but as a forum to inspire and motivate. Few would have believed in 1927 that hillbilly music would ever be a factor in a dramatic increase in college enrollment, but then again, who would have guessed back then that country music would grow into America's most beloved art form? Just like Reba's video character, country music has graduated and found its potential unlimited. Yes, there is a lot of life out there!

Holiday Bonus (1950)
I'll Have a Blue Christmas (Without You)

Written by Jay Johnson and Billy Hayes

As usual, Jay Johnson was running late. He had been slow getting started that morning, and the cold rainy weather wasn't helping at all. On top of that, his green 1939 Mercury convertible had developed a huge rip just above the driver's seat, and water was pouring through the growing hole onto his head. Pulling the car off to the side of the road, the forty-five-year-old Johnson rummaged among the papers he kept in his backseat until he found an umbrella. He pushed it through the hole in the canvas top, then hit the button allowing it to open. Shifting into first gear, he eased the car back onto the road, with the umbrella keeping most of the water out of the car. Jay continued on to the Stamford, Connecticut, train station.

A script and commercial jingle writer for radio, Johnson was on his way to New York, a daily commute that included a one-hour train junket. It was during these trips that Jay would catch up on the postwar news in the paper, work word puzzles, and scribble down inspiration for story lines and songs. His daughter remembers her father as a man driven by creative challenges.

"He often wrote or worked as he rode on the trains," recalled Judy Olmsted. "I am sure that if he were alive today he would have had a laptop computer. He loved to play with words. He made up all kinds of limericks and poems. He wrote for some of the top shows on radio and later on television too. He was a vaudeville veteran, played around with Broad-

way shows, and even published dozens of songs. Some of their titles were almost as funny as the lyrics. They included 'Peaceful,' 'Little Wedding Bells,' 'Telephone Fever,' 'Sunday Afternoon,' and one of my favorites, 'Peter Pan the Meter Man.' That title alone tells you how his mind worked."

On this particular rainy day, as the train chugged toward the Big Apple, Johnson pulled out an old piece of hotel stationery. The holiday season was just around the corner, and tunes like Irving Berlin's "White Christmas" were being written into many of the radio shows for which he worked. As Jay considered the long list of Christmas classics he could draw from for his scripts, an original idea began to take shape. At first glance it seemed almost too obvious. With the success of "White Christmas" and the tremendous impact of blues music during the forties, surely, Johnson thought, someone had combined the two concepts into a song. A number about a blue Christmas seemed so natural. Yet as he considered the idea, he suddenly and happily realized that no one had yet tackled this play on words. Picking up a pen he scribbled down his first thoughts.

I expect to have a colorful Christmas
tinged with every kind of holiday hue,
and though I know I'll find every shade in the rainbow,
this design of mine will be mostly blue.

These lines were destined to become the rough first verse of a lyric sheet which Johnson would call "Blue Christmas." Over the course of the next few days several more verses followed. Once Jay was satisfied with all his words, he met with friend and composer Billy Hayes.

Though no one recalls, Hayes probably offered a few suggestions about the lyrics. Long before the two men finished the song, Johnson's first two verses were dropped. Using the writer's later lines, Billy neatly wrapped the package with an appropriate musical score. The finished song was then sold to Choice Music.

It was copyrighted in 1948, and Choice Music began to shop their new holiday number. As a novelty and hillbilly specialty company, Choice most likely attempted to interest a number of Nashville artists in "Blue Christmas." If they did, no one noted the song's potential and jumped on board. The first act to record the tune was a pop band, Hugo Winterhalter and His Orchestra.

Winterhalter had worked as an arranger for the likes of Count Basie, Tommy and Jimmy Dorsey, and Claude Thornhill before putting together his own group. In late 1949 he had hit the charts for the first time with "Jealous Heart." When he recorded the Johnson/Hayes holiday offering in the earlier winter, Columbia hoped that it would land their new star in the top ten. Hugo's "Blue Christmas" did just that, topping out at #9. A year later the song would undertake another successful run up the pop charts for the band leader. Still, these modest numbers didn't forecast a long run on the hit parade. At that time "Blue Christmas" was far behind holiday standards such as "Silver Bells," "White Christmas," "Rudolph," and "I'll Be Home for Christmas" in both recognition and popularity. Most felt it would be soon forgotten.

Ernest Tubb must have heard the song during its initial Winterhalter release, because the Texas Troubadour worked it into his act at about that time. A year later, in 1950, he cut the number for Decca and took it to the top of the country charts. For the next five years "Blue Christmas" would become Tubb's holiday theme song and standard hit fodder for country radio playlists.

Before Tubb's "Blue Christmas," Gene Autry had scored big numbers with "Rudolph" and "Here Comes Santa Claus," but those songs were really children's numbers. With its lonesome message and clever lyrics, "Blue Christmas" was truly a hillbilly ode. It may have been written on an East Coast commuter train, but when Tubb vocalized it, it seemed to owe a great deal more to Nashville than New York. So many people identified it with Ernest Tubb that he was often referred to as "Blue Christmas's" writer. While he had contributed nothing to the song's lyrics or score, Tubb had put it on the map and shaped it into a country music standard. Because of the tall Texan "Blue Christmas" became country music's first true Christmas classic.

By the mid-fifties almost every country act was using "Blue Christmas" in their November and December shows. While still performed from time to time in pop music, by the late fifties the Johnson/Hayes number had seemingly established itself as a country epic. It was one song that had put some twang in the mistletoe. "Blue Christmas" probably would have remained strictly a part of the Music City genre if not for a young singer who had grown up idolizing Ernest Tubb.

Elvis Presley had listened to a lot of black blues and white Southern gospel during his youth, but he had also spent a great deal of time checking out certain country acts. The one and only time he worked the *Opry* he had even met a childhood hero, Ernest Tubb. It was probably Presley's affection for Tubb and his music that led him to record "Blue Christmas" on his initial holiday album. Yet Elvis's cut was far different from Tubb's or anyone else's. The rocker was the first to put real blues in "Blue Christmas." In one brief three-minute recording, Ernest had lost his lock on the song. It was now Elvis's Christmas standard.

Presley's recording of Johnson and Hayes's song would generate more royalties than all of Jay Johnson's other songs combined. It would also assure that this country classic would become one of the best-known holiday songs of all time. Since Elvis first cut it, "Blue Christmas" has been recorded by hundreds of artists from every musical genre. Yet in spite of its success in rock, pop, and blues, by and large "Blue Christmas" has remained as country as Ernest Tubb. It would be hard to imagine a country Christmas album or show without it. And for that reason the Jay Johnson and Billy Hayes song has become the gift that keeps on giving.

"I will tell you this," Judy Olmsted said with a laugh. "It wouldn't be Christmas at our house without 'Blue Christmas.'" And a host of country music fans would probably agree that while there are a lot of great holiday songs, a real country Christmas isn't complete until it's sung blue.

For those interested in becoming a songwriter or finding out more about songwriting—

The Nashville Songwriters Foundation and its staff have been a great help in putting together this book. The organization is a non-profit foundation whose purpose is to educate, preserve, and celebrate the contributions of the members of the Nashville Songwriters Hall of Fame. The NSF is governed by a thirteen-member board of directors who give their time and energies so that the songwriters' stories and songs will be remembered and revered by the general public and the industry.

Those interested in finding out more about the NSF should write

> NSF
> P.O. Box 121775
> Nashville, TN 37212-1775

The Nashville Songwriters Association International was founded in 1967 as a service organization which is dedicated to serving and protecting both the professional and aspiring songwriter in all fields of music. This organization not only informs its members how to submit music to publishers, but evaluates new songwriters' compositions and holds symposiums and seminars, as well as hosting many special festivals. The organization has three different levels of membership and is probably the first place aspiring country songwriters need to contact when they want to expand their craft.

Those interested in joining the Nashville Songwriters Association International should write

> NSAI
> 15 Music Square West
> Nashville, TN 37203